IMAGINING CITIES

The city has always been a meeting point for cross-disciplinary discussion within the debates of modernity and, more recently, postmodernity. *Imagining Cities* gives students access to the most exciting recent work on the city from within sociology, cultural studies and cultural geography.

Contributions are grouped around four major themes:

- The theoretical imagination
- Ethnic diversity and the politics of difference
- Memory and nostalgia
- The city as narrative

While these representations consider the interplay of past and present, imagined and substantive, the final section of the book links present and future in examining the idea of the virtual city. Here, the world of cyberspace not only recasts our imaginaries of spaces and communication, but has a profound impact on the sociological imagination itself.

Contributors: Roger Burrows, David Byrne, David Chaney, Julie Charlesworth, Allan Cochrane, Phil Cohen, James Donald, Max Farrar, Stephen Graham, Tim Hall, Barnor Hesse, Ruth Jamieson, Graham B. McBeath, Edward W. Soja, Ian Taylor, Stephen A. Webb, Elizabeth Wilson.

Sallie Westwood is Professor of Sociology and **John Williams** is Football Trust Research Lecturer, both at the University of Leicester.

IMAGINING CITIES

scripts, signs, memory

Edited by
SALLIE WESTWOOD and
JOHN WILLIAMS

LONDON AND NEW YORK

First published 1997
by Routledge
11 New Fetter Lane, London EC4P 4EE

Simultaneously published in the USA and Canada
by Routledge
29 West 35th Street, New York, NY 10001

Typeset in Baskerville by Solidus (Bristol) Limited
Printed and bound in Great Britain by
Biddles Limited, Guildford, Surrey

British Library Cataloguing in Publication Data
A catalogue record for this book is available from the British Library

Library of Congress Cataloguing in Publication Data
A catalogue record for this book has been requested

ISBN 0–415–14429–9 (hbk)
ISBN 0–415–14430–2 (pbk)

CONTENTS

FIGURES

CONTRIBUTORS

Roger Burrows is a researcher in the Centre for Housing Policy, University of York.

David Byrne lectures in Sociology at the University of Durham.

David Chaney lectures in Sociology at the University of Durham.

Julie Charlesworth is a member of the Faculty of Social Sciences, The Open University.

Allan Cochrane is a member of the Faculty of Social Sciences, The Open University.

Phil Cohen is Director of the New Ethnicities Unit at the University of East London.

James Donald is Reader in Media Studies at Sussex University.

Max Farrar is lecturer in the School of Cultural Studies at Leeds Metropolitan University.

Stephen Graham is a researcher at the Centre for Urban Technology, Department of Town and Country Planning, University of Newcastle-upon-Tyne.

Tim Hall is lecturer in Human Geography in the Department of Geography and Geology, Cheltenham and Gloucester College of Higher Education.

Barnor Hesse teaches Sociology at both the University of London and the University of East London.

Ruth Jamieson is a researcher of the University of Keele.

Graham B. McBeath teaches in the School of Social Studies, Nene College, Northampton.

Edward W. Soja is Professor in the Department of Urban Planning, University of California, Los Angeles.

Ian Taylor is Professor of Sociology at the University of Salford.

Stephen A. Webb is lecturing at the University of Derby.

Elizabeth Wilson is Professor of Media Studies at the University of North London.

ACKNOWLEDGEMENTS

We would like to offer generous thanks to all our contributors for their support in the production of this volume. Equally, our thanks to members of the Sociology Department, staff and students, especially James Fulcher, at the University of Leicester for their involvement in the 1995 British Sociological Conference, *Contested Cities*, from which this volume developed. We owe a special debt of gratitude to Robert Ash for his detailed and expert work on the text. Personally, Sallie Westwood extends warmest thanks to Rashpal Singh and Jitu Kachhella, who supported the conference and the book.

SW/JW

IMAGINING CITIES

Sallie Westwood and John Williams

> If the spectre of Communism no longer haunts Europe, the shadow of the city, the regret of what has died because it was killed, perhaps guilt, have replaced the old dread. The image of urban hell in the making is no less fascinating, and people rush towards the ruins of ancient cities to consume them touristically, in the belief that they will heal their nostalgia.
>
> (Lefebvre 1996: 142–3)

The city has always been a locus of research and discussion for sociological discourses generated by the debates with and around modernity and, more recently, the volatile terrain of postmodernity. This volume brings together some of the most recent and exciting work on the city from within sociology, social geography and cultural studies. The cross-disciplinary nature of this collection should be read as a further sign of confirmation of the resolution of the longstanding debate on the 'specificity of the urban'; that is, whether specifically urban, social and spatial forms can provide an appropriate object for theorisation for writers drawn from across the 'social science academic coalition' (Soja 1989: 69). The main themes of the book derive from the notion of *imaginaries*, whether these relate to literary productions, notions of urban myth, memory and nostalgia in the city and its environs, or to the sociological imagination re-cast within the changing realm of new technologies and forms of communication.

The book is organised around five major themes. The first of these is the *theoretical* imagination and how sociologists and geographers are currently theorising the enormous socio-cultural, economic, technological and spatial changes that are effectively re-inventing the city. From the recently 'rediscovered' work of Simmel onwards, sociologists and others have generated a sociological imagination with which to frame the city and urban life, and the first section of the book elaborates on the range of current debates within (and outwith) the discipline. One of the crucial, constitutive elements of cities throughout history has been their diversity in relation to spatial and economic divisions of labour and in terms of *ethnicities*. Ethnic diversity and the politics of difference generated by such diversity is the second major theme of the book and this section includes chapters that address the binaries of the local and global, nation and citizen, home and away, and black and white. These binaries are often constructed through an imagination which looks back to some time of greater certainties and this form of retrieval of the past is addressed in the collection's third theme on *memory and nostalgia*. These are contradictory phenomena offering both a subaltern story kept alive through a folk history and local practices or by personal memory, but also re-cast by media systems, capital and politics in order to be consumed as a heritage myth. The new and the old come together in the fourth theme of the book which offers a discussion in relation to literary and cultural forms that *narrate* the city in complex and contradictory ways. This narrative imagination can be seen in the literary canon and heritage and in the ways in which city centres and civic buildings and spaces are re-framed for the current urban world. While these representations bring the past and the present together, the final section of the book elaborates the present and the future in relation to the idea of the virtual city and the world of *cyberspace* which not only re-casts our imaginaries of space and communication, but also has a profound impact on the sociological imagination.

THEORISING CITIES

Although we begin this collection with a section on the theorisation of cities and the urban, the suggestion that there is a separate category here for theoretical practice is demolished throughout this book and we use the heading by convention and for ease of explication only. Sociological work on the city has consistently sought ways in which to frame urban forms and to interrogate the consequences of urban concentrations of wealth and power. The well-known discussions involving Castells (1977), Harvey (1973) and Saunders (1980) in the 1970s and early 1980s emphasised, especially, the political economy of the city and the importance of collective consumption and struggles in this realm. These interventions, as Soja reminds us in this volume, provided structural accounts of the city and its politics which, Soja suggests, have been overridden by the more recent emphases upon the local and studies of locality. Soja calls here for a revival of interest in the more 'macro' concerns of earlier theorising and offers a series of headings to provide a lead for generating a contempory overview of urban forms on a more structured basis. Such a project, of course, calls forward just the kind of imaginative thinking that is the central theme of this volume, but to move in this direction is not without its problems.

Some of the difficulties associated with the politics of 'imagined cities', for example, recently found expression in London through the 'Art and Power' exhibition at the South Bank's Hayward Gallery. This event was organised as a facsimile of the 1937 Paris exhibition in which the artistic and architectural projects of the fascist and socialist states met. The exhibition offered a glimpse of the 'heroic' art and architecture of Albert Speer in Berlin and Mussolini in Rome, plundering, as it does, images from the past as an expressive means to the glorification of a fascist future. It is a powerful vision, indeed, intended to be so, and a reminder of why the grand narrative – whether of the city or the nation – is now so negatively assessed. The critique of the fascist vision is found within the exhibition manifest in the shape of the Spanish pavilion; this is a deceptively light structure, boasting no columns or imposing massive statues and certainly no pretentions to a grandiose scale. Instead, the pavilion is a seductively simple building sporting a curved totem pole capped by a stylised heart. It reminds the worlds of the 1930s and today that celebrations through art and architecture can be very different from those designed to evoke the intimidating power and ambitions of the state. Elliott (1995: 31) in his introduction to the exhibition suggests, persuasively, that: 'The dictators of the 1930's were the apotheosis of modernity. By looking simultaneously at both the past and the future, they were able to sustain the fantasy of being able to stand outside their own time.'

While such political dictators sought to stand outside time there were other inter-war social commentators who used art and film effectively to provide a critique of modern urbanism, most famously the Austrian-born sceptical modernist film director and writer, Fritz Lang. Lang's social and political concerns were already apparant in *Dr Mabuse, the Gambler,* made in Berlin in 1922, and which contained pointed allusions to post-First World War social and economic conditions in Germany. But in *Metropolis* (1927), Lang used images of high-tech landscapes and routinised and de-humanised workers cast against mechanistic and steeled cityscapes to inscribe a futuristic vision of the urban-industrial world of capitalist development and authoritarian politics; it was a terrain theatrically re-visioned, of course, through the lens of scientism and the mutant chaos of the late twentieth century in Ridley Scott's seminal *Blade Runner* (1981).

While these kinds of artistic visions articulated and re-interpreted for a mass audience the myths and fears of the modern and late-modern world, sociologists have, perhaps, more usually sought ways in which to 'domesticate' or suppress such fears through accounts of the ordered and 'organic' city from the Chicago School onward; accounts which largely emphasised the patterns and coherence associated with Park and Burgess's famous concentric circles or the routinised focus of much urban sociology and geography upon metropolitan zones and the separation of functions within the city. The ordering of the city had its counterpart in urban planning and architecture, producing, for example, the most extraordinary confluence of rural and urban in the British notion of the 'garden city', a reference to the suburban dream of green spaces, but on an individualised basis, and a development explored by Charlesworth and Cochrane in this volume as they provocatively peer at Britain's Milton Keynes – 'an anglicised and sanitised lotusland' – through the prism of contemporary Los Angeles. In fact, this reference to the garden city could be read differently, following Bauman (1991) and his account of the 'gardening state', defined by its ability to order the population and separate out 'legitimate' plant life from the weeds. This is, perhaps, to overwrite authoritarian and domesticating discourses in urban theorisation, though it does call up some familiar themes from early ecological theory. As Ellin (1995) suggests, for example, there was also a more democratic, populist impulse evidenced in the work of Frank Lloyd Wright and other lesser-known architects in the United States and elsewhere from the 1930s onwards.

The shift from the challenges to history and tradition posed by 'modernism' to what Lash and Urry (1994: 3) have termed the radical exaggeration of 'postmodern' theorisations of the city and the urban, has disrupted the discourses on order and privileged those on chaos and the unintelligibility of the city as an organic form. As the 'postmodern' city has hyperbolically accentuated the processes of increased turnover time, speed of circulation and the disposability of subjects and objects, arguably the pessimistic prognoses on the prospects of theorising such shifts have been somewhat misplaced (ibid.) Instead, as Byrne contends in this volume, chaos and complexity may constitute fruitful ways towards understanding developing urban forms and cities at the end of the twentieth century. His approach should not be mistaken for the kind of postmodern nihilism exemplified, for example, by Baudrillardian excess or by artistic visions of urban alienation such as in Paul Auster's bleak novel, *In The Country of Last Things* (1988). Byrne does, for example, return to forms of *collective* struggle and the capacity of collective subjects to have an impact on city develop- ment. In fact, current theorising about the city tends to celebrate the quixotic and the flux of the urban world, and the diversity of the cityscape. But, as with earlier theorists, the emphasis of such scholars has consistently been on the cities of the metropolitan core and, of late, on California's Los Angeles as some kind of paradigmatic case of urban development. If LA of the early 1970s embodied for Banham (1971) the great bourgeois vision of the good life, twenty years on, it seemed, we were all, eventually, destined to head down the open freeway; as Sharon Zukin (1991: 220) has famously put it, we are fascinated with LA 'because we think it shows us the future'. The work particularly of Davis (1990, 1992) and Soja (1989) has had a major impact on the way in which Los Angeles has been mistakenly treated as a trajectory for future urban forms rather than as a peculiar case of the urban landscape. Instead, we would do well to heed the words of Lefebvre (1996: 143) when he argues that 'The city and the *urban* cannot be recomposed from the signs of the city, the *semanthemes* of the *urban*, although the city is a signifying whole. The city is not only a language but also a practice.'

The vision of Los Angeles as the punitive and privatised segregated city evoked in Mike Davis's work is also echoed in some recent accounts of cities as cyberspace. Bauman (1988), for example, seems to see the cyber option as a retreat into a fortified and technologised private world, safe from the dangerous spaces occupied by the oppressed, rather in the way that the LAPD (Los Angeles Police Department) and city fathers in California have shaped the forbidding 'apartheid' ecology of the city against the claims for free passage from the resident gangs and other citizens from South Central LA. Stephen Graham in this volume takes a rather wider perspective on the wiring-up of major cities. Whereas cities were seen as spatial containers of wealth and resources, economic, cultural and political, the new technologies deconstruct spatial bound- aries and work across conventional geographies. As Graham cogently argues, one of the defining features of telecommunications is its *invisibility* which allows urban theorists to ignore its form and impact and to hold on to basically outmoded views which demote the importance of the 'information city' and the importance of electronic spaces.

Considering the fate of the city and generating new worlds and urban spaces is possible not only in the imagination and through futuristic novels (see Burrows in this volume) but through the celebrated computer programme SimCity which allows all of us to be urban planners for a while. This is a programme in which the key elements and spatial arrangements of the city can be moved, changed and invented, which suggests the programme has enormous potential for community-based city planning and negotiations over space and resources. Via this virtual city collective it may be possible for subjects to elaborate and act upon a series of priorities.

It is the *practice* of the city – to return to an earlier point – that has also been the major concern of sociologists in relation to the long tradition of 'community' studies and of ethnographic accounts of urban neighbour-hoods, particularly of those living on the margins of mainstream urban economies. Such approaches are well represented in the current collection too. Latterly, however, influential sociological accounts of the city have been re-cast through a langauge derived from post-structuralist forms of theorising. The key themes of this 'new direction' are reflected here in the major sections of the book but what underpins this new account may be briefly summed up as follows: a) a decentred account of the social which offers a series of available sites in which the practices of urban life are produced, reproduced and changed; b) an emphasis upon spatiality and the indivisibility of the social and the spatial; c) the encoding of urban practices into social/spatial relations of time.

The decentring of the social implies a radical shift away from the notions of organic wholes and systems which seemed indispensible to earlier generations of social theorists. Instead, 'society' is understood to be fractured and constantly in process in relation to its constitution and reconstitution. This has major implications for the ways in which the city and the urban are understood as a series of overlapping sites, following Foucault, which are permeated by power relations. These ideas have been developed recently, particularly in the work of Laclau and Mouffe, both together (1985) and individually (1994), in relation to the political moment predicated upon a series of engagements and re-engagements which cannot be read off from a privileged moment of class-based antagonisms. In such accounts the primacy of social class gives way to a multiplicity of struggles and confrontations, involving a wide range of constituencies and social actors, with many of these struggles, in fact, relating to the cityscape. What is so interesting about this vision of the city, as a multiplicity of dramas and places, is the ways in which this has been so clearly understood and celebrated in the non-metropolitan world and has been expressed so vividly and affectionately in, for example, the writings of Salman Rushdie on Bombay. Anyone from the life world of metropolis who has visited the great non-metropolitan centres – Cairo, Bombay or Mexico City spring to mind – cannot fail to be impressed by the experience of the cityscape above all else as a living, peopled locale; and as places which, despite ongoing problems of poverty, homelessness and pollution, in some intelligible ways, work.

Consistent with the theoretical shift in the decentring of the social has been the reinscription of space, spatiality and place into social relations generating an ever-growing literature following the seminal work of Lefebvre, who sees the social and the spatial as indisoluble. This is not the moment to rehearse many of the tautological arguments around space and spatiality (see, instead, Massey 1995 and Farrar in this volume) but to suggest that conceptualisations of place and space are discontinuous and that this has major implications for the theorisation of the city. It is to suggest, quite simply, that the city is *many* cities and that place-positionality has an important impact on the ways in which subjects understand, negotiate and live in cities. As Massey (1995: 284) suggests: 'One of the most powerful ways in which social space can be conceptualised is as constituted out of social relations, social interactions and, for that reason, always and everywhere an expression and a medium of power.' Given this under-standing, it is not surprising that much recent academic work on cities has concentrated upon specific localities *within* cities using ethnographic fieldwork data in order to elaborate narratives of city life that no longer claim to represent 'the urban' but, instead, are *stories* from the city. While these are important contributions to the burgeoning store of 'lived histories' hewn from urban spaces, Squires (1994) is surely right to point to the ways in which such approaches romanticise the city and promote a sense of the local that is artificially distanced from the real conflicts of urban life. She goes on: 'New "urban romanticism" or new "localisms" seek a cohesive city life, one which avoids real conflicts and fails to confront real diversity; and does so through physical enclosure and exclusion' (ibid: 89). In this volume, too, both Elizabeth Wilson and James Donald critique utopian visions of the city, of a landscape impossibly cleansed of the 'normative' tensions, cleavages and conflicts of urban existence.

One of the key theoretical problems for local, ethnographic work on the city has been the issue of time – long known in anthropology as 'the ethnographic present'. Local ethnographies provide a 'slice of life' but in a stills frame from which it is difficult to generalise and to examine social processes, given the rather 'static' form of ethnographic research. Farrar's work in this volume provides an important corrective, charting as it does the history of popular visions and cartographic blindness which together produce the 'visible invisibility' of the Chapeltown area of Leeds. By using Shields' (1991: 30) work on 'social spatialisation', Farrar is able to recode sites and geographic spaces which have become associated with particular values, historical events and feelings. Farrar also incorporates conceptions of the famous time–space compression that marks the era of late modernity. Time, understood in this way, is not confined to temporality and to its linear unfolding but is bound to social constructions – Farrar talks, briefly, of 'Black People's Time' as a complex form of accommodation and resistance to Greenwich Mean Time. *Capitalist* time organises production and profit and simultaneously generates a conception of 'free time'. Farrar agrees with Lash and Urry (1994) that time (and space) are resources which can be manipulated and exploited by dominant social forces. In this sense, cities are not 'invented' by spatialities but by time, and specific cities (and locales, to follow Giddens) will have very different conceptions of time which are bound to a historicised past and which may be re-invented and expressed in and through the visions of the powerful, as evidenced in the plans for Berlin and Rome in the 1930s. Alternatively, cities might be 'time*less*', for example, in relation to the enduring symbolic power, for both Jews and Muslims, of a city such as Jerusalem. Urban time appears to be transparent, organised for business and the transportation of people across the spaces of the city and routinely expressed in the preoccupation with timetables, starting and finishing times, opening and closing times. But, even these urban forms of time have important specificities. A 'global' city such as London, one (with New York and Tokyo) of the world's 'big three' financial and communication/information centres, turns out to be no city for late night, pleasure-seeking insomniacs – they are much better off in New York!

While the emphasis in this volume is on the socio-cultural relations of the city and the ways in which such relations are theorised and lived, this focus cannot, and does not, marginalise or underplay the significance of *economic* relations in defining and transforming cityscapes. The localities of the city are part of a wider set of relations, an ensemble of the economic, political and cultural moments which are also shaped by the effects of the changing global and national positions of cities bound, as they are, to the changing fortunes of capitalism. The growing importance, in global terms, of the Pacific Rim economies, for example, has rapidly transformed the 'town' of Auckland in New Zealand into a diasporic city with rocketing real estate prices and the arrival of multinational banks and casinos. The global shift which has occurred here, and which is represented in the impressive but 'placeless' Auckland architecture and by her new trading partners, is another reminder that in an era of time–cost and time–space compression it is *relative* location, that is, how one is connected to the new circuits of communication and capital, which becomes ever more important (Brunn and Leinbach 1991: xvii). The familiar cultural and economic reference points of such locales – the ubiquitous MTV and CNN, the 'McDonaldisa-tion' and 'Coca-Cola-isation' of almost all major cities, for example – alerts us, sensitises us, as David Harvey suggests, to the localised *differences* between cities. But it also alerts us to the global flows of 're-organised' capital, to the intensity of the global circulation of signs, objects and subjects between cities, and to a new stage of international cultural domination – a new and depthless form of imagining – by what Lash and Urry, following Bourdieu, have called 'symbolic violence':

> Postmodern and late capitalist symbolic violence comes through the final nihilism of ... reducing time to a series of disconnected and contingent events, as exemplified in the pop video and the advent of the 'three minute culture'.
>
> (Lash and Urry 1994: 15–16)

or, as Rattansi (1995: 346) suggests, through the sheer scale of *sign saturation*.

Given the coterminus central significance of massive capital and financial flows for the above model, we can only speculate on the scenario for the *financial* centre of London and for the capital itself if the EU partners reach agreement and the common currency, the 'Euro', takes off; conversely, who knows what the future might hold for a 'traditional' centre of finance capital such as 'The Square Mile' if the EU and the 'Euro' simply 'melt into air'. That non-metropolitan cities have histories bound to the articulation of governance and capital is also clearly expressed in the recent changing, and declining, fortunes of Calcutta, recently revived by the liberalisation of the Indian economy, historically the major city of imperial India.

While there is no generic periodisation of cities, as Sudjic (1993: 3) argues, the 1980s were crucial for the transformation of western cities, a time in which 'the industrial city finally shook off the last traces of its nineteenth-century self and mutated into a completely new species'. An exaggeration, perhaps but one which forces us to reconsider our vision of western cities and to acknowledge that the changes which have occurred to them have had ramifications throughout the metropolitan core, a fact which is so clearly expressed in the chapter in this volume by Ian Taylor and Ruth Jamieson on the consequences of de-industrialisation in Sheffield for the social construction of white, working-class masculinities. In fact, their account of lifestyles and strategies for existence among the young urban poor in Sheffield clash harshly with the *nostalgic scripts* produced by just the forms of corporate advertising which are emblematic of the wider shifts in global networks which now confine 'the lads' to the 'grafting' of petty crime and drug use.

Importantly, while the changes in the constitution of cities of the late twentieth century are occurring *structurally* in some of the uneven and discontinuous forms suggested above, changes have also been occurring, of course, in relation to the *subjectivities* of those living through this complexity. Theorising changes in the city, therefore, foregrounds one of the key problems for sociology more generally, the relationship between the psyche and the social. Consistent with our account of the decentred social we also posit a decentred subject interrelated in a variety of sites within the urban landscape in ways that call forth a multiplcity of subjectivities and a range of struggles over the meaning of city spaces themselves:

> Theoretically, city spaces cannot restore the lost certainties of identity, centre the decentred subject, precisely because they, themselves, are produced in the multiple discourses of urban spatiality. Resonant with politically contested meaning, they are sites of struggle which themselves are decentred, rendering the sort of identity formation that they engender always contingent.
>
> (Keith 1993b: 208)

This kind of theorising is a key element in the focus upon *difference* which is privileged in the multi-ethnic, diasporic urban world, consistently one of the defining features of the city.

RACIAL/SPATIAL IMAGINARIES

One of the most powerful ways in which social formations and cities are decentred is through their constitution as racialised forms. Historically, cities have been racialised since the earliest times into the quarters of medieval Europe, the ghettos of yesterday and today, and the more ideologically impelled apartheid cities of South Africa and racially divided cities such as Abijan of the former French West Africa and Nairobi in British East Africa. The 'geographies of exclusion' (Sibley 1995) which mark so much urban space are not only demographically delineated but, as the work of our contributors Cohen, Hesse and Farrar argues so cogently, are imaginaries linking the social and the psychic, placing 'race' at the centre of the cityscape and reproducing within Britain the centrality of the couplet 'race' and nation. This is not an innocent articulation but one which, instead, sustains racism and racially motivated violence. Consistent with a Foucauldian account of governmentality, racism comes to rest on the body, using the visibility of the body as a major signifier but also as a site for racial abuse and violence. The visibility of ethnicised 'others' produces the global cities with which we are familiar but it also allows racism to operate as a disciplinary mode in which the fact of being seen provides optimum conditions for surveillance and for identification as an alien and threatening presence. In this sense, calls for safer cities become emotively tied to 'the dreadful realisation that while the medieval fortress town has been a place of safe retreat against the external enemy, the enemy was now within the gates' (Cohen 1985: 211). This visibility of the 'other' is part of biopower which shifts the field of vision beyond the institutional sites in which racism is deployed, to the generality and diffuseness of racism as a regime of power which is constitutive of subjects, subjectivities and resistance. Diffuse and general as forms of commonsense racism may be, they are also constructed within time and space and it is spatiality which is ever present in encounters benign and violent.

Phil Cohen in his 'narrative cartography' of the white population of London's Isle of Dogs in this volume elaborates some of these themes bridging the gap between detailed empirical research and the broader theorising about cities. This work is also a long way from the 'romantic', utopian accounts of cityscapes which 'magically' omit the violence and paranoia of some city sites (Robins 1995a), meshing, as it does, story and territory, plot and map and, in doing so, successfully excavating and interrogating popular imagery of the East End as a 'dense concentration of dangerous difference'. Cohen's discussion of images of East and West London also recall the racialised and spatialised popular imaginings associated with visioning these locales in turn-of-the-century London (Walkovitz 1992).

Hesse, for his part, focuses on the problem of 'whiteness' in imagining the nation in a British city, to the occlusion of its racialised history. This 'hegemonic structure of "whiteness"' also calls forth a 'white amnesia', what Stuart Hall called a 'decisive mental repression' (Hall 1978: 26), which has overtaken the collective memory of the British people about the links between race and Empire. This 'fictive ethnicity' of 'whiteness' is, on the one hand, a discursive attempt to imagine and represent the nation as a closed system of differences while, on the other, the historical formation of the nation is itself relegated – the 'shrinking' of the nation – to a symbolic abstraction as locality is elevated to the concrete heritage of indigenous 'whiteness'. In the routinised oppression of racial harassment, Hesse contends, the body of the 'other' is 'naturally' viewed as a surface for inscription of a 'white' appropriation of the city and for the exercise of the disciplinary logic of 'whiteness' and white governmentality.

Some of the issues raised in these detailed accounts of the complex interweaving of history, race, nation, identity and territory are important for our deliberations on the relationship between spatiality and power, and they are ones to which we will return. Racialised spaces have been elaborated elsewhere through the work of Cohen (1988), Wacquant (1989), Hesse (1993a), Keith (1993b) and Winant (1994), to mention only some of the writers who have been concerned to name the processes as constituting 'nationalisms of the neighbourhood' (Cohen 1988) or re-territorialisations, following Deleuze and Guattari (1988), which are central to the ways in which racialised imaginaries in cities become the focus of struggles and the definitions of insiders/outsiders, included/ excluded. Conversely, however, decentred cities deconstruct binary notions, for example, inner city and outer suburb expressed physically in the rise of 'Edge City' (Garreau 1991) with housing, workplaces and shopping malls developed beyond the conventional, geographical city limits. However, there has been little attention to the racialisation of edge cities and the ways in which these developments provide enclaves against multi-racial, diasporic populations, their populations living, instead, within a myth of forced homogeneity, apeing the 'white flight' from the cities of earlier eras in the States and the UK.

The racialisation of city spaces is central to any analysis of urban forms but, like class relations or sexualities, it does no justice to the complexities of racisms, ethnicities and identities to discuss 'race' as though it existed by and for itself rather than within the complex articulations of gender, class and religious identities. The ways in which religion has been, and is currently, racialised across Europe in particular offers one more moment in which the anatagonisms of diasporic cities are exemplified. The physical landscape of the cities of Britain, and elsewhere, is currently being changed by the Jewish *eruv* (the enclosure for ritual purposes of a specific space by means of poles and wires) and by the growing number of Hindu and Sikh temples, and mosques from the great diversity of Muslim 'communities' present in Britain. These buildings mark the presence of the South Asian diaspora and the sense of belonging in Britain which is often cruelly disrupted by the politics of these sites. Invariably, extant, usually white residents complain about noise and traffic, about people and the 'alien' presence constituting a politics of space which has nothing to say about faith and religion but is organised around discourses of the nation, culture and belonging. Those who complain run against the time and to an imagined homogenity of the neighbourhood. The re-insertion of the sacred into the urban world is a dramatic intervention and a real claim for space, a reminder that not all the grand narratives have been shaken by the postmodern turn.

NOSTALGIA/MEMORY

The arrival within the cityscape of *eruvin*, temples and mosques might be construed as a nostalgic response to displacement – nothing could be more misguided. These religious buildings and practices are constituted in the present with a vision of the future, one in which the designated visibility of people of Jewish and South Asian descent in racist discourses has been re-inscribed in the urban landscape. However, nostalgia and the imaginary city of the past are fused in popular culture especially, perhaps, in Britain where the heritage industry turns the relics of industrial cities into theme parks (Hewison 1987). Equally powerful are the soap operas that recreate the northern working class and the East End of London, favourite location for film makers, TV producers and sociologists. The very size of audiences for these programmes, their longevity and their consequent importance for channel schedules are testimony to their near unshakeable hold on the public imagination. These imaginaries thrive on a largely benign account of community and on a romance located within the rough and ready warm heartedness of, mainly, white working-class folk, particularly the starchy and strong female characters (though, arguably, recently the intensification of competition between the main TV channels has thrust the storylines of even these texts into the realm of the hyperreal). The inclusionary cultures of these localities and practices are suffused with notions of Englishness and belonging which exclude (despite their sometime inclusion as characters in the soaps) the 'Other British' – the myriad and diverse peoples who are part of the nation.

The inability to work with difference is also part of the ways in which popular narratives from TV, tabloids, novels and songs actually *domesticate* the city, taking out the *risqué* element and making it safe – for some. These discourses act as an alternative to the dangers of city life that belong with another genre of popular writing exemplified in detective stories (see Young 1996) and film noir but which are sanitised and represented in the ever-popular British police series on television. Like the advertisements discussed by Taylor and Jamieson in this volume, these are representations of masculinities and gender relations which figure strongly in the nostalgic re-presentations of city life. This kind of consumption of nostalgic images is both cruel and instructive. The lives of the disenfranchised 'little Mesters' discussed in Chapter 9 are highly spatialised – they have clear 'mental maps' of the city – but their form of 'protest masculinity' and their 'work' at theft on the streets of the city reflects, in fact, their lack of the kind of rootedness and placeness given to their forebears by their role in the local industrial structure.

Nostalgia is, however, as Elizabeth Wilson argues, rather more ambivalent than the preceding account suggests. Lowenthal (1985: 8) characterises contemporary forms of nostalgia as 'memory with the pain taken out'.

For Wilson, however, nostalgia conjures memories, feelings of the past and evocations drawn from senses which are themselves socially and discursively constructed: in Proust's phrase, 'our arms and legs are full of torpid memories' (quoted in Lash and Urry 1994: 241). But such feelings are lived in the present as sentiments, as pleasures and yet are also bound to loss and discomfort with a familiar world removed and now remodelled within the imagination. The romance of nostalgia is bound not only to a past 'world we have lost' but to a present and the representations that celebrate and romanticise poverty and urban privations. In effect, by retrieving the past from the detached viewpoint of the present – would we really want to go back? – we reappropriate the present. Wilson also has an important message about women and the city; messages about 'cities of danger' (Valentine 1990: 101) underwrite inescapable aspects of city life, but to suggest rationalist solutions to the perceived urban threat or to talk only about safety for women is also to invite the heavy yoke of impossibilist risk-free homogeneity.

As Chaney suggests in relation to suburbia, it is the invocation of community which marks so many urban imaginaries and the discourses that construct a collective subject and identity. In part this is related not to sentiment but to the intimate knowledge of place that generates a sense of belonging (Westwood 1990). This is gathered over time and holds within it a sense of the history, of time and memory in relation to place as a living, changing urban and social milieu. Importantly, as Bhabha (1986: xxiii) reminds us: 'Remembering is never a quiet act of introspection or retrospection. It is a painful re-membering, a putting together of the dismembered past to make sense of the trauma of the present.' As 'liveability' in cities and especially facilities for education have become recent key attractors for employers and employees, post-industrial cities may pretend not to be cities at all but try to market themselves as 'safe' semi-rural suburban enclaves (Mulgan 1989: 270). However, these utopian aspirations of surburban existence are always played out against dystopian visions and myths about the potential dangers posed by the threat of urban disintegration; by the 'Other', the urban stranger against whose intrusion the suburban community is set. For Chaney, the contradiction between this idealised sense of 'community' and the kinds of social fragmentation produced by the privatisation of suburban spaces and the rise of com-petitive individualism is resolved in the mythical domain of 'tradition' and its appeal to strains of leisured authenticity.

NARRATING CITYSCAPES

Commonsense accounts of the city are, as James Donald elaborates, sustained and produced through the myriad imaginative cityscapes nar-rated by literary and cinematic productions. As we have already suggested, novels, poetry and film provide us all, and sociologists and cultural theorists in particular, with a never-ending commentary on the city, the urban, city people and institutions, the 'real' and the fictive more and more woven together in intertextual discourses. These 'texts' are complex cultural products which form part of the ways in which we talk about ourselves and meditate upon the fate of the peoples of the late twentieth century. The work of Richard Wright is exemplary in this respect, a confluence between literature and sociology foregrounded in his long introduction to the classic study of Black urban life in the US, *Black Metropolis* by Horace Cayton and St Clair Drake, published in 1945. Thus, novels and films are instructive and offer us another language in which to pose key questions and to search for answers. They constitute a 'narrative space' in which, as Sennett (1990: 190) suggests, 'The novelist held up a magic mirror. It showed images of the city that were more legible than they were to the urbanite using his own unaided sight on the street'. Sennett is not writing here about the crude sentimentalism of 'second order' novelists like Elizabeth Gaskell but rather about the passionate imaginations of Dostoyevsky in relation to St Petersburg and of Balzac in Paris, making of Paris a lived entity in which places become characters.

Cinema currently does similar work; the recent thriller, *Candyman*, for example, treats the white, female, urban anthropologist as intrepid explorer in relation to popular urban fears. These fears are bound, predictably, to the 'others' of the city of Chicago, the lives of the black urban poor and the violence of the Southside. The projection onto this black population, specifically onto the black men, of the sexualised and violent fantasies of the main white female character are in a double take exposed as such with the urban anthropologist, no longer the intrepid explorer but the dangerous, murderous killer of the film's sub-plot. This is a tacky realisation and is at some distance from the polished aestheticised violence, discontinuous narratives, wit and general style of, for example, Tarrantino's *Pulp Fiction*. But it evokes 'real' urban schisms and cleavages and plays with some of the 'normalised' conventions of late twentieth-century urban screen violence. *Seven*, an urban fable about redemption and the city serial killer, is, perhaps, more interesting. The 'victim' here is the city itself but the text is also seductive for its various allusions to the complexities in the (post)modern city of relations of generation, 'race' and gender; to the catastrophic allure of the city when measured against the arcadian promise of upstate; to the bright surfaces of modern cityscapes and the subterranean and dangerous spaces they conceal; and to the forced tyranny of technologised pursuit over theorising and scholarship – in fact, the killer is eventually successfully tracked via the skilled library craftsmanship of Morgan Freeman's tired, humanistic, retiring black cop.

While novels and writing 'produce' the city for readers in their accounts of places such as Dublin or New York that render these cities familiar to all, there are alternative narrations generated by the practices of urban planning and the dreams of city elders and financiers. It is as well to remember, too, as Donald points out in quoting Doreen Massey, that most of us continue to live in arcane spaces doing arcane things; we go to the movies to *get* to New York. In this book we are grounded in these matters by, primarily, two chapters. In the first, Hall explores the relationship between cultural markers and place representation by focusing on the place imaging and marketing of the International Convention Centre in Birmingham in the UK. In late capitalism cities are packaged as centres of consumption, not production. There is much talk these days of the post-production *Creative City* (Landry and Bianchini 1995b); of the need for 'the creativity of being able to synthesize, to connect, to gauge impacts across different spheres of life, to see holistically, to understand how material changes affect our perceptions, to grasp the subtle ecologies of our systems of life' (ibid.: 11). Hall's account of the 'symbolic regionalisation of places' and of urban regeneration and cultural relocation in the English Midlands charts the local and global struggles over the promotion of Birmingham as 'city of spectacle' as, in the words of David Harvey, aesthetics come to replace ethics in urban planning (quoted in ibid. 4). This account of the re-imagination of sites within the city as theatre and spectacle is instructive because it highlights local contestation and the consequent marginalisation or enclosure of other local cultural spaces. In the second, Charlesworth and Cochrane discuss how the dreams of urban planners bound to the vision of Los Angeles become Anglicised in the 'edge city' of Milton Keynes, a utopian moment. This is not a narration beyond the themes with which we began, for Milton Keynes, in its very naming, presents part of the ongoing story of Englishness and the ways in which in its conception it reproduces the 'whiteness' and highly gendered spaces of suburbia, characterised by subtle – and not so subtle – processes of social segregation; it also separates itself from the diversity and racial mixtures of the metropolitan core – London. Milton Keynes is famous for its grid-pattern road network, its shopping mall and its fake cows in the green fields, bringing together a space designed around the car and yet with multiple references to rurality and the rural idyll – a new white world, as the author's put it, of car-borne consumption and rural villages. Yet, with the Open University also in its midst, Milton Keynes is high-tech and global in its concerns, from the course units that travel the world to the peace pagoda.

Milton Keynes has not yet been lovingly described or interwoven within a work of fiction in the way of a Los Angeles or Sydney, Calcutta or Bombay; each of these cities, in their turn, have been made both glamorous and dangerous, inviting the reader to hop on a plane or, more simply and definitely more cheaply, inhabit the pages of the book. The city is not simply context or setting for novels, it forms the spatial texture of the novel; as Donald puts it in this volume, the text is actively constitutive of the city. In Doris Lessing's novel *The Memoires of A Survivor* the narrator lives behind a window on the city and watches, stunned and enfeebled by the pace of change in one small corner of London, a voyeur rather than a *flâneur* (for a discussion of the *flâneur* as *man* of pleasure see Wilson 1995a). She wants distance from a world that threatens. It is a very melancholic novel quite unlike the powerful narrative of *The Four-Gated City* which is both a product of, and productive of, London, recognisable and crafted in one. In another mode, it is theorists of the city who re-invent literary themes in their analysis. Cuthbert (1995), for example, writing an account of contemporary Hong Kong entitles his paper 'Under the volcano: postmodern space in Hong Kong'. Literary borrowings pepper the sociological literature and are increasingly in evidence in post-structuralist geographies, but the attempt to merge sociological theorising and the novel has been advanced most recently through the importance afforded technological innovations and it is to this we turn in the final theme of our volume.

VIRTUAL CITIES

While cities such as Mexico City and most especially cities of the Pacific Rim, such as Hong Kong, grow into mega-cities – Hong Kong will be a city of 40 million, a megalopolis, on current projections by the year 2005 – and theorists continue to revise and refine their views of the 'postmodern city' (Watson and Gibson 1995), a new 'genre' of city theorising is being developed in relation to the arrival of virtual reality (Sherman and Judkins 1993). The issues involved here go to the very heart of the notion of imagining and imagined cities and involve past, present and future, technological innovations and, of course, the literary forms that these innovations have produced. Consequently, Burrows in this volume suggests that the futuristic novels of William Gibson provide a sociologically relevant source for the development of theories about the urban and its imaginaries. Rejecting the utopianism of much of the current phase of work in this area, Burrows opts instead for the deterministic chaos theory of De Landa, enquiring provocatively, *en passant*, has sociology been parasitic on the cyberpunk tradition?

William Gibson's cyberpunk scene is no longer a distant realm – though not yet science fact – as the increasing enthusiasm for the Internet and 'net relations' suggests. With every town now having its own cyber café and *Sociology* launching its own electronic journal, the future looks good for sociological cyborgs. The importance of the Internet is not only in its capacity to make available huge data banks, set up interrelationships between like-minded people from around the globe and offer football bulletin boards; it is a sign of the postmodern era, a signifier of a globally interconnected world, a purveyor of goods and ideas in a 'time–space' compression second to none.

For all the hype and the many words written and spoken on and about the Web, it is only recently that political economy has re-entered the screen following the ongoing battles between Bill Gates of Microsoft fame and the inventors of Netscape, Firecrest. These rivals are involved in a struggle for control of the Internet. Share prices in Firecrest have risen from 37p to 215p before falling to 165p in the last few months. Somewhere, as was the case with the South Sea bubble, suggests Victor Keegan (*Guardian*, 11 December 1995) the market punters believe that there is money to be made out of the Internet and a cyborg-capitalist future promises huge returns. The contestations are taking place in the US between the big companies, Apple and IBM for the hardware and for and against Bill Gates and Microsoft for the software. The outcome of these struggles will have major implications for the development of the Internet and the politics of knowledge, the intellectual property and cultural capital of the next century.

These issues raise, in part, some of the themes explored in the final chapter of this collection, by McBeath and Webb. These authors consider the importance of 'virtual community' in the selling of the Web and the various contortions that are in play among cyber surfers in order to sustain a vision of community. The issues raised here foreground the links between subjectivities and cyberspace. As in our earlier discussion, the decentring of the social is reproduced within the Internet, where a series of sites offer any number of 'homes' to individuals who negotiate these spaces and their relations within and between them. McBeath and Webb, rather pessimistically, regard the designation 'community' as misleading in a situation where a series of detached screen-watchers interact electronically. Theirs is a Raymond Williams-inspired assault on the Internet as a community of 'feeling'. But as an 'imagined community' it seems to us that identities collectively inscribed in cyberspace are no less valid or authentic than the myriad identities understood as imaginary forms of belonging.

The sense of belonging offered within the diverse spaces of cities throughout the world is, in part, constructed in relation to the sense of identity that cities offer to the strangers and locals within the cityscape. We would concur with Watson and Gibson (1995: 262) when, in concluding their discussion of 'postmodern politics and planning' they write, 'the division between the discursive and non-discursive terrains and between the "imaginary" and the "real" needs to be crossed'. It is our hope that this volume too disrupts the binary 'real/imagined' and provides novel ways in which theorisations of the city may be developed in the future. This, as Richard Rogers (1996) has argued so persuasively in the 1995 Reith Lectures and elsewhere, cannot be achieved without an imaginative leap beyond the negative appraisals of the current urban landscapes and away from the nostalgia for a safe, domesticated world. We celebrate the creativity of the city in all its forms and, as paid-up metropolitans, welcome the revival of sociological interest in the city to which this volume contributes.

Sallie Westwood and John Williams
Sociology Department
University of Leicester

Part I

THEORISING CITIES

1

SIX DISCOURSES ON THE POSTMETROPOLIS[1]

Edward W. Soja

Between the Watts riots of 1965 and what are now called the Rodney King or Justice riots of 1992, the urban region of Los Angeles experienced one of the most dramatic transformations of any comparable region of the world. For the resident Angelenos of the early 1960s a radically different, an 'Other' Los Angeles seemed to be developing beyond their control or understanding. And it would increasingly, over time, replace many more familiar urban worlds with shockingly new ones. Over the same period of about thirty years, a group of local scholars have been trying to make practical and theoretical sense of this radical restructuring of Los Angeles and to use this knowledge to understand the often equally intense urban transformations taking place elsewhere in the world. What I would like to do here is draw upon the work of what some, perhaps prematurely, have begun to call the Los Angeles School of urban studies, and to argue that the transformation of Los Angeles represents both a unique urban experience and a particularly vivid example of a more general sea change in the very nature of contemporary urban life, in what we urbanists have called the *urban process*.

Some have been so entranced by this urban restructuring that they proclaim it to be the most extraordinary transformation in the nature of urbanism since the origins of the city more than 6,000 years ago. Others, only somewhat more modestly, describe it as the second great urban transformation, after the tumultuous emergence of the nineteenth-century industrial capitalist city. I tend to see it as the most recent of a series of dramatic crisis-driven urban restucturings that have been taking place over the past 200 years. But however one interprets the magnitude of the current changes and sets them in a comparative historical framework, there can be little doubt that something quite exceptional has been happening to the modern metropolis during the last quarter of the twentieth century. Making sense of these new urban processes on the basis of how they differ significantly from the past thus becomes, in my view, even more necessary than tracing origins in an unfolding history of urbanization and urbanism as a way of life.

I have recently chosen to use *postmetropolis* as a general term to accentuate the differences between contemporary urban regions and those that consolidated in the middle decades of the twentieth century. The prefix 'post' thus signals the transition from what has conventionally been called the modern metropolis to something significantly different, to new postmodern forms and patternings of urban life that are increasingly challenging well-established modes of urban analysis. As will become clearer in my discussion of the six discourses, there are other post-prefixed terms and concepts packed into the postmetropolis, from the notion of post-industrial society so familiar to sociologists to the more recent discussions of post-Fordist and post-Keynesian political economies and post-structuralist and post-colonial modes of critical analysis. Before turning to these discourses, however, I want to make a few more general introductory observations.

First, as I have already suggested, the changes that are being described or represented by these six discourses are happening not only in Los Angeles but, in varying degrees and, to be sure, unevenly developed over space and time, all over the world. Although they take specific forms in specific places, they are general processes. Furthermore, these processes are not entirely new. Their origins can be traced back well before the last quarter of this century. It is their intensification, interrelatedness, and increasing scope that makes their present expression different from the past. I also want to emphasise that when I use the term postmetropolis as opposed to the late modern metropolis, I am not saying that the latter has disappeared or been completely displaced, even in Los Angeles. What has been happening is that the new urbanisation processes and patternings are being overlain on the old and articulated with them in increasingly complex ways. The overlays and articulations are becoming thicker and denser in many parts of the world, but nowhere has the modern metropolis been completely erased.

What this means is that we must understand the new urbanisation and urbanism without discarding our older understanding. At the same time, however, we must recognize that the contested cities of today and their complex relations between social process and spatial form, as well as spatial process and social form – what I once called the socio-spatial dialectic – are increasingly becoming significantly different from what they were in the 1960s. While we must not ignore the past, we must nevertheless foreground what is new and different about the present. Looking at contemporary urban sociology, this suggests that we can no longer depend so heavily on the 'new' approaches that flowered so brilliantly in the 1970s with such classic works as Manuel Castells's *The Urban Question* (1977; French ed. 1972), David Harvey's *Social Justice and the City* (1973) and the pioneering world systems sociology of Immanuel Wallerstein. These were, and remain, powerful and incisive inter-pretations of the late modern metropololis, Castells's *monopolville* and *ville sauvage,* the 'wild cities' that consolidated during the post-war boom and exploded in the urban crises of the 1960s. But the late modern metropolis, to coin a phrase, is not what it used to be.

Many of the insights developed by these theorists and analysts are still applicable and, I must add, the radical politics they encouraged is still possible. My argument, however, is basically that the changes have been so dramatic that we can no longer simply add our new knowledge to the old. There are too many incompatabilities, contradictions, disruptions. We must instead radically rethink and perhaps deeply restructure – that is, deconstruct and reconstitute – our inherited forms of urban analysis to meet the practical, political and theoretical challenges presented by the post-metropolis.

Another preliminary observation complicates things even further. While urbanists continue to debate just how different the new metropolis is from the old and precisely how much we must deconstruct and reconstitute our traditional modes of urban analysis, the postmetropolis itself has begun to change in significant ways. Beginning in the eventful year of 1989 in Berlin, Beijing and other major world cities, and punctuated in Southern California by the Spring uprisings in 1992 and the postmodern fiscal crisis of Orange County in 1994, the postmetropolis seems to be entering a new era of instability and crisis. There are growing signs of a shift from what we have all recognised as a period of crisis-generated restructuring originating in the urban uprisings of the 1960s to what might now be called a *restructuring-generated crisis*. That is, what we see in the 1990s may be an emerging breakdown in the restructured postmetropolis itself, in postmodern and post-Fordist urbanism, and also perhaps in the explanatory power of the six discourses I will be discussing.

My last introductory comment refers to some recent developments in critical urban studies, an exciting new field that has grown from the injection of critical cultural studies into the more traditionally social scientific analysis of urbanism and the urban process. While I consider my own work to be part of this increasingly transdisciplinary field, I have recently become uneasy over what I perceive to be a growing over-privileging of what has been called, often with reference to the work of Michel de Certeau, the 'view from below' – studies of the local, the body, the streetscape, psycho-geographies of intimacy, erotic subjectivities, the micro-worlds of everyday life – at the expense of understanding the structuring of the city as a whole, the more macro-view of urbanism, the political economy of the urban process.

The six discourses I will be presenting are aimed at making sense of the whole urban region, the spatiality and sociality of the urban fabric writ large. They are precisely the kinds of discourses being hammered at by those micro-urban critics who see in them only the distorting, if not repressive, gaze of authoritative masculinist power, the masterful 'view from above'. A primary tactic in fostering these often reductionist critiques of macro-level theorizing has been a kind of epistemological privileging of the experience of the *flâneur*, the street-wandering free agent of everyday life, the ultimate progenitor of the view from below. There is undoubtedly much to be gained from this ground-level view of the city and, indeed, many of those who focus on more macro-spatial perspectives too often overlook the darker corners of everyday life and the less visible oppressions of 'race', gender, class and sexuality. What I am most concerned with, however, is the degree to which such micro-level critiques have been unproductively polarizing critical urban studies, romancing agency and the view from below to the point of labelling all macro-level perspectives taboo, off-limits, politically incorrect.

The six discourses I will now turn to are, in part, an attempt to recapture and reassert the importance of a macro-urban tradition, not in opposition to the local view from below but drawing on insights that come directly from the significant work that has been done on the microgeographies of the city by a variety of critical urban scholars. Understanding the postmetropolis requires a creative recombination of micro and macro perspectives, views from above and from below, a new critical synthesis that rejects the rigidities of either/or choices for the radical openness of the both/and also. With this little plug for an explicitly postmodern critical perspective and after a more extensive introduction than I had originally planned, we are ready to begin examining the six discourses.

The six discourses are already familiar to most of you and, in one form or another, they weave through a large number of the papers presented at this conference of the British Sociological Association. I have discussed them before in a chapter in *Postmodern Cities and Spaces*, edited by Sophie Watson and Kathy Gibson, and they will be elaborated at much greater length in my forthcoming book, *Postmetropolis*.[2] I list them below with brief descriptions and a selection of sub-themes drawn from what will be six separate chapters in *Postmetropolis*.

1   FLEXCITY: on the restructuring of the political economy of urbanization and the formation of the more flexibly specialised post-Fordist
industrial metropolis.
   • the primacy of production
   • crisis-formation and the Great U-Turn
   • the ascendance of post-Fordism
   • the empowerment of flexibility
   • getting lean and mean
2   COSMOPOLIS: on the globalisation of urban capital, labour and
culture and the formation of a new hierarchy of global cities.
   • the primacy of globalisation
   • the 'glocalisation' process
   • the glocalization of discourse in New York and London
   • the vanity of the bonFIRES
   • reworlding Los Angeles
3   EXOPOLIS: on the restructuring of urban form and the growth of
edge cities, outer cities and postsuburbia: the metropolis turned inside-
out and outside-in.
   • paradigmatic Los Angeles
   • deconstructing the discourse on urban form
   • rosy reconstitutions of the postmetropolis: the New Urbanism
   • exploring the darker side of the Outer and Inner City
4   METROPOLARITIES: on the restructured social mosaic and the
emergence of new polarisations and inequalities.
   • a new sociologism?
   • widening gaps and new polarities

- the 'truly disadvantaged' and the 'underclass' debate
- the new ethnic mosaic of Los Angeles

5 CARCERAL ARCHIPELAGOS: on the rise of fortress cities, surveillant technologies and the substitution of police for *polis*.
- cities of quartz: Mike Davis's Los Angeles
- further elaborations: interdictory spaces in the built environment
- taking an Other look at *The City of Quartz*

6 SIMCITIES: on the restructured urban imaginary and the increasing hyperreality of everyday life.
- the irruption of hyperreality and the society of simulacra
- cyberspace: the electronic generation of hyperreality
- simulating urbanism as a way of life
- variations on a theme park
- scamscapes in crisis: the Orange County bankruptcy

Rather than going over these discourses in detail, I will use what I have just outlined to select a few issues that I think may be of particular interest to a gathering of urban sociologists. Given the challenge of brevity, the critical observations will be blunt and stripped of appropriate (and necessary) qualifications. My intent is not to offer a well-rounded critical presentation of the discourses but to use them to stimulate debate and discussion about how best to make sense of the contemporary urban scene.

The first discourse, on the post-Fordist industrial metropolis, rests essentially on the continued intimate relation between industrialisation and urbanisation processes. In Los Angeles and in many other urban regions as well, it has become perhaps the hegemonic academic discourse in attempting to explain the differences between the late modern (Fordist) metropolis and the post(Fordist)metropolis. It has also entered deeply into the recent literature in urban sociology as a theoretical framework for understanding the social order (and disorder) of the contemporary city. In Savage and Warde's book on British sociology, for example, there is a clear attempt to redefine and reposition urban sociology around this post-Fordist industrial restructuring.[3]

In some ways, this has been a peculiar embrace, for urban sociologists have contributed relatively little to the industrial restructuring literature and to the conceptual and theoretical debates that have shaped the first discourse. They have instead been content primarily with detailed empirical studies of the new capitalist city, leaving its theorisation and explanatory discourse to geographers, political economists and other non-sociologists. How can we explain sociology's apparent retreat from playing a leading role in conceptualising the new urbanisation processes and the post-metropolis, especially given its pre-eminence in explaining the development of the late modern metropolis in the post-war decades?

Part of the answer may lie in a persistent if not growing 'sociologism', a retreat back into tried-and-true disciplinary traditions of both theoretical and empirical sociology. Even when seeming to reach beyond disciplinary boundaries for theoretical and practical inspiration, such sociologism tends to seek ways to make what is new and challenging old and familiar, that is, absorbable without major paradigmatic disruption or radical rethinking. I think something like this has been happening in sociology with respect to the new discourse on post-Fordist urban-industrial restructuring in particular, and more generally with many other post-prefixed discourses. One vehicle for this retreat back into the disciplinary fold in the face of new challenges has been the continued appeal, especially in the US, of one form or another of the post-industrial society thesis developed within sociology decades ago. Continued use of the term post-industrial is jolting to a discourse built upon the persistent importance of industrialisation and the production process. What has been happening to the industrial capitalist city is much more than the decay of manufacturing industry and a shift to a services economy. De-industrialisation has been occurring alongside a potent re-industrialisation process built not just on high-technology electronics production but also on cheap labour-intensive forms of craft production and the expansion of producer-oriented services and technology. These shifts, often to more flexible production systems and denser transaction-intensive networks of information flow, are creating new industrial spaces that have significantly reshaped the industrial geography of the late modern or Fordist metropolis. Continuing to see the new urban restructuring processes through the eyes of the post-industrial thesis makes it difficult to comprehend the more complex and still production-centered discourse on post-Fordist urbanisation.

Similar problems arise from continued attachment to the politically more radical traditions of urban sociology that developed in the 1970s and early 1980s, especially reflecting the pioneering work of Castells and others on urban social movements and the politics of collective consumption. Here too a lingering consumptionist emphasis makes it difficult to comprehend the production-centred discourse on post-Fordist urbanisation and industrial restructuring. That much of this post-Fordist discourse also centres around explicitly spatial concepts and analyses complicates matters still further, given the recent attempts by such British sociologists as Peter Saunders to de-emphasise space and spatial analysis in the conceptual frameworks of urban sociology. Such efforts have been particularly constraining with regard to the participation of sociologists in the wider debates on postmodernism and critical cultural studies, both of which have experienced a pronounced spatial turn since the late 1980s. But this takes me into another discussion that I cannot expand upon here.

Sociologists have played a much more important role in the second discourse, on globalization and world city formation. In some ways, despite their interrelatedness and complementarity, the first and second discourses have often developed in competition, each seeing itself as the most powerful explanation for the new urbanisation and urbanism. This constrains both discourses, but I will comment here only on how the discourse on global cities has been weakened by an inadequate understanding of the industrial restructuring process as well as by a touch of the sociologism mentioned above. I can summarise my comments around a playful phrase I once used to express my discontent with the approaches being taken to the study of New York as a 'dual city' standing at the apex of the world hierarchy of the global 'capitals of capital'.[4] The phrase was 'the vanity of the bonFIRES and it referred to what I saw as an over-concentration on the command and control functions of the FIRE sector (finance, insurance, real estate) in the global cities literature and a closely related overemphasis on two tiny sites where these commanding bonFIRES appear to be burning most brightly, Wall Street in Manhattan and The City in London, along with their tributary yuppified offshoots (Battery Park City, the World Trade Center, South Street Seaport, Canary Wharf, the Docklands).

There are several weaknesses I see arising when the discourse is narrowed so tightly. First, there is a tendency to see world city formation as creating an increasing sectoral and geographical detachment from manu-facturing industries on the one hand and the productive base of the regional economy on the other. This may fit well to the post-industrial and de-industrialisation models of urban change and accurately describe some of what has been happening internally within New York City and London. But it distorts the general debate on globalisation and world city formation, especially with regard to such postmetropolises and major manufacturing regions as Tokyo and Los Angeles (and, I might add, the re-industrialising regional hinterlands of Greater New York and London).

I do not want to deny the importance of these research and interpretive emphases, but rather to note the dangers of a sort of Manhattanised or Londonised myopia. In addition to oversimplifying the connections between the financial and industrial sectors, and between the central city and the larger metropolitan region, such myopia also tends to inhibit more comprehensive and sophisticated understanding of the spatiality of global-isation and the new cultural politics of identity and difference being spawned in global cities. This, in turn, widens the breach between more sociological studies of globalisation and the increasingly spatialised cultural studies approaches to interpreting the postmetropolis.

The third discourse focuses on what I have described as the formation of Exopolis, a process that, on the one hand, points to the growth of Outer Cities and Edge Cities and other manifestations of the rather oxymoronic urbanization of suburbia and, on the other, to a dramatic reconstitution of the Inner City brought about both by an outmigration of domestic populations and the inmigration of 'Third World' workers and cultures. The social and spatial organisation of the postmetropolis seems as a result to be turning inside-out and outside-in at the same time, creating havoc with our traditional ways of defining what is urban, suburban, exurban, not urban, etc. Perhaps no other discourse is raising such profound challenges, not only for urban sociology but for all of urban studies as it has been conventionally constituted.

A few examples from Los Angeles can be used to illustrate this deconstruction and reconstitution of urban form, and of the traditional vocabulary developed to describe it. Such classic examples of American suburbia as the San Fernando Valley and Orange County now meet almost all definitions of being urbanised. They are highly heterogeneous agglom-erations of industrial production, employment, commerce, cultural and entertainment facilities, and other characteristically 'urban' qualities such as gangs, crime, drug-dealing and street violence. To continue to label these areas 'suburban' is to misrepresent their contemporary reality. Similarly, most of what we continue to label the Inner City of Los Angeles – including the urban ghettoes and barrios of South Central and East Los Angeles – would appear, especially to those familiar with cities in the eastern US, Europe and Asia as characteristically suburban.

I have used the term Exopolis to describe this discourse because of its provocative double meaning: exo- referring both to the city growing 'outside' the traditional urban nucleus and to the city 'without', the city that no longer conveys the traditional qualities of cityness. This radical deconstruction/reconstitution of the urban fabric has stimulated many other neologisms for the new forms emerging in the postmetropolis. In addition to those already mentioned, including Exopolis, there are post-suburbia, metroplex, technopoles, technoburbs, urban villages, county-cities, regional cities, the 100-mile city. It has also spawned self-consciously 'new' appproaches to urban design, such as the New Urbanism in the US and, in Britain, the related neo-traditionalist town planning so favoured by Prince Charles; and, at the same time, much darker interpretations of the social and environmental consequences of the restructuring of urban form, exemplified with noir-like brilliance in the work of Mike Davis. Here too, then, the discourse has begun to polarise in potentially unproductive ways, creating the need for more balanced and flexible, yet still critical and politically conscious, approaches to interpreting the changing built environment and social geography of the postmetropolis.

The fourth discourse explores the restructured social mosaic and is probably the discourse that has attracted the largest number of urban sociologists. It is especially attuned to the intensification of what I describe as Metropolarities: increasing social inequalities, widening income gaps, new kinds of social polarization and stratification that fit uncomfortably within traditional dualisms based on class (capital–labour) or race (white–black) as well as conventional upper-middle-lower class models of urban society. As with the discourse on urban spatial form, the discourse on the changing social forms and formations in the postmetropolis has instigated a new vocabulary. Yuppies (including such extensions as yuppification and 'guppies', or groups of yuppies) and the permanent urban underclass (or 'the truly disadvantaged') head the list, but there are many other related terms: dinks (double-income/no kids families), upper professionals, the new technocracy, the working poor, the new orphans (both youth growing up fatherless and motherless and the elderly abandoned by their children), welfare-dependent ghettoes, hyperghettoes, and so on.

Whereas the first two discourses tend to present themselves as capturing (and effectively theorising) the most powerful processes causing the restructuring of the late modern metropolis, the second pair concern themselves primarily with the empirical consequences of these processes. A more explicitly spatial emphasis is infused within the discourse on Exopolis and this, I would argue, creates closer ties to the practical and theoretical insights of the discourses on post-Fordist industrialisation and globalisation. The discourse on metropolarities, while certainly not aspatial, seems to be developing with a relatively simplistic perspective on the complex spatiality of the postmetropolis and, in part because of this, with an inadequate understanding of the links between cause and effect or, more specifically, the restructuring process and its empirical consequences.

Perhaps the best example of this conceptual gap has been the work of American sociologist William Julius Wilson and his associates, which today dominates the contemporary representation of the Chicago School of urban studies. While there is much to be praised in this work on the permanent urban underclass and the truly disadvantaged, it is filled with oversimplified notions of post-Fordist industrial restructuring, location theory and the relations between urban spatiality and the urban social order. Much of what I noted earlier about the constraining effects of sociologism is relevant here, as are my comments on the growing disjunction between theoretical and empirical work in sociological studies of the postmetropolis. Not all of urban sociology suffers from these constraints, to be sure, but I suspect they are more widespread than most of you think.

If the first pair of discourses on the postmetropolis emphasises the causes of urban restructuring and the second pair its empirical spatial and social effects, the third pair explores what might be described as the societal response to the effects of urban restructuring in the postmetropolis. In Los Angeles as well as in many other urban regions, the fifth discourse, on what I call the emergence of a Carceral Archipelago, has been dominated by the work of Mike Davis. In *City of Quartz* (1990) and other writings, Davis depicts Los Angeles as a fortified city with bulging prisons, sadistic street environments, housing projects that have become strategic hamlets, gated and armed-guarded communities where signs say 'trespassers will be shot', and where the city is surveilled and patrolled by a high-tech space police. What his work suggests is that the globalized post-Fordist industrial metropolis, with its extraordinary cultural heterogeneity, growing social polarities and explosive potential, is being held together largely by 'carceral' technologies of violence and social control, fostered by capital and the state.

What I want to question here is not the validity of Davis's depictions of Los Angeles but the degree to which his work has been 'romanced' by other urbanists, especially on the left, to the point of narrowing all the discourses on the postmetropolis to his politically appealing radical view. I once described *City of Quartz* as the best anti-theoretical, anti-postmodernist, historicist, nativist and masculinist book written about a city. For those who eschew abstract theorization because it takes away from good empirical work and radical political action, who find the whole debate on postmodernism and postmetropolises inherently conservative and politically numbing, who feel much more comfortable with the good old historical materialism of Marx rather than this new-fangled spatial and geographical stuff, who appreciate the gritty streetwise pluck of the truck driver-*flâneur* operating on his home ground, and who recoil from the presumed excesses of postmodern feminist critiques, Mike Davis has become a heroic figure. I can only add here that such romancing seriously constrains our efforts to make practical, political and theoretical sense of contemporary world, and weakens our ability to translate this knowledge into effective radical action.

Finally, we arrive at the sixth discourse, on the postmetropolis as Simcity, a place where simulations of a presumably real world increasingly capture and activate our urban imaginary and infiltrate everyday urban life. A key concept here is that of the simulacrum, roughly defined as an exact copy of something that may never have existed. Stated bluntly and with a nod to the work of Jean Baudrillard, the argument is that such simulations and simulacra, and the hyper-real worlds they define, are more than ever before shaping every aspect of our lives, from who and what we vote for to how we feed, clothe, mate and define our bodies. With this expansive blurring of the difference between the real and the imagined, there is what Baudrillard defines as a 'precession of simulacra', a situation in which simulations increasingly take precedence over the realities they are simulating. Our lives have always been shaped by these hyper-realities and by the specialized manufactories that produce them, from religious institutions to Hollywood and Disneyland.[5] Most of the time, however, one chose to go to these manufactories, usually passing through some gate and paying for admission. Today, again more than ever before, hyper-reality visits you, in your homes, in your daily lives.

At the very least, this Simcity discourse needs to be addressed seriously in contemporary urban studies, not just at the micro-scale of everyday life but also in macro-scale analyses of urbanisation and the social production of urban space. My own work has increasingly focused on this precession of simulacra and the growing hyper-reality of urban life in the postmetropolis, in part because I suspect that this restructuring of the urban imaginary is playing a key role in the emerging mode of social regulation associated with what the French regulation theorists define as the new regimes of capitalist accumulation (arising, I might add, primarily from the processes described in the first two discourses). There is so much to be discussed here, but too little time and space to do so. I offer instead some telling vignettes on what I call the 'scamscapes' of Orange County.

Orange County is one of the richest, best-educated, and most staunchly right-wing and Republican counties in the US. It has been a focal point for the local discourse on post-Fordist industrial restructuring and an exemplary case for my own discussions of the formation of Exopolis and the increasing hyper-reality of urban life.[6] In the hyper-real worlds of Orange County there has developed a particularly effulgent scamscape, my term for an environment in which the real and the imagined are so blurred that it encourages fraud and deceit as appropriate if not routine forms of behaviour. Orange County was one of the centres for the notorious Savings and Loans scandal that is costing the US untold billions of dollars to resolve; and it has been the most active area in the country for defence industry frauds. In one recent case, it was discovered that a plant making 'fuzes', switching devices that control whether or not nuclear missiles would explode, failed to test their products primarily because everyone genuinely believed the sign posted on the factory's walls: 'We make the best damned fuzes in the United States'. If so, why bother to test? Just confidently tick 'excellent' after every government query. Also representative of the scamscape are the 'boiler rooms', sort of high-tech sweatshops that are centres for all kinds of telemarketing frauds and scams. Nowhere are there more of these boiler rooms than in Orange County, and they are reputed to make higher profits than the drug dealers. In one of these busy hives of hyperfraud, a sign was found that captures the core of the scamscape's deceitful honesty. It said: 'we cheat the other guy and pass the savings on to you!'

In late 1994, the Orange County scamscape exploded in the largest municipal/county bankruptcy in US history. Exposed in the aftermath of this stunning declaration was a system of county and municipal governance that routinely ran the county's public economy as if it were a form of the popular computer game, *SimCity*, with a *sim*government serving *sim*citizens in what was essentially a *sim*county. Making the bankruptcy even more hyper-real was that the key figure, the county tax collector who was gambling the *sim*county's money in the financial cyberspace of exotic derivatives and leveraged synthetics, had a more than appropriate Orange County name: Citron! In this bastion of the new fiscal populism and small government is better government, this fountainhead of entrepreneurial unregulated capitalism, home of both Disneyland and the Richard M. Nixon Library and Birthplace, the proud centre for the foundational achievements of an ultra-conservative postmodern politics that cheats the other guy and passes the savings on to you, the simulation game broke down – and there was no button to push to reboot.

Also revealed by these events is the extraordinary degree to which government, politics and civil society in the US are being shaped by the precession of simulacra and a spin-doctored game of simulations. And from what I know of Thatcher's legacy, Britain today cannot be too far behind. This leads me to some brief conclusions. Like it or not, we are all living in an increasingly postmodern world that is creating new contexts and new challenges that cannot be effectively responded to by clinging to older ways of thinking and acting politically. The city and the urban still remain sites of contestation and struggle, but the social processes and spatial forms, and the spatial processes and social forms that define these struggles are now significantly different from what they were even ten years ago. Moreover, there are now some ample signs that the predominantly neo-conservative and neo-liberal forms of postmodern society and the postmetropolis that have consolidated from three decades of global and local restructuring are beginning to explode from their own success/excess. Such events as the Los Angeles Justice riots of 1992 and the Orange County bankruptcy of 1994 are not just local, isolated disturbances, but part of what may be emerging as a restructuring-generated global crisis. This makes it even more urgent for the Left and all other progressive thinkers and actors to resolve their internal divisions and act together to create an effective and emancipatory postmodern politics and a conceptual framework for an also explicitly postmodern critical urban studies that is appropriately and effectively attuned to the realities and hyper-realities of the contemporary moment.

N O T E S

1   This chapter is adapted from a keynote address presented at the annual meetings of the British Sociological Association. Leicester, April 12, 1995.

2   See Edward W. Soja, 'postmodern urbanization: the six restructurings of Los Angeles', in Sophie Watson and Kathy Gibson (eds), *Postmodern Cities and Spaces*, Oxford: Blackwell, 1995: 125–137; and *Postmetropolis*, forthcoming from Blackwell in 1997. At the time of the presentation from which this chapter is drawn (April, 1995), the discussion of the six discourses on the postmetropolis was contained in Part III of a manuscript entitled *Thirdspace: Journeys to Los Angeles and Other Real-and-Imagined Places*. Subsequently, it was decided to break the manuscript into two books. The first, with the title just mentioned, was published in 1996 by Blackwell.

3   Mike Savage and Alan Warde, *Urban Sociology, Capitalism and Modernity*, New York: Continuum, 1993.

4   See 'Poles Apart: New York and Los Angeles', in J. Mollenkopf and M. Castells (eds), *Dual City: The Restructuring of New York*, New York: Russell Sage Fondation, 1991: 361–376.

5   References to simulacra abound in the Bible and throughout the practices of Christianity. For faithful Catholics, statues of the Virgin Mary or Christ on the cross are not merely symbols but *real* presences, just as the communion host and wine *are* Christ's body and blood. One must actually behave as if these simulations are real.

6   Edward W. Soja, 'Inside Exopolis: Scenes From Orange County', in M. Sorkin (ed.), *Variations on a Theme Park: The New American City and the End of Public Space*, New York: Hill and Wang/Noonday Press, 1992: 277–298.

2

IMAGINING THE REAL-TIME CITY*

Telecommunications, urban paradigms and the future of cities

Stephen Graham

INTRODUCTION

> The chaos of American urban sprawl belongs not just to the city of
> steel and glass, but also to the other city – the phantom city of media
> and information. With most resources devoted to it, it is the cyber-city
> which is accelerating faster than the real urban space.
>
> (Channel 4 1994: 4)

How can we imagine the 'real-time' city? What does the growing mediation
of urban life by telecommunications imply for the way we view space, time,
place and the 'urban'? What becomes of urban areas when a growing range
of their constituent elements and processes – economic, social, cultural –
can and do become mediated via instantaneous flows of voices, information, images, services, money, capital and labour power, switched over
sophisticated telecommunications links between increasingly ubiquitous
computers? Does the city have a future when one of its key original roles –
that of supporting communication through concentration and propinquity
– may cease to matter? Are the traditional roles of urban areas as economic
dynamos of capitalism, and as the social and cultural crucibles of modern
life, simply evaporating in some transition to a 'post-urban' society where
the informational, communicational and transactional fabric of society is
'telemediated'?

This chapter explores these questions by examining the debates and
difficulties associated with imagining cities in a world shifting towards
increasingly pervasive and 'real-time' electronic flows. At the outset of this
exploration, it is important to establish the parallel but contrasting
communicational functions often ascribed to both modern cities and

*Thanks to Patsy Healey for her comments on the ideas that led to this chapter. Thanks
also to Richard Naylor and Vicki Belt for their comments on an earlier draft.

telecommunications links. On the one hand, it is traditionally popular to imagine the classic industrial metropolis as a giant generator of communication – economic, social and cultural. In 1966 Deutsch wrote that 'any metropolis can be thought of as a huge engine of communication, a device to enlarge the range and reduce the cost of individual and social choices' (Deutsch 1966: 386). Industrial cities grew cumulatively by providing all the 'external agglomerations' that physical concentration of employment, services, administration, transport and communications infrastructure and social and cultural facilities made possible. The time constraints inhibiting information exchange, communication and transactions were overcome or reduced by minimising the frictional effects of distance between activities in space. In other words, *space was used intensively to overcome time.* To a considerable extent, then, the classic 'Fordist–Modernist city' of the post-war boom, underpinned by specialised and integrated industrial economies, could be considered as an internally integrated locus of 'mass production, mass consumption, social interaction and institutional representation' (Amin and Thrift 1994). It was from this sense of the bounded, unitary city as a 'special place', separated from others by the frictional effects of Euclidean space, that the political and cultural power of urban places was seen to derive.

The shift away from the classic industrial metropolis is a multi-faceted restructuring process. But the growing telemediation of the economic, social and cultural life of the city is a key element of the challenge to this notion of the city (W. Mitchell 1995). It forces us to re-imagine urban places. This is because, at the most fundamental level, telecommunications and computer or telematics networks can be seen to have the opposite functional effect to the industrial city – that is, *they help overcome space and distance by minimising time constraints,* rather than the other way round. To use Marx's maxim, telecommunications 'annihilate space with time'; they are 'essentially based on an indifference to the notion of boundaries' (Negrier 1990: 13). Where quality telecommunications links exist, distance constraints can effectively collapse altogether (subject, of course, to the cost of using them and the technical and organisational barriers involved). Because they operate through flows of electrons or photons at or near to the speed of light, they overcome spatial barriers by minimising – or even eliminating – temporal barriers. They help overcome space/time barriers, and support the instantaneous or rapid mobility of information, messages, services, capital, images and labour power that are necessary to link widely dispersed sites into fast-moving and integrated economic, social and cultural systems.

Looking within the tensions between cities and telecommunications, with a view to understanding how we might imagine cities in a world shifting rapidly towards reliance on cheap and pervasive real-time flows, based on 'tele' interactions, this exploration has three parts. In the next section I set the context by investigating the problems that have beset attempts to treat telecommunications as a central focus of research within urban studies and urban planning and policy making. In the second section I review some of the most influential efforts to imagine cities in a world of pervasive real-time flows. In particular, I focus on two sets of influential analyses: one utopian and optimistic, based on predicting a telecommunications-based 'end' of the city; and another critical, often dystopian, approach highlighting the emergence of an ensnared, polarised and corporatised urban world based on telecommunications. Finally, I try to build on these by developing a new perspective for imagining how 'real-time' cities – that is, cities where all their constituent functions become hooked up to real-time telematics networks – might be understood.

TELECOMMUNICATIONS AS A PARADIGM CHALLENGE TO URBAN STUDIES, PLANNING AND POLICY

> Where the early market economies grew out of the temporal and spatial regularities of city life, today's are built on the logical or 'virtual' regularities of electronic communication, a new geography of nodes and hubs, processing and control centres.... Networks of computers, cables and radio links [now] govern where things go, how they are paid for, and who has access to what.
>
> (Mulgan 1991: 3)

The pervasive application of advanced telecommunications to urban life challenges many of the underlying assumptions in urban studies about how we can imagine cities and the processes of urban development, that have been built up since the emergence of industrial metropoli. As a consequence, empirical research tracing the links between cities and telecommunications is much rarer than speculative and generalised debate about how future cities will be 'impacted' by future technological advances (see Graham and Marvin 1996). The 'paradigm challenge' of telecommunications to urban studies has three aspects: the challenge of invisibility; the challenge of conceptualising space and time; and the challenge to urban planning.

First, whilst the Internet is beginning to make telecommunications more visualisable, it is easy to diagnose the historic *invisibility* of telecommunications in cities as a key reason for their neglect by urban studies. Unlike other visible infrastructures, such as roads, railways and airports, the effects of telecommunications on cities tend to be salient to only a few. New telecommunications networks tend to be largely *invisible* and *silent* or, at most, relatively hard to discern, weaving through or under the fabric of cities, using very little space. Urban telecommunications networks consist of underground networks of ducts and cables or aerial lattices of wires over which speed-of-light flows of electrons or photons carry information. Radio and satellite-based telecommunications networks rely on the truly invisible flows of electromagnetic radiation across space between antennae, transmitters and aerials. This fundamentally hidden nature of telecommunications distinguishes it from virtually all other aspects of urban development. Michael Batty suggests that 'much of that [telecommunications-based] change has a degree of invisibility which does not characterise traditional economic and social activity' (Batty 1990).

Second, it can be argued that the relative lack of empirical research on cities and telecommunications is closely related to the way space and time have tended to be conceptualised in urban studies. Crucial, from our point of view, was the general treatment of space and time in approaches to studying the development of the industrial city up to the late 1970s. Especially in the 'scientific' period which prevailed between the late 1950s and mid-1970s, positivist epistemologies dominated, approaching cities and social structures as though they developed within the *external environments* of an 'objective' time and an external, physical and 'Cartesian' space (Lefebvre 1991: 1). Space was treated as an absolute object *within which* human life was played out, a Euclidean notion based on enclosure and exclusion (Emberley 1989: 745) and 'a passive arena, the setting for objects and their interaction' (Massey 1992). Urban space was to be understood as a Cartesian object to be inspected through 'perspectival vision' (Jay 1988), first through art and later through maps, aerial photographs, remote sensing and mathematical spatial modelling of urban structures spread out across a Euclidean plain. As Ed Soja argues, until very recently 'geography ... treated space as the domain of the dead, the fixed, the undialectic, the immobile – a world of passivity and measurement rather than action and meaning' (Soja 1989: 37).

Meanwhile, the importance of time in social life was also seen to echo classical Newtonian physics, to be a simple, invariant, *container* for urban and social life, an elementary measure of duration and succession (Lash and Urry 1994: 237; Giddens 1979: 202; Emberley 1989: 745). In this view, cities grew by overcoming the effects that distance and time delays produced, inhibiting movement and interaction. Through intense concentrations of activities in Euclidean space, information flows, communications and transactions became more efficient, both within tightly integrated cities and within networks of interlinked national systems of cities.

Such absolute and objective views of time and space were closely wedded to the broader elaboration of modernity. Massive industrial metropoli were the dominant economic, social, cultural and political constructions of modern industrial society between the early nineteenth and mid-twentieth centuries. They became closely woven into these wider 'modern' treatments of time and space – with their abstract and rational systems of measurement and partitioning, their regular and routinised patterns for work, sleep and leisure, their rational grid-like plans and their soaring skyscrapers. Cartesian and abstract notions of space and universal, absolute ideas of time became infused into everyday conceptions of the urban world (see Kern 1983). Understanding of 'modern' cities was dominated by 'a visual space of discrete points, planes and boundaries engendering the notions of spatial exclusivity, enclosure, visibility and distance as well as those of association and order' (Emberley 1989: 747).

But such absolute conceptual treatments of time and space, and such imagining of cities, made it difficult, if not impossible, to fully appreciate the importance of advanced telecommunications. They tend to result in telecommunications being seen as technologies which can overcome space and time *constraints*, rather than as technological networks *within which* new forms of human interaction, control and organisation can actually be *constructed* in real (or near real) time. To allow this to happen, new approaches are needed which adopt fully *relational* views of space and time as 'time–space', so acknowledging the social construction of reality within which telecommunications have effects (Healey *et al.* 1995). As Bruno Latour argues:

> Most of the difficulties we have in understanding science and technology proceed from our belief that space and time exist independently as an unshakable frame of reference *inside which* events and place would occur. This belief makes it impossible to understand how different spaces and different times may be produced *inside the networks* built to mobilise, cumulate and recombine the world.
>
> (Latour 1987: 228)

With the pervasive application of digital mass and personal communications networks across the globe, images, symbols, information, data and communications contacts now simultaneously and instantly saturate the postmodern urban world. And as more sophisticated telecommunications emerge which support graphical environments and 3D interactions in 'virtual' spaces, constructed with software, so telemediation begins to occur in tangible spaces and 'places', which are more and more similar to the familiar environments we inhabit in cities. Ideas of bounded, integrated and mechanical cities, separated from each other by the frictional effects of distance, no longer capture the meshing of urban functions into pervasive lattices of real-time functions that criss-cross the globe based on computer networks. This leads to a sense of the opening up of urban elements to be tied intimately into global flows, rather than though intense place-based 'relational webs'. 'The overall impression is of the fragmentation of the city's component parts, rather than any idea of the city as an integrated, functioning whole' (Gold 1985: 98).

The third and final reason for the neglect of telecommunications has been the difficulties faced by urban planners and policy makers in understanding city–telecommunications relationships in the post-war period. Urban planning and policy was heavily influenced by the positivist theories of urban development that emerged during the 1950s and 1960s. Planners concerned themselves with economic and social modernisation and the need to improve the *locational efficiency* of cities and urban regions. They tried to plan their cities as approximations of the 'perfect' physical systems predicted by theory, a technical, rational process that would be socially neutral in its effects, helping to secure a single 'public interest' (Rydin 1993; Boyer 1986). 'Most planners share a conviction that the physical and locational variables are key determinants of social and economic behaviour and of social welfare' (Webber 1964: 85).

These ideas focused the attention of planners on the need to improve the *physical* mobility of people and goods within cities, and to locate physical facilities and land uses with maximum efficiency within a unitary, integrated city (Webber 1968: 1093). New Modernist environments – urban motorways, mass housing schemes, comprehensively redeveloped city centres – were superimposed on the fabric of the chaotic pre-modern city, leading to 'rational' and improved patterns and processes of urban life (Boyer 1986). The basic assumption was therefore an environmentally determinist one: that 'by changing the *physical and the locational environments at the places* in which families live out their lives and in which groups conduct their business, the lives and the businesses can be improved' (Webber 1964: 84; emphasis added).

Once again, though, telecommunications were largely ignored in these considerations, particularly in Britain (Graham 1995) and the United States (Mandelbaum 1986). Their intangibility meant that they had never stimulated the urban political movements that led urban planning to intervene in roads, railways, airports and the built environment. As Mandelbaum argues, 'the concept of an urban communication infrastructure was not expressed in local institutions comparable to those which realized public concerns with education, environmental quality, housing or transportation' (ibid.: 134). Responsibility for regulating and developing the slow-moving urban telecommunications infrastructures of the time fell outside the planners' remit, resting usually with distant, centralised public bureaucracies or virtually autonomous public and private enterprises.

To make matters even more difficult, urban planners and local governments inevitably have to deal with bounded and enclosed jurisdictional definitions of urban space. This leads to further difficulties in taking account of real-time flows of capital, information, services and labour power that continually and invisibly puncture these boundaries. Noting this, Nigel Thrift comments 'it has become increasingly difficult to imagine cities as bounded space–times with definite surroundings, wheres and elsewheres' (Thrift 1993: 14). Emberley remarks that 'one can see that such [bounded] models continue to operate within conceptions of sequential, durational time and enclosed, exclusive space' (Emberley 1989: 767; see Graham 1996). The challenge to planners is therefore to develop new ways of thinking and acting that reflects the growing telemediation of urban life. Some progress is being made here, however, especially in France. A recent communications plan for Lille argues, for example, that:

> the traditional concepts of urban and regional planning are today outmoded. The harmonious development of areas towards equilibrium, the correct sharing out of resources, providing support to complementary developments within the city ... these ideas have given way to the impression that spaces are fragmented, atomised and strongly competitive ... the insertion of telecommunications into the city makes the development of spaces more complex and introduces today a third dimension into urban and regional planning [after space and time]: this is the factor of real-time.

DISCOURSES OF DEMATERIALISATION:
CYBERSPACE UTOPIAS AND URBAN DYSTOPIAS

The difficulties faced by the urban studies and planning communities, in analysing and conceptualising telecommunications-based urban development, has left the terrain open for a wide range of more general speculations on how future cities might be influenced by the radical extension of telecommunications. Two broad perspectives have dominated here. First, there is a long history of futuristic and utopian commentary where telematics are seen as departure points for a new humanistic and decentralised post-urban society. This is seen to herald various degrees of social equality, liberation and the transcendence of the limitations and problems derived from the old industrial city. Second, there are a wide range of dystopian and critical scenarios – many of which stem from critical theory – where telematics are seen to be closely woven in with the onset of a more polarised and disempowering urban world. Interestingly, however, there are often some surprising parallels between certain parts of these two strands of work, in their predictions of a shift towards a 'dematerialised' society which is no longer attached to the specific qualities offered by urban places. It is worth briefly looking at these in turn.

Cyberspace utopias: the anything-anywhere-anytime dream

Various strands of commentary, from the 1960s technological forecasters to the 1990s 'cybernauts', have predicted some pervasive shift to a tele-mediated, utopian and effectively *post-urban* age (Stallabrass 1995). Whilst these strands vary, a remarkable degree of commonality exists in their assumptions about how current advances in telecommunications will influence cities. As with the often-related approaches deriving from technological determinism, the 'logic' of telecommunications and electronic mediation is interpreted as *inevitably* supporting urban decentralisation or even urban dissolution. As Gillespie (1992) argues, 'in all ... utopian visions, the decentralising impacts of communications technology are regarded as unproblematic and self evident'.

This is often linked with an underlying anti-urbanism, leading to predictions of electronic interactions in 'electronic spaces' constructed by telematics hardware and software supplanting those in urban places. Gold (1990: 22) suggests that underpinning many futuristic visions is 'a prevailing hostility towards the metropolitan city and a social philosophy that aims to break up the mass society and recreate smaller communities. In these visions a new urban order arises in which people can move back to the "natural" surroundings of the countryside while still retaining close connection with their workplaces and with the culturally-enriching aspects of city life.'

These sorts of ideas have a long history. Goldmark (1972), for example, predicted that telecommuting to work would liberate people from the 'conditions of extreme density within the confines of cities and their suburbs' that they were forced to endure as a result of the growth of the great industrial metropolis. People, he argued, were 'physiologically and psychologically unprepared for' this 'unnatural' life; cities were the areas where 'problems of crime, pollution, poverty, traffic, education etc. are the greatest' (ibid.). The resulting home-centred society therefore overcomes the environmental, social and political problems associated with the industrial city.

A new convivial, democratic and environmentally sustainable society of home-based small-town or rural life therefore becomes possible (see Toffler 1980). Of course, the other effect of this shift is the virtual dissolution of the great industrial cities that become little more than centrifuges for the 'export' of their contents. The key axis emerges as the interplay between the individual in the 'electronic cottage' (ibid.) or the 'smart home' (Mason and Jennings 1982) and global lattices of telemediated flow; the dynamic linking social groups and the city evaporates. 'Whereas, in the past, life at home was often confining and oppressive', write Mason and Jennings, 'the home centred life of the future may be exhilarating and mind-expanding, thanks to worldwide networks of electronic communication' (ibid.: 35). Computer-based access to electronic spaces 'will bring into the home environment many of the facilities and services we now often travel many miles to obtain at schools, libraries, offices, theatres etc.... It will provide a new focus for human life – a twenty first century version of the hearth that was so long an essential feature of the "home" in every age and civilisation.' Telework will replace physical commuting to work; tele-education and tele-health will replace schools, universities and doctors; tele-services will replace face-to-face services; teleshopping-based 'virtual' malls will eventually supplant town centres and out-of-town retailing (Sheth and Sisodia 1993).

Usually, futurists go on to argue that this will iron out geographical differences, totally redefine cities and make location virtually irrelevant. Negroponte (1995: 165) believes that 'digital living' 'will remove the limitations of geography'. Telematics networks will replace physical concentration and will also overcome the need to travel, and solve many of the problems which futurists and utopianists see as the results of concentration in industrial cities. Naisbitt and Aburdene (1991: 329), for example, see 'a new electronic heartland of linked small towns and cities as laying the groundwork for the decline of cities ... in many ways, if cities did not exist, it now would not be necessary to invent them ... truly global cities will not be the largest, they will be the smartest'. But such predictions of urban decline have attracted a range of followers beyond the utopianists and futurists. To Marshall McLuhan, for example, the emergence of the 'global village' meant that the city 'as a form of major dimensions must inevitably dissolve like a fading shot in a movie' (McLuhan quoted in Gold 1990: 23). Webber, in his assertion that society was on the verge of a 'post city age' predicted that

> for the first time in history, it might be possible to locate on a mountain top and to maintain intimate, real-time and realistic contact

with business and other societies. All persons tapped into the global communications network would have ties approximating those used in a given metropolitan region.

(Webber 1968)

Cities will therefore 'vanish' as their chief *raison d'être* – face-to-face contact – is substituted by electronic networks and spaces (Pascal 1987: 59). New rural societies will emerge, as people exercise their new freedom to locate in small, attractive settlements that are better suited to their needs (Goldmark 1972).

Interestingly, many of the current 'cyberspace' debates in the media and the press surrounding the Internet follow similar lines of reasoning, alleging the fundamentally empowering and liberating importance of electronic 'cyberspaces', or the emerging 'information superhighway', based on the Internet (see Stallabrass 1995). Here, too, the almost universal assumption in their speculations is that we are moving to a world where *all information will be available at all times and places to all people*. For example, Godfrey and Parhill (1979: 10) declare: 'all information in all spaces at all times. The impossible ideal. But the marriage of computers with existing communications links will take us far closer to that goal than we have ever been.'

Often, these commentaries are breathless and excited, offering tantalising future glimpses of how remarkable advances in new technologies will determine future lifestyles that are incalculably 'better' than those today. Almost always, this future state is offered as a scenario where, as Eubanks (1994) believes, 'potentially huge benefits are to be had by all'. Maisonrouge (1984: 31) argues that 'modern information processing capability creates a society where everyone has an equal opportunity to be information literate . . . telecommunications and the computer are making information accessible to everyone'. Santucci (1994: 16) predicts that a 'truly planetary consciousness will spring from the establishment, at world level, of bidirectional information highways accessible to all individuals'. Through the humble personal computer and modem, it is argued, individuals can now shape, participate in and interact with a vast range of new multimedia spaces rather than merely being passive consumers of a narrow range of TV, newspapers and radio as in the past (Leary 1994; Negroponte 1995). The explosion of the Internet makes massive information resources available on all subjects all over the world to be accessed from anyone's desk. This occurs irrespective of location, disability, gender, 'race' or other characteristics that have led to repression and subjugation in previous eras.

Increasingly, many futurists predict that the burgeoning capability of computers and the plummeting costs of telecommunications bandwidth mean that the transmission of voices, data and images will shift to the creation and transmission of whole virtual environments which are remotely accessible. 'The transmission of place itself will start to become possible' (Negroponte 1995: 165). Such virtual reality (VR) technologies will lead to a culture based on the notion of:

'being there'. You will buy one terminal that will integrate all the capabilities [of a phone, video, camcorder and computer] together. Then we will be able to enter the real world from a distance – to go to the Olympic Games, Wembley Stadium or Wimbledon or whatever from our living room or office. We will be able to have new experiences and go to places we've never been before. I would guess that we will see 40 years experience crammed into just a five year period.

(Cochrane quoted in Harrison 1995: 7)

All this will 'enhance the individual, to break down the walls between individuals', so creating a humanistic 'cultural renaissance' of truly histor- ical proportions (Rushkoff quoted in Channel 4 1994: 15). In theory, interactive cyberspaces can be constructed *ad infinitum*; consequently utopianists stress that cyberspace can be seen as an infinite resource offering perpetual solutions to the finitudes of the real urban world. Don Mapes even suggests that 'we have to do away with our territoriality. The good news is: Cyberspace is big. It's basically infinite. Earth is limited, it's finite. In cyberspace, if you don't like it, you can move out to the next frontier. There's always another continent in cyberspace' (Mapes quoted in Channel 4 1994: 19).

Urban dystopias: beyond *Blade Runner*

A highly contrasting stream of commentary on the telemediation of urban life has emerged from a disparate group of critics (for example, Mike Davis), novelists (such as William Gibson), philosophers (for example, Fredric Jameson) and social theorists (such as Manuel Castells and Paul Virilio) (see Graham and Marvin 1996, Chapter 3). Whilst far from homogeneous, such perspectives centre on highlighting the dystopian tendencies in the processes alleged to be under way – usually in North American cities – toward more polarised, fragmented and divided cities. Here the new capabilities that telematics bring are alleged to put cities increasingly at the mercy of globally operating corporate economic power; to trap them in an increasingly violent spiral of decay, poverty and polarisation; and to underpin the packaging of urban landscapes into commodified fragments which are tightly controlled to maximise consump- tion. To Davis (1992: 2), for example, the reality of contemporary Los Angles already goes beyond what he calls the 'Wellsian' caricature in Ridley Scott's *Blade Runner*. Rather, he builds on William Gibson's science fiction to map out the highly polarised and militarised urban present of LA, where telematics underpin both the social segmentations, the surveillance and control, and the maintenance of spatial power within the fragmented metropolis.

Three interlinked shifts are usually highlighted in critical treatments of telematics-based urban development. First, stress is placed on the degree to which telematics-based shifts in work, social interaction and urban culture are promoting heightened social polarisation within cities. Telematics-based changes in the lifestyles of affluent and mobile elites are seen to perpetuate the wider advantages they enjoy because of economic restructuring, the erosion of the welfare state, and their physical shift away from urban cores into affluent suburban or 'exurban' communities (Castells 1985). Those in poverty, meanwhile, become physically trapped in inner urban cores, beyond the economic and technological mainstream of society. To Davis (1993: 12), the danger is that 'urban cyberspace – as the simulation of the city's information order – will be experienced as even more segregated, and devoid of true public space, than the traditional built city'. 'South central L.A.', he writes, 'is a data and media "black hole", without local cable programming or links to major data systems. Just as it became a housing/jobs ghetto in the early twentieth century industrial city, it is now evolving into an electronic ghetto within the emerging information city.'

Second, the emergence of a paranoid and 'fortressed' home-based culture, particularly in the United States, is highlighted, based on spiralling fears of the 'Other' in the postmodern city. Fear of crime and social alienation with urban life are seen as key supports to the trend toward the 'cocooning' of the middle classes, in enclaves that are further and further away from the old urban cores. Broadly, the argument here is that people are exploring the 'electronic spaces' based on telematics because they are increasingly alienated by the processes of change under way in many American cities. Far more so than in Europe, for example, the urban middle classes have scattered to be 'cocooned' in suburban areas which have little genuine public space. Such suburbanites are increasingly paranoid about crime and the incursions of different social groups, leading to physical gates and electronic surveillance systems being installed, which furthers their isolation and fear. And so the cycle continues. In other words, 'virtual cities' in electronic spaces, based on systems like the Internet, with their informal 'electronic cafés' and interactive discussion groups, are an electronic *antidote* to the depressing reality of real urban life. They are a form of 'world rejection' (Schroeder 1994: 524), allowing social connection to occur whilst people become disconnected from the urban world. The clear risk here is that 'telematically linked communities could fragment our larger society, enabling each of us to pursue isolation from everything different, or unfamiliar, or threatening, and removing the occasions for contact across lines of class, race and culture' (Calhoun 1986). A recent Channel 4 (1994: 5) television programme commented that access to telematics networks for shopping, leisure and work 'looks safe indeed compared to urban decay. Paranoia, violence and pollution are eating away at the soul of America, driving it inward – to the protection of the home, private security, entry codes, and video-surveillance-controlled gated fortresses.'

Many critics, meanwhile, highlight the ways in which city centres are being redeveloped along postmodern lines as 'themed', enclosed and commercialised districts (Davis 1990; Sorkin 1992; Christopherson 1994). These centres are dominated by large retail and leisure chains, and many 'undesirable social groups' are purposefully excluded to maximise consumption and profit. Here, too, it is alleged, informal public space is squeezed out through commercialisation (D. Mitchell 1995). But, whilst the unregulated and anarchic nature of the Internet may currently offer solace for alienated suburban Americans, some critics argue that it, too, is now becoming commercialised as one vast 'electronic shopping mall' – so mirroring the narrow and commercialised orientation of most American malls and downtowns. So this antidote may just be temporary. Some critics have recently started to raise interesting questions about the ways in which *electronic spaces* may be subject to similar patterns of commodification and control as urban landscapes are – with the shift toward the 'themed' packaging of urban landscapes for consumption (Sorkin 1992; Boyer 1993). It is alleged that corporations are increasingly attempting to 'package' electronic spaces for the purposes of *electronic* consumption in ways that closely relate to, and increasingly actually join with, the wider commodification of urban space.

Fred Dewey draws attention to the (admittedly untypical) example of Las Vegas. Here, 20 million visitors a year now spend $4.5 billion in themed hotels and gambling and leisure spaces. An increasing attraction, though, is a range of enormous complexes filled with the latest virtual reality entertainment technologies such as the 'Virtualand' centre. In these, participants explore electronically constructed worlds for pleasure which have many similarities with the themed physical environments within which they are placed (Channel 4 1994: 5). According to Fred Dewey, such trends represent a blurring of the differences between electronic spaces and urban places, as both succumb to commodification, simulation and packaging for individualised consumption. He argues that:

> we are already very much inside a 'virtual' environment, and what's really being impoverished is the world of real experience, and people interacting with each other. . . . What's developing now is an entirely new form of controlled environment. We already find malls, theme parks and themed environments. These provide safe, secure environments where people can interact. It looks very much like public life, but in fact really isn't, because the environments are owned and controlled and heavily regulated by, generally, large global corporations. People interact somewhat randomly, but the actual experience is entirely manufactured – all of its terms are defined ahead of time. The experience is very similar to going through virtual reality. While this provides a kind of vitality, at the same time it's based on leaving behind the mess of real urban life. Everyone expects that the Cyberworld is not going to have these kinds of parameters and controls. This is extremely unrealistic.
>
> (Dewey quoted in Channel 4 1994: 5–6)

Finally, the commodification of all digital information by giant corporations to be sold on-line via cybernetic systems of production, distribution and consumption is stressed (Mosco 1988). Schiller and Fregaso (1991: 202), for example, argue that 'the concerted drive to privatize telecommunications should be viewed as an effort to create a thoroughgoing global foundation for systematic corporate exploitation of information'.

The combined effects of these trends is widely viewed, particularly in the North American literature, as the complete collapse of the public sphere of the postmodern city. Emberley (1989: 754) believes that 'what is obvious is that the possibility of space being invested with human meaning, such that it could be interpreted as "place" has evaporated here'. To Michael Sorkin (1992: xi) 'computers, credit cards, phones, faxes, and other instruments of instant artificial adjacency are rapidly eviscerating the historic politics of propinquity, the very cement of the city'. Edward Soja remarks that Los Angeles is now

> divided into showcases of global village cultures and mimetic American landscapes, all-embracing shopping malls and crafty main streets, corporation-sponsored magic kingdoms, high-technology based experimental prototype communities of tomorrow, attractively packaged places of rest and recreation all cleverly hiding the buzzing workstations and labor processes that keep it together.
>
> (Soja 1989: 246)

The end of public space in cities is seen as part of a shift to a 'society that expects and desires only private interactions, private communications and private politics, that reserves public spaces solely for commodified recreation and spectacle' (D. Mitchell 1995: 121). Cyberspaces become the 'new frontier of public space' which supersede the material public spaces of the modernist city (ibid.: 122). On the economic front, Castells (1989) argues that, whilst key global cities such as London and New York are emerging as nodes of profound economic power, within the global informational economy, this is part of a wider economic shift from a 'space of places' to a 'space of flows' where places only have economic meaning through their configuration in global telematics networks dominated by multinational capital: 'the supersession of places by a network of information flows is a fundamental goal of the restructuring process' (Castells 1989: 349).

Paul Virilio has argued that the new urban era is marked by the use of telecommunications and telematics to support what he calls an 'urbanization of *real time*'. This follows the previous era of the 'urbanization of *real space*' – that is, the *physical* building of industrial cities (Virilio 1993: 3). Because time barriers are being so comprehensively challenged by the global 'instantaneity' of telematics, Virilio argues that the physical boundaries of cities – what he calls the 'urban wall' – 'has given way to an infinity of openings and enclosures' (Virilio 1987: 20), where telecommunications and telematics networks interpenetrate invisibly and secretly with the physical fabric of cities. Distance and space boundaries collapse and the ability for individuals to be 'telepresent' through real-time interactions at any location means eventually that the very practice of physical concentration or movement seem likely to be overcome. 'Everything arrives so quickly that departure becomes unnecessary' (Virilio 1993: 8). To Virilio, this challenges accepted notions of the nature of cities and urban life. What he calls the 'unity of place without unity of time' emerges which 'makes the city disappear into the heterogeneity of advanced technology's temporal regime. Urban form is no longer designated by a line of demarcation between here and there, but has become synonymous with the programming of a "time schedule". Its gateway is less a door which must be opened but an audio-visual protocol – a protocol which reorganizes the modes of public perception' (Virilio 1987: 19). Virilio predicts the ultimate cocooning of the urban masses, and the evaporation of the place-based meaning of the city, as the urbanisation of real time displaces and overcomes the need for movement and concentration in cities. 'The city of the past slowly becomes a paradoxical agglomeration in which relations of immediate proximity give way to interrelationships over distance' (Virilio 1993: 10). Startlingly, he predicts a 'growing inertia' as citizens cease to travel physically and instead operate their tele-interactions from home. This shift, he argues, 'is ultimately felt in the very body of the city dweller, as a terminal citizen who will soon be equipped with interactive prostheses whose pathological model is that of the "motorized handicapped", equipped so that he or she can control the domestic environment and enter a vast range of global networks without undergoing any physical displacement' (ibid.: 11).

REIMAGINING THE REAL-TIME CITY: URBAN PLACES, ELECTRONIC SPACES

I should note that in both these summaries I am guilty to some extent of caricaturing complex and diverse arguments for the sake of brevity and clarity. Both the utopian and the critical discourses on cities are diverse, contested and heterogeneous. Not all predict some simple 'end' to cities; not all imply that telematics are the inevitable motors of some 'post-urban' shift. Nevertheless, I would argue that whilst much of this commentary offers some useful insights into how we might imagine the real-time city, both the utopian and, to a lesser extent, the dystopian visions can often be criticised as being partial, oversimplified and technologically deterministic. The main problem in many of the more simplistic utopian or dystopian approaches is that, in their simple recourse to some all-encompassing 'vision of heaven or hell' (Harrison 1995), they tend to assume there is a single future for all places and all cities. Simple determinism is common. Utopian approaches tend to resort to technological determinism – current or future urban changes are often assumed to be determined by technological changes in some simple, linear, cause and effect manner. Dystopian approaches, on the other hand, can often be accused of social determinism – the urban implications of telecommunications are seen to be the result of the simple imprinting of some global capitalist political economy onto cities. In both, the 'urban impacts' of telecommunications often appear to be apparently homogeneous, linear and direct. As with much social research on technology, there is a tendency in many approaches to invoke what Gökalp calls 'grand metaphors' of the nature of telecommunications-based change in cities. In the utopian literature especially, modern telecommunications tend to be seen as an autonomous agent which somehow induces a 'shock', 'wave' or 'revolution' to sweep across all cities in the same way. Most often, analysis centres on speculations concerning the 'impacts' of telecommunications on *future* cities in a general and vague way. *Actual* telecommunications-based developments in *real* contemporary cities are rarely analysed in detail, a device which conveniently allows the complex relations between telecommunications and contemporary cities to be overlooked (Robins and Hepworth 1988).

In fact, any assumption of the simple and pervasive 'end' of the city seems misplaced. The pervasive application of real-time technologies to cities is part of a shift to a *new type of urban world*, rather than a *post-urban world* (Graham and Marvin 1996). The dominance of cities cannot be simply disinvented – they represent an incalculable sunk investment and the dominance of urban systems shows much inertia. Whilst cities are often spreading out to be vast, multi-centred urban regions linked into global networks, not all of the place-based relational webs that rely on adjacency and propinquity within cities can, or will, be superseded by telematics. Often these webs – the new industrial spaces, the research and development parks, the high-level corporate and financial services, the centralised back-office functions, the social, leisure and shopping activities, the clusters of educational and innovational activities, the massive transport infrastructures – are actually strengthened by the shift to tele-mediation. This is because telematics allow large cities to extend their strategic dominance by 'acting at a distance', and dominating what goes on in other places, in a volatile and global economic environment.

Many effects of telecommunications, in fact, seem to support new types of urbanisation, which often strengthen and remake place-based relational meanings in cities. London, New York and Tokyo, for example, have managed to maintain or extend the place-based relational meaning, that derives from their functions as global command and finance centres. As Castells (1989) and Sassen (1991) have demonstrated, their crucial roles as global transport and telecommunications hubs, along with their concentrations of scarce skills, social and cultural advantages, tacit information, and the importance of face-to-face exchanges at the apex of corporate power, have all reinforced the positions of these cities. They now function as key command, control and financial centres, for globally scattered multi-national corporations as well as an integrated global financial marketplace (Sassen 1991; Moss 1987). The key strategic role of certain cities in a global society has led some to speculate that the centrality of certain cities might actually be reinforced by shifts to a world dominated by real-time flows (see Knight and Gappert 1989). Landry and Bianchini (1995a), for example, note the 'rebirth of the city as the real driver of economic and cultural change ...' in an era when the powers of nation-states seem increasingly transcended by globalisation. Parkinson (1994: 83), meanwhile, argues that 'major metropolitan areas, situated at the centre of communications networks and offering easy access to national and international institutions, the arts, cultural and media industries, are, if anything, becoming more attractive to international finance houses, corporate headquarters and producer service companies'. The continuing importance of cities is shown by the way they still dominate telecommunications investment and use (Graham and Marvin 1996: Chapter 4). Cities have the greatest concentrations of demand, the most sophisticated users, and are increasingly attractive to telecommunications operators in an increasingly market-driven regulatory era. It is clear that whilst telematics 'produce a new and more elaborate temporal order', these effects actually tend to 'erupt within the spatial order of the old city' (Wark 1988). So space and time, and speed and distance are thrown together in new and often bewildering ways within the physical arenas of dominant cities. As Mulgan (1991: 13) suggests, 'information technologies continue to be most revolutionary not in creating the new out of nothing but rather in restructuring the way old things are done'.

In fact, what seems to be emerging – far from being a renaissance in rural ways of life – is a *more totally urbanised world*, where rural spaces and lifestyles are being *drawn into an urban realm*, because of the time–space transcending capabilities of telecommunications and fast transportation networks. This represents not the death of cities and the renaissance of genuinely rural ways of life, but the emergence of a 'superurban' and 'super-industrial' capitalist society operating via global networks. Equally, there is little evidence to support the idea that growing telecommunication flows substitute for transport and physical movement in the emergence of some totally cocooned and immobile home-based culture. Rather, our society seems to be moving toward a reliance on more intense flows of *both* physical and electronic communication. Certainly, in terms of economic processes and with the communications patterns of affluent global elites, physical and electronic communications encourage each other through mutually reinforcing feedback effects. The complex positive interactions between transport and telecommunications make this increasingly clear (Graham and Marvin 1996). Advanced telecommunications actually stimulate massive transport flows (for example, tourism, global conferences and just-in-time logistics shipments); they are used to control, monitor and facilitate ever-intensifying transport movements; they help increase the capacities of road, rail and airline networks; and they limit the negative effects of transport congestion (as with the use of mobile phones, for example).

What we need, clearly, are new 'relational' concepts of the 'urban' which address the continuous interweaving of place-based relations and flows with electronic ones. The 'urban' can now be seen as a locus for many social, economic, institutional and technological networks spread out over diffuse and extended regions (see Healey *et al.* 1995). But there is now no *necessary* correlation between physical propinquity and relational meaning – as was so often assumed in positivistic formulations and absolute ideas of time and space (ibid.). Such meaning, however, still occurs and is still very important. Notions of 'community' are required which take account of the fact that geographical neighbours may or may not have meaningful social contacts with each other, whilst they may each link into geographically stretched 'virtual communities' based on phones and electronic media (Jones 1995). Approaches to 'urban culture' must similarly address the fact that urban public space may or may not emerge as a common cultural arena, but that this will interact with the forging of diverse cultural identities via both passive mass media (for example, transnational television) and interactive electronic media (such as the Internet) (Morley and Robins 1995). Finally, concepts of the 'urban economy' must address the fact that firms may or may not create linkages with adjacent or local firms, whilst they are likely to be tied into geographically stretched transactional and linkage chains, based on advanced telecommunications. Thus it is clear that complex combinations of electronic propinquity in the 'non-place urban realm' (Webber 1964) and place-based relational meanings based on physical propinquity and transport need to be considered in parallel. Place-based and place-bound ways of living, and the social, economic, institutional and cultural dynamics that can arise where urban propinquity does matter is still critically important in shaping how cities and localities are woven into global lattices of mobility and flow (Amin and Thrift 1994; Healey *et al.* 1995). The vast city region, tied intimately into global grids of electronic flow and held together by electronic as well as place-based connections, is still a *meaningful* place (Wilson 1995b). And for large sections of urban populations who, without access to either physical or electronic communications, remain physically trapped in the traditionally marginalised life of the impoverished, the talk of the 'death' of cities through 'universal interactivity' is little more than absurd. It is also easy to forget that distance decay and the frictional effects of distance are still critical in influencing the vast majority of social interactions and physical flows. Indeed, the vast bulk of electronic social relations operate over small distances within extended urban regions in ways that are related closely to the immediate face-to-face contacts of people at work and home.

The mistaken assumption of a universal post-urban shift also means that the contingency and diversity in city-telecommunications relations is usually overlooked (see Pool 1977). An over-reliance on the American literature is particularly unhelpful; not all cities will be affected in the same way as Los Angeles or Las Vegas. Different cultural, political-economic and social contexts will mean that different advanced industrial cities, and the diverse groups who inhabit them, are likely to be affected very differently by advanced telecommunications. Neither technological nor social determinism are helpful here. Telematics, whilst biased, are to some extent *indeterminate* in their effects in cities, depending on how they are used and socially constructed, within prevailing social, cultural and political-economic contexts (see Hill 1988; Graham and Marvin 1996). Their impact is not pre-defined to somehow shift us automatically to some post-urban world. Effects will be different for different cities; complex combinations of positive and negative effects are likely to develop; and there will be a diverse terrain of winners and losers in the shift to telemediated urban development. Some examples illustrate the need for a fine-grained perspective to capture the complexity and contingency at work. Europeans, for example, have been shown to be much less interested in tele-mediated social interaction and consumption than Americans (Bannister 1994). Women have been shown to use the basic telephone in ways that support distant social and familial links (that is, for 'intrinsic' communication), whilst men tend to use it 'to get things done' or for 'action at a distance' (that is, for 'instrumental' communication) (Moyal 1992). Different nation-states have been shown to produce diverse trajectories of telecommunications development because of their political, cultural and geopolitical variety, leading to very distinct urban telecommunications developments in different cities (De Gournay 1988; Dutton, Blumler and Kraemer 1987).

In fact, it seems likely that urban telecommunications developments are socially constructed in diverse ways and that such contingency is recursively linked with the diverse shaping of urban places (see W. Mitchell 1995). This makes the simple prediction of generalised 'post-urban' state unhelpful. This means that it is helpful to replace the notion of the 'urban impacts' of telecommunications by looking at how urban places and the electronic spaces accessible through telecommunications might recursively interact and be socially constructed together (see ibid.). A starting-point here is to look at the complementary characteristics of urban places and electronic spaces (see Figure 2.1; Graham and Marvin 1996).

It is parallel systems linking presence in urban places with presence in electronic spaces that seem to be the defining social constructions of contemporary urbanism as the current trends towards the development of 'intelligent buildings', 'smart homes', 'tele-villages', 'teleports' and 'cyber-cafés' make clear (see Graham and Marvin 1996; W. Mitchell 1995). For example, both urban places and electronic spaces are subject to similar processes of inter-linked social struggle, as between the demands of social equity, public space and local accountability and the commodifying

Urban places (Based on buildings, streets, roads, and the physical spaces of cities)	Electronic spaces (Constructed 'inside' telematics networks using computer software)
Overcome time constraints by minimising space constraints	Overcome *space* constraints by minimising *time* constraints
Territory	Network
Fixity	Motion/flux
Embedded	Disembedded
Material	Immaterial
Visible	Invisible
Tangible	Intangible
Actual	Virtual/abstract
Euclidean/social space	Logical space

Figure 2.1 Characterising urban places and electronic spaces

tendencies of global commercialisation. Murdock (1993: 534), for example, draws the striking parallel between the 'fortress effect' generated by many postmodern office buildings, and the development of vast, private 'dataspaces' on corporately controlled networks, arguing that, 'here, as in territorial space, a continuous battle is being waged between claims for public access and use, and corporate efforts to extend property rights to wider and wider areas of information and symbolization'. The clear conclusion here is that urban studies must explore the complex and recursive interactions between urban places – as fixed sites which 'hold down' social, economic and cultural life – and electronic spaces – with their diverse and real-time flows of information, capital, services, labour and media.

3

CHAOTIC PLACES OR COMPLEX PLACES?

Cities in a post-industrial era

David Byrne

There is also an element of 'chaos' which is intrinsic to the spatial. For although the location of each (or a set) of a number of phenomena may be directly caused (we know why x is here and y is there), the spatial positioning of one in relation to the other (x's location in relation to y) may not be directly caused. Such relative locations are produced out of the independent operations of spatial determination. They are in that sense 'unintended consequences'. Thus, the chaos of the spatial results from the happenstance juxtapositions, the accidental separations, the often paradoxical nature of the spatial arrangements that result from the operation of all these causalities . . . the relation between social relations and spatiality may vary between that of a fairly coherent system (where social and spatial forms are mutually determined) and that where the particular spatial form is not socially caused at all.

(Massey 1992: 81)

And there again it might not! The point of this chapter is that it doesn't – that instead of alternatives of simple linear determination, represented in discussions of the urban and spatial by both the explicitly positivist and linear accounts of traditional social ecology and the implicitly positivist and linear (if only in the last instance in theory but in practice, always) Althusserian-derived structuralism which underpinned the old 'new radical geography'[1] on the one hand, and the absolute indeterminacy of the postmodernist project of the new 'new radical geography' on the other, we will do far better if we think about causal processes which are neither linear nor indeterminate, but are instead complex.

It is certainly possible to accept that modes of causality vary along (not between, a word which necessarily conveys the meaning of absolute categorical alternatives) a continuum from simple linearity to absolute indeterminacy, particular if we think of the complex in Waldrop's useful phraseology as describing systems on 'the edge of order and chaos' (1992), but that is something very different from the false alternatives of simplicity and the unknowable. Indeed, I find it useful to think of linear determination in the modern tradition – sure, certain and simple knowledge, as a thesis, and the indeterminancy and absolute uncertainty of the postmodern perspective as an antithesis. Complexity is the unity of these opposites in a new and fruitful synthesis – a synthesis of the greatest significance not merely because it provides us with new tools of contemplative knowledge to use in describing the world, but far more importantly because it emphasises the capacity of agency in changing it. The penultimate part of this chapter will pick up this theme in terms of a complex fix on politics and policy.

First I will introduce some key terms. I do not have the space here for a general account of the nature of complexity and of its potential in association with realism for providing a general meta-theory for all science. For that see Waldrop (1992), Casti (1994), Lewin (1993), Baker (1993) and (especially) Reed and Harvey (1992). Instead, in the central section of the chapter I will use concepts drawn from the field to illustrate an argument about the nature of urban space, and in particular about its potential for becoming divided into two quite distinctive socio-spatial forms, characterised by different economic and cultural relations, and equally distinctive relationships with both political activity and governmental management through policy regimes. In other words, I will consider in complex terms the situation generally described by the expression 'the dual city' and the processes which generate such dualism, and I will use some analyses of census data for Cleveland and the Leicester urban area in the UK to illustrate what this means 'on the ground'. However, some initial conceptual clarification and positioning is appropriate. I will attempt this by means of a brief review of linear modern urban theory, and 'chaotic' postmodern urban theory, and will contrast both with a complex post-postmodern programme.

A DIALECTICAL DEVELOPMENT OF URBAN ACCOUNTS?

As a preliminary to such a discussion three things need to be done. The first is to clarify the distinction between the scientific usage of the word chaos and its popular usage, 'chaos' (the popular usage is indicated in this piece by inverted commas). The second is to consider the place of agency as against structure in modern and postmodern urban accounts and to compare these with a complex account of agency in general. The third is to get a complex fix on the appropriate scale for understanding the city.

In popular usage 'chaos' implies absolute indeterminacy, disintegration and the uselessness of knowledge – the postmodern condition in summary. The scientific usage of chaos deals with situations where very small variations in initial conditions lead to very different outcomes – the usual illustration relates to the mathematical description of weather where variations in initial conditions of the order of the force of a butterfly's wingbeat can produce hurricanes, whilst the absence of that force produces a calm. To this extent, the initial idea of chaos does involve indeterminacy, but a strict distinction has to be made between random developments and chaos, because in chaotic contexts complex causal systems may generate stability around 'strange attractors' (see Littell's novel *The Visiting Professor* (1993) for a very readable account of this). In other words, in popular usage 'chaos' never leads to order, whilst in science order emerges from chaos. As Baker puts it:

> order and disorder, order and change, are no longer presented as irreconcileable opposites but as dimensions of the same process. Order generates chaos and chaos generates order.
>
> (Baker 1993: 127)

This is very important because it leads us towards the idea of order as an emergent property. If we think synthetically we should be struck by the resonance of ideas. Emergent properties, as in Kauffman's *The Origins of Order* (1993), are central to ideas about complexity. Massey says:

> precisely that element of the chaotic, or dislocated, which is intrinsic to the spatial has effects on the social phenomena that constitute it. Spatial form as 'outcome' (the happenstance juxtapositions and so forth) has emergent powers which can have effects on subsequent events. Spatial form can alter the future course of the very histories that produced it.
>
> (Massey 1992: 84)

In saying this, she is dealing with emergent properties, although in a characteristically structuralist way. The structures can have causal effects, but can people?

Traditional social ecology and the Althusserian new geography generally either ignored conscious human agency or explicitly dismissed it. In traditional ecology the model was one of a simple social Darwinism in which urban social ecologies were the product of social competition. Of course, there was much more to the Chicago School than this, but this simple linear determination remained the basis of its account of urban forms. Castells (1977) dismissed this approach on the grounds that it provided no account of socially determining structures which produced the effects observeable in the urban world. He then proceeded to an account which not only explicitly *dismissed* collective agency, but also ignored the social significance of the internal organisation of urban space. His account might have been realist in that at its centre lay the explanatory force of the notion of a capitalist mode of production, but it remained simply linear in that it (and subsequent related approaches, particularly in the work of Harvey and Massey) retained a strong conception of determination, whatever the qualifications applied about 'last instance'. The general account based on the 'post-Fordist' approach, with its emphasis on the determinative character of capitalism's flexibility in production, remains essentially linear in the same way.

It is important to note that the notion of linear determination is not applicable even to the simplest instance in a complex world – the form of attractor called a torus, or in plain language a doughnut. There is a very strong correspondence, indeed an essential identity, between descriptions of the torus attractor, where each new phase is different from that preceding it, but remains within a set of boundaries defining the phase state as a whole, and the weak usage of determination characteristic of the approaches of Williams (1980) and Thompson (1978). It also corresponds essentially with Lefebvre's comment that social relations are reproduced as capitalist but never exactly as they were at the beginning of the production/reproduction cycle.

The linear accounts of the 'old' new radical geography often assert that they are realist in form, but they are so only to a very partial extent. Typically, the grand system accounts rely on a realist justification for the specification of the causal mechanism which drives their system – mode of production in the original account, secondary circuit of capital in Harvey, flexible specialisation in post-Fordism – but they do not develop the realist account of complex causation in any very serious sense. Local studies have been more properly realist in that they have taken the idea of contingency seriously, and studies which have emphasised the role of policy (e.g. Dickens *et al.* 1985, in their cross-national and local investigation of housing policy) have moved towards a fully realist account which begins to resemble the complexity programme.

In simple and commonplace terms, modern accounts of urban form belong in the structural determinist set which comprised one of Dawes' two sociologies. Postmodernist accounts, in contrast, emphasise agency above all else, but do so in a way which dismisses any conception of structure or causal understanding. People do something or other in circumstances which don't seem to matter very much and without any way of under-standing what might inform their actions. The central argument is well expressed by Kelly, Davies and Charlton in a book dealing with 'Healthy cities':

> The core idea of postmodernism is that the social and moral conditions obtaining in the world at the present time mark a fundamental break with the past. In art, form displaces content; in philosophy, intrepretation displaces system; in politics, pragmatism displaces principle; and in science 'chaos' [my inverted commas] replaces order.
>
> (Kelly, Davies and Charlton 1993: 159)

A clear example of a coherent postmodernist account of urban process, and by implication urban form, is provided by Graham (1992),[2] although there is a realist tinge to her approach which actually gels well with a complexity-founded programme of understanding. Graham's epistemological position (which she calls 'overdeterminist') can be expressed in summary by a quotation:

> knowledges are fully constitutive social processes rather than depend-ent reflections of an independent real. . . . Like other social processes, knowledges differ from each other in the ways in which they are constituted and in their social effects, but they cannot be ranked hierarchically on the basis of their closeness to or distance from a

single, objective or unchanging 'reality'. In other words, the 'truth' of particular knowledges is not adjudicated in a universal forum but is particular to certain social settings and validation practices.

(Graham 1992: 398)

The problem is that there are at least two possible readings of this passage. One, which fits well with the argument proposed here, is a rejection of linearity and prediction (complex theory deals with explanation, not prediction) and a recognition of the role of agency in constituting reality – people make history. However, another, and stronger, version involves the rejection of anything real external to the immediate context of the actor. That is what I regard as the postmodernist fix and it is the one Graham herself adopts when she argues for 'treating class as an analytical entry point rather than a social essence' (1992: 403), and goes on to say:

this approach to social analysis requires acknowledging the existence and 'validity' of other entry points and other forms of social knowledge, as well as the other politics they may promote. In this way, it constitutes a postmodern strand within Marxist discourse, one which explicitly theorizes its often antagonistic coexistence with other Marxisms and with non-Marxist approaches to social analysis. . . . In an overdetermined social totality, class processes – like other social processes – are continually reshaped as they interact with all other aspects of social life. This ceaseless reconstitution opens the way for an ongoing politics of class transformation, a politics which recognizes an infinity of points of intervention in the constitution of class and other social processes. Social transformation, then, is not something that takes place in a cataclysmic upheaval or a systemic transition; it is an aspect of everyday life.

(ibid.)

I very much agree with a lot Graham says, and she is an atypical proponent of the postmodern account despite her self-identity in those terms. Nonetheless, an argument for a 'ceaseless reconstitution', 'an infinity of points of intervention', and the notion that social transformation does not require systemic transition (there are other forms of systemic transition than cataclysmic upheaval, although as we shall see we cannot disregard the possibility of that form), necessarily reduces politics to a matter of individual assertion of style, or at best a matter of social movements constituted separately from any complex fundamental structural reality. People may be making history, although in practice to abandon the notion of systemic transformation is to abandon the prospect of any fundamental reconstruction of the world, but there are no real circumstances to this.

Essentially, Graham's account oddly combines (although this oddity is characteristic of the postmodern source of this element in it) a notion of infinite possibilities, a popular version of 'chaos', with a notion of continuous reconstitution within limits. It is, as we shall see, a torus. Indeed, to that limited extent it shares the general conservatism of postmodernism. Despite the notion of chaos and indeterminacy which is so central to the postmodernist position, in the end nothing very much changes except surfaces. There is a very considerable clue to postmodernism's character in this emphasis on surfaces – we can see but we can't understand what made what we see, and if we lack that understanding we can do nothing very much. Graham is actually an uncharacteristically active and optimistic postmodernist – class can form the basis of an identity politics and people have the capacity to act. And yet her theory of knowledges really provides no analytical framework for the informing of that action. Perhaps the complex synthesis can do that.

To understand the complex approach to agency we have first to clarify the nature of the kind of systems in which agency might matter. Reed and Harvey do this for us:

> This new science studies physical systems that are governed by an evolutionary dynamic that is of a far from equilibrium nature. Unlike their conservative, self-equilibrating counterparts with which we in the social sciences are most familiar, far-from-equilibrium configurations are inherently historical and intensely innovative. Because of these tendencies, far-from-equilibrium systems exhibit capacities for spontaneous change and long range tendencies towards evolutionary behaviour. Their internal dynamics are ontologically unique in that they are predicated upon a set of self-replicating, non-linear feedback mechanisms that promote increasing structural complexity.
>
> (Reed and Harvey 1992: 359)

A further, crucial property of such systems is their sensitivity to initial conditions. This means that their evolutionary paths depend on the relationship between timing of peturbation and exact initial conditions and are inherently unpredictable, but not inexplicable, over time. Here explanation becomes essentially historical – the charting of the history of the system. There is no point in trying to deduce what will happen from a description of its present state, but we can understand how it got there. However, this does not render history merely contemplative. Nicolis and Prigione (1989) have pointed out that in social systems 'peturbations of far-from-equilibrium conditions can originate in the values and actions of humans themselves' (see Reed and Harvey 1992: 370). All dissipative systems have to be understood as being characterised by a dominance of information over energy with information representing both order and the orgins of disorder. In dissipative systems which contain consciousness things can be made to happen and an understanding of how things have happened in the past can be the basis on which things are made to happen in the future. People can make history but not in circumstances of their own choosing.

Before turning to the main part of this chapter, which is a discussion of urban social division in terms of the butterfly and higher order attractors, I want to say something about the scale of the central programme of urban and regional studies in recent years. In particular I want to criticise the emphasis on generating hierarchies of localities as a way of providing an account of the local expression of global restructuring. Although I don't propose to use all the properties of the term, yet, it is interesting to consider the idea of a fractal:

> Fractals are curves that are irregular all over. Moreover they have exactly the same degree of irregularity at all scales of measurement. . . . If you start looking from a distance (i.e. with a long ruler), then as you get closer and closer (with smaller rulers) small pieces of the curve that looked like formless blobs earlier turn into recognizable objects, the shapes of which are the same as that of the overall object itself.
>
> (Casti 1994: 232)

It is argued here that the actual expression of the consequences of global restructuring in advanced capitalism is expressed not among places but within them – that studies which emphasise the distinctiveness of localities, and especially of whole city regions, have been using too long a ruler, and that we need to look within cities, at intra-, not inter-, urban differentiation, if we are to find the expressed consequences of what is certainly a phase state change. This gets us away from the absurdities represented by Lash and Urry's identification of Newcastle as a post-industrial welfare city – contradictions of daily experience ought to be challenged. The point is, to paraphrase Hill and Feagin (1987), that there is no longer one Newcastle, even understood as a torus attractor, but at least two and possibly many Newcastles.

I would take the fractal idea down to the level of neighbourhood in urban analysis and household in accounts of social structure, but would then treat these as indivisible classical atoms. Complexity provides us with a very good way of understanding the range of possible trajectories of households and of the individuals originating in them. The conception of a butterfly attractor as descriptive of household/individual possible phase states is profoundly pessimistic for simple talent/energy-based models of individual or household social mobility.

Toruses, butterflies and beyond – an alternative way of thinking about dual cities

The idea of fractal contains more than the notion that scale of measurement matters. It is a general description of the geometry of a chaotic system. If we think of social structure as having a Euclidean geometry, then we assume that it completely fills the space it occupies. However, this is not the case in nature or, by implication, in the social world. Here, fractals are estimates of the degree to which a system occupies a region in an outcome basin.[3] When the region occupied is small we have high order – in chaos the system may occupy almost any location in an outcome field and we cannot say where it will end up.

Young and Kiel (1994), on whom I will draw heavily in this section, offer an excellent summary of the character of non-linear attractors. Of especial interest to us here is the torus, characterised by self-similiarity, and the butterfly in which whilst 'a system may vary markedly from one iteration to the next still it is very probable that it will wind up in one of two fairly stable if very different outcome regions' (ibid.: 6). Self similiarity describes the sort of system which reproduces itself within limits, but never in exactly the same form. It is possible to predict that the system will be within boundaries but not where it will be within those boundaries:

> When a key parameter of a torus increases in value, one region inside it can expand to form a tongue: when it exceeds a given value, that tongue expands to form another wing of the attractor.... The Feigenbaum number for the transformation of a torus into a butterfly attractor is 3.0. That is, when a key parameter exceeds 3 times its value in a previous iteration, it forces an outcome basin to expand into two distinct causal fields.
>
> (ibid.: 5)

Young and Kiel suggest that: 'The fact that there are two natural outcomes for a system whose internal parameters have not changed is foreign to most scientific thinking' (ibid.: 5). I don't agree, although my reasons for not doing are highly particular. In traditional Engels-derived linear Marxist accounts, changes in key parameters, the transformation of quantity into quality, do produce phase state changes, changes in the mode of production. However, only one outcome is possible. When Castoriadis (see Hirsh 1981) offered us the alternatives of 'socialism or barbarism' he offered us two phase states – a butterfly attractor.

Let me look for resonance in urban theory. I want to go further into the fractal world than Baker (1993) who, pertinently and properly, points out the clear relation between the use of the concepts of 'centre' and 'periphery' in a range of sociological work, and the interplay of autopoetic and dissipative elements in social life. This can be done by scouting for signs of attractor recognition in descriptions of urban space. Let me present a representative selection.

1 Lash and Urry's account of urban division when they articulate:

> a socio-spatial analysis of today's 'underclass' who inhabit a space characterized by a deficit of economic, social and cultural regulation. In such spaces older organized capitalist social structures – industrial labour market, church and family networks, social welfare institutions, trade unions – have dissolved or at least moved out ... unlike the spaces of the city centres and the suburbs they have not been replaced by the information and communicative structure.
>
> (Lash and Urry 1994: 8)

All the necessary elements are here – change in fundamental parameters and the creation in consequence from a torus form to a butterfly form in which spaces are one thing or another.

2 Sassen's use of centre and periphery in an intra-urban context (very reminiscent of autonomist notions of 'underdevelopment' – see Byrne 1995b):

> Recent research shows sharp increases in socio-economic and spatial inequalities within major cities of the developed world. . . . One line of theorization posits that this represents a transformation in the geography of centre and periphery, rather than merely a quantitative increase in the degree of inequality; it signals that peripheralization processes are occurring inside areas that were once conceived of as core areas whether at the global, regional or urban level, alongside the sharpening of peripheralization processes, centrality has also become sharper at all levels.
>
> (Sassen 1994: 54)

3   Fainstein *et al.*'s sense of unease with their attempt at a conventional and linear account of 'divided cities':

> The point of the comparison is to hold economic roles as constant as possible so as to determine their importance relative to other variables in producing social outcomes, and to investigate the sources of differences in national traditions and public policies.
>
> (Fainstein, Gordon and Harloe 1992: 1–2)

but then:

> Of course the rather linear model linking common economic changes with differentiated outcomes provided no more than a point of departure for the research. The causal linkages between the various factors outlined above are complex and not unidirectional.
>
> (ibid.: 18)

4   Hegedus and Tosic's introduction to a special issue of *Urban Studies* dealing with post-industrial cities and Van Kempen's continuation of the theme:

> It seems a long way from the neatly organised social segregated city of the human ecologists to the rather vague and confused image of the post-industrial city, which is hidden behind the dual city concept . . . if social polarization is a more complex phenomenon than mostly is understood, then also the dual city which is supposed to reflect this process, represents a more complex reality than the clear social divide the term suggests. It [the dual city concept] suggests, in sum, that there are two urban realities instead of one, which are spatially discrete and only have the name of the city and some public spaces, or maybe not even that, in common: a city of 'despair and squalor' and a city of 'power and splendour', which can be some blocks or streets away from each other only.
>
> (Hegedus and Tosic 1994: 990)

5   Esser and Hirsch's recognition of the effect of agency in relation to complex change:

> It is likely that it [the post-Fordist town] will be far more varied

than the standardized type of town marked by fordism, because of the social and regional heterogenization process. It is not only 'objective' tendencies and capital strategies, determined by the world markets, which will be important, but also the outcomes of political social conflicts in the towns themselves. . . . The fact that the social-spatial structure of towns is always the result of political-social power relations, conflicts and compromises under given economic structural conditions, which vary historically and in the context of particular struggles, is more true today than ever before.

(Esser and Hirsch 1994: 93)

Of course, there is a fundamental disagreement contained in the above – a disagreement about whether the notion of duality, in terms of complex attractors the butterfly, is adequate in describing cities, or whether it is necessary to move towards some more complex account (Marcuse's quartered city for example – 1989). This is an empirical matter and I will attempt an empirical account below. However, I want for the moment to stick with torus/butterfly transformation. Let me draw again on Young and Kiel:

If we want to maintain the integrity of a market economy with its many advantages then there must be such forms of linear feedback with which to defeat the transformation of the Torus which describes, say, frequency of entry into the market for essential goods and services by race, class and ethnicity. If not, the market itself may split into two or more attractors: one oriented to those with discretionary income, and the other to those without. As income inequalities between minority groups, economic classes or nations grow, more and more capital is attracted to the basin of production allocated to luxury goods and less and less to the production basin in which essential goods are produced.

(Young and Kiel 1994: 15)

This chapter is about the spatial form of such developments, the way in which such attractors manifest themselves in space.

There is one further point worth making here. The essence of complex systems is that they have a history with development by bifurcation BUT – and it is a very big but indeed – not all outcomes are possible. This is the key idea behind strange attractors, which has been most coherently developed by Kauffman (1993) in relation to evolutionary biology. This is the difference between chaos and randomness – in a chaotic world certain things are more likely than other – all is not contingent. Kauffman points out, in contradistinction to Gould's (1989) emphasis on complete contingency in evolutionary development, that there exist 'rugged fitness landscapes' in which there are areas of stability and points of change. The character of such landscapes themselves is not static but changes in response to environmental change and co-evolutionary competition among species. The effect is that only some phenotypes, not all, are possible, and that evolution moves towards such phenotypes (critics have frequently noted the correspondence of this account with the platonic conception of ideal forms) exemplified by the remarkable phenotypical correspondence between wolves and their marsupial equivalent at the end of a very long evolutionary separation. However, nothing is absolutely stable because other changes change the landscape. Nonetheless, things may be 'relatively permanent' – a key idea in the realist conception of structures.

The relevance of this to the present debate is that it allows for a taxonomy of possible urban futures, and suggests that policy should act as information in modifying the direction of development towards those which people want to achieve, not those which they don't. It makes historical accounts rather more than the screechings of the owl of Minerva. Sure prediction is not possible, but creation is – to quote, yet again, O'Connor (1982) – not a matter of what will happen but what can be made to happen. We should note that the idea of fitness landscape can be applied at different levels. Implicitly, concerns with localities have been concerned with a global fitness landscape within which localities are positioned. My argument for neighbourhood is an argument for a much more finely drawn fitness landscape in which local intra-urban variation reflects global parameters, rather than those parameters being reflected at the whole locality level.

We must note that the butterfly attractor form for industrial cities, with the possibility of neighbourhoods ending up in the urban ghetto wing, is not inevitable. I am at one with Young and Kiel about the desirability, if possible – and it may not be possible – of preventing the fully developed emergence of such forms with their tendency to self-reinforcement and development into ever more complex and malignant differentiated phase states. But we must remember that not every phase state in a complex development is possible. It may be that we can't go back to the good old universal Fordist Torus – that our political and policy options are about going forward to the best possible urban phenotypes which derive from the complex development of a differentiated urban structure. But we must not forget that this can be a convergent process, and if it can be, it should be made to be.

Now I turn from this theoretical exposition of the dual city as butterfly attractor to see if it can be established as real, and can be illustrated by the use of quantitative investigations founded on the idea that complex procedures are the best way to investigate a complex world. What follows may not appeal to those who have promoted innumeracy to an epistemological principle, but the maths are really very simple in concept and all computation is done out of sight. What matters is not deductive mathematical reasoning, but rather the willingness and ability to understand a complex world through a quantitative account.

LEICESTER AND CLEVELAND COUNTY – TWO SKIPPERS

Skippers are the commonest 'non-flashy' butterflies to be found in our countryside. They aren't glamorous, like peacocks or red admirals, but there are a lot of them and they are an important part of the ecosystem. My interest is in industrial cities – the urban equivalent of skippers. In England some 14 million people live in the metropolitan counties and in the big county districts such as Leicester, Nottingham, Derby and Bristol which are cities by any criteria. If Tyne and Wear is anything to go by the actual population of these cities is really about 40% greater if you include suburban parts of their journey to work areas (in Leicester this would include Blaby and Oadby and Wigston), so we can safely say that some 20 million people in England live in industrial cities outside the Greater Metropolitan Area of London. Another 10 million live in large towns like Darlington, Ipswich, Preston, Swindon, etc. and their suburbs, which are essentially mini-cities. The question is what is the *form* of these places?

What follows is an examination of Cleveland County, which is pretty well a complete industrial city (although even here parts of North Yorkshire are really its suburbs) and the Leicester urban area (Leicester, Blaby, and Oadby and Wigston). The product is a straightforward urban ecology generated for each place by a cluster analysis using enumeration district level data.[4] In hierarchical fusion methods of cluster analysis an agglomeration schedule is generated at each fusion which shows a coefficient measure. Large changes in this coefficient indicate that two very different things have been fused. The easiest way to intepret this is by graphing out coefficients at fusion levels. The very large change in slope of the graph for both Leicester and Cleveland when two clusters are fused into one indicates that very different things are being joined together. Table 3.1 indicates that this is so.

Essentially, both cities can be divided into two sorts of area respectively made up of households which are owner occupier, car owner and work-rich on the one hand, and not car owners and much more likely to be social tenants and work-poor on the other. The variables used in generating these clusters were percentage households with car, percentage households work-rich, percentage households work-poor, and percentage households containing a child in which no adult was employed. The very high degree of concentration of social housing in the poorer cluster in both cities is especially noteworthy, given that tenure variables were not used in the classification. Obviously these clusters are not tight. There is a range of variation in key variables within them. However, as Figures 3.1 and 3.2 indicate, when the distribution of a key descriptor variable (car ownership) is organised by cluster, we find a very clear bimodal pattern. This pattern persists for all variables except percentage of households owner occupied, and in Leicester, percentage of population describing themselves as 'white'. The tenure patterns absolutely support the contention that social housing is now a residualised tenure of the poor and owner occupation contains households at all social levels. The ethnicity pattern reflects the diverse class background of Leicester's 'other than white' population.

If we look at the proportion of each city's population in each cluster we find that Leicester does indeed look like a two-thirds/one-third society, whilst Cleveland is beginning to be a half and half society. These descriptions make sense. They correspond with everyday experience and

Table 3.1 Cluster descriptors Cleveland and Leicester

	Mean percentages for clusters			
	Cleve Cl 1	Cleve Cl 2	Leic Cl 1	Leic Cl 2
White	97	99	76	81
Males economically active	66	74	76	68
Econ. act. males full time	55	75	72	62
Econ. act. males not working	37	11	10	25
Females econ. act.	38	42	57	43
Econ. act. females full time	37	47	56	54
Econ. act. females part time	39	41	31	27
Males potential workers not working	48	18	14	33
Hhds owner occupied	37	88	82	32
Hhds private tenants	5	3	8	7
Hhds social tenants	56	7	8	59
Hhds no car	65	22	27	60
Hhds with child and no worker	47	12	13	44
Hhds with child lone parent	28	7	7	29
Married females full time	12	22	30	22
Hhds work-rich	19	42	44	23
Hhds work-poor	48	28	26	45
No. of EDs in cluster	490	632	570	261

with popular conceptions people have about the social structures of the localities in which they live. Such conceptions are in fact a very important part of people's repertoire of social knowledge and cluster analysis, used here in an explicitly exploratory sense, accords very well with such knowledge. Let me emphasise something very strongly. In severely de-industrialised Cleveland, probably the purest industrial city in the UK, rather more than half the population are living well and prosperously, if, in household terms, potentially insecurely.

We have to ask is there anything new about this sort of socio-spatial organisation in the 'post-fordist', 'post-industrial', 'post-whatever' period? The answer is simple. Yes, there is. A comparison of these patterns with those Robson (1969) identified for Sunderland and which the present author has identified for 'Northern Tyneside' (Byrne 1989) and Cleveland (Byrne 1994) during the industrial era of full employment, show that industrial cities are now differentiated in a way in which they previously were not. They have indeed changed from toruses into butterflies. Complex models suggest that we should look for changes in key variables which have increased by about a factor of 3. An examination of census data for Leicester and Cleveland shows that male non-employment (adult males who are neither retired nor students and are unemployed or permanently sick, as a percentage of adult males working, unemployed and permanently sick) increased by some three times between 1971 and 1991. Detailed examination of data at the household level from the Cleveland Social

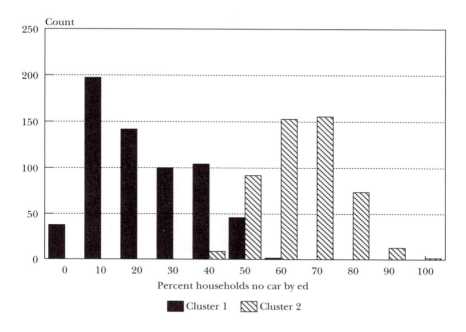

Figure 3.1 Cleveland households, no car

Survey (see Byrne 1995a) suggests that it is this change in male employment which is the crucial factor in determining household forms, and, hence, socio-spatial differences. I don't want to reify Feigenbaum numbers but here we have one and we have the phase form which it suggests would occur.

It is very important to recognise that the poorer areas are not just ghettoes of the non-employed. Although nearly half of the households with children in these areas in both Leicester and Cleveland contain no employed worker, more than half do contain workers. Even at the ED level (which is too small to stand for neighbourhood – I see neighbourhoods as constituted from the aggregate of spatially adjacent EDs in the same cluster) very few EDs have over 70 per cent of child-containing households having no worker. Likewise, although the variable work rich is bimodal in both cities, the poorer clusters do contain work rich households – this makes sense if we think of the logic of poor households which can get over benefit trap levels by having multiple employment. Work-rich households can be rich in poor work, and my guess is that in these areas that is exactly what they are. The work-poor households in the affluent cluster are predominantly households of retired people, who are probably not poor. Note that in this account the existence of unemployment matters to those in poor work precisely because the unemployed are a reserve army against them.

The character of socio-spatial division suggested by these analyses is

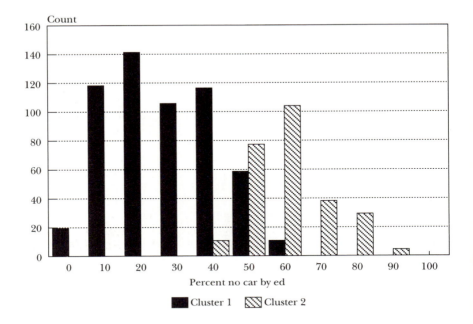

Figure 3.2 Leicester households, no car

certainly one which follows the form of a butterfly attractor. It is a division between affluent possessors of resources and employment and the non-affluent, but most of the non-retired, non-affluent households are dependent on wages (perhaps in combination with benefits – the sociological significance of our reinvention of Speenhamland is immense) rather than on benefits alone. The division is a division within work, rather than between workers and workless.

POLICY MADE IT – CAN POLICY UNMAKE IT?

Two sorts of policy in interaction have created this butterfly form. One relates to government management of the UK labour market at the national level. The other is a consequence of detailed urban policy programmes over the last decade, as these have been written on the residential matrix created by housing policy in this country since 1919. It would be easy to blame globalisation and the inexorable impact of a globally competitive capitalism for these situations. That is what 'capital logic marxism', much reproduced in 'new geographies', does in fact do (see Byrne 1995b). Of course, global tendencies do matter, but the assertion of their absolute importance and of the impotence of any political interventions is profoundly ideological. If we remember that the dominant social group in poor areas in industrial cities are workers, then we might wonder about the absolute significance of global competitiveness, especially as many of these workers are employed in service employment which is necessarily local in orientation and which is not part of a global competitive system.

In practice, employment policy and the legislative destruction of the capacities of trade unions for effective industrial action have created a context in which many men and women with poor jobs are faced by a massive reserve army of labour, which is constantly called into use against them, and by police prevention of traditional forms of job, wages and conditions protection. It is true that the reserve army is a reserve army against all of us, but reserve armies are useful only to the degree that their members are appropriate and competent replacements for employed people. This is much easier for Macjobs and general labouring, cleaning, etc. than it is for skilled and/or credentialised employment. To this extent, a malignant interpretation (and in my view a proper one) to be placed upon the operation of those key actors in urban programmes, such as City Challenge, the Training and Enterprise Councils (TECs) in providing low level training and 'work habit forming', is that this is a way of keeping a reserve army constantly in being and up to the mark.

However, my focus here is on the urban component of policy, because it is in this domain that the elected governments of cities (not one of the districts in my English industrial city category is now governed by the Conservative Party) still have some capacity for action. I want to present my argument here somewhat 'backside foremost'. Before discussing the extent to which recent urban policy has generated a butterfly complex form in the socio-spatial organization of cities, I will review the potential of complex founded policies in practice now.

Such policies come in three, potentially contradictory, forms. Blackman, Keenan and Coombes (1994) have recently illustrated the use of data flows as a way of describing the changing status (phase states) of locales within a city. They have shown that a sudden increase in the departure of 'five year residents' from particular small areas within west Newcastle prefigured a social collapse into 'chaos'. In policy areas there are now a number of quantitative data streams from management practices which can highlight the potential occurrence of such changes. One model of urban policy becomes literally cybernetic – the city is steered by responses to data indications, responses which take the form of resource inputs, exactly as a ship (the Starship Enterprise perhaps) is steered in response to sensor information in similar data streams. Information guides the implemenation of small energy changes which may be stabilising – Young and Kiel's stabilising feedback. This sort of fine tuning is possible given the nature of administrative data streams and is an important part of policing and housing management practice. Such complex-based responses are essentially technocratic but have important political implications.

Another policy form involves the acceptance of the existence of different urban realities and the development of distinctive policy regimes which operate in those different realities. An extreme version of this is what is often called, by medical analogy, triage, but which in urban practice generally reduces to biage. Policies operate in one sort of locale and in the other sort policies do not operate at all. There was a period on Tyneside before the 1991 riots when local residents in poor areas argued that the police had ceased responding to their calls for assistance. However, generally speaking, what we find are different regimes of action rather than one of action and one of inaction. A very clear example is provided by the operation of English state secondary schools. These can now generally be classified into those which are concerned with realistic achievement and credentialism, and those which are essentially about containment without achievement. The character of the school regime is simply a function of the social character of the spatially bounded area which it serves. UK state education is now very much differentiated in these ways.

This sort of policy form generally characterises political life in both the US and the UK. My understanding from Internet debate is that in US elections the occupants of the poorer half of the butterfly attractor simply don't vote anymore. In the UK it is evident that formal politics at the national level is effectively directed towards the interests and behaviour of those in the affluent wing. The poor are politically relevant only as a source of disorder and crime, and responses are designed around the exclusionary maintenance of order in affluent areas and the affluent social world. Eversley's (1990) angry critique of the UK planning system as it has adapted to the service of development capital describes a planning system working to this end. Indeed the physical expression of such exclusion through the privatisation of forms of space, shopping areas, streets, etc., which were public is now common.

The last potential form of complex-based policy is creative – it is neither the fine tuning of stability maintenance nor the acceptance of a divided social world. Rather it seeks to make new social worlds in the city. The argument I want to present here is the complete opposite of that presented by Cartwright (1991) in an article which includes a very useful survey of central ideas in chaos theory. Cartwright argues that:

> Most planners assume that, given enough information, they can anticipate what is going to happen in a particular situation, and can thus determine how best to act to promote, defer, deflect, or divert it, as may be desired. Chaos theory suggests that, on the contrary, some systems are inherently unpredictable and can never be fully under-stood, no matter how much effort or expense is devoted to trying.
>
> (Cartwright 1991: 53)

He goes on:

> Finally, and perhaps most important of all for planners, is the fact that chaotic systems are predictable only on an incremental or local basis. . . .On a global or comprehensive basis, chaotic systems are unpredictable because of the cumulative effects of various kinds of feedback. But on an incremental or local basis, the effects of feedback from one time period into the next are perfectly clear. This is a powerful argument for planning strategies that are incremental rather than comprehensive in scope and that rely on a capacity for

adaptation rather than on blueprints of results.

(ibid.: 54)

This is Oakshottian conservatism as planning – we can only know a little so 'ga canny'. It seems to me that Cartwright has missed a fundamental point made by Nicolis and Prigione (1989). Reed and Harvey argue that Nicolis and Prigione's contention that 'each human system constitutes a unique realization of a complex stochastic process whose rules can in no way be designed in advance' (1989: 238), supports a 'world view that presumes the naturalness of both disjunctive developments and of asymmetrical structures that carry within themselves inherent tendencies for periodic self-negation and radical change' (Reed and Harvey 1992: 371). Stochastic processes are exactly processes which are random in the short term but whose outcome is directional – a drunkard's walk – the rambling English drunkard may have gone to Birmingham by way of Beechey Head, but s/he got there. What this means is agency. It is precisely the human capacity to imagine and seek to construct a future which is so crucial to understanding the potential of trajectories within a complex world. Of course this does not guide us towards 'blueprints', towards the imposition of centrally designed plans from on high in the best Leninist tradition. But neither does it leave us with only the market as a method of information processing and decision making.[5] Instead, a participatory democracy has the capacity for collective realisation of urban and other futures. As Young and Kiel argue:

> The holistic nature of Chaos dynamics requires a democratic politics which involve all significant sectors of a population; in a complex society, that means every adult citizen. One cannot plan on abandoning whole sectors of a population without long term costs.
>
> (Young and Kiel 1994: 15)

If this looks like Council Communism, Zapatistism, the style of Brazilian basic Christian communalism, Aragonese anarchism, anarcho syndicalism or whatever, who should be surprised? It is precisely the belief in the creative capacity of people which underpins all these positions. There is much that resonates with ideas about complexity in Ursula le Guin's *The Dispossessed*. We can get more from science fiction than nightmares from *Blade Runner*.

I think this argument for a creative engagement with complex urban realities, based on a clear Gouldian understanding of the historical process by which we got to where we are now, can be illuminated precisely by a consideration of how the present butterfly form of industrial cities has developed, and of the role of housing and planning policies in its creation. It seems to me that this can best be done by understanding how the Left Keynesian universalism of British urban planning in the post-war years was displaced by a Right Keynesian particularism in the 1960s, and how this created an urban matrix on which 'catalytic planning' has tried in vain to write a post-industrial, service led, exclusionary form. Perhaps the most important thing in all of this is to recognise just how evidently that last project has failed, in contrast with the enormous success of the two preceding it. Things would be even more complex had it succeeded!

Britain's post-war planning, the planning system put together behind the slogan 'Never Again' (see Hennessy 1993), was a strange mixture. Its political foundation was mass democratic, but its implementing form was technocratic. Nonetheless, it is very important to note that, despite every sort of technocratic and resource pressure to develop post-war public housing forms on the basis of mass flatted estates, this was never done in England outside London during this period, and even in London it was done only to a limited extent. Much of the account of the history of council housing which has been attempted by, among others, the Political Economy of Housing Workshop was precisely about the contrast between the physical arrangements and social character of public housing of this period (and of the 1920s) in contrast with technocratic solutions to slum clearance as developed during the 1930s and 1960s/70s. This was the basis of social division in the 1970s when the Community Development Projects were set in place to deal with an urban disintegration which was to be fifteen years in coming.

The crucial policy change in establishing the matrix of housing forms was the shift towards a Right Keynesian policy form of urban reconstruction through the development of mass owner occupation, a reversal to the policy form of the 1930s. It is very important to note that in every city I have examined no significant area of owner occupied housing developed during this second period is in the poor wing of the butterfly. It is true that some inter-war housing in west Newcastle has passed into that condition, but this is very unusual. However, good council housing estates of the 1920s, 1940s and 1950s are now generally poor and deprived. The abandonment of social housing as a universal tenure set up the basis on which even that very large part of it which was not in origin or for most of its history ever the locale in which poor people lived, is now exactly that.

In contrast with the enormous physical transformation of industrial and other cities from the 1940s to the 1970s, much of it by immense peripheral construction of outer estates in both the public and private sectors, events since 1979, which have been informed by policy regimes directed towards the reconstitution of land and property markets in cities, have been trivial in their effects on spatial forms. It could be argued, using the vocabulary of complexity, that policy sought to create an attractor state which did not exist in the range of possible attractors. In essence, the effort to create socially exclusive elements constructed around high incomes generated in financial and producer services was attempting to create a form which was available only within the complex urban spaces of world cities, and which was highly contingent even there. It is now clear that the local and temporally specific financial market conditions which sustained such forms were very unstable, in contrast to the enormous stability of Fordist level suburban prosperity which persists as the basis of the affluent wing in butterfly cities. The fitness landscapes set by global economic conditions and the place of urban development within it were very temporary. At the end of more than a decade of operation the New Right Urban programme in the UK, which began with the Local Government Planning and Land Act of 1982, has achieved very little. These policies could certainly be interpreted as positive reinforcing feedback in creating divided cities, but they have not, in industrial cities at least, generated a more complex form with a clear social divide between the elite and the prosperous masses. Contemporary urban policies following on from City Challenge through the mechanism of the single regeneration budget are control mechanisms directed at the poor attractor state, but they are in no way resolutions for its condition.

Such resolution plainly requires a set of policy initiatives which re-cast labour market, income replacement and urban policies on a scale which has not been seen since 1945. It is illuminating to contrast the structuralist pessimism which informs the recent Borrie Commission *Report on Social Justice* (1994), larded as it is with pessimistic talk of globalisation, with the radical and creative commitment of the Church of England's *Faith in the City* (Archbishop of Canterbury's Commission 1984) of a decade earlier. The latter asserts that people are made in the image of God and have creative capacities. As an atheistic former Catholic catechist I might deny the non-human creator, but I remain convinced of human capacity. I am not going to proceed to a full specification of a radical programme of reconstruction here. The point of this chapter is to try to present a framework for understanding the situation to be dealt with, and to assert that the task is actually a do-able one.

METAPHOR OR REALITY?

I want to conclude this chapter by posing a question about the utility of chaos/complexity theory in sociology. Does it describe the social world, or is it simply something which gives us a very powerful set of metaphors for handling the development of complex social systems? I am going to argue that it is really an account, and there is a very important reason for asserting that argument. Despite postmodernism's interest in ecological social movements, the postmodernist position has never grasped the crucial significance of the ecological assertion of the non-independence of people from the natural world, and from limits which the natural world imposes on human action and development forms. The production of the built environment, and the social environment which is intrinsically linked to it, is not a limitless activity. There are Gaian limits, for example on the continued reliance on car-borne transport, just as there were Gaian limits imposed on earlier industrial cities by the capacity to remove human waste products from them.

If we apply the commonly utilised logistic (s-shaped) curve to describe urban evolution we may well be in the flat bit at the top where the capacities of systems for innovation and new developments are minimal, compared with for example the public health successes of the early and mid-nineteenth-century 'Healthy Cities' movement when the system was moving up the steep bit of the curve. Certainly the minimal impact of contemporary 'Healthy Cities' progammes compared with their nineteenth-century precursors would suggest that this is the case. In an interesting article De

Greene has argued that 'the US national and world economies are in the phase of depression of Kondratriev Number Four, and the world natural environment is in a precariously metastable state' (1994: 171). If he is right then the imperatives for action are not merely derivatives of a general problem of social order. As we approach a millenium, apocalyptic prounouncements are certainly in order.

NOTES

1   The way in which many of the personnel of the old 'new' radical geography shifted directly from essentially positivist styles of research and methodological exposition to Althusserian structuralism is worth noting. Even those who seem to have read Marx have only read some Marx and have read Marx in a capital logic style. See Byrne (1995b).

2   Graham's critique of the relationship between regulation theory perspectives and 'tendential modification' economic regeneration policies adopted by 'Left' local governments is wholly persuasive. Her argument for a politics of class is   likewise attractive and coherent. Where I differ from her is in my belief that her 'overdeterminist' epistemology offers no foundation for such a politics other than a moral one.

3   Young and Kiel (1994: 42) define an outcome basin thus:

> The region in a larger basin of outcomes to which a set of initial conditions (causes) drives a systm or set of similar systems. A system is said to be 'attracted' to that region, hence the pattern of nonlinear dynamics seen in such a basin is called an attractor. Imagine a saucer inside which spins a marble. The path of the marble is the attractor, the whole region is the basin. Since the path is a nonlinear function of key parameters, that area can be considered a causal basin. There can be a number of such basins/attractors in a larger outcome field.

4   For a description of the organisation of census geographies see Marsh and Dale (1993). For an account of cluster analyis see Everitt (1974).

5   The general New Right critique of planning, best articulated in the work of Hayek, is of course predicated exactly on the unmanageable complexity of modernity. It is therefore ironical that one of the major uses made of complex nonlinear dynamic models is in the analyis of financial markets. This approach requires considerable mathematical competence, not available to people who have failed A level maths, hence the Leeson/Baring's fiasco.

Part II

RACIAL/SPATIAL IMAGINARIES

4

OUT OF THE MELTING POT INTO THE FIRE NEXT TIME

Imagining the East End as city, body, text

Phil Cohen

I have been dogged for years, from as far back as I can remember, by the impulse to return to a place where I have never been – an imaginary and actual island ... sometimes the shore shines and is bright with miraculous possibilities, sometimes it is the manifestation of my most secret fears . . . the chance has come to return to this island and I will take it only because it is no longer my story.

(Ian Sinclair, *Down River*)

People do not live in places but in the description of places.

(Wallace Stevens)

SPLIT PERCEPTIONS

There seems to be a growing division in urban studies between those who continue to accord primacy to the spatial economy of cities and the processes of their globalisation, and those who argue for the strategic importance of cultural and political geographies in which the local, however problematically, still holds its explanatory place.[1] This relates to a number of different, but linked, arguments here which need unpacking. Some have to do with scales of analysis; others with the kinds of theoretical models and research methodologies which should be used to analyse urban structures and processes. Some approaches, for example, continue to use centre/periphery models, or models of unequal exchange to explain both the international migrations of capital and labour and struggles over the distribution of urban amenities and resources. For others globalisation represents a qualitatively different kind of world disorder, associated with space/time compression and the impact of information technologies, making the former models and their related politics largely redundant. In the new post-Fordist spatial economy, locational decisions and identities have been transformed into fluctuating variables determined opportunistically by the space of information flows, and/or the logic of flexible accumulation rather than being tied to locally embedded structures of historical circumstance and geographical constraint. Finally, there is the argument that globalisation can only be understood as part of a larger discourse of post/modernity of which the metropolis is a key symbol and site. It is here that Difference and the Other – other sexualities, races, nations and peoples – are both concentrated and dispersed, contained and marginalised within the framework of homogenising technologies of power.

Whether the local is seen as a site of defiant resistance to the global, its unwitting and reactionary accomplice, or a point of vertical transcendence, depends first and foremost on what is given a habitation and a name under its rubric, and then on how that accommodation is evaluated. Most social historians and urban ethnographers are methodologically committed to teasing out particularisms of place and time even if only to make them tell a larger tale; cultures and consciousnesses tend to be given an active and often heroic role in these accounts. Political economists tend to a more sanguine view; they have fewer local loyalties and stress the social structures which overarch the fabrics of urban life. In contrast, semiologists and communication analysts are almost by definition into urban imagineering and the global information flow; they become acutely uncomfortable if asked to do anything as pedestrian as study social relations on a housing estate for signs of these post/modern times.

Geographers, who have added cultural and political to the physical and economic tags of their trade, have been able to move between these registers more easily than most, which is why perhaps the discipline has moved so centre-stage. But even they have not been able to entirely avoid the ancient quarrel between those who see the city as primarily a material infrastructure for accommodating a diversity of social functions, and those for whom it is essentially a space of representation for imagining and regulating the body politic. Richard Sennett in *The Conscience of the Eye* (1990) cites Isodore of Seville as first making the distinction in the sixth century between *urbs/urban* (the stones laid for the practical purposes of shelter, commerce and warfare) and *civitas*, the structures of feeling, ritual, custom and belief that take form within it; this rests on a division between profane and sacred space which finds its contemporary academic resonance in what we might call the prosaics and poetics of socio-spatial analysis. The first concentrating on the logistics of urban policy, planning and administration, the second on the lived cultures and narratives through which the daily business of living, loving, working, travelling and playing around in the city are conducted by different groups of citizens.

According to Sennett, this intellectual schizophrenia derives from the original Judaeo-Christian split between secular and spiritual city, which is resumed, but not resolved in the modernist dialectic between the global heights of profane power commanded by state and capital, and local spaces of private or public retreat organised around purified identities and communities constructed 'from below'. Sennett's project is to overcome the alienation of these two orders from each other in and through what he calls the multicultural city, a city which is to be organised around a prosaic poetics of difference 'made by all'. What this might mean in practice is never made clear! Indeed his whole argument about urban multicultural-ism, like so much else in the debate about the local/global city, rides at a hyper-real level of generalisation, propped up by a few quasi-normative examples, but effectively immunised from detailed empirical research. How then to go about bridging that gap?

QUESTIONS OF METHOD

This is the central issue which a group of us are trying to address in a new research programme which is looking at models of community safety and racial danger in two of London's Dockland communities and two matched areas of Hamburg.[2] One dimension of this study involves examining how the local/global is constructed by differently placed individuals and groups, by men and women, children and the elderly, by the native born and the immigrant, by national minorities and majorities, by the powerful and powerless, by policy makers and community activists. Our starting-point is the sense that one person's microcosm might be another person's macrocosm, one group's bridge, another's filter, a space that was sacred to one community might profane another's sense of what was central or peripheral to their world.

The pilot study which was carried out on the Isle of Dogs in 1994 was, amongst other things, designed to establish what methodology might be appropriate for the larger, comparative study.[3] It quickly became clear to us that the usual kinds of approach to mental mapping or time geography were not going to be of much help; they reproduced the very split between urban prosaics and poetics which was part of the problem. We tried getting people to describe their daily movements and communication networks, and then answer questions about the whys and wherefores. While this provided a snapshot which might be useful for assembling a gallery of urban ideal types, it hardly provided adequate contexture for the stories people might actually have to tell about where, in a deeper sense, they were coming from. To access this 'other scene' meant devising a more sensitive way of eliciting the spatial inscriptions of life histories, and mapping the symbolic landscapes of longing and belonging which inform people's sense of place, origins and identity. In other words we needed to find methods appropriate to a *narrative* cartography to help us unravel the complex webs of meaning spun around that deceptively simple equation – story : plot : territory : map. As we quickly discovered this was easier said than done.

We chose as our thematic focus our informant's sense of home, and its relation to the life journey. While our long-term aim is to explore the various political, social, psychological, economic and cultural articulations of these constructs, for the pilot study we decided to anchor the enquiry to people's sense of safe, dangerous and contested space. We showed our informants photographs of key locations in and around the Isle of Dogs, asked them to identify particular places which they frequented or avoided, and then to tell us stories about them.[4] Partly this approach was forced upon us by the area we chose for the study. The Isle of Dogs in the East End of London was in many ways an obvious choice for a study of this kind. Here after all we had an area which had been a gateway of world trade in the age of Empire, where international commerce had apparently provoked an intensely insular culture and community of dock labour. More recently this working-class localism had come up against the global information city, as represented by Canary Wharf and the superintendent London Docklands Development Coporation (LDDC); it had also mobilised against the diasporic presence of the Bangladeshi community whose settlement in the area coincided with the closure of the docks. Here, if anywhere, it seemed was a case study in localism as a reaction formation to the global flows of capital and labour, in the era of space/time compression.

Yet, as we were to discover, there were other, less obvious island stories waiting to be told which did not quite fit these terms of reference. It was, for example, a story of a white working-class ethnicity whose racialisation could not be explained in either purely local or global terms – it was neither simply a legacy of inbreeding or of Imperialism. The imagined histories and geographies which many of our white informants unfolded for us evoked a space and time compressed by technologies of power which were not so much centred on concentrations or dispersals of capital and labour as on the articulations of bodies, cities, and texts.

THE BURDEN OF REPRESENTATION

Many of the stories we heard from our white informants involved drawing a line between those habits, habitats and happenings which supposedly belonged to and strengthened the backbone of the nation, and those which undermined it because they derived from an alien source. This distinction between 'backbone of the nation' and 'race apart' in a sense subsumes the sacred/profane division, and invests it with a specific class dimension. It is one which has played an especially important part in the cultural formation of the English working class and the ideology of white labourism.[5] In the stories we collected about safe and dangerous spaces we found that many of the key images and metaphors derived from this same repertoire. It was used, implicitly or explicitly, to discriminate between indigenous and immigrant populations, and between different parts of the Island, different historical generations of East Enders, and between those who were genuine cockney East Enders and others who were not. This discourse of invidious comparison rendered the local as the locus of an inside story, comprising an authentic or organic view from below; whereas the global was seen as a conglomerate of disparate outside forces, united only in the attempt to impose a false homogenising view of the future of the area.

It seemed impossible to fully understand the white Islanders' own stories without relating them to those other accounts in which the East End symbolises the state of the nation or race, and in which particular localities are made to signify the essence of what the East End as a whole has been made to mean in this larger narrative. To put it another way, we could not understand the cultural geography of the Isle of Dogs without also understanding this wider history of representations.

In the mid-Victorian period, public attention shifted from the dark satanic mills of early industrialisation, epitomised by Manchester, to the causes and consequences of urban degeneration exemplified by slums and rookeries of London. The grand narrative of the East Ender has been elaborated by countless social commentators, philanthropists, missionaries, urban reformers, journalists, novelists and, last but not least, sociologists. No area in Britain has been more written about, more exploited as a source and site for the projection of public anxieties about proletarian combination or sexual promiscuity, the state of the nation or the degeneration of the 'race'. And often the whole lot at once.

There are important differences in style and emphasis between these accounts but they all turn on the distinction between east and west; this tale of two cities, two nations, and sometimes two 'races' remains central to the discussion of how, and if, the body politic should be strengthened or reformed to deal with the consequences of social inequality.

In many cases the pictures of disease, depravity and disorder which were drawn with such lurid detail were the preamble and rationale for local schemes of moral education and social reform based upon no less imaginary communities of civic well-being, national health, or racial integrity. Whether it took the form of designing model dwellings, providing rational recreation, reforming the sweating system, or relieving poverty, the project of improving conditions of life and labour in the East End was intimately tied to the regulation of local family and community relations. Moral panics focusing on the spectacle of gangs of unemployed youth terrorising the neighbourhood, girls selling themselves on street corners, men brutalising or abandoning their wives and children through gambling or drink, ensured that whatever actual relief of distress was achieved by these means remained secondary to the reduction of alarm amongst the middle classes. Although similar images were applied to other working-class areas, and other parts of the country, they were articulated with particular vehemence in the East End of London. For here, in the heart of the metropolis, within a stone's throw of the City, and within easy marching distance of Parliament and the West End, was a dense concentration of dangerous difference, where poverty wore a foreign face and people from far-flung corners of the Empire might yet strike back.

One of the things the LDDC has tried to do is to revise the historical relation of mutual voyeurism and vicarious emulation entailed in these descriptions of east/west relations. According to this new version of the script, there is no longer any need for East End boys to go looking for West End girls in expensive Soho nightclubs, when they could be found living next door on the Isle of Dogs and taken to one of the new local discos. And there was no need for young women or men about town to go slumming in search of East End rough trade when they could meet them downtown at Canary Wharf.

So we are offered a vision of harmonious reintegration of east and west, an area where rich yuppies and poor cockneys, Bangladeshi and white English families could happily co-exist within pleasurable reach of each other's otherness and without treading on each other's toes. This was one of the key plots through which the inside story of the area's development was told from the vantage point of outsiders. At the same time this official iconography of multiculturalism was projected onto a narrative map of modernity, progress, and urban regeneration in which the presence of the poor, the unemployed, the elderly, indeed almost anyone who did not conform to the dominant image of the economically active entrepreneur, was effectively sidelined. These 'locals' simply did not show up in the global view – taken with the wide-angled telephoto lens. They were, at best, an ornamental backdrop to the yachting marinas and neoclassical piazza parlours, at worst, an acute embarrassment which pointed up the discrepancy between working-class territory and middle-class map. The LDDC storyline sought to reverse the surface terms of the dominant urban discourse: now it is the East End's turn to become the preferred habitat of the glitterati, the centre of multicultural excitement, in contrast to the dreary 'commercialism' of the West End or the cultural wasteland of the City. At the same time the LDDC's promotional strategy conserved the basic ideological plot centred on the opposition between backbone of the nation and race apart. And it is to this deeper grammar of urban imagineering we must now turn.

CITIES, BODIES, TEXTS

From the standpoint of governance, the western city has to be represented as a rational, ordered whole, especially when its superficial appearance is one of chaos and fragmentation. The aim is to disclose the hidden organising principles in order to subject them to conscious planning and control. The social sciences have obviously played a key part in this, especially in disseminating models from one country to another. Nevertheless, there remain important national differences in the way large cities have been imagined, observed, written about, and governed. Metropolises in the US and Germany have frequently been compared to gigantic engines of production and complex servo-mechanisms, melting pots and waste disposal systems, prisons and asylums. In all these cases the city is imagined to be a crucible, or microcosm, of the whole society, containing all its disparate elements and holding them together in some kind of dynamic equilibrium. Since the eighteenth century the city-as-container has been assigned its own special chemistry, even an alchemy, in which different classes and ethnic groups learn to co-exist and contribute their separate identities to the making of a common cosmopolitan culture. This imaginary is, of course, haunted by the fear that the elements will prove too combustible to be contained in this way. As Ted Johns said of the East End, 'it's not so much a melting pot as a boiling cauldron' (from interview with the author). To stop it boiling over, however, requires the pouring of oil on troubled waters, taking the matches away from anyone who might be tempted to light the flames of resentment. This makes for a compelling narrative which keeps us on the edge of suspense, for it is always a case of 'the fire next time'.

This dramatic trope of a multicultural city was never popular amongst the urban squirearchy in Britain and their anti-industrial temper drew them to other, safer analogies. The workings of cities were compared to those of bodies and texts, not because of any affinities of natural symbolism, but because the available disciplines which studied bodies and texts furnished strategies of urban and civic analysis with which the elite felt more at home. Comparative anatomy, parasitology, epidemiology, on one side, classical philology, biblical exegesis and literary aesthetics on the other provided the models and metaphors with which this stratum thought, felt, dreamt and lived its relation to the city. The first set of discourses made it possible to represent the city as Other, and then to isolate the Other in the city, to distinguish and classify the diseased habits, habitats and happenings associated with 'the race apart'. The second set of analogies made it possible to identify and celebrate those elements which might be assimilated into the national culture and provide a backbone for the body politic. Here uniquely, and only for a time, the two cultures of Victorian science and humanities collaborated to common purpose and effect.

Many commentators have been struck by the more obvious medical analogies – cities that are equipped with lungs, arteries, bloodstreams, bowels, hearts, and faeces. Galen's theory of humours connects with Harvey's model of circulation to put flesh on the bare bones of bourgeois fears of social contagion and racial degeneration. Less well notated are the textual analogies. To many observers, processes of urban growth seemed to have turned the Victorian city into a foreign language or an illegible text. The purpose of the urban explorers was to decipher its vernacular codes, parse its sentence structures, translate its idioms into a more familiar language and, if they were professional *flâneurs*, read the exotic signs between the lines of more pedestrian desires. This was an active method-ology which permitted the working-class city to be read and written about in a way that rendered it both fascinating and a safe topic for conversation and concern in the middle-class drawing room.

The concatenation of these two image repertoires produced an essen-tially rural pre-industrial model of the city as an organic community. The body analogy furnished a naturalistic image of urban growth and regenera-tion; it was more often used to represent its antithesis – processes of blight and decay caused by parts that become dysfunctional, or parasitic, thereby disrupting the harmony of the whole. At the same time images of urban health or disharmony are rendered into an intelligible and narratable text, with a storyline which unfolds more or less teleologically, and features heroes and villains, bearers of good news and bad. We need perhaps to consider what it is about bodies and texts which enables them to be so easily articulated into metaphors of urban inclusion and exclusion, and also what it is about cities that either resists or welcomes such configuration.

Bodies and texts are alike in that they both have beginnings and endings. But the consequences of physical and narrative closure are somewhat different; with bodies it is always the end of the storyline, but texts have an afterlife; they may go out of circulation rather sooner than bodies, but they normally survive their authors death somewhat better (even if only in the literary graveyard of the British Library!). So if you want to imagine an eternal city you'd better construct it like a Labyrinthine Library after Borges. As to the marking of boundaries, bodies have non-negotiable limits rather than margins. Texts, in contrast, have margins which offer a space for others to stake their claims to authorship; and just because it is only a simulated dialogue there are no limits as to what may be said. Bodies have excitable zones, which usually require real or imaginary others to set them going, and these may be no-go areas for strangers; whereas texts have footnotes which are dispensable and whose main function is to familiarise the reader with the author's intellectual world. Each analogy thus offers a different strategy for mapping territories of difference and desire in the city, and the choice is determined as much by aesthetic as ideological purpose.

There is one final area where bodies and texts most neatly coincide and that is in the depiction of the relationship between dominant and subordinate cities. Bodies have invisible insides and visible outsides, texts have legible surfaces and depths of meanings hidden 'between the lines'. Through their conjugation we get the notion of a hidden urban under-world as an ultimate repository of inside stories and a socially transparent overworld where everything is on the surface, legible and light. It is through this moral binary that the relationships of east and west in the capital city have been largely articulated. This split image of the Victorian metropolis not only corresponded to an actual social polarisation – the eastward displacement of the labouring poor from Westminster and Covent Garden and evacuation of the middle class from Bethnal Green; it answered to an actual crisis in intellectual and aesthetic representation.

With the growth in the size and complexity of metropolitan centres in the nineteenth century, the attempt to sum up the city as a whole in a single all-embracing statement became an ever more overwhelming and encyclo-pedic task. Booth's was the first and last attempt at a comprehensive social cartography of London. Usually mapping took the more modest form of a simple enumeration of instances without any attempt to trace their inter-connection. The picture of London as a visual spectacle changed too. The urban panorama or diorama increasingly gave way to the synechdocal view – the choice of particular locations or perspectives as symbolising the essence of the city. Inevitably these tended to be places associated with the exercise of various kinds of power – highly visible parts that exercised control over the now invisible whole. The one exception to this underwrites the rule. The enduring popularity of the view of the Thames from the City up to Tower Bridge and down to Westminster stems from the fact that the river provides a single line of articulation connecting so many different symbolic centres, on both sides. London can still be imagined as forming a single, if complex, entity stitched together by social bridges. The LDDC appropriated this image in its attempt to rewrite the history of a divided city in a new global vision of the enterprise culture with the slogan 'go with the flow'. In this vision, the river is used to naturalise the movement of new capital and labour from west to east and to portray them as a new force binding together and rejuvenating (rather than dividing or destroying) the

Dockland communities on north and south banks.

When it came to representing the Other London, however, the body/ text code came into its own. For this was a code which specialised in generating metaphors of otherness by making the more visible parts stand for the disreputable whole, as well as drawing the line between those parts which were redeemable and those which were not. This code held special implications for the way immigrants and ethnic minorities were regarded and treated – in particular for the dividing lines which were drawn between those elements which were assimilable and those which were not. There were those who were a force for renewal, and those who were undermining natural growth, those whose cultures were regarded as translatable and those which remain inscrutable one from another. It is the latter, of course, who are made to represent the chaotic flux of urban life, the anarchic vitality which is subverting rational organisation. And let us note here that race is represented in one of two ways. First as a symptom of something wholly outside the text, or at least highly resistant to penetration by the methods of textual exegesis, inherent in a particular kind of social body, configuring its meaning in ways which are beyond negotiation or change. Alternatively, 'race' is primarily a matter of textual discrimination, a function of classificatory strategies applied to the decoding of cultural and linguistic forms which operate independently of their physical embodiment, and are altogether less fixed. This double standard of representation is thus deployed to further sort the ethnic minority from the immigrant.

EXPLANATIONS OF 'RACE'

In some recent accounts of the urban exploration literature there has been a tendency to regard these stories of the East End as hallucinations or figments of the bourgeois imagination, having little real impact on the people who live there. Stalleybrass and White (1986), for example, argue that when the top people in late Victorian society sought to get to the bottom of East End lives they only discovered their own anal erotic fantasies, fantasies which had been unconsciously repressed as a necessary condition for the assumption of a superior civilised posture. Hence the voyeuristic obsession with insanitary conditions and the imagery of sewers, pollution, germs and dirt which is used to characterise the moral status of the 'lower orders' and their habitats as the breeding grounds of vice. However, I think that to read the Victorian slumming literature in this way is to be carried away by its own, rather calculating rhetorical excess. It may perhaps be a valid comment about the opium-induced delirium of the 'orientalised' crowd produced by a Thomas De Quincey as he strolls around the East End markets. In most cases it would be more precise to say that these urban explorers were horrified to discover the open drains and middens, the slum tenements with no water, heating or light, the physical evidence of lives so different from their own. But this material phenomenology of poverty also excited a sociological imagination about its causes and consequences in a way which provided, in some cases only, a space of representation for these fantasies.

The hallucination model has the unacknowledged pay-off that it leaves the lives of real East Enders, the real 'inside story' intact, if invisible, in the opacity of its material self-reference outside the text, outside modernity. In this account East End cultures remain pure, or at least unpolluted by the perverse imaginations of these civilising missionaries, resisting the oppressive disciplines of capital and the corrupting delights of cosmopolitanism. Impurities, such as racism, have then to be explained by factors which are purely intrinsic to the East End itself, a natural home-grown peculiarity of this particular section of the English working class, a symptom and symbol of its pre-modern materialism. Husbands (1982), for example, in his study of East End racism, argues that it can be explained by the persistence of a culture of racial vigilantism based on a 'laager' mentality amongst a hard core of indigenous white East Enders in areas like Hoxton and Shoreditch, which has subsequently diffused to other areas. He writes of:

A profoundly materialistic culture, it implies a very limited and confused perception of social structure, and a corresponding readiness to apportion blame in inappropriate directions. Its political sophistication has been similarly limited; was long resistant to sustained mobilisation by the left, and even in its more recent voting has had a narrowly pragmatic and poorly articulated ideological basis. A continual readiness to engage in right wing racial exclusionism suggests the persistence of a 'rootless volatility' which was also a feature of working class politics in 19th century.

(Husbands 1982: 328)

In what is more an assumption than argument, Husbands deploys the historical stereotype of the East End working class as a race apart, trapped between an inert body and a volatile temperament, their racism symptomatic of a congenital stupidity brought about by inbreeding.

Another popular explanation argues the opposite case. The civilising mission was all too successful. From the 1890s the mass of East Enders were transformed from dangerous denizens of the underworld into cheerful patriotic cockneys through the combined and cumulative influence of outside forces, the Labour Party, the Church, state education, better housing and sanitation, rational recreation and self-improvement provided by the settlements, clubs and mission, even the music hall played its part. They all somehow worked together to produce this mysterious alchemy, which tamed the beast and turned it into that peculiarly English hybrid, the yeoman in overalls, who is terrifically traditional and only modestly modern. If racism enters into this story it is as a foreign import, something injected into the local body politic as part of the process of inoculating it against its own worst inclinations. If the dockers marched in support of Enoch Powell and his racialised version of romantic little Englander nationalism, or if more recently some of the Islanders could be heard voicing the slogans of white supremacism, it was only because they had internalised the underlying plot of the outsiders story and learnt only too well how to improve themselves by drawing the line under their own feet.

Versions of both these arguments could be found in the media coverage of events surrounding the election of a BNP candidate in a by-election on the Island in 1994. They were also taken up by academic commentators, anti-racist organisations and even by Islanders themselves. Yet I do not believe either argument does justice to the intricacy of the negotiations which have taken place between the insider stories constructed by people who live in the area and the accounts produced by professional middle-class observers.

MIMICRY, MASQUERADE AND MYTHS OF ORIGIN

Given the massive burden of representation which the East End – and, by proxy, East Enders – have had to carry, it would be surprising if strategies had not developed to lighten it in various ways. It is no coincidence that the East End should have been such a prolific creator of youth cultures which are particularly good at this game. From the masher and swell of the 1890s to the mod and crombie of the 1960s, local youth styles have impersonated upper- or middle-class forms of dress and deportment, associated with the models of propriety and enterprise to which East Enders were supposed to defer. Unlike the ritual transvestism of the early urban explorers (who dressed up in carefully disinfected secondhand clothes bought from the street market in order to pass as labouring poor), these youth styles contained elements of irony and parody aimed at the very cultures they sought to emulate. The mashers' scarf was part of coster rig, not the rich young man about town. The cut of the crombie coat, combined with jeans, caricatured the well-dressed city gent. Such features signal the presence of mimicry and disturb the social simulation game, even as they convey the message 'this is play'.

There are other strategies for turning the official East End success story inside out. The very features which are highlighted by outside middle-class observers as characteristic of the essential cockney or authentic East Ender can be exaggerated in ways which simultaneously make nonsense of the stereotype. For example, the original boot boys were Victorian shoe shine boys, orphans and destitutes from the street rescued by missions, such as Dr Barnardo's in Stepney, and organised into brigades to go out and mend or polish the boots of the bourgeoisie in Regent Street or Pall Mall. There was no more effective image of child rescue for fundraising purposes than the spectacle of the erstwhile waifs and strays transformed into honest service and happy with their lot. We may suspect that even the original boot boys had a somewhat different inside story of their lives as they spat on those well-to-do shoes and rubbed them up to a shine. A story, perhaps, closer to that of latterday boot boys who wear their Doc Martins as a symbol of physical hardness historically associated with costers and dockers . For it is this now almost defunct culture of manual labour and increasingly dysfunctional version of masculinity which has so fascinated generations of middle-class observers of the East End. A male physicality at once envied, feared and despised, especially by those who secretly or openly wished to participate in a bit of male bonding with the rough trade as part of their moral reclamation of the working class.

Another model of narrative transformation is to be found in certain post-war romanticisations of the old East End in films and TV series, and in the autobiographies of professional East Enders like Dan Farson, Ralf Finn, Dolly Scannell and a host of others. The picture of slums redeemed by warm, close-knit family and neighbourhood life, the cosy cockney village, with its friendly pubs and markets spiced with a bit of safe ethnicity, and naughty but nice sex, communities united against adversity, but not usually against class adversaries, the heroic stories of self-help, self-sacrifice and self-improvement, all this seems not only to have touched a chord of nostalgia amongst the yuppies, but amongst working-class people as well. The defence of traditional East End values of solidarity and tolerance is as common a refrain in left-wing propaganda, as mourning their passing is in the life stories of the older generation who grew up in the area between the wars. It is difficult to know whether we are dealing here with invented traditions, and sentimental idealisations which owe their origin and power to the workings of political rhetoric or collective false memory. Or whether this sense of imagined community draws on real historical material, structures of life and labour which have been dismantled by the malign confluence of post-Fordism and Thatcherism, but which are being remembered selectively to dramatise feelings of loss.

Even if we shelve the issue of whether these accounts of a 'world we have lost' do correspond in some way to 'the way it really was' we are still left with the question of their symbolic function in the present. Do these stories offer the new generation of East Enders a more engaging image of the area than the narratives of drabness and dereliction, exotic multiculturalism, or gothic horror which are otherwise on offer? Or is the evocation of a lost community spirit really a coded statement for a racism which refuses to recognise the black and Asian presence as an integral part of community, and blames them for its demise? Does the attempt to construct a 'real' East End from below through some kind of 'authentic' inside story really break with the dominant representations? Or does it function as a defence against the anxiety of outside influence, producing a racially exclusive, nativist definition of who belongs in a way which mimics the larger narratives of nation in which the East End story has traditionally been told?

Certainly with the advent of Thatcherism a new imagined community of 'race' and nation was constructed around the espousal of Victorian values and enterprise culture; the materialisation of this project in Docklands meant, inevitably, that the terms of local negotiation shifted. Increasingly, the stories told by white Islanders, in an attempt to define and defend an authentic East End way of life over and against those forces which were seen to be destroying it from inside and out, came more and more to resemble the official versions of that larger Island story which the Falklands war had done so much to revive. In fact, this connection had already been implicitly made in the campaign which the Islanders had organised against the LDDC plans for Canary Wharf. For all its socialist inspiration, the campaign increasingly fell back on a populist rhetoric which relied subliminally on the Falklands factor. The image generated was of a long-established, indigenous population of British stock brutally attacked and driven from their own land by the dictatorship of foreign capital. In a sense, the campaign provided the essential missing link between the grand narratives of 'race' and nation relayed in the media, and myths of local origins and entitlement which drew on an oppositional discourse of popular rights and sovereignties. It was this fatal connection which facilitated the growth of white working-class nativism on the Isle of Dogs. This dual process of racialisation inevitably gave a new lease of life to the self-image of Islanders as belonging to a tight knit homogeneous and long-established community which had been deserted or betrayed by its traditional friends and besieged by alien forces of change. Instead of explaining this outcome as the simple triggering of an immanent local peculiarity by a conjuncture of dis-advantage or as the expression of a generalised false consciousness within a historically declining manual working-class culture, our analysis focuses on a specific, racialised articulation of the East End story. By the same token, there is nothing inevitable or permanent about the local hegemony of this storyline. It is made up of different elements whose internal tensions can be exploited and ultimately unravelled. Its rationale can be challenged. There are alternative versions of the East End, and even of the cockney story, which move the search for a viable white working-class identity in another less racialised direction. But that, as they say, is another story.[6]

NOTES

1   I am grateful to Professor Peter Jackson of the Geography Deptartment, Sheffield University for his very helpful comments on this text, and especially these introductory remarks. The discussion following the presentation of the paper at the BSA Conference was also useful in helping me to clarify some of the main points.
2   'Finding the Way Home – Young People's Models of Community Safety and Racial danger' is an ESRC-funded project by the New Ethnicities Unit in collaboration with Michael Keith and Les Back at the Centre for Urban and Community Studies, Goldsmiths' College.
3   The pilot project was funded by a PCFC grant at the University of East London. I would like to thank my research assistants, Tarek Qureshi and Ian Toon, who carried out the fieldwork, and the many individuals and organisations on the Isle of Dogs and elsewhere who made it possible for us to undertake this project at a very difficult time.
4   Fieldwork based accounts of the research can be found in 'The Other East', *Demos 6* (1995), 'Backbone of the nation, race apart – conflicting narratives of the East End', *Dockland Forum 20* (1995) and 'Local habitation and a name' in Rustin (1996).
5   See Cohen (1996).
6   See Runnymede Trust (1995).

5

WHITE GOVERNMENTALITY*

Urbanism, nationalism, racism

Barnor Hesse

> When, in a crisis the traditional alignments are disrupted, it is
> possible, on the very ground of this break, to construct the people
> into a populist political subject: with, not against, the power bloc; in
> alliance with new political forces in a great national crusade to make
> Britain 'Great' once more.
>
> (Stuart Hall: 1989)

> And it is only too true that those who are most responsible for this
> racialization of thought, or at least for the first movement towards that
> thought are and remain those Europeans who have never ceased to set
> up white culture to fill the gap left by the absence of other cultures.
>
> (Frantz Fanon: 1967b)

INTRODUCTION

There is a problem of imagining the nation in the British city. It a problem of
'whiteness'.[1] But this is not so easily defined given the hegemonic preoccupation with governing the 'racialised other'. What concerns me here is how and
why the nationalist imaginary[2] increasingly invokes the regulatory structure
of 'whiteness' in appropriating the political and cultural experiences of
British cities. Mazzoleni (1993: 293–4) has suggested that the imaginary of
the city has an anthropomorphic projection and that the habitation of the city
is lived as one's body is encountered, as a recognisable and inimitable
physiognomy. However, where the city is imagined as the nation's sibling and
conceived as the white body's double, the concept of 'otherness' becomes a
racialised alien intrusion, a difficult cultural virus. This nationalist imaginary
circulates both opaquely and pointedly in diverse social discourses which
insist that the racialisation[3] of the city is a recent trend, reducible to the

*I would like to thank the following usual and unusual suspects for providing much needed
critical insight at different stages into different aspects and different versions of this chapter:
Denise Noble, Dhanwant K. Rai, Bobby Sayyid, Ernesto Laclau, Farish Noor, Paula Williams
and Chas Holmes.

other's sudden incursion. But, as I shall argue, racialisation cannot simply be collapsed into the temporality of the post-war experience. In this sense what might be described as the cultural problem of 'whiteness' refers not only to the occlusion of its racialised history, but also to its resistance to questioning as a racialised identity, particularly where it insinuates and conceals itself discursively as the horizon of universal representation. It is a 'white mythology' which 'has erased within itself the fabulous scene that has produced it, the scene that nevertheless remains active and stirring, inscribed in white ink, an invisible design covered over in the palimpsest' (Derrida 1982: 213). This hegemonic structure of 'whiteness' forgets its contested antecedents, it forgets what 'others' remember; in effect this 'white amnesia' represses the historical context of racism because the threat of the 'racialised other' absorbs all attention.

My approach to a late twentieth century illumination of this begins from the analysis of a social margin, the site of the apparent exceptionalism of racial harassment.[4] In effect this signifies disruptions in the unqualified circulation of 'whiteness' as the source of national representation in imaginaries of the city. At the beginning of the century this found dynamic expressive force in the urban emergence of the so-called race riots of 1919 (Liverpool and Cardiff, Bristol, London, Glasgow), 1948 (Liverpool) and 1958 (Notting Hill, London; and Nottingham). The scale and intense duration of these patterns of racial harassment subjected geographically specific black communities to extreme and highly visible forms of violence and terror by white gangs, resulting in sustained escalations of defence and counter-attack (see Fryer 1984; Ramdin 1987; Gordon 1990). In the 1950s the clarion call 'Keep Britain White' captured media attention; in the 1960s 'Nigger hunting' entered the British public's imagination; and in the 1970s 'Paki bashing' was a familiar refrain in everyday vocabulary. The street or a series of streets and places of residence, recreation and worship in racially pathologised and socially impoverished neighbourhoods became the terminus of the 'white city's' limits. To challenge the cultural-urban difference of immigrant and indigenous black/Asian settlements was to snipe across a racialised border. The social margin where the city became contested nationalistically as 'a site of identification' (Mazzoleni 1993). It is here that we can begin to trace an urban genealogy of 'whiteness' that has, as bell hooks suggests, a terroristic structure:

> To name that whiteness in the black imagination is often a representation of terror. One must face written histories that erase and deny, that reinvent the past to make the present vision of racial harmony and pluralism more plausible. To bear the burden of memory one must willingly journey to places long uninhabited, searching the debris of history for traces of the unforgettable, all knowledge of which has been repressed.
>
> (hooks 1992: 172)

What I offer in the rest of this chapter is a 'deconstruction'[5] of racial harassment and racial terror in white appropriations of the British city.

RACIAL HARASSMENT AND THE CITY

It is often forgotten that racial attacks and racial violence have long been part of the British way of life, especially during the twentieth century. According to one estimate during 1970–89 there were seventy-four racist murders of black and Asian people (see Gordon 1990). However, prior to the 1980s there was virtually no official recognition of the daily and varying incidence of racial harassment. It was only in 1981 that Home Office research estimated that Asian people were fifty times more likely to be attacked on racial grounds than white people, and black people thirty-six times more likely. In 1982 the Policy Studies Institute suggested that the incidence of racial harassment was probably ten times the Home Office figures. This should be borne in mind when considering the findings of the Home Office's second survey in 1987. This put the figures for the Asian and Black communities at 141 and forty-three respectively (see Hesse *et al.* 1992). Although the struggle to raise the profile of racial harassment has been well documented (ibid.), it still persists as a phenomenon which appears both to outrage all sense of British decency and to exemplify the nation's indignation at post-war 'black immigration'. What this nationalist '*double entendre*' suggests is that while racial harassment may be seen as an exception to the rule of Britishness and its surrogate tolerance, even tolerance like Britishness has its limits. The 'respectable racism' which emerges from this nationalist formulation circulates within the same discourse that has come to define the terms of the unprecedented proliferation of racist assaults and murders during the 1990s in south and east London.[6] The disturbing concentration of these factors together with the rise to public prominence of the racist sentiments of the British National Party really do oblige us to rethink our understanding of the social dynamics of 'whiteness' and to theorise the implications of this thinking. The discourse of racial harassment may not be as marginal as some of us continue to believe.

Discursive formation of racial harassment

As I have argued elsewhere (Hesse 1993a) the social experience of racial harassment is the victimisation of communal location. What is statistically defined as an incidence is better analysed as a scenario. It is socially processual, it combines various types and levels of recurrent victimisation. There are four key dimensions to this. The first, 'multiple victimisation', describes how different forms of verbal and physical abuse may be experienced simultaneously. The second, 'cyclical victimisation', describes how racial harassment is experienced as repetition, over varying periods of time (e.g. every day, week or month). The third, 'secondary victimisation', points to the problems victimised communities have in reporting their experiences to public agencies who cannot perceive or refuse to address the logic of racism. And finally there is 'spatial victimisation' where black or Asian communities experience dangerous limitations on their freedom of movement and residential safety.

In order to understand the discursive construction of this 'racial victimisation scenario' we need to move beyond an analysis determined by exceptionalism and the polarisation of the criminal and law-abiding or the racist and anti-racist. A reinscription of this polarization can be drawn from Cohen's (1988) discussion of the intrapenetration of concepts of 'property and propriety' in the spatialisation of white working-class communities. He suggests this defines a 'quasi-biologically constituted community' as a natural urban phenomenon, where the rights and privileges of spatial ownership are asserted as a heritage and strategies of social closure are deployed as a right. Cohen describes this development as 'neighbourhood nationalism'. In this context we can unravel three urban levels of 'white' articulation in racial harassment which displace the idea that its discourse is exceptional. First there is the 'racialised asymmetry of local residence'. This is spatially contingent, it expresses itself in a presumed right to abuse, violate or dis-establish the routinisation of the Black or Asian habitation. This ascribes 'illegitimacy' to the presence of Asian and Black people in the 'locality'. It is invoked randomly and opportunistically in a range of forms in order to disrupt the incorporation of a racially proscribed 'other' within a proprietorial sense of place. Second there is the 'racialised nationalism of local governance'. This expresses the strategic idea that the local concerns of 'non-whites' are an illegitimate consideration for legal or policy intervention and that local politics ought to privilege white patriality. Third there is the 'racialised lack of geographical sovereignty'. This is spatially recurrent and suggests that British/English identity has become diminished by the intrusion and proximity of the 'non-white' and therefore 'non-British' and can only be retrieved through the spatial visibility of white domination. Racial harassment in the sense I have given it is a discursive formation (Foucault 1972). It displays a spatial regularity in its logic of meaning despite the dispersal and various levels of its forms; it uses 'whiteness' to reclaim the city.

On this basis racial harassment establishes meaningful correlations through the implications and consequences of a diverse array of activities that 'name, defame and claim' contested racialised spaces in the city. What produces a regularity in this dispersal is a nationalist imaginary that modifies the relation between and incorporates the coherence of abuse, spitting, assaults, intimidation, damage to property, arson and murder. This imaginary raises to the ground anything which is 'other' than 'white' in the city. It establishes its own national configuration in a spatial frontier which sustains a relation of exteriority with a 'non-white' inner-city, a local 'racial outside'. Intensely localised, racial harassment secretes a nationalist narrative in the spatialisation of a 'whiteness' that attempts to inherit the city. But why is the narrative of nationalism so significant? An interesting possible answer is provided by Bhabba, who argues:

In the production of the nation as narration there is a split between the continuist, accumulative temporality of the pedagogical, and the repetitious, recursive strategy of the performative. It is through this process of splitting that the conceptual ambivalence of modern society becomes the site of writing the nation.

(Bhabha 1994: 145–6)

What I want to consider now is how nationalism provides a split surface of inscription for the discourse of racial harassment to re-write the Britishness of the city.

SPLIT SECRETION OF BRITISH NATIONALISM

According to Balibar (1991: 86) the nation is constituted by the narrative of a retrospective illusion; at least two narrative structures are particularly significant. The first nurtures the idea that 'generations which succeed one another over centuries on a reasonably stable territory, under a reasonably univocal designation, have handed down to each other an invariant substance'. The second sustains a belief that 'the process of development from which we select aspects retrospectively so as to see ourselves as the culmination of that process, was the only one possible, that is, it represented a destiny'. In this way the narrative structures of 'project and destiny are the two symmetrical figures of the illusion of national identity'. But nationalism is also a strategically organised illusion or imaginary and this necessarily involves a 'programme of unification and a postulate of homogeneity' (Bauman 1992: 683). Historically the programme of nationalism in its European genesis set its sights on the 'exclusive rights to a territory, a population, a populated territory' (ibid.). This imaginary could only express and refine itself through the deployment of particularist strategies which claimed the right to administer, tame, proselytise, segregate or evict different populations depending on whether they could be depicted as naturally inside or outside the 'nation'. Nationalism, according to Bauman (1992) always contains an ambiguity which results from the 'interplay of inclusive and exclusive tendencies' and requires as much investment in the specification of the national-self as the national-other. However, the boundary is not as transparent as the desires of nationalism would wish. Where the boundary cannot be clearly specified or where its parameters are unstable, the apparent coherence of the nationalist ambiguity turns into the incoherence of nationalist ambivalence. The motivational logic of nationalism appears unrelenting because the:

> Nations of the nationalists are constantly at war – an unwinnable war – against their own inner ambivalence. Fighting, as always, its inner incongruity in a re-projected form of The Other, nations focus their self-defence on locating, segregating, disarming and banishing the strangers rather than enemies: those aliens in their midst who are the crystallizations of their zealously, but ineffectively suppressed ambivalence.

(ibid.: 687)

Bauman's suggestion of a nationalist distinction between 'strangers' and 'enemies' should not be read as a 'natural' demarcation. What it points to is the nationalist difficulty in sustaining the reductionist polarity between national-identity and national-otherness. The difficulty is posed by 'national-differences' which are neither reducible to identity or to other-ness but could be either. Elsewhere Bauman (1991) has referred to this in Derridean terms as 'undecidablity'.[7] Bauman described the 'stranger' as disrupting the settled, oppositional discursive terrain of 'friend and foe' and therefore precluding an easy resolution of that dispersal of cultural elements which escape the binary, identity/non-identity. What results is an excess of meaning within and beyond the horizon of nationalism. This is the locus of Bauman's conception of the 'stranger', ambivalence and undecidability. It is also the context in which we should understand Bauman's further claim that:

> Nationalism, that quest for a uniform world without contingency, turns out ambivalence as its' 'productive waste', and cannot but turn it out continuously and on a never diminishing scale. Lest they should suffocate under the growing heaps of ambivalence, nations are called to be vigilant against strangers in their midst – the false pretenders who claim soil and blood that are not their own, outspoken detractors of the sanctity of national symbols or (worse still) deceitful flatterers drowning their alienness in the mendacity of praise.
>
> (Bauman 1992: 687)

But this undecidabilty which deconstructs the nationalist discourse does not only create the problem of deciding friend from foe, but of friend from stranger and foe from stranger. This excess of meaning constructs nation-alism as the contingency of a 'decision'[8] in an undecidable national terrain. There are two contingencies which nationalism as a 'decision' confronts. These are perhaps best encapsulated in the paradoxical reversibility of the relation between identity, difference and otherness. Connolly (1991: 64) suggests an identity establishes itself in relation to socially organised and recognised differences. Nationalism then, despite its programme of homo-geneity, needs to negotiate differences of ethnicity, gender, sexuality, class, 'race' and present itself as their 'logic of equivalence' (see Laclau and Mouffe 1985). The first contingency arises where the status of the national identity is perceived as threatened or contaminated. Maintaining identity 'involves the conversion of some differences into otherness, into evil or one of its numerous surrogates' (Connolly 1991: 64). The second contingency reverses the first. This emerges where national identity perceives itself as incomplete or lacking in some vital dimension, here the difference transmuted and added to identity marks it as the essence of purity or superiority. Nationalism then both expels and absorbs difference. The nation is constitutively split between the difference which subverts identity and the difference which subverts otherness. Only the nationalist illusion of project and destiny can displace if not eliminate this split. As we shall see, it is this structure of nationalism which underlines a racial crisis of British identity in the post-war period.

A post-war white genealogy

It is conventional for commentators on 'race' in Britain to point to the post-war period as the crucial turning point in the racialisation of national politics because of primary immigration from the Commonwealth and the legislative responses of central government. Usually what this fails to recognise is that the late 1940s and 1950s is also the period of the dissolution of Empire and a shift in the racialisation of British identity and nationalism. During this period the Conservative government was concerned both with 'black' immigration and the future of the Empire. This was a time when the process of decolonisation intensified in the African, Caribbean and Asian colonies; it was also the decade of the 1958 'race' riots in Nottingham and Notting Hill. I characterise this post-war/post-colonial period as the movement from the politics of 'race' as Empire to the politics of 'race' as Nation. Stuart Hall (1978) has argued this is the period which inaugurates the 'forgetting of Empire' and the idea that 'race' is 'nothing intrinsically to do with the condition of Britain'. Hall's observations are an important intervention in the understanding of what I described above as 'white amnesia', particularly where he writes of:

> the profound historical forgetfulness – what I want to call the loss of historical memory, a kind of historical amnesia, a decisive mental repression – which has overtaken the British people about race and Empire since the 1950s. Paradoxically, it seems to me, the native, home-grown variety of racism begins with this attempt to wipe out and efface every trace of the colonial and imperial past.
>
> (ibid.: 26)

Thus 'race' comes to be seen not as a social and political relation with British historical antecedents, but the cultural or biological property of a contingent Black and Asian population. In this way the emergent national discourse conceives 'race' as a cluster of issues which can be repressed in the idea of the nation because they have no intrinsic location. Yet it is precisely the trace of Empire which is effective in structuring the racial dislocation of post-war/post-colonial British identity.

At the beginning of the twentieth century Britain was already racialised and had been for over 200 years. Its identity was synonymous with Imperialism. The historical expansion of Empire in Africa, Asia and the Caribbean defined a discursive sequence in the logic of imperial identity. Each colony was not only a British possession, but the colonised peoples were defined as British subjects through a logic of equivalence in which each was not French, not German, not Belgian and so on. The idea of a British nativism, a territorial exclusiveness, does not emerge at this point for two reasons. First, Britishness is a unity of different statuses, colonised subject and Imperial subject. The colonial subject is the difference, the excess added to British identity which elevates it to a superior essence. Second, the mythical spatiality of a pure British nation is not put into question. Although the colonial relation establishes the exteriority of a British secondariness, this does not begin to threaten the national project and destiny of identity until the colonial relation is increasingly turned into a relation of migration throughout the twentieth century. It is in the shadow of the declining British Empire, after the time 'when Britain stood alone', that the racial dislocation of British identity takes a radical spatial turn in the city. At this point, the catalyst of post-war immigration and the reinforcement of Black and Asian settlement introduces an acute antagonism between the spatial proximity of non-white colonial Britishness and Imperial white Britishness. Britishness becomes valorised as whiteness, whiteness becomes nationally spatialised and the racialisation of residential co-presence enters the 'organization and meaning of space (as) a product of social translation, transformation and experience' in the city (Soja 1989: 80). An interestingly sympathetic account of the emergent local nationalist demand for spatial propriety can be found in Rex's lament on the white experience of Handsworth, Birmingham during the 1960s. Although this is not necessarily Rex's intention, he describes the racial legacy of Empire in the ambivalence of Britishness and the urban genealogy of whiteness:

> what happened was nothing less than a disaster. The Soho Road, for them suddenly came to look like a street in Bombay, and little knots of West Indian boys stood around on the streets wearing strange Rasta locks and little Rasta hats, and sometimes these boys would get into trouble with the police. These Englishmen [sic], who'd grown up in Birmingham and had learned to think of the peoples of the Empire as their inferiors, now found that they were supposed to live as neighbours. They felt threatened and destatussed [sic]. The one thing they said repeatedly was, 'we weren't asked'. And that's quite true. They weren't.
>
> (Rex 1978: 17)

Between the late 1940s and late 1970s a deep crisis of national identity was experienced through a constitutively Imperial, split sense of Britishness. The contours of the spatial anxiety around 'race' were captured in the attempted distillation of patriality through immigration legislation which formalised a racist ideal of national belonging and institutionalised a national pastime of agonising over Britain's racial-spatial density. Not only did this facilitate the politicised themes of 'race' that endured throughout the 1970s and early 1980s (see Solomos 1989); it harboured the underside of the less well-scrutinised features of white appropriations of the city where configurations of cultural identity, locality and neighbourhood became icons of national contestation. Vital elements of this appropriation are discussed at length in Smith's (1989: 105–45) important but relatively neglected study of the emergence of 'racial segregation' in Britain.

Smith's analysis suggests that segregationism overlaps and interacts with racism and nationalism. She defines it as a 'system of beliefs which seeks justification for racial exclusivity within national boundaries'. The main expression of this was the practice of residential racial segregation which, once cut loose from its former colonial moorings, found anchorage in Britain's post-war housing policy and urban geography. The context for this was the process of decolonisation and the replacement of the Empire with the ideals of the British Commonwealth. Nevertheless, Imperialist assumptions were sufficiently intact to confer an exemplary Britishness on both the formerly colonising and colonised subjects. For example, the 1948 Nationality Act 'reasserted the Imperial ideal that anyone born under the crown could claim equal privilege as a British subject' (ibid.). This, however, could not conceal the ambivalence of national identity which was now caught between British particularism and the incorporative tendencies of Imperialism; and white universalism and the expulsionist tendencies of racism. The spatial dimension of this national ambivalence was stimulated by the development and proliferation of the pre-war 'coloured quarters' (see Little 1948/1972) in English cities and this excited a governmental concern with spatial clustering. Initially perceived as a temporary phase of immigration, it was expected that economic growth, regional development and social mobility would produce the dispersal of 'immigrant' communities and that assimilation would follow through the adaptation of the more 'civilised' British way of life (Smith 1989: 114).

This should not of course suggest that 'race' was perceived as a domestic or intrinsic social policy concern at this point. In fact 'throughout the 1950s, immigration and its effects (including segregation) were viewed in the context of foreign (rather than domestic) and colonial (rather than European) policy' (ibid.). Up to the early 1960s there was no policy context in which the existence of 'racial inequality, discrimination and disadvantage' could be acknowledged, officially national racism or the 'colour bar' did not exist. The initial 'post-war phase of non-interventionism', together with the absence of clear government directives, had two devastating economic and social consequences for the spatiality of Black and Asian communities. First, government support for the privileging of the white British in employment was guaranteed. Employers instituted colour quotas and limited the skilled and supervisory posts to white employees. Second, this marginal position in the labour market was exacerbated by marginalisation in the competition for housing, as employers gave no thought to the provision of accommodation and public housing subsidies did not exist. The spatiality of racism received an indelible national imprimatur at this conjuncture:

> Contrary to the welfare ideal, black Britons received virtually none of the benefits associated with council housing for at least 15 years following the war. This exclusionism was to squeeze New Commonwealth immigrants into the deteriorating remnants of the privately rented sector and into the least attractive portions of the owner occupied housing stock. A legacy of government inaction became the first link in a chain of events tying residential differentiation to the structures of racial inequality.
>
> (Smith 1989: 115)

Most commentators agree that the racialisation of national British politics intensified from the 1960s onwards (see Solomos 1989). What is less discussed is 'the extent to which the cultural politics of "race" reveals conflict over the production of urban meanings' and how those meanings which are racialised situate themselves as 'contending definitions of what city life is about' (Gilroy 1987: 228). What has also escaped discussion as a central feature of these contending definitions is the imaginary of the city/nation as an appropriation of paradoxical whiteness.

THE PARADOXES OF BRITISH WHITENESS

For, 'the British nation' the national past is interred in a post-war imaginary evoked by popular cultural investments in the Second World War, the welfare state, Imperial consciousness and the monarchy (cf. Wright 1985). This post-war social periodisation provides contemporary Britain with a racially nostalgic structure for the dialogics of everyday life. It constitutes part of what Wright (ibid.: 5) describes as British society's 'cultural manipulation' which occurs through 'endless public invocations of the national identity and tradition'. However, this fails to emphasise the racialised logic of that cultural manipulation. It is not sufficient for any discourse simply to invoke itself in order to guarantee the order of its identity, it needs to specify limits and frontiers of exclusion. In the case of British nationalism this cannot occur through an infinite enumeration of its own particularisms. The paradox is it can only appeal to the comparative universalism of whiteness in order to define the excluded, yet whiteness is not intrinsically British. In so far as the racial aesthetics of the British nation comprise a population and a landscape, it is the exclusive particularism of the former which in remaining impregnable must delimit the inclusive particularism of the latter, exemplified by its susceptibility to 'racial invasion' (cf. Gilroy 1987). This is one of the ways in which 'the nation has become a key figure in British politics' (Wright 1985: 141) and racialised whiteness the dangerous supplement[9] of a 'fictive ethnicity' (Balibar 1991: 95–9).

The role that whiteness plays in the imagination of the British as a community is paradoxical because rather than defining some final version of a 'natural' ethnic or racial foundation, it points to its mutability and incompleteness. It is used as a necessary criterion of ultimate authenticity but is ultimately insufficient. Its involvement in the production of a fictive ethnicity illustrates the nature of this paradox. Balibar describes a fictive ethnicity as something which is not identical with the nation but indispensable to it. It refers to ethnicity as if it were not an invention (cf. Sollors 1989) but of natural origin. Balibar suggests this can only be resourced in two ways, through the 'metonym of language' or the 'metaphor of race'. Although they operate together in representing the people as a nation inscribed in nature, they diverge as well as complement. Language expands the inscriptive range of the nation. Immediately transactional and provisionally translatable it creates a national imaginary through a language community. But this is 'not sufficient to produce ethnicity' because it is too permissable, it does not prescribe a destiny and in assimilating anyone it holds no one. In the context of nationalism then the nation cannot be based on a language community, it needs a supplement, 'an extra degree of particularity, or a principle of closure, of exclusion'. This establishes the logic of the search for a common 'race'. Whereas the language community created equality between individuals by naturalising the social inequality of linguistic practices, the race community dissolves social inequalities: 'it ethnicizes the social difference which is an expression of irreconcilable antagonisms by lending it the form of a division between the "genuinely" and "falsely" national' (Balibar 1991: 100). In this way British national inscription is contracted through racism; the metaphoric auxiliary of this is 'whiteness'. The form of 'whiteness' which carries the destiny of racism is:

> not an 'expression' of nationalism, but a supplement of nationalism or more precisely a supplement internal to nationalism, always in excess of it, but always indispensable to its constitution and yet always still insufficient to achieve its project, just as nationalism is both indispensable and always insufficient to achieve the formation of the nation or the project of a nationalization of society.
>
> (Balibar 1991: 54)

I recognise that Balibar does not discuss 'whiteness' as such but this is what I think emerges when racism is added to European nationalisms. 'As a supplement of particularity, racism first presents itself as a super-nationalism' which is based on the 'integrity of the nation', consequently it 'induces an excess of purism' (ibid: 59). The excess is the structural logic of whiteness, it evokes the spirit of Gobineau rather than Herder. The problem is that 'whiteness' creates a logic of purism which runs counter to the nationalist objective of populism. The paradox is intrinsic, it can only be concealed and it is only through the exclusion of designated impurities (e.g. the immigrant, the Black, the Asian) that the nationalist authentication of Britishness can be restored. But this restoration cannot take place through any conceivable particularity of Britishness, only the addition of 'whiteness' can secure the symbolic act of suture. Thus the self-sufficiency of Britishness becomes attenuated at precisely the point at which universalism is present. This is because 'whiteness' circulates within the imperial discursive economy of Europe/non-Europe and the globalisation of the West. There are two significant dilemmas here for a British nationalist imaginary. First, an unreconstructed British nationalism cannot avoid reinscribing a split sense of Britishness, particularly within the major cities (e.g. the authentic nationals and the artificial citizens). Second, any nostalgic return to the imperial visibility of whiteness in order to repair the split and exclude the unwanted racial material cannot avoid the dislocation of British identity being experienced as a perpetual crisis. It is the misrecognition of this and an apparent unremitting desire for 'white hegemony' which leads to racial antagonism.

RACIAL ANTAGONISMS AND THE SOCIAL CONTRACTION

My excursions into the unfolding disciplinary realms of 'whiteness' has a great deal of relevance for approaches which address the politics of nationalism within the city. This is illuminated by the way racialisation underlines the contestation of social relations. Paul Gilroy (1987: 27) describes this as a 'racial antagonism'. This is the primary basis for understanding the way in which 'racial meanings, solidarity and identities provide the basis for action'. Racial antagonisms are constitutively contingent because: 'Different patterns of "racial" activity and political struggle will appear in determinate historical conditions' (ibid.). I have tried to develop this theoretically elsewhere (see Hesse 1993b: 171–3); here I want to specify the relationship between British nationalism and 'whiteness' in the spatial determination of racial antagonisms. At the level of social relations and the constitution of the British nation, a racial antagonism can be said to disrupt, constrain and facilitate both the formations of 'whiteness' and 'multiculturalism' (i.e. the relative, differential configurations of 'race', gender, sexuality, ethnicity) in the regulation of the 'social'. That these formations are each inscribed in the determination of the other requires that we specify the logic of this antagonism and its racialisation. The approach I adopt has been initiated by Laclau and Mouffe who argue that an antagonism describes a relation which subverts the possibility of any totality. It is not an objective relation as such but a social relation which 'works' to disrupt objective relations; in other words it exposes the limits of every objectivity:

> the social only exists as a partial effort for constructing society – that is, an objective and closed system of differences – antagonism as a witness of the impossibility of a final suture, is the 'experience' of the limit of the social. Strictly speaking, antagonisms are not internal but external to society; or rather they constitute the limits of society, the latter's impossibility of fully constituting itself.
>
> (Laclau and Mouffe 1985: 56)

It is important to understand that the emergence of 'white society' is a discursive attempt to represent the nation as a closed system of differences. What I have referred to as an antagonism emerges through the logic of a 'constitutive outside' (see Laclau 1990), which describes the excluded relational elements (e.g. the non-whites, multiculturalism) against which the privileged social identity (e.g. whiteness) is defined. In this sense antagonism is an account of the process that eventuates in the 'dislocation' of social identities, describing how identities are blocked in their attempts to constitute themselves fully. Racial antagonisms in Britain are a contested experience of the cultural limits of the city where the assertion of 'whiteness' against the representative possibilities of the multicultural actually affirms *both* in the complex articulation of the nation. In other words the very idea of white Britain is already prefigured both in the Imperial legacy of a split sense of Britishness and in the anatomy of racial antagonism where white identity is dependent for its expression at all on the very racialised others it sees as blocking its full expression. As I have argued elsewhere: 'Black and Asian people are crucial to the existence of white society' (Hesse 1993b). It is these conditions of possibility in the differentiation of British national identity which the political discourse and logic of racial harassment seeks to repress, by founding the authenticity of the nation not simply in nationality in the first instance but in locality in the final instance. This discursive move is captured in the following observation by Balibar:

> By seeking to circumscribe the common essence of nationals, racism thus inevitably becomes involved in the obsessional quest for a core of authenticity that cannot be found, it shrinks the category of nationality and disestablishes the historical nation.
>
> (Balibar 1991: 60)

The shrinking of the nation occurs spatially on two mutually enforcing levels. First, the city-contraction of nationalism. National identity begins to refer less to the nation than to the region or the neighbourhood. The historical formation of the nation is perhaps relegated to a symbolic abstraction while the generational formation of locality is elevated to the concrete heritage of indigenous 'whiteness'. The localisation of heritage and the territorialisation of 'whiteness' becomes counter-posed to the discourse of political citizenship. What links this dynamically to the spatialisation of racial harassment is the second level. This is perhaps best described as the 'nativisation' of nationalism. What I am thinking of here involves Britain's importation of the anthropological construct 'native'. Generally its use has not been to refer to people born in certain places who belong to them, but rather as a reference, 'for persons and groups who belong to those parts of the world that were and are distant from the Metropolitan West' (Appadurai 1992: 35–6). It seems to me that part of the legacy of 'white amnesia' (e.g the forgetting of racism and the historic racialisation of 'whiteness') involves the curious but duplicitous cultural practice of projecting the discrepancies of the 'other's' experience onto the dislocations of the experience of 'self'. Hence the British nation is referred to as if it is experiencing 'colonisation'. The nationalist imaginary intones piously an anthropological litany in which the 'British native' on its own soil in the metropolis is incarcerated in the 'contaminated' localities of its natural setting as an endangered species. This perverse advocacy of British native rights brings together the two levels of shrinkage in the idea of nation in the pragmatism of 'white territorialism'. This establishes a linkage between, 'territoriality, the assertion of imperial white identity and racial harassment among various individuals and groups in white communities who regard themselves in racial or cultural terms to be defending their space against change and transformation' (Hesse *et al.* 1992: 173). In the context of racial harassment the body of the other is viewed as a surface of inscription for the shrunken visibility of a 'white' appropriation of the city. For the 'white' body of neighbourhood nationalism the 'zone outside the body, occupying its surrounding space, is incorporated into the body' itself (Gorzs 1994: 79). It is 'reterritorialised' (see Deleuze and Guattari 1994). In this way any intrusion (e.g. immigration, multiculturalism) into this 'bodily space is considered as much a violation as a penetration of the body itself' (Gorzs 1994: 79). It is probably for this reason more than any other that the discourse of racial harassment in the city justifies itself, without qualification, in the defence of the nation against the 'threat' of being overrun or the 'fear of being swamped'[10] and in paranoiac anticipation of those events violates the integrity, relations and context of the 'other's' body. The culmination of this analysis has a direct echo in Wieviorka's cogent formulation:

> From this point of view, racist violence represents a mode of resolution of tensions in which these are taken out on a scapegoat in the wake – and this is the key point – of a loss of social and cultural bearings, or a destructuring of social, political or community relations, or the – real or imagined – risk of such a destructuring.
>
> (Wieviorka 1995: 70)

CONCLUSION

What I have been trying to formulate in this chapter is what might be described as the disciplinary logic of 'whiteness' which emerges in resolute form whenever the cultural formation of the British nation is called into question by the racialisation of spatial dynamics in the city. In recent years the proliferation of racist abuse, violence and murder in relation to Black and Asian populations has continued to highlight an acute national identity dislocation in the post-war/post-colonial settlement. What I have tried to theorise are the conditions which make possible, and frustrate the dissemination of, 'whiteness' in the regulation of that dislocation. But there remains a profound political dimension to this deconstruction which I can only address schematically in this conclusion. I want to consider the hegemony of 'whiteness' as a structure of what Foucault has described as 'governmentality' (see Burchell, Gordon and Miller 1991). The focus here is not government in a reductive statist sense but rather the specific ways in which the conduct of individuals or of groups might be directed. For Foucault (1986: 221–4) government designated a wide area in so far as it described those activities which structured the 'possible field of the action of others'. Governmentality as a relation of power has expansive and restrictive senses. Expansively it describes the deregulation of power relations in a multiplicity of social networks which interact and interface in numerous ways where there is no 'primary and fundamental principal of power which dominates society down to the smallest detail'. In the restrictive sense it describes the increasing regulation of power relations through the securing of compliance to state control. Understood in these two senses governmentality can be defined as the 'conduct of conduct', a strategic activity that aims to shape, guide or affect the conduct of persons and communities, including the government of the state, the self and others. The most important thing to note is that governmentality is not reducible to what can be identified as the political domain. It is a rationale of governing which encapsulates both an activity and a mode of comprehending that activity; it determines who can govern, what governing is and what or who is governed (Burchell, Gordon and Miller 1991: 1–3). It is in this politically intrusive and socially pervasive way that European racism, as a relation of regulating the subordination or excommunication of the 'other', has always sought its articulation not simply within the general structure of a 'colonial governmentality' (cf. Bhabha 1994; Thomas 1994) but, more complexly, within a 'white governmentality'. Although my formulation of this is provisional, I describe it as: a preoccupation with government which valorises 'whiteness' in the conduct of European activities as the source of legislative culture and the conduct of the 'non-white/non-European' as variously a threat, a resource, a fantasy or an epigone to be regulated by that culture (cf. Said 1978, 1993; Mudimbe 1988, 1994). What is remarkable about this is not so much its entrenched institution in the regime of modernity, but that its extremely mundane routinisation in the social encounters of everyday life in Britain seems to pass through the discourse of social science unnoticed even by the super-critical sensitivities of postmodern thought.

It seems useful therefore to say something strategic about how we might begin to think about the operationalisation of 'white governmentality'. This means asking questions about how 'race' becomes problematised within and beyond the state (e.g. in the streets and communities of the city) and defined as a problem of government. In other words we need to know, as Rose and Miller (1992: 175) suggest, 'those dreams, schemes, strategies and manoeuvres of authorities that seek to shape the beliefs and conduct of others in desired directions by acting upon their will, their circumstances or their environment'. By drawing on this analysis it is possible to identify at least two significant strategies of 'white governmentality'. The first can be described as 'nationalist political rationalities'. This incorporates a moral elaboration of appropriate directives, an epistemological characterisation of the objects and subjects of governance and a distinctive idiom which makes this amenable to political deliberations. Generally 'white govern-mentality' develops this through techniques of surveillance (cf. Foucault 1979; Hunt and Wickham 1994) which affirm the 'crushing objecthood' (Fanon 1967a: 106) of the 'racialised other'. This entails the deployment of representational strategies which assume the right to oversee, interrogate, celebrate or include/exclude the 'racial other' in any social field.[11] The second strategy can be described as 'racist programmes of government'. This is less discursive and more pragmatic, it is focused on the rectification of problems and the practical resolution of anxieties, for example, fears of 'black mugging' or 'Muslim fundamentalism'. Here 'white governmental-ity' relies on technologies of the body (Foucault 1979) which aim to control and discipline conduct through populist racist ascriptions and moral panics which inform the limitations placed on the 'racial others' spatial mobility, economic status, political participation and social visibility.[12] In the British city the practice, incidence and impact of racial harassment is lived under the virtual aegis of a 'white governmentality'[13] which pervades the national configuration of social and political life.

NOTES

1   In this chapter the generic sense of 'whiteness' refers to its various contradictory ruses, plays and strategies of concealing and revealing the relational terms of its racialisation; and in forgetting or deploying the logic of its implication in racist discourses.

2   It has become fashionable to cite Anderson's (1983) anthropological concept of a nation imagined as limited, sovereign and as a community. But this needs to be distinguished from what is meant by an 'imaginary'. The concept is taken from Jacques Lacan (see Benevenuto and Kennedy 1986). The imaginary has been used in political theory (Laclau 1990) and cultural theory (Bhabha 1994) as a conceptual tool in understanding the logic and limits of social discourses. There are four dimensions of an imaginary which are relevant to the discussion of 'whiteness' and nationalism in this chapter. First, it is the 'absolute limit which structures the field of intelligibility' (Laclau 1990), in other words it is a social horizon. Second, it refers to the recognition of social incompleteness and the desire for fulness in any social vision (ibid.). Third, the desire for fulness requires negotiation with a 'constitutive lack', which is 'simultaneously alienating' and 'potentially confrontational' (Bhabha 1994). Fourth, the imaginary oscillates between two forms of identification, 'narcissism and aggressivity' (ibid.).

3   'Racialisation' is important in the understanding of social processes and social identities. Discussions can be found in Fanon (1967), Miles (1989, 1992), Goldberg (1993), Anthias and Yuval-Davis (1991), Keith (1993a) and Small (1994). Miles (1989) attributes the first use of 'racialization' to Fanon (1967b: 73–74; see abstract on first page of this chapter). My reading of Fanon is a little more structured than Miles allows and perhaps a little less circumspect than Fanon. In my view Fanon suggests racialisation is dialogical but that it is the idea of Europe which initiates the first move or constitutes the first term. This establishes the pattern of defining people formations as gendered collectivities of visibly distinctive bodies, otherwise classified in the European gaze as 'races'. On this reading racialisation occurs on three levels. First, the reduction of diverse cultural representation to the limited iconography of 'races'. Second, the hegemony of 'white culture' which eliminates dialogue with 'other cultures' in the global representation of the universal. Third, social contestation around and through different conceptions of 'race' (cf. Keith 1993.) and between differently racialised identities (cf. Small 1994). This dimension can also be described as a racial antagonism (cf. Gilroy 1987). These three levels taken together enable me to concur with Miles' (1989: 76) summary that racialisation refers to the 'historical emergence of the idea of "race" and to its subsequent reproduction and application'. But it is important to argue as Goldberg does (1993: 42–45) that 'race' is the 'discursive object of racialized discourse' and that this 'differs from racism', although the two are linked. I see the intervention of racism as instituting a hegemonic form of regulating relations of racialisation, it eliminates the possibility of relativism. This hegemonic regulation takes two socially uneven co-existent forms. The first, 'social hierarchy', includes the 'racialised other' within the social's 'mainstream' but only in the position of subordination to a racially dominated structure. The second 'social incommensurability', excludes the 'racialised other' to the social's 'margins', in the position of excommunication from a racially monopolised structure. Often what is analytically described as racism simply refers to strategies and interventions which attempt to introduce, sustain or elaborate the structures of these social formations.

4   I use the term racial 'harassment' in order to convey the processual logic at work in this phenomenon and its recurrent destabilising impact.

5   Deconstruction as associated with the work of Jacques Derrida (1976) should not be confused with the idea of dismantling or taking something apart in order to reconstruct it. This sociological misconception misses the significance of Derrida's philosophical insights. Deconstruction as a phenomenon emerges from the semantic entanglement or conflictual logics within a 'text' or 'experience' where areas of meaning cannot be fixed or settled and are resistant to being settled once and for all. The 'method' of deconstruction exposes the limits of the 'decidability' of meaning within a text and correspondingly the extent of 'undecidability' (see Gashè 1986 for a quasi-methodological account). See notes 7–9 below.

6   The 1990s have seen an upsurge in racist atrocities and fascist activities in London, particularly in the south and east. In February 1991 a Black teenager, Roland Adams (15),

was stabbed to death in Thamesmead, South London by a white gang having been approached at a bus stop. In April a young Black man, Orville Blair (25) was also stabbed to death, apparently for taking part in a local burglary. Shortly afterwards local graffiti appeared with the words 'Two nil'. A year later in July 1992 an Asian teenager, Rohit Duggal (16) was murdered. In April 1993 another Black teenager Stephen Lawrence (18) was also stabbed to death in Thamesmead while standing at a bus shelter. The London Borough of Greenwich, where all these events took place, was described as 'Britain's racist murder capital'. Throughout this period the headquarters of the British National Party, less than two-and-a-half miles from where Stephen Lawrence was murdered, became the focus on an anti-racist campaign to have it closed down (see the *Voice*, 12 March 1991, 7 May 1991, 21 May 1991, 20 August 1991; the *Guardian* 25 May 1991, 17 October 1991; the *Independent Magazine*, 12 June 1993). Meanwhile in East London in September 1991 it was reported that Asian families on the Teviot housing estate in Poplar were under seige having experienced 250 racial attacks in the past ten months. In September 1993 an Asian teenager Quaddas Ali (17) was attacked by seven white men and one white woman while walking in Stepney. The attack left him critically injured and subsequently connected to a life-support machine in hospital. Later that month the British National Party won a council byelection in the Isle of Dogs. During the election campaign the Liberal Democrats distributed leaflets advocating that council houses should be passed onto tenants 'sons and daughters'. The local Labour Party condemned this as privileging the tenancy of white ancestry. After his election victory BNP councillor Derek Beakon declared: 'The British people are no longer prepared to be second class citizens in their own country. We've had enough, we are going to take our country back'. In February 1994 Asian teenager Muktar Ahmed (19) was walking in Bethnal Green when he was assaulted by twenty white youths. The assault left him with a detached scalp, severely fractured skull and permanently disfigured face. All these events took place in the London Borough of Tower Hamlets which 'has long had the highest incidence of racial assaults in the capital' (see the *Guardian* 12 September 1991; 'Runnymede Trust', October 1993, March 1994; *New Statesman and Society*, 18 February 1994).

7   Derrida (1987, 1981) suggests 'undecidablity' refers to the logic in a system of signification which sustains both coherence and incoherence in which meaning is irreducibly incomplete, and where the construction of what makes sense or can be defined is beyond semantic mastery. Thus it is the logic or syntax within which the generation of meaning takes place that creates the possibility of indeterminacy. Even in a classical opposition between two terms, the element of undecidability emerges where the meaning of an item: cannot be allocated exclusively to either one of the two terms; could be defined as any one of the two terms; is not itself a third term; and continually disturbs the demarcation line drawn between the two terms. In the relation between identity and otherness what is different from both identity and otherness, is undecidable. Therefore in order to establish what is identity and what is otherness, a 'decision' is required which cuts across or blocks the untamed excess of meaning (see also Gashé 1986). See note 5 above.

8   Derrida (1973) has given an important weight to the concept of 'decision'. He suggests it is a theoretical choice or a discursive intervention to secure a definition within a textual experience, which is taken in the face of competing and incomplete alternatives (e.g undecidability), where there is no pre-existing guide or ground for the decision. In this sense Laclau (1994) has argued a 'true decision is something other and more than an effect derived from a calculating rule', this is because the 'decision has to be grounded in itself, in its own singularity'. As both Derrida and Laclau note in their citation of Kierkegaard, the moment of decision is the moment of madness.

9   The supplement or supplementarity (see Derrida 1976) describes a discursive element which has to be added to an apparently foundational discourse in order to shore up the appearance of an originary foundation. In terms of my argument the desire for the original nation adds the element of 'whiteness' to the idea of its foundation. This fails to recognise that not only is the significance of 'whiteness' an imperial addition to the history of the nation, but its significance is irreducible to the singularity and insularity of Britain. Hence 'whiteness' becomes a dangerous supplement in so far as once added it threatens not only to transform the particularist idea of nation into the universal idea

of 'race', but to prescribe racism as more important than nationalism.

10   This recalls Margaret Thatcher's famous 'swamping' statement on nationwide television in 1978 shortly before she was elected as prime minister. According to Thatcher, 'people are really rather afraid that this country might be swamped by people of a different culture. The British character, has done so much for democracy, for law, and done so much throughout the world but if there is any fear that it might be swamped, then people are going to be rather hostile to those coming in' (Solomos 1989: 129).

11   An illustration of this occurred in September 1995 when Sir Roger Bannister, a sports scientist, told the British Association that Black athletes had natural anatomical advantages and that their superior physique was confirmed by the increasing incidence of all Black sprint finals. Many in the media who felt that the description of these views as racist was yet another instance of the so-called 'political correctness' lobby were in fact defending as fair comment the legitimacy to seek explanations in social behaviour in the bodies of Black people. That this process of racialised body objectification hardly seems to arise when the excellence of white athletes in all white finals is on display demonstrates the extent to which this technique of surveillance is culturally assumed as a right.

12   In July 1995 the Metropolitan Police Commissioner, Sir Paul Condon, announced he wanted to hold a meeting with Black community leaders. His intention was to discuss the high incidence of young Black men involved in 'mugging' offences in particular parts of London, prior to a police targeting operation. This played on the idea that there is something called 'black crime' but not 'white crime'. In assuming that there exists a Black community with leaders who somehow convene or represent that community, this offers up the colonial imagery of a barely tolerated people who have to be governed, whose leaders cannot control their youth and whose youth have to be restrained. Technologies trained in relation to the Black body thus acquire the cultural commonplace of reasonableness.

13   'White governmentality' legitimates if not the deployment of racism then at least its cognitive rationale. It is important to stress here that racism is 'non-reversible', since to argue otherwise is to assume it has a normative direction and to ignore its constitutive implication in an asymmetrical relation of governance.

6

MIGRANT SPACES AND
SETTLERS' TIME

Forming and de-forming an inner city

Max Farrar

This chapter critically examines current sociological and geographical conceptualisations of space and time in relation to the processes which have formed an inner city area of Leeds, England. This area, known as Chapeltown, contains the majority of the city's black residents. The chapter analyses some of the ways in which diverse human agents historically created and continue to use this territory. Simultaneously, it investigates the impact on social relationships of disparate senses of time among the various historical and present occupiers of this space. The overall argument is that, while the effect of global economic forces and the time–space shifts identified as characterising the condition of postmodernity are clearly evident in this locale, and signs of fragmentation and ghettoisation abound, the diversity of the population, and the rootedness of many residents in modern and traditional time–space, provides a social coherence, and a resource for resistance, for many of the people who live in the area.

NAMING AND PLACING THE TERRITORY

Visitors to Leeds will only find Chapeltown if they acquire 'local knowledge'. This knowledge – held by anyone who has been in the city for even the shortest time – places Chapeltown quite precisely on the north-east edge of the city, bounded by major roads, with Chapeltown Road bisecting it in two. On the largest scale maps, Potternewton is the name given to this area. Richard Hoggart's description of his childhood around Potternewton Lane, and his characterisation of this area today as 'a kerb–crawlers magnet [with] many of its houses in multiple occupancy' (Hoggart 1988: 36) reflects the gap between the maps and local knowledge. Large-scale maps include the word 'Chapeltown' within an area of the city which both the maps and local knowledge call Chapel Allerton. Sack has demonstrated that in pre-modern times 'even the more abstract calendars and maps of imperial officials were laden with mythical–ritualistic meanings' (Sack

1986: 77). Harvey states that this changed with the Enlightenment. 'Maps, stripped of all elements of fantasy and religious belief ... had become abstract and strictly functional systems for the factual ordering of phenomena in space' (Harvey 1989: 249).

But the modern map of Leeds is not 'abstract and strictly functional' when it comes to ordering the space popularly known as Chapeltown. If you can find the name on a map you go to a different place from that dictated by local knowledge. The map is not a simple 'instrument of power/knowledge' (Gordon 1980: 74); Foucault later agreed that 'the plan is not always an account of relations of power', saying: 'No. Fortunately for the human imagination, things are a little more complicated than that' (Rabinow 1986: 255). It is the human imagination which is interfering with our modern mapping, for all its claims to scientific accuracy. The large-scale map of Leeds bears a pre-modern imprint of a 'delicate green, commonly known as Chapel–Town Moor' (Thoresby 1816) in the heart of contemporary Chapel Allerton. As Ralph Ellison (1952) famously demonstrated black people are rendered invisible by whites. The smaller-scale Leeds' maps erase Chapeltown altogether. But while the cartographers make Chapeltown invisible, the myth-makers insist on representing the black residents of the territory everyone in Leeds knows as Chapeltown. This 'visible invisibility' – the contrast between popular vision and cartographic blindness – is maintained by the mix of social motivations which come into play as soon as popularly named Chapeltown becomes the topic of discursive manoeuvre, with the various representational categories reflecting the values and ideologies of 'race' and sex held by their proponents.

Nor can science provide us with objective data about the people who are resident in popularly named Chapeltown. In no time at all the 1991 census on a CD-Rom will produce an enumeration district analysis of the area known as Chapeltown. The area contains almost 14,000 residents, of whom 28 per cent are African, Caribbean or Black Other, 28 per cent are South Asian and 39 per cent are white. Overall unemployment stands at 32 per cent: 29 per cent of white men, 32 per cent of South Asian men and 36 per cent of black men are registered as unemployed. But in inner city areas throughout the country, unknown numbers evaded the surveillance of the census (Simpson and Darling 1994), and a small but significant group of men neither engage in waged work nor register as unemployed. A figure of 20 per cent for female unemployment provides no useful information about the situation of women in an area in which, for a large section of the population, domestic relationships are prescribed by religious and patriarchal requirements, rather than material need. Maps and census statistics cannot be taken literally. The plot thickens when we turn to sociologists' and geographers' efforts to think about the conceptual problems we face in analysing the inner city.

THEORISING SPACE

Keith and Pile have rightly criticised the jumble of metaphors and concepts which threaten to engulf our discussion of space. After listing a bewildering variety of terms, they conclude that 'it is rarely clear whether the space invoked is "real", "imaginary", "symbolic", a "metaphor–concept" or some relationship between them or something else entirely' (Keith and Pile 1993: 1–2). The confusion seems to arise from Lefebvre's pioneering effort to establish 'space' as a material force: 'Space has its own reality in the current mode of production and society, with the same claims and in the same global process as merchandise, money, and capital' (Lefebvre 1979: 286). Sayer has condemned Lefebvre's 'sloppy statements' on space, accusing him of using 'space' when he should use 'territory' (Sayer 1985: 60), but the real danger in some of Lefebvre's statements lies in his tendency to reify 'space'. Thus, when Lefebvre (1979: 290) tells us that '[t]his formal and quantified abstract space negates all differences, those that come from nature and history as well as those that come from the body, ages, sexes, and ethnicities', we are tempted to believe that 'space' has some power of its own, independent of the agents who occupy it. The understanding of space as *social space*, 'permeated with social relations', 'shaped and moulded from historical and natural elements' (Lefebvre 1976: 31) is extremely helpful, so long as it is not compressed into a reified and deterministic shorthand. While it might be right to argue that '[t]he spatial is *partly* constituted by the social, but is reducible neither to natural or social constituents' (Sayer 1985: 59), the most interesting topic for sociology is that element of space which *is* constituted by social activity. As Sayer (ibid.: 52) argues: 'Space makes a difference, but only in terms of the particular causal powers and liabilities constituting it' – a view reinforced by John Urry (Urry 1985: 28). Ed Soja, however, in his enthusiasm for Lefebvre, appears to have rejected Sayer's and Urry's strictures. He presents us with the kind of tautology that characterises some of the current writing on space: 'Spatiality is a substantiated and recognisable social product, part of a "second nature" which incorporates as it socialises and transforms both physical and psychological spaces' (Soja 1989: 129). Soja defines 'spatiality' as 'socially produced space', and he offers a definition of 'second nature' on the same page. Employing these definitions, we see that Soja is arguing that:

> Spatiality [i.e. socially produced space] is a substantiated and recognisable social product, part of a 'second nature' [i.e. the transformed and socially concretised spatiality (socially produced space) arising from the application of purposeful human labour] which incorporates as it [i.e. socially produced space] socialises and transforms both physical and psychological spaces.
>
> (Soja 1989: 80n)

This seems to amount to the notion that social space produces more social space, which, apart from being circular, is no help whatsoever in understanding the social processes involved.

But the concept of 'spatiality' is contagious and it appears in Keith's informative study of riots and policing in London in the 1980s:

> These locations [Notting Hill, Hackney, Brixton] were not neutral spaces in which riots occurred. Instead they were resonant with

contested meanings; the social relations of conflict between the police and the local Black communities were sedimented through time in particular places lending these locations distinctive senses of 'spatiality'. The events of 1981 in these three places were only comprehensible if we understand the manner in which this sense of spatiality mediated antagonism. Such spatiality draws on the symbolic readings of these locations, but these readings were never transparent or universal; they were sites of political struggle, constitutive rather than incidental to the patterns of violent conflict.

(Keith 1993a: 154).

Keith opens this part of his discussion with a quote from Lefebvre ('Space is political ... the production of space can be likened to the production of any particular kind of merchandise'), but he seems to have adopted Soja's notion of 'spatiality' in an effort to understand police–black relations in the urban setting. What sense can we make of the suggestion that these conflictual relationships have been 'sedimented' with the result that the locations in which they have occurred have a distinct sense of 'socially produced space' about them? And that these events can 'only' be understood if we employ the concept of 'spatiality'? Some parts of most British cities *are* staked out by people (black and white) whose relationships with the police are characterised by persistent antagonism, and both the police and the occupants behave in routinised ways when they come into contact in that territory. But it confuses matters to conceptualise such processes in terms of 'socially produced space'. This formulation fixes the territory, the actions and the relationships too permanently. Moreover, it is not 'spatiality' which mediates the antagonism.

The land on which these interactions are taking place is better thought of in Giddens' (1984: 375) terms of 'locale' (a 'physical region involved as the setting of interaction, having definite boundaries which help to concentrate interaction in one way or another'), because this concept neatly captures the idea that it is the relationships between people in that place which interest us. It is what people *do* that counts, and using 'spatiality' in Soja's sense of the word detracts from the particular strategies employed by the police and the occupants of the area. Sack's (1986: 19) notion of territoriality, which he defines as 'the attempt by an individual or a group to affect, influence, or control people, phenomena, and relationships, by delimiting and asserting control over a geographical area', captures these processes far more effectively than Soja's 'spatiality'. The wars of position employed by police and their antagonists in their efforts to control a territory will partly depend on their respective understandings of the lie of the land (an instructive topographical metaphor) and the balance of forces in any particular territory. To direct our attention to 'socially produced space' as the intermediary in this process is to mis-direct us from human agency to an ill-defined structure.

Rob Shields has theorised the way that territories can be 'read'. He is concerned with 'the logic of common spatial perceptions accepted in a culture ... the recodings of geographic spaces [in which] sites become associated with particular values, historical events and feelings'. Sites become symbols of good and evil and states of mind, 'zones of the social imaginary'. He directs attention to 'the pre-constructed cultural discourses about sites' and the 'questions of power which lie behind conventions' (Shields 1991: 29–31). But he moves into a more structuralist vein when he defines 'social spatialisation' as:

> the fundamental coordination of perceptions and understandings which allows for the sociality of everyday interaction and the creation of durable social forms and institutions. . . . As a fundamental system of spatial divisions (e.g. subject–object, inclusion–exclusion) and distinctions (e.g. near–far, present–absent, civilised–natural) spatial-isation provides part of the necessary social coordination of percep-tions to ground hegemonic systems of ideology and practice.
>
> (Shields 1991: 46)

Social spatialisation manifests itself in conversation where places are referred to metaphorically, and where place-images are generated through over-simplification, stereotyping and labelling (Shields 1991: 46–7). The link with Soja's notion of spatiality is clear, but Shields' approach has an empirical focus on the precise mechanisms by which a territory acquires social definitions. If Lefebvre, at his best, ensures that we think of territory not as the physical elements of which it is composed, but as the product of human labour and social meaning, Shields (cued at least partly by Lefebvre) directs us to consider the impact of the discourses which people construct in their effort to make sense of locales. While 'spatialisation' might be a concept which is now suffused with too many meanings to bear the weight that Shields wishes it to carry, the need to analyse the multiple representations which people attach to certain locales is well established. In the discussion which follows of the settlement in Chapeltown of Jewish and black people, the underlying spatial practices of 'inclusion–exclusion' will prove highly relevant.

THEORISING TIME

In everyday speech, many residents of an urban area of black settlement would readily comprehend a phrase such as 'black space' or 'black time' in terms of their effort to forge discourses and practical activities in a particular part of town which are, to some extent, 'free' from the discourses and practices which they associate with a coercive white power structure. Establishing nearly autonomous territory is the conscious aim of all sorts of actors in the black inner city – in churches, mosques, temples, community centres, clubs, pubs, and in certain 'open' spaces. This is the sense in which I might use the term 'black space'. Similarly, it is likely that they would respond knowingly to Homi Bhabha's 'dialectic of various temporalities – modern, colonial, postcolonial, "native"' (Bhabha 1990: 303) – as soon as his proposition that different cultures apprehend time in different ways, and that these contrasting senses of time often conflict, became clear. But, just as the differential meanings of space need to be analysed, and the diversity of practices that go into the staking out of these places must be recognised, so too does Bhabha's formulation of time need to be scrutinised.

Lash and Urry present a resumé of sociological approaches to time, highlighting Durkheim's argument that 'time in human societies is abstract and impersonal and not simply individual . . . it is socially organised'. Citing Evans-Pritchard on the absence of a sense of time as a resource among the Nuer, and Bourdieu's demonstration that the Kabyle have constructed a social-time system which is hostile to clock-time, they argue that modernity is characterised by a different approach to time. 'Clock-time is central to the organization of modern societies and of their constitutive social activities. Such societies are centred on the emptying out of time (and space) and the development of an abstract, divisible and universally measurable calculation of time' (Lash and Urry 1994: 224–5). Bhabha is perhaps getting at these sorts of distinctions between societies in his notion of 'modern' and 'native' time. But Lash and Urry take the discussion further than this. They acknowledge Giddens' contribution to the analysis of time in late modernity – in particular his thesis of 'time–space distanciation' – but argue that he has missed another important feature:

> Giddens' account . . . does not sufficiently address a further characteristic of modern societies. It is not merely that time (and space) are disembedded from social life, but that time (and space) have developed as independent resources which can be manipulated and exploited by dominant social forces (and resisted of course). The emergence of time and space as independent resources is one of the defining characteristics of modern society.
>
> (ibid.: 235)

This idea that time is a resource to be manipulated is borne out in some practices in the black inner city – a point to which I will return. In drawing attention to the uses of time, we move away from the simplistic notion that, within any one type of society (e.g. post-colonial society), there might be a single sense of time. However, Lash and Urry want us to make an even more radical break with the existing sociology of time than this. They propose a move towards a more aesthetically sensitive discussion of time, quoting Irigaray's view that 'your body remembers. There's no need for *you* to remember'. This provokes an approach to conceptualisations of time in the black inner city via people's efforts to ward off the effects of age and the approach of death through bodily transformations of skin, flesh, muscle and hair. Further investigations in this area would be highly productive, but there is no room for them here.

CONSTRUCTING CHAPELTOWN'S SPACE

In applying these theoretical insights to a discussion of space in the main area of black settlement in Leeds, I am going to highlight a few social practices from a long list of possible examples. My main focus is on the human interventions in the landscape which resulted in the mixture of buildings, roads and 'open spaces' that characterise the territory now. This will substantiate, in broad terms, Lefebvre's point that this land has been politically constructed. I will trace some of the contrasting representations of this locale that have been established over the past 200 years. Over the past fifty years, these representations are inextricably linked with the settling in this territory of migrants – Jewish people, Caribbeans and South Asians in particular – and I will make some preliminary remarks about the perceptions of space and time that those groups might have brought with them. More briefly, I will discuss the effects of the recent changes in the circulation of money and of information in the daily life of the area. This will provide a vehicle for an argument about the implications of global-isation on the space–time of the city of Leeds, and on (popularly defined) Chapeltown in particular.

Early history

In 1344 William de Brugges, John Stuule, William Manlivey, Robert Raisin and William de Killingbeck conspired to steal the land which includes Chapeltown. Archivists have demonstrated that the original document of sale is a forgery (HCRO D/EP T4466). This is the first record in a long history of chicanery over the territory we call Chapeltown. By the end of the eighteenth century ownership of this land is a matter of dispute. Two of the major landowners have, by now, acquired peerages and between 1767 and 1801 Lords Cowper and Mexborough are in and out of court disputing who has legal entitlement to the land each of them occupies. Behind the lawyers' machinations lay physical violence. Thomas Stanton, one of Lord Mexborough's people, is in court on 20 July 1776 charged with entering the 50-acre farm of Richard Sykes, a tenant of Cowper's, and 'ejecting him with force of arms' (WYAS MEX 838).

But, by the middle of nineteenth century, the dominance over this land by the rich is established and their boundaries fixed in law. Ownership of most of the land to the west of Chapeltown Road is held by Lord Mexborough and Earl Cowper has most of the land to the east (up to and well beyond Roundhay Road). The nouveau-riche Mr Brown has most of the rest of the area we call Chapeltown, and much more besides (Ward 1960). This control of large swathes of land by only three people has had a major impact on the way that the territory was divided and sold into building plots in the latter half of the nineteenth century. The archives of Brown's and Cowper's papers contain documents which attest to their keen interest in obtaining the best possible price for the land and they insisted on selling large plots so that substantial, middle-class homes would be built. They achieved this aim in the 1870s, 80s and 90s despite Cowper and Mexborough both failing to find buyers when they put land on the market in 1845 (Treen 1982: 170). It seems likely that the transformation of this territory from farming to housing was stimulated by a different kind of material intervention in the landscape – the arrival of the horse-drawn tramway in Chapeltown in 1875. The road, now called Chapeltown Road, has its earliest traces on a map of *c.* 1580, and it was extensively rebuilt as the Leeds–Harrogate turnpike road in 1752 (ibid.: 162). The 1876 Street Directory shows that, in the south-east corner of Chapeltown, Spencer Place, Louis Street and Leopold Street have been developed, as has a small part of the centre of the territory (Newton Grove and part of Reginald Terrace). The Spencer Place residents' occupations show us a middle-class suburb-in-the-making: engineer, upholsterer, leather manufacturer, cigar merchant, corn-factor, draper, merchant, manager, solicitor, wine-merchant, reverend and the like. Over the next thirty years, almost all the land will be developed for middle-class housing (Holmes 1876).

In Chapeltown, the sometimes abrupt changes in housing style reflect both the pattern of the sixteenth-century field lay-outs (Ward 1962: 158) and the strictly commercial decisions of the late nineteenth-century estate agents and solicitors. Ford and Warren, estate agents, 'rather jumped' at the offer of one shilling a yard for a strip of land 'which would be very difficult to sell' (WYAS BEP 3 January 1896), no doubt because it was so close to a stream. The houses built there were some of the smallest terraces in Chapeltown. (When the Chapeltown Community Association campaigned for their demolition in the mid 1970s the stream was running up the walls of the houses closest to it.) Ford and Warren bemoan the failure to control every aspect of the building in the area. One decision, they complain, 'removes all line of demarcation between the better houses and the cheaper ones which is most necessary if we are to sell our land to best advantage' (3 January 1896). The landed gentry stamped their class upon this land with their original acquisitions, by fair means or foul. Now, when they come to realise their profit, consciousness of intra-class status demarcations prevalent in Victorian England is inscribed in the landscape of Chapeltown.

A novel published in 1929 provides an almost anthropological portrait of the formation of a middle class in this suburb between around 1880 and 1920 (Stowell 1929). This is a curiously coded work. The name of each street in today's Chapeltown can be 'read off' the street names used in the book if you have detailed knowledge of the history of the area. Only in the past five years has the historic (pre-suburbanisation) name for part of the area – Button Hill – found its way onto a street sign. The novel is called *The Story of Button Hill.* It has a tone of voice somewhere between ironic critique and reverence for the people and its territory. This is a locale which, until the 1914–18 war, is deeply at ease with itself, conscious of its mission to establish in 'Button Hill' all that is to be admired about the values and lifestyle of its class. Even the invasion of the working classes (living 'in the slum districts of Lambswell [Sheepscar] and Tannersdale [the leather tannery is still in operation], lying like dirty puddles at the bottom of the hill' (Stowell 1929: 12)), 'provoked' by a pro-Boer Button Hill resident, is easily repelled by the resounding voice of the area's MP and a 'Now, you bounders ... here's your first bath' counter-attack by hose-wielding local chaps (ibid.: 84–92).

We can, therefore, agree with Lefebvre that the processes by which this land has been transformed – particularly evident in the extensive production of bourgeois housing in the late nineteenth century – are intensely political, and reflect the various material and ideological aspirations of the landowners, the estate agents and the people who occupied these houses. The claim that this space 'is a product literally filled with ideologies' (Lefebvre 1976: 31) might be one way of expressing this point, but it seems to me to suffer from its somewhat abstract formulation. Worse, it might be read as implying that ideologies get cast in stone when they 'fill' space. As we shall see, the relationship between ideology and territory in this locale shifts with alarming rapidity.

By the end of Stowell's account of the neighbourhood – this concept now enters the discussion because, above all, Stowell has established the idea that Button Hill was an area in which 'neighbourly' social relationships were actively created – a discernible sense of decline has set in. There is a clear 'spatial' dimension to his description of this change. For Stowell, the rot has already set in by 1919 as 'industry' has 'stealthily, insidiously' crept up Chapeltown Road with the conversion of 'three of the larger detached houses' into 'makeshift premises for firms of ready-made clothing manufacturers, wooden sheds being erected indiscriminately over lawns and flower-beds'. In case we do not immediately spot this reference to the Jewish rag-traders moving north from their original area of settlement, we are informed that another house has become 'a Jewish maternity home'. Worse still, further to the south of the territory 'The proletariat, enjoying the first fruits of victory, have invaded [several streets] and are paying fantastic weekly rents' (Stowell 1929: 373–4).

Jewish settlements

Eastern European Jewish migrants originally settled (between 1870 and around 1900) in the Leylands (now the site of the West Yorkshire Playhouse in the city centre), then moved a mile or so out to the North Street area, and then, from the 1930s onwards another mile north into Chapeltown. Their entry brought with it considerable prosperity and social organisation. But its original physical location in the Leylands was one of appalling overcrowding and insanitation (Ravetz 1973) and the situation in North Street was not much better, as an interview with Mrs Hassell, a white, Christian woman who often passed through the area in her childhood reveals:

> Oh, the pong was terrible. It wasn't these people's fault. They had an up and a down, and a cold water tap, and you could have about ten people living in a house ... but it wasn't their fault, it was bad sanitation in the streets and that. There were no baths in the houses, they'd use the local baths.

(Farrar 1988: 36)

The move from these warrens of yards, back to backs, makeshift tenements, workshops, pubs and so on which are familiar to all students of nineteenth-century working-class housing, into the spacious middle-class houses, with their front and back gardens, their wide streets and two parks, marked a major change in the lifestyles of Jewish settlers in Leeds. By 1956 they had established, according to local journalist Ronald Stott, 'a Little Israel in full working order', with Kosher shops, representative organisations, clubs and 'at least six major synagogues' (Stott 1956). The Jewish presence is visibly established in its built environment. But if Stowell's is an ironic, sympathetic insider's account of this neighbourhood, Stott's is an outsider's account which, for all its respect for the Jews of Leeds, stamps them irredeemably as 'Other'. For Stott, the Jews are a 'transplanted civilisation'. Following the conventional picture of this migration as having been forced by Russian pogroms (a view somewhat undermined by Gartner's (1960) authoritative account), Stott tells us that:

> It was natural for them to keep together. For while the Jew moves in the normal life-stream of the place of his adoption, he must often in many things remain slightly apart. He must live as an integral part of his exiled minority whose saga of suffering has taught it that strength and defence can only be found in a close-knit communal life.
>
> (Stott 1956)

There is no hesitation here over the use of the words 'them' and 'the Jew'. This, however, is an extremely complex text which is open to several readings. Jewish 'difference' may be being explained (as a response to persecution), or it may be being signalled as highly problematic:

> Leeds Jewry, while often giving service to the city, remains an outpost of an ancient civilisation, loyal to the age-old doctrines, precepts, customs and beliefs of the race – its faith undimmed and undoubted by the passage of centuries by wanderings, by persecution.
>
> (ibid.:)

This may suggest that Jewish people 'often' give service to the city, but their prime loyalty is to their 'ancient civilisation'; they will never really serve the city, 'like we do' because they are primarily devoted to their 'race'. Bauman (1989: 38–9) has argued that Christianity endowed the Jews with a 'sinister fascination', lacking 'unconditional loyalty' and symolising 'anomaly and aberration'. These assumptions underly Stott's journalism. His biologically absurd notion that Jewish people constitute a 'race' reminds us of another part of the story of Leeds Jewry. Mrs Hassell chose to recall that 'people talk about racialism now, but they *want* to know what they [Jewish people] went through' (Farrar 1988: 36). Anti-semitism found its spatially defined targets: towards the end of the First World War gangs would roam the Leylands hurling stones through the windows of Jewish homes, recalled Louis Teeman (Naylor 1975). Even in 1940, the British Union of Fascists, with its vitriolic anti-Semitism, could command 722 votes at a parliamentary by-election in the Leeds North East constituency (of which Chapeltown is a part) (Benewick 1972: 292). In Stott's account, the persecution of Jewish people is a thing of the past, but the sub-text might be that Chapeltown is now the locale of an alien culture and, while it may contain admirable features ('if there is one feature more impressive than any other in the Jewish character it is this love of family life'), its presence, architecturally encoded in the territory called Chapeltown, is a cause for concern.

Both aspects of Shields' approach to 'spatialisation' are therefore relevant here. First, Chapeltown is described by both Stowell and Stott in terms which heavily rely on the readers' ability to imaginatively identify with, and abstract meaning from, the shape of its buildings and the uses to which they are put. Second, both accounts are predicated upon an 'us' and 'them' binary opposition – a 'self'–'other', 'inclusion'–exclusion' categorisation – which is presented in such 'taken-for-granted' terms that we are justified in assuming that this is a structuring category for the authors and, presumably, for the majority of their readers. With the advent of a novel and journalism about Chapeltown, we have texts which allow us to analyse the construction of representations of the residents and the territory, crucial moves in the social production of the area called Chapeltown. I am using the concept of 'representation' here as a reference to 'the process and the product of making signs stand for their meanings (O'Sullivan *et al.* 1994: 265). Lefebvre's reference to 'spaces of representation' as the conceptualisation of space more or less conforms to this definition of representation. Lefebvre, somewhat obscurely, uses the term 'representational space' to convey the idea of 'lived space' (Lefebvre 1991: 40). I shall confine 'representation' to the encoding of social meanings in discourse.

Black settlers

As Jewish people steadily migrated further north into Moortown, and as migrants from the Caribbean began to occupy these houses from the late 1950s onwards, representations of Chapeltown ceased to exhibit Stott's cautiously phrased concern about the 'otherness' of the residents of this territory. (Some of the following examples are analysed, along with other material, in Farrar (1996).) Two devices seem to be employed in the assertion that black residents are utterly different from whites. First, the locale is mediated as a 'mecca of vice' (Smith 1974) or a ' "red light" suburb' (Cooke and Blankley 1977). The association between black people, sex and vice had long been set in the popular imagination by the time it found its way into the government's thinking in the early 1950s. A Cabinet Working Party of 1953 highlighted one police report that there had been 'a marked number of convictions of coloured [sic] men for living on the immoral earnings of white women', and then claimed that 'this practice is far more widespread than the few prosecutions indicate' (Carter, Harris and Joshi 1987: 10–11). The 'red light', 'mecca of vice' characterisation of Chapeltown indicates the way in which white fantasies can locate themselves in a particular territory. The reports are intent on specifying quite precisely the streets in which fantasy – and, for those that actually stop their cars and make a contract, activity – can take place. Smith's (1974) front-page newspaper report in the Leeds' evening newspaper included, both in its headline and its opening sentence, the street called Hamilton Place, along with a photograph of this otherwise unremarkable stretch of tarmac, paving and buildings. But, despite the headline and photo, Smith's story placed prostitution more widely than in this one street. He interviewed residents of Cowper Street, Louis Street and Francis Street (all within half a mile of

Hamilton Place), all of whom confirm the view (originally stated by a Leeds magistrate) that these streets are teeming with prostitutes ('"Sometimes as many as 50 young lasses and they're always busy", said Mr Alphonse Klamec'). (Having walked and driven along these streets throughout the 1970s, to the present, I can pitch my impression against Mr Klamec's: I have never seen more than half a dozen 'working girls' at any one time.) Cooke and Blankley (1977), writing for a national paper, were less concerned with street names, but equally interested in representing Chapeltown in terms of its fantasy life and its built environment. Stating where one of the so-called Yorkshire Ripper's victims was found, they wrote: 'This street is in the area's rubble–strewn bedsitter land. Many of the converted Victorian houses are occupied by prostitutes.' The event, and the subsequent torrent of writing and film, which most effectively implanted the representation of Chapeltown as a site of dangerous sexuality was the succession of murders carried out by Peter Sutcliffe ('The Yorkshire Ripper'). Between 1975 and 1977, Sutcliffe killed six women in the Chapeltown area. Yallop's book about Sutcliffe's career uses the device of imagining Sutcliffe's internal monologue to establish a portrait of Chapeltown's streets, clubs and pubs as polluted and corrupted by women working in the sex industry (Yallop 1981). The power of the 'Ripper' saga in enforcing Chapeltown's reputation lies in the silence 'Ripper' narratives have about 'race'. The white public's association of prostitution with black men is never mentioned, so can never be publicly contested, but Chapeltown's blackness underlay its darkest hours.

The second device consists in the depiction of black settlers as a 'colony within'. During June 1973, a specially designed block featuring a black woman with a black child containing the heading 'THE COLONY WITHIN' introduced each of a series of articles in the *Yorkshire Evening Post*. The overt purpose of these articles appears to be to provide a forum in which (white) professionals can deploy their expert knowledge on the black citizens of Leeds, alerting (white) citizens to the existence of racial prejudice and the 'quiet unrest that could lead to black revolution' (Naylor 1973). Just as Stott's seemingly sympathetic portrait of Chapeltown's Jewish citizens in the mid-1950s encoded other attitudes, so these articles provide another message. The lead describes Chapeltown as the 'melting pot for immigrants from many lands for many years', reminding readers of the anomalous presence of the Jews in Leeds, and conjuring up a notion of difference 'melting away'. The most telling phrase, however, is the repeated 'colony within', reminding readers of the former status of black subjects within British colonies – and the bloody history of decolonisation. A 'colony within' suggests the loyalty test: instead of difference melting, perhaps white Leeds is experiencing a permanent alien wedge in its midst. The next day's article is headlined 'You can't legislate against the heart', providing a clear rebuttal to those who think that prejudice might be eradicated by laws or education.

Representations of Chapeltown seeking distance from the 'mecca of vice' trope are heavily reliant on reference to the bricks and mortar which constitute the place. Peter Lazenby's (1980) 'Chapeltown – a special enquiry' series in the Leeds' paper featured the plight of two families located in damp, dangerous and overcrowded council-owned accommodation. But such efforts are few and far between. Those obsessed with deviance repeatedly return to architectural descriptions of the territory. Franks' (1986) damning portrait for *The Times* includes the obligatory photograph of buildings with boarded up windows. Franks maps the places where the 'rapings, muggings and stabbings' take place, and where you can 'pick up just about any drug you want' with matter-of-fact precision. While the concern with prostitution and housing conditions seems to have slipped out of the media, contemporary moral panic about crime and drugs is given its territorial location in Chapeltown today. Vivek Chaudhary's work shows that even a newspaper which has resisted racist discourses will unquestioningly employ the standard narrative devices of journalism, and exhibit the preconceptions of those for whom the inner city is 'obviously' 'hell' (Chaudhary 1994). Again, Chaudhary spatialises his story extremely precisely around the Hayfield Hotel, a pub/club on Chapeltown Road ('The pub from hell'), and employs a metaphor as though it can be taken as literal. (For a more detailed critique of this article, see Farrar (1995).)

Territorial control

If all this can be taken as confirmation of Shields' approach to 'spatialisation' as 'the recodings of geographic spaces [in which] sites become associated with particular values, historical events and feelings' (Shields 1991: 30), it also has consequences of the kind which Sack summarises as 'territoriality' (Sack 1986: 19). Not only is police activity in Chapeltown – perhaps the most overt strategy for controlling residents of the territory – determined at least partly by the 'red-light' metaphor, a more subtle form of control, this time over material resources, has been exerted by building societies in their lending policies for people wishing to purchase property in the area. A research project in the late 1970s found 'significant differences' in lending policies for predominantly white inner city areas compared with those with 'ethnically mixed' populations, with the mixed areas getting less favourable treatment. The effect of the negative representations that we have just examined is made clear by the researchers:

> The discriminatory effects of loan decisions do not seem to arise as the result of clear-cut and consistent building society policies.... [Rather] they seem to be the end product of subjective attitudes held by housing exchange professionals that 'black areas' are a 'bad risk', and should be avoided, or the 'risks' minimised by offering less favourable terms.
>
> (Stevens *et al.* 1981: 1–2)

But, if state agencies and public bodies exert their power over this locale, it is important to stress the countervailing influence of Chapeltown's political and social organisations. I have attempted elsewhere (Farrar 1981, 1986, 1992) to demonstrate the effectiveness of a myriad of protest groups over the past twenty-five years in their demands for social justice and material resources. The transformation of the physical landscape (in the form of new housing, renovated old houses, community and religious centres, traffic-calming measures, constructed play-space, new schools and a health centre) is testimony to the ability of these organisations to get some of their views heard by those who control resources. Their tactics have in some cases been spatial in the most dramatic sense – such as violent street-based confrontations with the police in 1975 and the burning down of several buildings on Chapeltown Road in 1981 (Farrar 1981). In many others, the drama has been less intense, but the organisations have been equally focused on marking out their power in spatial terms by invading the Education Committee's meeting in the Civic Hall (Root Out Racism in Education, 1987–8) and by successive demonstrations along Chapeltown's streets (which I first witnessed in 1971). More recently, the organisers' increased political confidence has been evidenced by decisions to march out of Chapeltown and into the city centre to make a physical presence known to the legal establishment by taking up space outside the main police headquarters, the police station in the Bridewell (part of the Town Hall), the Magistrates' Courts and the Civic Hall (both in protest against police activity: 'Black Direct Action for Equal Rights and Justice', December 1994 and 'Chapeltown Defence Campaign', December 1990).

Territorial control takes another form, which has a fundamental effect on the patterns of sociability within Chapeltown. The media's moral panic about Chapeltown, spatialised, metaphorical and imbued with fantasy as it is, contains a mystified notion of anti-social, pathological actors. While this representation must be deconstructed and resisted, there are groups of young men who use Chapeltown as their territory for activities which contradict the law and break the moral values which underlie neighbourly social relations. While they form a tiny proportion of the total crime in the area, the most socially significant of these activities – because they are experienced bodily – is personal assault with robbery (carried out, according to the media by 'muggers', which, with its unconscious significa-tion of 'niggers', might be read as a code for 'violent black youth'). The location for this activity has been carefully specified by the police. In 1993, there was an average of fourteen robberies of this type per week in the square mile around the lower end of Chapeltown Road – 22 per cent of all the robberies in the whole of West Yorkshire (Hellawell 1994). While the teenagers responsible for most of these assaults were less than twenty in number, their effect on the ability of Chapeltown's residents to utilise the physical space of the area is immense. Since the jailing of one of their leaders, the number of robberies in the division has dropped – but only by 19 per cent (and the precise area concerned is larger than the 'square mile') (Coward 1995). The 'square mile' referred to may seem small, but it covers a large number of houses, and the mobile presence of robbers in this area inhibits the movement of all people. The occupation of the territory at the top of Chapeltown Road, around the Hayfield Hotel, by an older, small group of men specialising in street sales of drugs similarly marks out a territory in which movement by people who neither want to trade with nor associate with this group is heavily restricted. An urban myth is perpetrated by taxi drivers, who repeatedly tell their customers that they are regularly attacked on Chapeltown Road. The fact that there were only ten such attacks in 1993–4 and twenty-three in 1994–5 (Heptinstall 1995) does nothing to allay the fear felt by the drivers, which is transmitted widely and taken at face-value in Chapeltown and throughout Leeds. The constituents of this locale name themselves 'Front-Liners', indicating the way that actors employ spatial metaphors in their self-characterisation. Placing themselves in a line, they heighten and mask their visibility (in the front of public gaze, in the face of police telephoto lenses placed at nearby surveillance points) with their particular uniform of hoods and hats. Both the Goffmanesque (Goffman 1971: 114) and the structuralist senses of 'front' and 'back' are relevant here. In occupying 'their' space and engaging in their trade so prominently, the Front-Liners disrupt pedestrian traffic in the region of the Hayfield Hotel; while the activities of the street robbers were at their highest point (during 1993–4) many residents were reluctant to walk anywhere at any time. In an area where only 41 per cent of households have a car (OPCS 1991) and where much social intercourse takes place in public spaces, the fear engendered by these activities has enormous consequences for social relationships.

Globalisation: space

This activity, which deforms the relationships of community in the area, should be understood in the context of global economic restructuring. Unlike their predecessors, these men do not even have the choice of waged, legitimated work. Given decisions they made at an earlier stage – in the classroom, faced, no doubt, with teachers who lacked the material and personal resources to deal positively with them – many of them have excluded themselves from the educational and training centres that exist in Leeds. Global economics are not abstract for them. Contrary to Murray (1990, 1994) and Dennis and Erdos (1992), then, I am stressing the effects of the removal of waged work in a context of economically and racially-structured institutions, rather than of the collapse of the nuclear family, on the young black men of the inner city. But, echoing some of the views of Campbell (1993), I would draw attention to the difficulties these men have in constructing their masculinity (Farrar 1994b, 1994c). It should also be stressed that, just as the media infuse their interpretations of the inner city with myth, sociologically informed, close participant observers such as myself find it extremely hard to claim a firm grasp on the 'real' (Farrar 1994a).

While global economic forces have contributed to the creation of a small class of criminals in Chapeltown, they have also affected patterns of sociability in the area in more subtle ways. There is evidence that Leeds, having de-industrialised in the 1960s and early 1970s, has suffered less, and re-orientated its economy towards services more successfully, than other cities in Britain (Fazey 1993; Haughton and Whitney 1994). Lash and Urry claim that Leeds, along with Düsseldorf and New York, is a global city which has 'effected a successful transition to a post-industrial economy' (Lash and Urry 1994: 152). But, even in a successful city, there are significant areas where there is little or no potential for free-market capitalist enterprise. Lash and Urry (ibid.: 19) argue that: 'Goods, labour, money and information will not flow to where there are no markets ... [thus] there has been an emptying out of economic space of many institutions'. Since these institutions provide 'spatial, social and cultural governance ... there is a deficit of institutional regulation and it is followed by an outflow of subjects'. This analysis is not exactly borne out in Chapeltown. Economic activity within the area *has* been significantly reorganised, and the number of small shops, particularly on Roundhay Road, has been drastically reduced. Since shopping, like walking and encountering friends in public places, is a primary mode of sociability, with implications for the normative regulation of everyday life, this depletion of opportunities for social interaction is important. What has happened, however, is that internal norm-setting has been replaced by externally imposed norms of quite a different type. Where ordinary people once regulated each others' lives by their value-laden conversations, they now find themselves regulated by contracts. In the place of the small shops we now find offices for building societies, housing associations, solicitors, and extended premises for the banks. Quite literally, these institutions, by their manipulation of the supply of money or tenancies, hold the power to control their everyday lives to an unprecedented degree. Far from 'emptying out', it is arguable that the global restructuring of the economy of Chapeltown is engendering a process in which the people are 'filled out' with the rules of new commercial and voluntary institutions. Earlier forms of association – casual interactions while shopping – still take place in the corner shops and the main road grocers' shops (mainly run by local Asian traders). But the other growth area in the local economy, the large number of Asian restaurants, seem to provide conviviality mainly for white people who drive into the area (often for a take-away only).

Globalisation: time

The relationships that are established between inner city residents and the new kinds of institutions (such as banks and rent offices) are based on money and information. Both of these are manipulated in time. Black residents of Chapeltown are compelled to operate in a complex time-frame which bears the mark of their (or their parents') former lives in the Caribbean, Asia or Africa. Their transition from migrant to settler is not as simple as that formula makes it sound. A client's relationship with a bank, building societies, landlord or betting shop is constituted by the agreement to spread financial transactions over long or short periods of time. In agreeing to pay money to a building society in the long-term expectation of receiving the deeds to the property at the end of the mortgage period, the client accepts the society's power to remove his or her family from the property if the contractual agreement is broken. The experience of anxiety, spread out in time, sometimes, apparently, interminably, that goes with this should not be underestimated in a situation in which employment arrangements are subject to the vagaries of a post-industrial economy. In contrast, the immediacy of the potential reward at the betting shop must be an attractive option – a response to, and a provocation of, financial anxiety – and it is striking now to see young women using the bookies on Chapeltown Road. All these transactions are dependent on the rapid and accurate transmission of information inside the institutions and between the institutions and the client. It has been frequently observed that the super-fast transfer of information in digital form along fibre-optic cables has in recent years transformed our experience of space and time.

Not only has the legitimate world of banking, betting and renting been radically changed. Digital information in the cell-net telephone system has transformed another part of the local economy. No longer does the customer for drugs have to search out his or her supplier by knocking on the door of several possible houses, or risk police surveillance or worse by approaching a Front-Liner. He or she simply phones a number and make the connection. The entrepreneur's ability to conquer both space (he or she can remain mobile without limiting his or her trade) and time (he or she can work day and night, and can abolish the distinction between work-time and leisure-time) is enormously enhanced by the simple acquisition of a cell-net phone. Trade can expand dramatically and risks can be cut proportionately. The purchaser conquers the dead time of searching for and waiting for his or her supplier.

This implies an easy transition to postmodern economics by the inner city residents, but the situation is much more variegated and complex. If the 'muggers' are seen as postmodern vagabonds (Farrar 1994c) and the drug-dealers as postmodern deviant entrepreneurs, those who use the modern financial services, the multi-media bookies and the computerised housing associations similarly exhibit characteristics of the old and the new. As migrants, and the children of migrants, they operate with equal facility in multiple time-worlds. When Clinton Cameron, recently arrived from Jamaica, looked out the window of a tailoring factory in the early 1960s and decided to get a job on the buses so that he could see the world (of Leeds), he spatialised his experience, but he, like his compatriots who shifted jobs (changed places) whenever anyone treated them badly (Farrar 1986), also operated in a time frame which was different from the one they had utilised in their countries of origin. This should not be assumed to be a simple 'traditional/rural'–'industrial' contrast of time-orientations. Most Jamaican migrants had industrial or workshop experience in their countries of origin and even those from the small island of St Kitts-Nevis (the majority community in Leeds) had experienced the time-frame imposed by sugar-plantations run as a farming industry (and resisted with all the disciplined organisation of the unionised labour movement) (Richards 1989). (Paul Gilroy (1993) establishes the emphatically modern consciousness of dia-sporic, post-slavery Africans with his concept of 'the black Atlantic'.)

For some South Asian migrants to Chapeltown, it might be the case that the time-frame of traditional society was carried to Britain. The majority of Indians and Pakistanis now resident in the area originated in the Punjab or

Mirpur where they worked as small-scale farmers or artisans, and the majority of Bangladeshis had similar occupations in Sylhet. For farmers, time is regulated more by the rise and fall of the sun and the long passage of seasons than by a clock. But there are no reports of a difficult transition to the clocking-on and clocking-off required by the industrial occupations which they originally filled in Leeds (manufacturing garments or metal goods), nor do today's service sector occupations seem to have any greater time problems for South Asian workers than their white counterparts. It might be the case, however, that time is stretched within the religious practices of Islam and Sikhism (the two main South Asian religions in Chapeltown) in a way that differs from Christianity. Many ritual practices will take place over what seems to a Christian to be a long period of time. If they are not stretched (in the way that weekly acts of worship, and the annual experience of Ramadan are), they may be repeated (as in the five times a day prayer of an orthodox Muslim) in a way which is unfamiliar to all Christians outside the monasteries. While this utilisation of time has limited implications for economic activity (it might make the worker less flexible about how he or she will spend her weekends and Friday mornings) it is likely to have profound effects on the social organisation of the inner city. The long-term and regular occupation of a place specifically devoted to the belief systems of your own ethnic group, the persistent reinforcing of its structures of religious meaning, and, no doubt equally important, the routinised socialising with fellow members before and after the ritual, will inevitably bind most members more closely with their group. Although there is some evidence that attendance at mosque or temple is not as 'taken-for-granted' among young South Asians as it once was, the consensual nature of the activity, with its focus on other-worldly, rather than this-worldly concerns, over considerable periods of time, is a fundamental feature of most people's life in the South Asian communities.

But even if time passes in a different way, and with a different meaning, in the place of worship, the transition to other ways of using time seems to be effortless. South Asian businessmen and women are as digital as anyone, European, Caribbean – whoever has an interest in conforming to the conventions of modernity and postmodernity seems to adopt Greenwich Mean Time with ease. Lash and Urry point out that, nowadays, people are increasingly 'reflexive' in their relationship to time – they are well able to appreciate the rhythms (what I am referring to as the 'time-orientations') of other cultures and other periods of history (Lash and Urry 1994: 227). In agreeing with this, I would merely point out that, in the inner city, many people do not need to travel, or study history, to gain that understanding: they contain that knowledge within their own conscious and bodily experience, and they act as time-travellers and cultural voyagers in the durée of their day.

While Caribbeans came to England well-experienced in modern time, it is undeniable that the 'pace of life' was (and is) faster in Britain than it was (and is today) in the small islands of the Caribbean. This is evidenced today in the conversation of any black person from Leeds who has 'gone home' to St Kitts-Nevis for a holiday. Without exception, they are picked out as

'English' by the high speed at which they walk. Further evidence of shifts in time-orientation lies in the expression 'Black People's Time' (BPT). (A parallel phenomenon in the USA is CPT or 'Coloured People's Time'.) The adoption of the imposed time-frame of modernity – the consensually agreed starting and ending time for any activity, regulated by a watch or clock that has a predictable relationship to Greenwich Mean Time (GMT) – is never a straightforward matter in the black inner city. It would be wrong to assume that this is a hangover from a 'less-developed' society in the Caribbean, where watches were less available. For a start, the ubiquity of watches in Britain is a relatively recent phenomenon; Caribbean towns and villages have as many public clocks per person as Britain, and the time-discipline of work and school is as long established there as it is in Britain. The use of BPT is better understood as a deliberate act of assertion and recalling of cultural difference. Within the inner city it only poses a problem if some black people have decided to adopt GMT while others are using BPT; this is most likely to occur when an event is taking place which is within the conceptual boundaries of modern, bureaucratic-rational action – such as a management committee meeting – when all members are expected to follow the time-rules explicit in that type of action. Members who adopt BPT in those circumstances are condemned for their inability to properly operate within two time-frames. In events within liminal zones (Shields 1991: 84), or when people are simply 'limeing' (playing), BPT will operate consensually, with everyone knowing at what time activity will *really* get going, and operating an individual decision about what time he or she will start and stop. Even this experience finds itself under pressure from the rational-legal regulation of time, since many such events take place in licensed premises and even if held in the open air, such as the carnival procession or the operation of Sound Systems in the park, the implementation of whatever arrangements have been made with the magistrates will be enforced. Until recent police activity, Chapeltown had a series of venues in which time stood still. From about 2am till 7am, at a Blues, people could stand in a dark place in which the absence of any time-based obligations allowed for an almost complete rejection of the outside world.

It is tempting to interpret BPT as a form of resistance to GMT – another way in which diasporan black people conflict with white European modes of being. But BPT is a more complex phenomenon than this. While there are many occasions when a black person will arrive late for a GMT event in order to express his or her resistance to what he or she expects to be going on at that event, and this may happen more often when the black person is attending a predominantly white event than when the event is organised (in GMT) by other black people, there will also be occasions when black people will express their disengagement with the organisers of black events by implementing BPT, just as white people turn up late for white events in order to publicly signal their disaffiliation. The problem in this scenario is the way that white people often mis-read the black person's time-orientation – either assuming that BPT is being used as an act of hostility, when, just as for white people, the black person may be late for contingent, non 'political' reasons. Alternatively, some whites will assume that the black person is (because of a disability inherent his or her 'blackness') incapable of operating accurately in GMT. My point is that the issue is not simply one of dominance by, or resistance to, GMT; frequently, complex choices are being made about which is the appropriate time-orientation to adopt in a particular situation. When Malcolm X said he never trusted anyone who didn't wear a watch (Blackside, Inc. 1994), he made very clear his allegiance to GMT, and his constant berating of people in the movement who arrived late shows that he expected his supporters to accept the predominance of GMT. This commitment to clock-time, and his 'fanaticism about learning' (Karim 1995: 228), indicates Malcolm's seriousness about modernity, his intention to use the knowledge provided by science, and the time-orientation which accompanies this knowledge, in support of black struggle. While many in Chapeltown would express the same kind of moral and intellectual commitment, their unwillingness always to put it into practice could be taken as an indication of a less intense commitment to 'scientific black struggle', than, say, Malcolm's, but not as a disengagement from modern, European, GMT.

CONCLUSION

By way of a conclusion I want to make explicit the implications of this analysis for the understanding of the social relations of this part of the inner city of Leeds. Chapeltown has here been conceptualised as a territory in which there is enormous diversity of spatially influenced practices and time-orientations. This diversity has been related, in part, to the long history of the territory and the political practices by which the locale has been formed; more particularly it has been related to the nature of post-war settlement of the area by migrants from the Caribbean and South Asia, and its representation in the white media. While this area has been heavily 'spatialised' by the mass media – in the sense that it has been represented in narratives which are pregnant with their authors' fantasies and fears – a closer observation reveals the complex effects of global forces on social practices in this territory. Spatially and temporally, these practices have been both 'emptied out' and 'filled out'. Economically, the emptying out of legitimate waged work for men, both within the area and (more impor-tantly) within the city of Leeds, has lead to a much greater occupation of certain streets by young men who gain income by force and by illegal sales. The restructuring of economic space – the replacement of shops by finance-based services – has changed the type of social regulation in these institutions, exercising greater external, bureaucratic-legal control over people than hitherto. But a long process of political struggle by black people has also resulted in the provision of numerous spaces in which some autonomy is claimed and preserved, filling out meanings used to sustain the cultural life of those who refuse to succumb to the homogenising, and often impoverishing, forces of global culture. There has been, in this chapter, an attempt to undermine the politically conservative representa-tion of the inner city in terms of a disorganised and disorganising underclass, without minimising the deleterious consequences of the emergence of a small group who do conform to some aspects of the conservatives' description. That description should be further modified after a consideration of the complex ways in which time is lived in this locale.

People of African descent are characterised as carefully manipulating a twin-time orientation, while the peoples from South Asia have been analysed in terms of movement between a religious time-frame and a modern time-frame. It should be stressed that, for both communities, there is no suggestion of a traditional time-orientation (even if it is guessed that those from a South Asian farming background might have arrived here with such an orientation). The clock-time of modernity (GMT) is the dominant feature in everyone's lives, for most of the time. But the ability to seamlessly shift into the time-frame appropriate to cultural practices which are outside those of the dominant European culture is seen as a source of social solidarity, and an antidote to some of the debilitating effects of economic restructuring.

Part III

NOSTALGIA/MEMORY

7

LOOKING BACKWARD

Nostalgia and the city

Elizabeth Wilson

For in the very temple of delight, veiled melancholy hath his sovran shrine.

> (John Keats, 'Ode to Melancholy')

Although the practice of academic research is meant to be an objective activity, one part of the 'postmodernisation' of such work has been a greater recognition of our subjective investment in it. The anthropologist and psychoanalyst, George Devereux, once wrote that all research is autobiographical, and this seems particularly clear in recent writings about urban space and cities. *City of Quartz*, by Mike Davis (Davis 1990) is a passionate, sorrowful love letter to 'his' city. Richard Sennett's walk up Manhattan to Fourteenth Street in *The Conscience of the Eye* (Sennett 1990) is autobiographical as well as analytical. François Maspero's *Roissy Express* (Maspero 1993) is even more explicitly personal – an exploration of the Paris *banlieues* by a dedicated Parisian. I, therefore, shall not apologise for beginning on an autobiographical note, and although I shall not explore the reasons why this subjective vein is so especially strong in urban writing, it must have something to do with the importance of place in any individual's sense of identity. It seems also to build on the feminist recognition of the importance of subjective experience and the insistence by feminists on the validity of the personal.

In the mid-1960s I lived in Leicester, and to return to this city – which I have barely visited for the past thirty years – naturally evokes a sense of the past and of change. I wasn't a sociologist when I lived in Leicester (and I'm not sure that I am now); I was just living with someone in the Leicester University Sociology Department. I was a social worker, and at that time sociologists were anxious to distance themselves and their profession from social work – a hangover from the historical perception of sociology as a discipline which, in this country, had initially developed to a large extent as a subject studied by social work students in order to help them understand the social context in which they were working. But the fear of Leicester sociologists in the 1960s that they might be contaminated by social work seemed utterly unnecessary since it was clear, even at the time, that this was a golden era for the Leicester University Sociology

Department. With Professor Ilya Neustadt at its head, it also had Norbert Elias – although his importance was not fully recognised then – and a whole number of students and young lecturers, many of whom are now extremely well-known and distinguished.

Since that period there has been a lot of stormy weather in academia, and in the 1970s and early 1980s sociology in particular came under attack, but in recalling the optimism of the 1960s I am not intending a nostalgic regret. Now, in the 1990s, although conditions of work within academia are, to varying degrees, difficult and perhaps are even further deteriorating, and although it has been argued that sociology has been marginalised by comparison with its intellectual dominance in the 1960s, I believe there can be more optimism about its future. The loosening up of discipline boundaries may have led to raids on the traditional concerns of sociology; there may have been gerrymandering here and there by geography, cultural studies and so on (and raids in the opposite direction, of course), but the spirit of enquiry persists, and the widening of parameters to include issues of varying forms of oppression and the investigation of activities outside the range of production, class and the family (not that it was ever quite so narrow as that) must surely be welcomed. To the extent to which issues of pleasure, leisure and consumption are to the forefront of sociological concerns today, perhaps we do all owe more of a debt even than we realise to Norbert Elias.

To return to a city in which you used to live is – especially if the gap is a long one – to be made sharply aware of the passage of time, and the changing fabric of cities congeals that process of the passage of time in a way that is both concrete and somehow eerie or ghostly. It reminds you that a city is neither of those two favourite figures of speech: a work of art or a diseased organism. It is a process, an unique, ongoing time/space event.

At the beginning of the twentieth century, Walter Benjamin and Siegfried Kracauer, writers who have become extremely important to us in the 1980s and 1990s, seemed to be especially aware of this, perhaps partly because Berlin, 'their' city, was then changing so rapidly. In an article entitled 'Streets without memory' Kracauer wrote of how the frenzied newness of this 'gold rush town', as he termed it, caused by the headlong march of capitalism, was wiping out all traces of the past. A building that has been torn down, he wrote:

> is not merely superseded but so completely displaced as if it never even existed at all . . . on the Kurfürstendamm it makes its exit without leaving behind any traces. . . . The new enterprises are always abso-lutely new and those that have been displaced by them are totally extinguished. . . . Many buildings have been shorn of the ornaments which formed a kind of bridge to yesterday. Now the plundered façades stand uninterrupted in time and are the symbol of the unhistorical change that takes place behind them. Only the marble staircases that glimmer through the doorway preserve memories: those of the pre-war world first class.
>
> (quoted in Frisby 1985: 140)

I would modify this view in the sense that the fabric of a city is not only always in process of changing, and not only is this change normally visible, but even when it is not, it becomes part of collective memory both informally and in the written and rewritten official and unofficial histories of cities. In cities change is continual, and the city changing through time has been likened to a palimpsest, that is to say, a writing block on which words are written, erased or partly erased and written over, time and again (Sizemore 1984: 176). Kracauer seems to be saying that the pace of change, its context, its dynamic, constitutes a denial of the passing of time, but I doubt if the denial has the effectivity he attributes to it: the pace of change, rather than effacing the past, may even intensify our memory of what is no longer there.

The notion of change is central to the experience of modern and contemporary urban life. In Leicester, in the 1960s, we were always being told that it was the wealthiest city in Europe. The way in which it was wealthy was interesting in that it had one of the highest rates of female employment, certainly in Britain and probably in Europe as well, in the knitting, textile and other factories; in other words this was working-class 'wealth' or rather the then much discussed working-class affluence.

Even then, despite its wealth, Leicester had what were termed 'pockets of poverty', and as a social worker I sometimes visited the most notorious, the Braunstone Estate. This was a lamentable example of the 1920s municipal fashion for council estates built on garden suburb lines, and by the 1960s it had degenerated into a place where there were weeds and couch grass growing on the lawns, old fashioned prams abandoned all bent and screwed up like enormous dead spiders, and where mothers used to talk about 'the cruelty' (the NSPCC inspector) coming to see them. In the popular sociological term of the period, Braunstone was a subculture, but, at least in retrospect, seems an extraordinarily benign and unthreatening place, bearing little resemblence to today's 'sink estates'. These are peopled, at least in popular stereotype, with the so-called 'underclass': hopelessly unemployed young men, single teenage mothers, and crack dealers – all seemingly supporting themselves by the resale of stolen 'white goods'. While I am sure there was poverty – and no doubt 'cruelty' and petty crime – among those Braunstone families, and although by 1964 there were, and had been, all sorts of moral panics about juvenile delinquents and rising crime rates throughout the land, by comparison with today there was amazing tranquillity and absence of perceived threat.

This was the mid-1960s – on the cusp between two myths: John Major's myth of the safe, secure 1950s, the nation at ease with itself, and the myth we now term 'the Sixties'. Without perhaps knowing it, or knowing just how, Leicester was changing.

J. B. Priestley had visited Leicester in 1934, when researching his book *English Journey*, and he had commented then on the city's blandness. He wrote:

> The citizens, who are proud of the place, boast that it is one of the cleanest manufacturing towns in this country, and they are quite right:

it is. They also boast that it has a very enterprising town council, and I have no doubt it has.... It is comparatively prosperous. You feel almost at once that it is a very worthy borough that is deservedly getting on in the world. But it is hard to believe that anything much has ever happened there. Actually it is very old and offers you a very rum mixed list of historical associations: for example, King Lear and his daughters lived here, if they ever lived anywhere; it is Simon de Montfort's town; the broken Cardinal Wolsey came here to die, and has now acquired a new immortality by having his name stamped on thousands of bales of stockings and underclothes; John Bunyan saw the siege here during the Civil War; and among its nineteenth century citizens was the original Thomas Cook, who ran his first little excursion out of Leicester station. But somehow you do not believe in all these goings on. The town seems to have no atmosphere of its own. I felt I was quite ready to praise it, but was glad I did not live in it. There are many worse places I would rather live in. It seemed to me to lack character, to be busy and cheerful and industrial and built of red brick, and to be nothing else.

(Priestley 1977 [1984]: 115)

It still seemed like that to me in the mid-1960s, and although by then there was a large Asian community in Leicester, that hardly affected the perceived sense of homogeneity.

These observations, whether justified or not, suggest that while the rapid pace of change in 1920s Berlin felt like a problem to Kracauer, it is also a problem if a place *doesn't* change, since then it appears somehow stagnant, and it is a further problem if a city is too homogeneous. Priestley clearly felt, and I felt, thirty years later, that Leicester was too homogeneous. The Asian community, if anything, reinforced the homogeneity of the rest.

Yet in spite of its blandness, or perhaps because of it, Leicester had inspired at least two British campus novels in the 1950s, *Eating People is Wrong,* by Malcolm Bradbury (1959) and Kingsley Amis's *Lucky Jim* (1954), as well as William Cooper's *Scenes From Provincial Life* (1950), which Philip Larkin described as the 'great Leicester novel' (Motion 1993: 238). Re-reading these in 1995 I have realised that it was not just Leicester that was boring in the early 1960s: life itself was astonishingly monotone in affluent society Britain. These novels reveal a world of bleakness and aesthetic poverty, erotic starvation and mental desperation, only partly alleviated by a feeling that the protagonists are engaged in a serious existential search for the moral meaning of life (and not even that in the case of *Lucky Jim,* a veritable compendium of anti-intellectual, anti-artistic and misogynist attitudes). It was not only the Leicester described by Bradbury and Amis that lacked the restaurants, clubs, music venues and other public entertainment spaces taken for granted by even the most impoverished student in the 1990s (there were only pubs, although the hero of Bradbury's novel does make one exciting excursion to the only coffee bar in town); this was just how things *were* when Harold Macmillan was telling us we'd never had it so good: a philistine intelligentsia groping fitfully towards hedonism through the gloomy penumbra of a decaying puritanism.

Bradbury at first seems to dismiss Leicester: 'There were, indeed, parts of the town in which one felt a real sense of place; but most of the time one felt a sense of anywhere' (Bradbury 1959: 19). But he then acknowledges its confident, civic Victorian splendour, created in 'a riot of Victorian self help':

> It was sheer Tawney: religion, and the rise of capitalism. . . . As business and non-conformity boomed, the former market town had erected Victorian Gothic churches, a Victorian Gothic town hall ... a temperance union hall, a mechanics institute, a prison, and a well appointed lunatic asylum [which later housed the university].
>
> (Bradbury 1959: 20)

Bradbury's London hero equated puritanism and provincialism, and in the late 1950s and early 1960s Leicester seemed caught in an indeterminate moment. What John Major misremembers as a world of moral certainty and quiet contentment was in fact a hesitance, or even a kind of blind, unknowing movement, a final abandonment of those provincial, puritan values as Britain moved, with something between a sidle and a lurch, towards the frivolity of the fully consumerised society.

Today, revisiting Leciester, I am more aware of the charm and gracious-ness of the redbrick Victoriana and of the Edwardian suburbs with their leafy gardens, their memories of moral solidity and civic responsibility and paternalism. They still speak of that lost 'provincial life', when the resonance of the word 'provincial' has almost disappeared. That sense of the contrast between provincial and metropolitan, the mainspring of the archetypal modernist hero's trajectory, has ceased to be. Who is not clothed today in the 'blasé attitude' which, for Georg Simmel, characterised only the urban person (Simmel 1950)? Balzac's Lucien de Rubempré felt like 'a frog at the bottom of a well' in Angoulême (Balzac 1979: 148), but today our sense of space and distance has destroyed this particular antinomy. Recently viewing on television the film of another provincial novel of the late 1950s, *Room at the Top* (Braine 1957), I was struck by how this sense of a whole discrete provincial world, a world vividly present in the film, the world of the proud, resolutely *local* Midlands or Northern English industrial city, has indeed disappeared.

My return visit to Leicester naturally set me thinking about the past and about nostalgia. To return, especially in circumstances I should have found astonishing in 1966, is not only a trip to a no-longer-existing past, but also involves an encounter with a no-longer-existing self. In retrospect it seems clear that I then projected onto the city of Leicester my own self-dissatisfaction and frustration. To live there, the heartland of 'provincial life', was to long to escape, and the raids I made with my partner to the mecca of the Biba fashion store in Kensington or boutiques in the King's Road – rushing up and down the then still new M1 in a bright turquoise blue minicar – were as much attempts to lose myself as to get shot of Leicester.

By a coincidence, my only previous return visit to Leicester was to see the Biba exhibition in 1993, and this exhibition was itself an exercise in collective nostalgia. Not only was I in a crowded room of middle-aged women, many of whom were walking round with their friends and exchanging memories: 'Oh – I had one of those', 'Don't you remember that?' – but the visitors' book was crammed with long autobiographical extracts, most of which played on the theme of the 'golden Sixties'. Everyone seemed to be 'wallowing' in nostalgia, as the cliché disapprovingly has it.

But I began to wonder then what nostalgia really is. Is it just a 'wallow'? Is it as sentimental and self-indulgent as that word suggests? Is it a simple longing for the past, a refusal to accept change?

Both change and nostalgia seem to be bound up with the contemporary debates about urban life and city space. On the one hand there are many laments at the pace of change (and as the quotation from Kracauer, above, shows the lament is not new). And change *can* easily seem too rapid, or too destructive. On the other hand Priestley's Leicester, and the Leicester of Bradbury and Amis, seemed stagnant and dull, and provincial life was always criticised because it never changed.

Perhaps this dissatisfaction is part of an apparent inability – at least in writings about cities – to put up with imperfection. Contemporary urban debates betray a very low tolerance for any sense of discomfort, so that there is a fine line between cities – or urban regions – being perceived as hideously dangerous and polluted, unplanned and chaotic, and being experienced as too gentrified, too prettified and transformed into museums and theme parks – a past congealed that will never change again. This hankering for *perfection* may have something to do with the long utopian tradition, the utopian literature on cities which, as Françoise Choay (1980) has demonstrated, bears such a close resemblance to the writings of architects. This must have influenced our perception of how cities ought to be, or what we have a right to expect. It is as if we have internalised a collective perception of the perfect city, and deviations from it become extremely threatening. Perfection, moreover, seems to be located either in the past or in the future. We rarely if ever accept, let alone embrace the present.

The search for perfect cities can lead, paradoxically, to a radical anti-urbanism. When in the mid-1980s I first had the idea of writing a book about the city, there were two themes that interested me: the issue of women in urban space, on the one hand neglected and invisible, on the other hand invoked as sinister embodiments of evil and disorder; and my perception – an oversimplified one as I later discovered – that the discourse on cities was indeed predominantly anti-urban. The two issues seemed to act together, both women's invisibility and the misogyny of the way they were written about when they did make an appearance seeming to legitimate a kind of 'progressive' anti-urbanism.

In seeking to create a different picture, using images and arguments circulating then and since in the literature on urban regeneration, I was, without realising it, part of trend in which urbanists of various kinds drew on concepts of the good city. In part this invoked a nineteenth-century metropolis such as had been described and explored by Baudelaire and Benjamin (and which was very unlike Victorian industrial cities such as Leicester, which embodied a rather different vision of the good city). From a more conservative perspective, Leon Krier and Prince Charles, from a more left position, Richard Sennett, Ken Worpole and others wrote lovingly of the *flâneur*, the pedestrian city, the city of many villages, the city of spectacle, setting against the nightmare city of crime, anomie and danger a vision of cities of pleasure and civility – itself perhaps easy to dismiss as a 'nostalgic' concept.

Nostalgia is a very different mood from the anger and determination to escape class society that was expressed, in however flawed a fashion, in Braine's *Room at the Top*. Then, upward mobility at the personal level was reflected at the level of city space by a thirst for the modern; urban planners believed that their large-scale plans would create wonderful new environments. These would solve social problems, ushering in a new era of leisure and consumerism.

The post-war rebuilding of the Birmingham Bull Ring, for example, was preceived as a miracle of the modern age. When it was opened, glossy leaflets were distributed which spoke of 'stiletto-proof' flooring and the revolutionary benefits of air conditioning, which would allow visitors to leave their 'top coats' at the door. In the promotional leaflets, the merits of 'continental' restaurants are detailed, along with the fatigue-breaking ease of travel by escalator and the introduction of Muzak – said to be 'the end product of 25 years research experience' – piped through the halls to create a 'warm, gay, [sic] and welcoming atmosphere' (Adams 1995). Tim Adams recalls that there was even a Cliff Richard film about the rebuilding of the Bull Ring. Sir Cliff played the part of a property developer and sang a song which went: 'Now I believe that you're a tough town and that's the way I like 'em/Concrete City I'm not that easily thrown'. But that was in the 1970s, after disillusionment had set in, when everyone knew about the Poulson and T. Dan Smith corruption scandal in Newcastle, when empty office blocks had become an eyesore and when tearing down city centres was no longer so fashionable.

Today, in 1995, when the Bull Ring itself is to be torn down and replaced by a more traditional vision of the city centre, we can, paradoxically, feel almost as nostalgic about the bright modernist optimism of the 1960s as we do about nineteenth-century Paris. Once an experience of urban life is safely in the past, we are able to invest it with a charm it lacked at the time. It is this shifting of perception that is sometimes dismissed as 'mere' nostalgia, but I am not convinced it is anything as simple as sentimentality.

It was Jane Jacobs who, in the 1960s, voiced most famously the reaction against massive urban redevelopments (Jacobs 1961). This was not, for her, a return to the past, but rather a preservation of the present, her Greenwich Village present. Yet although the developers were turned away from those particular twisting streets and low-rise buildings, change – albeit of a different kind – could not be held back, and Sharon Zukin charted the subsequent gentrification of this and other adjacents districts of downtown

Manhattan in the 1970s (Zukin 1982). Jane Jacobs and later Richard Sennett in *The Uses of Disorder* (Sennett 1970) argued that if the planners went away, city neighbourhoods would regenerate themselves. Both Sennett and Jacobs took an anti-statist stand in calling for the state to abandon its overweening, as they saw it, architectural and social engineering interventions in urban life. Sennett suggested that if the state withdrew from at least some of its regulatory and policing functions individuals and groups would be forced to confront their own conflicts and deal with them themselves.

Developing this argument, Kevin Robins (1995a) has pointed out that aggression and antagonism are inescapable aspects of city life. A key figure in urban culture is the stranger; the city is a place to which many different strangers come and encounters between strangers will not always be friendly. Even if individuals are not personally hostile, the more negative urban literature has repeatedly invoked a notion of the crowd as a dangerous entity pregnant with collective hostility and loss of control, ever ready to inaugurate a reign of disorder. The crowd becomes a kind of unnatural force of nature, the ruled threatening the rulers like a flood, a hurricane or a fire, and Robins explores the way in which the appearance of the stranger threatens the existing order, thus calling up the fear that is also expressed in fear of the crowd: that chaos will come. The appearance of the stranger sharpens the identity of the established resident, but often in a paranoid fashion, if the stranger is seen as a threat to that identity.

Robins suggests that this hostility need not be the end point and that it is certainly not the only component of the encounters of strangers. He quotes Georg Simmel who argued that the newcomer brings 'new and vitalising qualities into urban culture'. The stranger, says Simmel, has 'a distinctly "objective" attitude, an attitude that is a distinct structure composed of remoteness and nearness, indifference and involvement', and Robins argues that the diversity of communities and the encounters of strangers offers an opportunity to work through hostility and to arrive at dialectic and creative change.

This could raise as many problems as it solves, because if one side of the self-managed community is tenants' associations and watering your neighbour's pot plants, the other is urban vigilante groups, or the sort of situation that arose in a part of Birmingham where local Asian men became determined to get rid of the women – prostitutes – operating in their neighbourhood. There are no easy solutions to entrenched divisions of gender, race, class and simple moral expectation. Nor would Sennett or Robins argue that there are, but theirs is a refreshing alternative to the usual apocalyptic response to the perceived threat of violence and disorder in cities.

For, as Robins points out, the usual reaction by architects and urbanists to the perceived chaos and disorder of cities has not been to embrace, but rather to extirpate it, responding with plans for totally ordered and orderly cities based on complete rationalism. Indeed, this was part of a very long tradition of utopian writing. From its beginnings in Thomas More's *Utopia*, right down to *News From Nowhere* and Edward Bellamy's *Looking Backward*, the utopia is seen as the final solution, the creation of perfect cities which will never need to change any more (Choay 1980; Wilson 1992).

Robins argues that this kind of rationalism is not an adequate response to urban disorder, since it denies, suppresses or ignores our emotional and unconscious responses to every aspect of urban life. Urban life in its very being is a constant interaction of rational and irrational, order and disorder, harmony and friction. He further argues that what he calls the urban regeneration agenda is only 'the acceptable face of rationalism', and does not really deal with the problems of the disorder its vision of harmony confronts. Rationalism in this sense is a kind of perfectionism, the idea that the good city is one in which all problems have been eliminated.

Feminists writing about cities have also sometimes unintentionally produced rationalistic solutions in this partly negative sense to the perceived problems for women of urban living. The pressure to produce policies is understandable and in itself valid. Feminists are rightly concerned that cities should be safe for women, with, for example, better street and estate lighting at night and better public transport, and that they should be child-friendly. Yet to talk *only* about safety is somehow to suggest that on the one hand urban living in Britain *is* extremely dangerous, and simultaneously that it *can* be made totally safe (as well as to imply that it is problem specific to women). It is important to hold two separate visions of urban life in balance. Reforms, such as the reduction of private motorcar use and improvements in public transport, would do much to improve city life and increase its safety. But while risk can be reduced it can't be abolished, and risk taking as well as safety is an unavoidable element in urban or indeed any life.

Safety has tended to be associated with homogeneity, but, as I suggested earlier, cities that are too homogeneous come to seem to be lacking in some way. Homogeneity also goes against one of the main propositions of urban regeneration movements: the idea that cities are, and/or should be centres of diversity. This is surely an ideal to be pursued (although we need to remember that while diversity in the glittering city of consumption refers to a variety of entertainments, foods, fashion freaks, households and landscaped open spaces, diversity in impoverished areas of cities in so far as it exists is more likely to mean division – different kinds of people thrust together in unwanted proximity that breeds fear and withdrawal rather than neighbourliness and community).

Even contemporary visions of urban diversity too often seem to rely on reconstructing the past in the future. Is this a form of nostalgia? What is it about the *absent city*, the remembered but lost experience (or lost object of desire) that these sort of discussions evoke? Is it possible knowingly to recreate the sort of city that in former times sprang up spontaneously? In his Reith Lectures, Richard Rogers (1994) celebrated the Beaubourg (the Pompidou Centre) and its surrounding square, streets and the lively urban environment created by this spectacular arts centre, as he had every right to do. Yet that arts centre has substituted a largely leisure environment for the thriving markets that it displaced. Similarly, the new and resolutely postmodern Parc de la Villette, just inside the 'péripherique' motorway that encircles Paris, has displaced the abattoirs and a host of dependent small food processing businesses, bars and other enterprises that were dependent on the slaughter-houses. Both François Maspero (Maspero 1993) and Deyan Sudjic (Sudjic 1993) have acknowledged how this changes city populations; we become tourists in our own cities, suggests Sudjic. The Beaubourg and the Parc de la Villette, like hundreds of other environments in the western World, have been redesigned as leisure environments. We are *meant* to become *flâneurs* in these settings – municipal or heritage *flâneurs*. But am I alone in feeling that something has been lost once you are invited to do it? Or that perhaps there is a kind of alienation as we wander through 'our own' cities when they seem to have been taken over by tourists who are not even the 'strangers' referred to by Simmel, but crowds or groups of people who seem to be inhabiting an alternative universe which just happens to exist in the same space as our own 'real' city?

Many of us must have extremely ambivalent feelings towards the kinds of change I have outlined. It is this ambivalence that I miss in the Kracauer piece I quoted earlier, but which is clearly present in the writings of nineteenth-century writers such as Privat d'Anglemont (1861). To read d'Anglemont's articles and the writings of other nineteenth-century Parisian *flâneurs* is to be struck by the feeling that their wanderings and explorations into the poverty stricken and forgotten *quartiers* of Paris were tinged with the illicit. These journalists often likened the city to the American wilderness; indeed to invoke Fennimore Cooper became positively a cliché of the mid-nineteenth century, used by Balzac, Eugene Sue and Marx, among others. The whole point was the slight thrill of danger, or at least of the unexpected. Benjamin (1979) – later – went further and acknowledged the sexual, and sexually dubious, aspect of loitering and looking, most famously articulated in Charles Baudelaire's poem 'A Une Passante'.

These writers, though, were not looking only for the unexpected, and therefore new; they were looking for the unexpected that had been lost. Privat d'Anglemont hunted out survivals of eccentric professions and callings, forgotten tribes of gypsies, Italian puppet-makers and other medieval remnants and corners of the city that was soon to be Baron Haussman's.

Anyone who has lived in a city for a long time, or even visited a city on numerous occasions over the course of years, is confronted with this rather strange emotion, whereby something old and familiar, something which now exists only or almost only in memory, is endowed with a beauty it maybe never possessed at the time. Moreover, in cities, nostalgia operates particularly potently on impoverished, marginal out-of-the-way districts and corners. Privat d'Anglemont, for example, writing about his wanderings through Paris, occasionally calls himself to order, and says, 'well, really, all these frightful old buildings and alleys ought to be pulled down, they're breeding grounds for disease and crime, let's do away with them'; yet the bulk of his writing consists of a chronicle and catalogue of precisely these lost, forgotten, degenerated bits of the city and the curious characters who

inhabited them (but see Seigel (1986) for a somewhat different interpretation).

Nostalgia is part of the legacy of the romantic movement, and is an effect
of change, and the massive changes that take place in cities induce this
emotion to an intense degree. (The romantic movement was, after all,
originally a reaction to the intensification of the speed of change that came
with the industrial revolution.) Calls for urban regeneration or for some
kind of city that is different from what we actually have are also, of course
and paradoxically, calls for change; although sometimes the change that is
desired is a return to the past. Yet, if we could return to that past, would we
like it? We look yearningly at old movies and paintings, and dream of how
lovely those cities were. Maybe we would like to wave a magic wand and have
the Victorian Greek Revival public buildings of central Bradford rise again.
(They would certainly be an improvement upon what replaced them.) But
who would wish to return to the stifling snobbery and narrowness of the
Bradford of *Room at The Top*? Who could bear the Leicester endured by
Bradbury, Cooper and Philip Larkin – where boredom surely fused with
sexual repression to inflame the misogyny which resulted in Amis's deeply
unpleasant caricature of Larkin's real-life lover, Monica Jones (Motion
1993: 238–9), and more generally in Larkin's self-conscious nastiness? I can
afford to acknowledge the charm, the solidity and the calm of 1960s
Leicester only because I am no longer a resentful social worker, no longer
at the wrong end of the different, 'liberated' sexism of the 1960s. I can
enjoy the Biba exhibition because – although I *do* wish there was still a
Biba's (and I know that heaven will be a great big Biba superstore in the sky,
just like the one in the Derry and Toms building, where I'll be able to hang
out all day in the fake Art Deco showroom getting stoned with degenerate-
looking hippie angels) – I'm no longer so desperately (well, not quite
so desperately) dependent on fashion as a prop to bolster my defective
ego.

So what is nostalgia? If it is a looking back with regret at the past, if, in
other words, it is a sad feeling, then why do we talk about 'wallowing in
nostalgia' as though it were some kind of pleasurable indulgence like eating
too many chocolates or reading pulp romances? The *Shorter Oxford
Dictionary* defines nostalgia as a translation of the German *Heimweh*, or
homesickness, 'a form of melancholia caused by prolonged absence from
one's country or home'. This definition is surely inadequate, because
although understandable in terms of the need for a sense of belonging and
familiarity, of identity and roots, it doesn't address the *ambivalence* of
nostalgia. The phrase 'wallowing in nostalgia' suggests, to me at least, a self-
indulgence that is essentially sentimental. We surely disapprove of sentimentality because it lays claim to feeling (sentiment) without responsibility.
We feel sentimental about other people's babies and pets – because we do
not have to look after them. It is emotion on the cheap. Nostalgia is more
complex.

In 1930 a French historian giving a paper at the Musée Carnavalet in the
Marais district of Paris said:

> We are almost at the World's end here in this district of the 'Marais'
> – the marsh – now so deserted by society, so plebeian and commercial,
> but which for all its social degeneration has a beauty and poetry that
> have survived the upheavals of the past 30[0?] years. It is the remnant
> of a Paris where silent and provincial corners still exist. Where there
> are grass-grown streets, flanked by mansions that were not built
> yesterday – the mansions of the old aristocracy, full of memories.
>
> (Gillet 1930: 11)

I read this as a deeply nostalgic passage – and even more so for us today,
when we know that the Marais only just missed being completely destroyed
and redeveloped in the 1960s, and in fact has survived, not as a 'lost corner'
of Old Paris, but as the heart of gay chic and trendy gentrification. The
main feeling in this passage is, however, not a sense of loss, but a sense of
pleasure, and I think the pleasure with which the speaker undoubtedly
described the Marais was precisely due to ambivalence, or perhaps it is not
really ambivalence, but is rather the possibility of having an inherently
contradictory experience. He, a Parisian, delights in the un-Parisian nature
of this corner of his capital city; a city that, it turns out, is at one and the
same time a modern city and a provincial one, or rather it can contain
within its modernity an encapsulated experience of this other mood of
provincial melancholy. He can experience this melancholy without experiencing it, because actually he isn't living in the provinces. In addition, he
can vicariously enjoy the ghosts of the *ancien régime*, while, again, continuing
to be a modern citizen living in a republic. He can enjoy the present
through the lens of the past as he simultaneously enjoys the past through
the lens of the present. Thus for me, despite the dictionary definition,
nostalgia is not a pure sense of loss, nor is it the emotional self-indulgence
of mere sentimentality.

Ian Taylor and Ruth Jamieson (this volume) have written at length of the
loss to the men of Sheffield of the whole steel industry that once supported
and defined that community. They demonstrate the way in which advertisements – for beer, for example – play on a memory or invocation of this lost
community, its manliness and power, its harshness and yet, in a sense,
joyfulness. To look back at that community, that city and to compare it with
the devastation that has replaced it – and which the authors vividly describe,
pointing out that the lives of at least some young men in the Sheffield of
today constitutes a strange parody of the old steel mills ethic, only now
organised around petty crime and drugs – to look back at that is not, I
think, to indulge in nostalgia, but to experience grief and anger at the
devastation. These are emotions very different from nostalgia.

Perhaps the real secret pleasure of nostalgia is that it allows us, as we look
back at a past bathed in a rosy glow of melancholy beauty, at those lost
corners of the old city, at the same time to measure the distance we have
come – not in the sense necessarily of progress or improvement, but simply
in the sense of experiencing the reality of change, the passage of time, and
the existence of that great hinterland of 'lost time' that yet somehow is still
with us. It is the subtle pleasure of imaginatively experiencing the past from

the detached standpoint of the present. More seriously, and perhaps more valuably, it is the Proustian understanding, not of the remembrance of things past but of the retrieval of the past, a movement whereby we reappropriate the present by acknowledging and understanding that past. Yes: it surely contains an element of greater understanding, of detachment as well as attachment. Only by not just remembering but by confronting and reinterpreting the past was Proust's hero, Marcel, enabled to fulfil his destiny. Only by engaging in this way with the changing fabric of the city, and by acknowledging change as both loss and enrichment, can we adequately approach the experience of living in urban space. And, if nostalgia is itself a rather passive emotion, yet it can lead us towards a more active responsibility both for the past and for the future. For it is only by embracing both the past and the future of our cities that we can fulfil their potential in the present, using the awareness that nostalgia brings in order to move beyond it into an acceptance of and an active engagement in change.

8

AUTHENTICITY AND SUBURBIA*

David Chaney

A significant theme in contemporary thought has been a concern with distinctive tensions between processes of cultural globalisation on the one hand and local enclaves of innovation and opposition on the other (see for example Lash and Urry 1994). These tensions are usually held to have become particularly marked in the urban culture of later modernity as the optimism of the modernist imagination has turned sour. It is, however, surprising that the *character* of suburban culture has usually been ignored. It seems as if suburban inhabitants' acquiescence in the anonymity of everyday life cannot easily be accommodated in the new geographies of cultural change (see, for, example Bird *et al.* 1993). In this chapter I shall make a small gesture to redress this neglect by picking up the relatively neglected theme of *authenticity* in suburbia. Basically, my argument will be that in important ways the contradictions of collective identity in suburban settings have generated recurrent themes of a concern with authenticity in the appropriation of mass cultural forms. I will begin, and return towards the end of the chapter, by suggesting some general reasons for why this should be so: in a central section I will point to some aspects of a quest for authentic experience in recent British suburban life.

One way of approaching the theme of a dialectic between local and global is to turn to contributions to debates about the nature of the public sphere in later mass culture. These have emphasised the ways in which television makes public events available to domestic audiences. Thus, Scannell in an influential paper (1989) has argued that Habermas's concern with whether mass culture industries can provide emancipation through rational discourse is misplaced. Instead, Scannell argues that we should be more concerned with the ways television makes public life 'talk-about-able', an approach that Silverstone (1994; see also Corner 1995) has subsequently developed by emphasising what he calls the suburbanisation of the public sphere. In these perspectives a global political culture is incorporated in everyday life through audiences' active engagement with the gatekeeping mediation of television and other aspects of the discourse

*I gratefully acknowledge the help and advice of Andy Bennett in discussions and with references during the course of the preparation of this chapter. I would also like to dedicate the chapter to my friend, Bob Roshier, who has always been stimulating about our common history of suburban childhoods.

of actuality (on the significance of theories of the 'active audience' more generally see Moores 1993; Morley 1992 chapters 11 and 12).

The tenor of these ideas then is to emphasise the use or adaptation of mass cultural materials in the everyday life and the culture of local places such as suburban estates. While this is valuable as a corrective to a stultifying tradition that has been obsessed with the articulation of structural determinations, the forms and dynamics of the variety of ways of making such materials meaningful clearly still need to be explored. It is too easy to assume that there is a straightforward and unambiguous sense to the idea of a local, suburban, culture. In contrast I can easily point to three common, but contrasting, interpretations. First, are all those ways in which localities have sought to give themselves a distinctive identity either through the invention of local traditions or through an elaboration of some aspect of local history. An interesting version from my own locality of a combination of these strategies collected under a fictional mystique has been the recent development of 'Catherine Cookson Country' by local councils. In these cases the local identity is a bureaucratic enterprise, although often stimulated by local activists, and it serves a dual function of both boosting local pride and acting as a magnet to attract tourist visitors.

A second type of local culture is usually less clearly identified but exists in the multiplicity of affiliations that constitute local networks. I am thinking here of the variety of forms of music-making charted by Finnegan (1989) for Milton Keynes. In this and other cases it has been found that an amateur or semi-professional culture of local enthusiasts exists to give a distinct flavour to local experience, although it is one that has to be appreciated on the ground rather than from outside. Third, a local underground or alternative culture frequently exists to provide an enclave within which a national style or subculture is given a distinctive inflection (see for example Redhead (1993) and some of the issues about the idea of national culture discussed by Hebdige (1992)).

There are, therefore, a variety of ways of making a local cultural environment: ways that vary on dimensions such as the degree of organisation, the direction of the impetus to sustain local activities and the types of self-conscious positioning adopted in relation to the forms of national or global cultural industries. In every case though, for those concerned the relevant activities have a symbolic significance as well as their intrinsic rewards. The sense of cultural distinctiveness is evoked in an image or a story that is understood reflexively. I suggest that because suburbs are arbitrary places, a self-consciousness about local identity and local culture is inevitable. This does not mean that the local 'making' of culture is only located in suburban sites, but rather that a willingness to get 'caught up' in the consumption of local cultural images is particularly germane to suburban experience.

Suburbs are frequently presented as depressingly anonymous, ordinary places where the inhabitants seem only too eager to acquiesce in the conformity of conventional social mores. Neither rural nor urban, suburbs mimic some of the social characteristics of life in the former while remaining firmly located in the infrastructure of the latter. As well as lacking a clear identity suburbs resist planners' categories of purpose and function – endlessly growing, they defy any rational organisation of the metropolitan environment. The significance of anonymity has usually been explained by reference to the changing balance and meaning of public and private spheres in urban culture (Davidoff and Hall 1987; Fishman 1987; Jackson 1985: Stilgoe 1988). The first suburbs were created as a result of a growing antipathy amongst the entrepreneurial middle class to the threats posed to their respectability by the social heterogeneity and lack of order in urban culture. Processes of population growth, shifts in the size and character of occupational enterprise, urban development and slum clearance, etc. have all, throughout the twentieth century, created periodic surges in new markets for imitations of this process of suburban emigration.

Central themes for the individual social units which comprise a suburban estate will be domesticity and familialism; that is, values which emphasise the strength and intimacy of family or quasi-family relationships set within a dominating focus on privately owned settings – house, car, garden, second home, etc. Thorns (1972: 29) has reported that the core values of the 'suburban way of life' in Britain are: 1) a commitment to 'do-it-yourself' in home maintenance; 2) family and particularly child-centred relationships; 3) middle-class aspirations; 4) the significance of status symbols; 5) a high degree of social activity; 6) conformism in ethical judgements and behaviour; and 7) political conservatism. Also, Grossberg has argued that in 1950s America: 'suburbia grew 15 times faster than any other geographical sector of the country. . . . There was no great mystery about the motives: the suburbs were imagined as a better place to bring up the kids' (1992: 173; see also Fishman's emphasis on the suburb as a bourgeois utopia: 'a complex and compelling vision of the modern family freed from the corruption of the city . . . protected by a close-knit stable community' (1987: x)).

It is clear that in this context the home, and activities clustered around it, will take on a central importance as the grounds for identity. The symbolic status of these private settings will necessarily mean a great deal of financial and emotional investment in styling, furnishing, decorating, equipping. maintaining and defending these sites by their inhabitants. The suburban home is thus intrinsically linked to the spread of consumerism. Suburban culture and its activities endlessly generate new demands for objects, machines and decorations to display an appropriate commitment to the sphere that encapsulates these values. These then are localities of consumption not production, and it may be that images of cultural authenticity should be seen as a distinctive type of consumer good bought or appropriated from international cultural idioms.

Underlying *my* approach is the view that suburbs are anomalous places because they exist on two contradictory levels simultaneously. The first is a level of cultural ideal. While it may be trivialising the reference to describe suburbs as utopian places, I think it is appropriate to see them as harbouring utopian aspirations. As examples I will include the core theme of familialism and to this should be added a positive stress on communal integration in suburban values; the concern with active citizenship expressed through participation in a range of types of local association (see for example Bishop and Hoggett 1986); and a strong respect for tolerance and mutual privacy underwritten by the social homogeneity of any one estate and the powerful expectations placed on all inhabitants to conform to prevalent norms on tidiness and the upkeep of house and garden, etc.

Of course, one can point out that this vision is sustained by precise social differentiations between suburban districts, and powerful mythologies of ever-intensifying dangers of social breakdown articulated in frightening narratives of urban disintegration, criminal and particularly racial violence and social parasitism. (The urban 'other' to suburban values seems in the popularity of film and television dramatisations to both fascinate and repel suburban audiences.) The positive vision of the polite community is therefore dependent upon complementary nightmare visions of impolite disrespect, a contrast that underlies what Baumgartner has described, in relation to suburbs, as a culture of moral minimalism (1988). Suburbs, in his view, provide a utopian zone where the encroachments of strangers can be avoided, and where, in a form of moral order based on equality, autonomy and self-sufficiency, 'life is filled with efforts to deny, minimize, contain, and avoid conflict' (ibid.: 127).

The cultural form of the suburb is, however, also displayed at a second level of the material culture of public and private places. Here the integrative expectations of community and participation are undercut by the privatisation of public space and the use of lifestyle implements to display modes of identity. Both of these forms of competitive individualism are symbolised by the significance of the private car in suburban culture (a recurrent theme in the literature, but see in particular Jackson (1985 chapters 14 and 15)). The car exemplifies private use of public space - it symbolises social status, and provides a very precise expression of its owner's/user's social morality. A further mode of symbolism is that in everyday circumstances car drivers conform to an implicit but all-pervasive social discipline in order to maintain their individual autonomy.

The car as material culture not only symbolically encapsulates so many themes of suburban lifestyle, down to the depressing practical anonymity of the mass car market, but it also generates a distinctive topography or landscape for suburban places. By this I mean more than that a transport system privileging private cars necessarily generates a lot of roads, although it is important to remember that one version of the highway was invented in Los Angeles in 1930 to facilitate the limitless expansion of the decentred city. Two instances of suburban landscape generated by the predominance of the private car are, first, social institutions adapted to customers as drivers – for example motels, shopping centres, churches, sports stadia and eateries (on the more general significance of the latter see Ritzer 1992). The second instance goes back to the idea of the *incoherence* of the suburban landscape. There is a fragmentary indeterminacy to an ecological distribution generated by private transport. No longer tied to the radial spokes of central urban dependence, the ex-urban landscape overlaps a series of institutional functions in repetitious and arbitrary disorder.

The two levels of suburban existence I have described are complementary. But although they can co-exist, as in the politics of neo-liberalism, they also enable us to see a contradiction between community and the fragmentation of competitive individualism in the collective fictions of suburban experience. I suggest that although this contradiction is coped with ideologically in a variety of ways, one of the most important is through the resolution of being transposed to a mythological domain of tradition. This process of transposition is picked out and re-worked in various sub-dominant strains of authenticity.

The salience of tradition to suburban culture is most immediately apparent in the built forms of the new estates. In Britain only in seaside housing (and then possibly because they are by definition liminal places) have traces of modernist iconography crept with any regularity into the suburbs. Apart from these extravagances, the dominant tone of the housing is of a very highly predictable pitched-roof three-bedroomed semi-detached or detached house. Such houses generally lack ornamentation or any distinctive style, except for minor occasional details such as leaded windows. (The brutality of public housing provision is always indicated by pictures of tower blocks not repetitive rows of two-storey housing.) Slightly more ambitious houses will probably aim to mimic some of the features of an earlier epoch, presumably to create some association with the prestige and historicity of that era.

Thus, in the United States the colonial style quickly replaced Victorian Gothic in the twentieth century because it exemplified associations of early immigration, frontier spirit and rural solidity. In Britain the dominant style, so popular as to render its continued use as almost ironic, has been a mixture of fragmentary references to sixteenth- and seventeenth-century housing popularly known as Tudorbethan (on suburban aspirations see some of the essays in Oliver, Davis and Bentley 1981). Less ambitiously there has been a plague of quotations from the Georgian era, principally in doors and windows, which have sprouted as 'pasted on' additions to otherwise conventional brick boxes.

The deference to tradition in housing consists then in a combination of themes. First, a thorough-going refusal of anything redolent of modernism in any way; then, a frequent and usually ill-advised borrowing of historical reference; and, finally, an unchanging insistence on an orthodoxy of the lowest common denominator (the latter is particularly true of that other area of suburban display – garden design). This combination also holds true for institutional sites – in particular those seeking public endorsement such as shopping and leisure centres.

Other aspects of the use of motifs or forms of tradition (an invented nostalgia) to clothe the new societies of suburbia are the endorsement of institutional practices which seem to hark back to some unspecified 'traditional' past. Examples which readily occur are as varied as schools, at all age-levels, that require their pupils to wear uniforms which are inevitably drawn from a template incorporating anachronistic features such as short trousers and caps for boys, adopted from some mythical era (the 1950s?) when wealthy children attended schools with uniforms of this type.

Another instance is the likelihood of suburban families being church attenders and in particular marking the annual calendar through attendance at festivals such as Christmas and the perennial births, marriages and deaths. Finally, suburban shops, particularly small specialist retailers, seem increasingly inclined to re-stage themselves as historical survivals through an 'oldy-worldy' veneer.

A further aspect of the salience of references to traditionalism comes in the ease with which suburban politics can be dominated by constituencies oriented to the assertion of traditional values. I have referred to a suburban predilection for political conservatism and this is obviously part of the unquestioned rhetoric of traditional values. But more generally in relation to themes such as patriotism, the family, the educational curriculum, cultural orthodoxy, gender differences, state power and a dislike of strong welfare systems, a distinct political agenda has been formulated under the warrant of the supposed traditionalism of these values (most notoriously in Britain under a recent but short-lived slogan of 'Back to Basics'). This sort of agenda can obviously most easily be exploited by conservative political parties but it is sufficiently vague ideologically to be captured and adapted to a variety of political programmes.

The point of our present concern is not to comment on the integrity or validity of any of these values but to note how they commonly draw upon a metaphoric framework of tradition and nostalgia for the certainties of the past. The function of these metaphors is, on the one hand, to confirm the validity of the suburban utopian vision both as communal ideal and fear of the social incoherence of the public places of the city. While, on the other hand, the rhetoric of tradition makes sense, as I have said, of the inconsistency between communal ideal and the privatisation of the material culture by magically transposing the inconsistencies to a mythological sphere of commitment to the past.

To speak of the rhetoric of tradition as a magical resolution of difficulties in the communal consciousness of suburban life is a general frame of reference. More specifically, I suggest that the ideological orientation to a past represents values of seeking to transcend the ambiguities and inconsistencies of present experience, which in turn generate a persistent reference to ideas of authenticity (not least in relation to the touristic excursion – on tourism and the suburbs see Chaney 1994 chapter 4). A quest for authenticity can then act as a reflexive rationale, both appropriating mass cultural idioms for forms of local cultural activity and as a further point of reference for groups to use in constructing critical subterranean positions towards suburbia from within. This is the key ideological trick – a thematic value of authenticity can grow on overarching ideological orientations to tradition in a variety of ways that encompass critical dissent as well as conformist accommodation.

I shall explain what I mean by some uncontroversial examples from the history of popular music since 1945. Conventionally this history, quite rightly, privileges the development of successive musical idioms, from rock-'n'-roll through to punk, and how they have inter-penetrated with distinctive youth cultures (see for example Hall and Jefferson 1976; and Redhead

1990). The mass recording industry of the post-war world has, however, also facilitated a number of subordinate enthusiasms which occasionally break into the mass market but are usually pursued as a distinctive leisure interest or hobby by their followers. One of the most interesting of these was the traditional jazz revival in 1940s' and 1950s' Britain (Godbolt 1984, 1989).

The history of jazz in the US is a story of diaspora and development from roots in turn-of-the-century New Orleans to high modernist innovations playing to self-consciously avant-garde audiences. (Some aspects of the troubled ways in which American music has been appropriated in Britain are discussed by Frith (1988).) One of the unlikeliest inflections of that story is that the idiom of the earliest years rooted in a particular black community should be taken up and copied by middle-class young white men and played, initially, in the suburban pubs and rhythm clubs of South London. Subsequently, the style of Dixieland or New Orleans or traditional jazz has spread thoughout the nation's suburbs and can still be found being played in pubs and clubs enthusiastically by amateurs and semi-professionals.

While this sort of cultural transmission is fascinating in its own right, my immediate interest is concentrated on the almost cultic aspects of this new enthusiasm. It was not just that another music was being revived but that the mode of revival had to be authentic. As one might expect this meant that surviving exponents of the original style were venerated. In the 1950s and 1960s they were discovered and brought to Britain and their, by now, very elderly renditions were treated with awe. More polemically, the band of enthusiasts were caught up in doctrinal disputes over when this particular era which was being copied began and ended (did it for example include white musicians who were contemporary with, but possibly copying, black innovators?); what was the authentic instrumentation for the classic style? (thus the banjo achieved an almost iconic status as a rhythm instrument); and what were permissible as items in the repertoire? It seems clear then that this suburban enthusiasm was riven by agonised disputes over authenticity which were carried to the extent of violent factional splits, expulsions and loyalties. (The frequently amusing story of this revival has been told in a number of autobiographies – two good examples are Lyttleton 1954 and Melly 1977).

The revival of traditional jazz ran then in counterpoint to the dominant strands of the mass market for popular music, only briefly commanding a large-scale youth audience. We should also bear in mind, however, the brief but widespread popularity of skiffle as the bastard child of the traditional jazz revival providing a bridge to the subsequent 'discovery' of the blues (see Newton 1961: especially chapter 13). My second example of a quest for musical authenticity springing from suburbia had a more complex relationship with youth culture. In the middle and later 1960s a new idiom of popular music combined with a strong generational consciousness to generate a counter-culture or cultural revolutionary lifestyle aiming to attack a number of targets, such as military imperialism, educational institutions and even the capitalist state in France.

An important element in the cultural complex that became the iconography of this era was a process of discovery paralleling the earlier revival of traditional jazz. Initially an Afro-American style, the blues underwent a significant transformation as a result of the migration of Negro workers to Northern American cities. The subsequent committing of a new urban blues to vinyl underlay the British blues boom of the 1960s. It is a familiar refrain in interviews with, and biographies of, black blues musicians that they feel a mixture of gratitude and irritation with respect to the role of British groups and musicians such as the Beatles, the Rolling Stones and Eric Clapton in stimulating a revival of interest in their work. (Muddy Waters talking of Mick Jagger has said that, 'He took my music but he gave me my name' (quoted in Palmer 1977: 249).) Of course, the young men in British bands were also building on the inspiration of white American performers such as Elvis Presley and Carl Perkins who had been very aware of their borrowings from black performers (on the history of appropriations of black music see Bane 1992). It is, nevertheless, true that an enormous impetus to knowledge of and respect for black popular music had developed from a quest for authenticity in British suburbs.

The initial wave of the blues revival had a tremendous impact and become absorbed as an important inflection of youth culture that has remained significant ever since. In so doing, however, its roots in a suburban quest for authentic forms of expression quickly became lost to successive generations of pop audiences. Paralleling these commercial adaptations a variety of stubborn revivalists have continued to enjoy increasingly middle-aged white men playing a variety of types of blues music. In the live music performed in any British city an important strand is available informally in pubs and will consist of some pubs specialising in blues bands. From experience it seems that the audience for these bands is more middle-class, student-based and more suburban than for rock bands in pubs. Again one has to recognise that this identification with the perceived authenticity of discriminated culture is very much a minority strand within the cultural complex of suburban leisure tastes. But, precisely because the resonance of the music has spoken to a form of life that is at least considerably more intense than the stereotype of suburbia, it has provided a counterpoint that is not dissonant to the utopianism of more orthodox traditions. (Frith has aptly written of the adoption of 'black masks' by white middle-class audiences (1988: 50).)

My third example of a quest for authenticity in music largely based in suburban lifestyles is another instance of people looking to what they regarded as a disadvantaged or discriminated against culture. In this case, however, the movement did not look outside Britain but back, in complex ways, to peasant and/or industrial working-class cultures. The initial discovery and collection of *folk song* is usually attributed to a proto-nationalist consciousness amongst those who felt alarmed by the urbanisation of the nineteenth century, and saw a rural culture being absorbed into a growing mass culture (Burke 1978). Early collectors of folk song were often ideologically committed to a particular version of authenticity which led them to frequently bowdlerise lyrics and to frame notions of folk and rurality in idealised arcadian dress (Harker 1985). I do not need to trace the history of the folk song movement here, but it is important to stress that, although it has always been driven by an ideological contrast between an authentic other and an ersatz contemporary, the character of the ideological construction of authenticity has changed with the social constituency of enthusiasts.

The latest wave of folk song revival came very much out of the same cultural ferment in which the blues were adopted and copied. Over the last two decades there has sprouted a large number of folk clubs run by local enthusiasts which provide opportunities for all who want to perform, however amateurishly, as well as to listen to visiting (usually paid) performers. These clubs can use or take over all sorts of performance spaces but they usually do so in such a way that the venue retains a rather makeshift, impromptu air (the history of the recent movement and the style of performance, etc. are ably described in MacKinnon 1993). A local club may adopt a pub which is outside the town or in the city centre as its venue because it feels the right sort of place, but the membership and the support for the club are firmly suburban. These are not people singing to revive their own memories of a lost past but, in general, well-educated 30- to 50-somethings who are members of professional occupations seeking a mode of expression based in what appears to be a more authentic form of life.

It is not my purpose to question the consistency of the values of those committed to the folk song movement, but rather to note how it is another instance of identification by suburban residents with a culture that seems to offer the promise of a more authentic experience than their own. Once again the enthusiasts seek to preserve the otherness of the cultural form they are adopting by insisting on certain symbolic commitments. These are held to distinguish their version of popular song from what they see as the corrupted entertainments of the commercial popular music industry.

Two instances of this differentiation I can cite are the reluctance to use amplifiers in folk clubs (see MacKinnon 1993, especially 119–26), and the right of all to contribute to an evening's entertainment. The first consists of a widely shared feeling that electronic amplification constitutes some form of rubicon between amateur and professional production. The latter is not necessarily bad but it is held to be distorting, if not severing, of the performer's roots in the community. Similarly, the rule that a guest performance is interspersed with contributions from the floor seems to be insisted on in order to affirm the idea that 'stars' and 'amateurs' share a cultural community. The rules here are clearly symbolic but they function to mark off a distinct social occasion of performance.

These are then three modes of a search for authenticity. It can be objected that their relationship with suburbia is tenuous because others than suburban residents share these enthusiasms. This is true but it does seem to me that the suburban locations of their starting-points and the nature of their typical audience members is not coincidental. The continued strengths of these tastes do represent a more general theme of the value of tradition, in these cases in ways that are simultaneously critical rejections of at least aspects of the material culture of suburbia. But this is precisely why they function as a form of mythical resolution. There is no reason to think that the inhabitants of suburbia are not reflexively aware of the contradictions in the formulations of suburban places. Self-conscious ambivalence about suburban lifestyles may be more pronounced amongst those who live in older inner city suburban enclaves, but it is clearly not absent from the everyday discourse of suburban 'normality'. By clothing the contradictions of suburbia in the mythical guise of an identity that transcends the mundaneity of the here and now a complex process of a simultaneous accommodation and denial can be accomplished.

I hope I can make this proposal slightly clearer by pointing to an analogy with more general features of modern development. The idea that forms of collective experience in modernity can be discursively elaborated through mythical forms was given a powerful inflection by the publication of a collection papers edited by Hobsbawm and Ranger (1983). Briefly, they argued that the cultural imaginings of nationalism, faced with contradictions between the trans-historic essentialism of national identity and the actual historic novelty of nations as political communities, sought resolution at the level of myth by inventing traditions. Thus, institutions, organisations and movements have all sought to clothe their novelty in an obfuscating mist of imagined historicity. This idea has stimulated a wave of new ideas in our accounts of modernity but it does not have to be restricted to the emergent institutions of nationalism. My approach to suburban culture has clearly been based on an analogous idea to the reconciliation of tradition and modernity in nationalism. This is, that a concern with the authority of tradition can be seen to have been functional for the organisation of root metaphors for suburban culture.

The contours of a more general argument about the ambivalencies and paradoxes of later modernity are beginning to become apparent. This is a provocative approach that requires going beyond the surface meanings of cultural forms. My approach is interestingly complemented by Campbell's exploration of the spirit of modern consumerism: 'The central insight required is the realization that individuals do not so much seek satisfaction from products, as pleasure from the self-illusory experiences which they construct from their [the products'] associated meanings' (1987: 89). The hedonism of modern consumerism, it is argued, is to be understood as a search for the interdependence of pleasure and meaning in the endlessly renewing temptations that the market makes available. Thus it is not that consumers are fooled (or at least not all of them all the time), but rather that they accept a reflexive awareness of the (existential) absurdity of their own preoccupations (an approach I have developed at greater length in Chaney 1993: chapter 5).

Self-consciously nervous and anxious about the world constructed by contemporary consumers as suburban residents, taste provides a social vocabulary, a symbolic repertoire of membership and reference affiliations as a discourse that can be endlessly modfied and renewed in the imagery and narratives of mass culture. The spirit of modern consumerism in Campbell's account therefore aspires to transcend the physical limitations of its own material artefacts. It is a creative hedonism in which the pleasure sought is abstracted from any immediate and specifiable reward and transposed to a generalised quality of life even while recognising its impossibility. It is to this, 'self-illusory hedonism ... characterized by a longing to experience in reality those pleasures created and enjoyed in imagination' that 'the romantic ethic can be seen to possess a basic congruence, or "elective affinity"' (1987: 205, 206).

The provocation in Campbell's thesis is then that romanticism – traditionally the aesthetic 'other' of industrialisation because it offered a utopian refusal of pragmatic rationality - is in reality the hidden core of consumer materialism. Far from being the antithesis of suburban material culture, the romantic ethic swathes and persuades the promise of mass leisure and entertainment with the possibility of a quest for authenticity. Seen in this light the other passions of suburban dreams, such as feminism, the peace movement and environmentalism – even such mundane concerns as a quest for organic vegetables – movements seeking the preservation of local common land, and the values of secular asceticism in exercise, are further instances of romantic intimations of authenticity in the midst of conformity.

I have tried to show how what are frequently forms of cultural dissidence draw on more general ideological themes. In conclusion, and in order to indicate the complexity of these instances, I will cite another study of the politics of tradition in a suburban setting. This example is taken from Young's study of the suburb he calls Woodlands. In this prosperous ex-urban location local social organisation was characterised by the explicit declaration and celebration of communal identity. For many residents Woodlands was 'the Village' (Young 1986: 123). The significance of this elision of imputed rural values with communal identity was that residential activists were able to give the place a type of identity through, 'developing and expressing idealised versions of local history, asserting the existence and superiority of local tradition, [*and*] local rustic qualities' (ibid.: 124).

In this case, then, the utopian myth of a suburb transcending its phenomenal qualities provided a discursive context in which residential activists, such as the local amenity society, were able to resist the development plans of the urban corporation. Bureaucracy and all the other ills of the modern city could be posed as a demonic alternative against which a mythical quest for a different mode of authenticity was articulated; and then in turn made manifest through policies on how social arrangements should be inscribed in the landscape. Interestingly, this discursive mythology could not be used to close off political life within the suburb, as the same rhetoric of tradition was used by other residents who were critical of the policies of the amenity society. The quest for authenticity in suburban culture is therefore both mythical in function and endlessly contestable in character.

My more general conclusion is that the politics of mass culture are less likely to be about rhetorics of structural reorganisation based on competing class interests than about ideologies of authentic experience. To pursue this line of thought, though, might be held to be taking us too far from our initially limited ambitions. I began by raising the need to explore the dynamics of local cultures as they are articulated in the context of voracious cultural industries which are constantly marketing the specificities of lived experience as international idioms. I hope to have said something both about the meanings of invented traditions, and to have made a small contribution to the persistent neglect of suburban life-worlds.

9

'PROPER LITTLE MESTERS'

Nostalgia and protest masculinity in de-industrialised Sheffield

Ian Taylor and Ruth Jamieson

> Sons and daughters, dark and light,
> Toilers through the endless night,
> Turners all, the world around,
> Our heroines your history books ne'er mention,
> Rother sing a Don song of who we are.
>
> Lads and lasses, workers, grafters,
> Mam's on days and dad's on afters,
> Buffers, fettlers, datallers,
> Proper little Mesters, rollers, nailors,
> Rother sing a Don song of who we are.
>
> (Ray Hearne 'Rother Sing a Don Song' on Roy Bailey
> *Never Leave a Story Unsung*, Fuse records CFC 398 (1991))

The purpose of this chapter is to attempt an analytical application of what Bob Connell (1995) has called 'protest masculinity' to one particular urban context – the city of Sheffield – in the middle 1990s. We want to address the relationship between patterns of protest masculinity as an actual social practice and the pervasiveness in this particular north of England city of a series of nostalgic texts about a specifically local form of 'hegemonic masculinity' – the so-called 'little Mester', or 'master cutler' – which dominates the 'structure of feeling', to use Raymond Williams' term, in Sheffield. With this objective in mind, we will note, first, the importance of a particular body of new cultural texts (local industrial heritage museums and a literature in local urban nostalgia) and its representation of the urban and industrial past (in this case, of Sheffield) and also, implicitly, work, household life and masculinity. We will then discuss the representation of northern men in television beer adverts, and particularly a recent advertising campaign by the Sheffield-based brewery of Stones.[1] In the final section of the chapter, we will turn to an analysis of the vocabulary and rhetoric of a group of young men in Sheffield 'in trouble with the law', who were interviewed in 1994 as a part of an ESRC-funded research project.[2]

PROTEST MASCULINITY

The cornerstone of Bob Connell's celebrated earlier work on masculinity and the gender order is the concept of a 'hegemonic masculinity' – the set of taken-for-granted practices and understandings which work, apparently 'naturally', in a culture to support and reproduce the powerful domination of men over women (Carrigan, Connell and Lee 1985; Connell 1987). In his latest work (1995), Connell advances a more elaborated model of 'masculinities' and 'the crisis tendencies' which each of them currently exhibits. He stresses, in particular, that terms like 'hegemonic masculinity' refer to 'configurations of practices generated in particular situations in a changing structure of relationships' rather than to 'fixed character types' (1995: 81). He also attempts in this new text, amongst many things, to theorise the angry character of the complex and contradictory response of poor, largely unemployed young men to their current circumstances of life (an issue which was also the focus of Beatrix Campbell's compelling account of young men on Britain's council estates) – (Campbell 1993). Connell calls the set of gender practices of a set of these young men he encountered in Sydney 'protest masculinity' and he defines this as:

> a marginalized masculinity, which picks up themes of hegemonic masculinity in the society at large but reworks them in a context of poverty.
>
> (Connell 1995: 114)

Connell does not argue – and nor do we – that the relationship between the construction of gender identity at the individual level and the socio-economic context is direct and simple. What we want to suggest in this chapter is that the form of gender identity in place in particular localities will be inflected not only by actually-existing regimes of work but also by *nostalgic evocations* of such regimes, even in the aftermath of their dis-appearance. Neither is it our concern, we should emphasise, to argue that the gender practices, vocabularies and sentiments expressed by young men in Sheffield in the mid-1990s are fixed, coherent or exhaustive of all the forms of masculinity adopted by Sheffield men, whether in a similar situation (of worklessness) or a different position within the local labour market.

The list of 'gender practices' which Connell observed and discussed amongst a group of young men in Sydney in the early 1990s extended across 'violence, school resistance, minor crime, heavy drug/alcohol use, occa-sional manual labour, motorbikes or cars, short heterosexual liaisons' (ibid.: 110). Connell identifies some significant differences between this kind of masculinity and the familiar kind of profane proletarian masculinity associated with the earlier post-war era of mass manufacturing as discussed, for example, in the classic study of unskilled working-class young men in the 1970s by Paul Willis (Willis 1976, 1977). The kind of working life available in that period to Willis's young men – though poor by reference to the dominant middle and upper class (and also the skilled working class) – none the less allowed them to make a social and economic contribution to their local communities (and 'their' families) and it was also connected, in a more or less orderly way, to the reproduction of the existing social form (the Keynesian mixed economy). The young men interviewed by Connell in Sydney, however, exhibited a form of masculinity that did not appear to be located or 'founded' in any one set of institutions (of work or sport) or to perform any constructive role in the formal economy. It is from this recognition that Connell wants to understand these young men's particular display of agitated extroversion.

Connell's analytical strategy is to reference the work of Alfred Adler, the Viennese psychiatrist working at the time of Freud, on masculinity. Adler's arguments turn on the polarities between masculinity and femininity advanced by Freud, but pay particular attention to the ways in which 'femininity' was de-valued in the culture of western Europe in the early twentieth century, and, in particular, equated with 'weakness'. The body of Adler's clinical work was actually concerned to theorise the different types of responses to maternal domination, including the idea of a 'pampered style of masculinity' (involving marked egocentricity and the absence of any 'social interest') (Adler, in Anspacher and Anspacher 1958),[3] but also, importantly for our purposes here, the condition he called 'masculine protest' against feminine weakness, which might itself take different neurotic forms and which might be exhibited by young women as well as men. Strategies adopted to transcend feminine weakness could easily take on an extremely exaggerated form, involving considerable aggression and lack of care and self-discipline. The normal adult male, by contrast, according to Adler, certainly strives for superiority and has a firm sense of ego, but the maturity of the individual man is said to lie in the fact that a 'social interest' has developed and that an appropriate level of activity can be oriented to that interest.

A conventional sociological response to this kind of psychological approach would be to point to the absence of any analysis of the social and economic conditions (particularly of inequality or exploitation) that provide the 'conditions of existence' of any such failure of individual development. Connell's particular approach, however, involves the recognition that capitalist forms of social organisation (even at times of economic optimism) coincide both with 'hegemonic masculinity' and the problems which it produces, not just for subordinated women, but also for subordinated and marginalised men themselves, caught up in the demands of the hegemony. So Connell wants to argue, instead, that the achievement of real adult autonomy (sic) by men depends, certainly, on an absence of poverty, on the disavowal of the desire to dominate and colonise women, and on the absence of connected infantilist or neurotic blocks. It does *not* (and actually cannot) depend on the reproduction of the existing divisions of labour – that is, on the relationships of exploitation characteristic of an industrial class society (including the domination of women). There is no question but that the personal injuries involved in the problems resulting from the endemic poverty in some areas of our de-industrialised urban centres (like Sheffield) outweigh even 'the hidden injuries of class' described by Richard Sennett and Richard Cobb in their study of fully employed young men in Boston in the early 1970s (Sennett and Cobb 1973). But the disordered re-working in a protest form of certain themes of hegemonic masculinity, whose idealised imaginary form was itself problematic and exploitative, and whose actual achievement in practice is now *impossible*, means that the assertion of masculinity by severely disadvantaged young men takes on a desperate character – focusing on forceful involvement in crime and a heightened misogyny as a kind of neurotic over-compensation for lack of power in most other realms of life.

NOSTALGIA AND MASCULINITY IN SHEFFIELD

Dominating the main 'market street' in the Meadowhall shopping centre, proclaimed at the time of its opening in September 1990 as 'the largest shopping mall in Europe', and subsequently visited by 20 million people a year, is a large bronze statue, entitled 'Teeming'. The statue is a representation of the process of casting ingots (teeming) adopted in local steel-making in the early eighteenth century – which still played a part in the processes of production in that industry, with some modifications, until the closure of the mass of the larger steel-production plants in the early 1980s. The 'teeming statue' (crafted by a leading international sculptor, Ronald

Figure 9.1 'Teeming' statue, Market Street, Meadowhall Shopping Centre, Sheffield. *Source*: Meadowhall plc

Bell),[4] is 'iconic' in the sense originally meant by C.S. Pierce (quoted in Zeman 1977). That is to say, it 'partakes of the character' of its object (hard and hazardous manual work in steel, one of the two main sources of male employment in Sheffield until the late 1970s) – that is, it bears some perceivable relation, from the point of view of 'local knowledge' and recent 'social memory', to the reality it purports to represent. Students of semiotics have argued that the signifying power of icons lies in their capacity to re-narrate a well-known story. Representations of the steel-worker – and also (slightly differently) the cutler – in 'street heritage' and on television advertisements certainly have a particular resonance in the city of Sheffield in that they closely resemble the artefacts and tableaux presented in a number of well-known, heavily patronised industrial museums in the city, such as the Abbeydale Industrial Hamlet and the Kelham Island Museum, products of the veritable explosion of industrial heritage sites that occurred across the north of England during the 1980s. Another highly visible iconic representation in Sheffield, at present, is the picture of a forgeworker that was painted onto the gable-end of Castle Street in Sheffield in 1985–6.[5]

The appearance of iconic representations of the masculinity of male industrial workers on the landscapes of the street and in the Meadowhall shopping mall in Sheffield parallels the constant production in the mediascape itself – that is, in television drama, comedies and commercial advertising – of a series of images of northern men, particularly working-class men, in boyhood (the Hovis advertisements),[6] adolescence (most

Figure 9.2 Gable-end image of Sheffield forgeworker, Castle Street, Sheffield (design: Mr Paul Waplington) 1986. Photo: Ian Taylor

recently, in a very contemporary way, in some episodes of *Cracker*), family life (*Bread*), adult life (*The Boys from the Blackstuff* and *Aufwiedershen Pet*), and 'retirement' (*Last of the Summer Wine*). A particularly powerful site of television imagery of northern masculinity on television is in advertisements for beer or lager.

We are not aware of any dedicated historical study of 'northern male images' in television advertising, though any such study would clearly have to encompass a classic series released by Tetley's of Leeds in the 1980s depicting actually-existing industrial workers of the north of England – that is, in a period before the onset of the massive crisis of local manufacturing industry and local labour markets.[7] The mix of elements (or the *bricolage*) which make up the content of these iconic representations of a version of northern working-class masculinity in television advertisements and drama vary across the different media and over time, but there are also certain constant themes (most obviously, the emphasis on a firm connection made between masculinity and hard, physical work – 'graft', as it would be called in Sheffield).[8] This kind of representation seems to be preferred even for men's work which actually does not involve the same degree of muscular power as the work of the steel forgeman – and certainly nothing like the labours of the ultimate exemplar of physical work, the coal miner. The 'discursive frame' in the representation of the northern working man in these advertisements has not generally been attentive to the calibration of different physical demands in work, or, indeed, to different requirements of skill or 'graft' attaching to particular worker-positions. The dominant image within the advertisements for beer is most often that of the 'grafting' artisan/labourer 'downing his pint' – at the end of a working shift, or, perhaps, during a break from it.[9] A telling variation of this theme appears

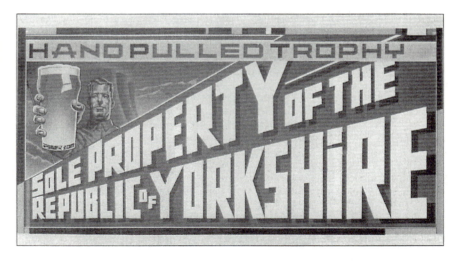

Figure 9.3 Whitbread Trophy billboard advertisement, South Yorkshire, early 1990s

in the new advertising campaign launched at the end of 1994 for William Stones' 'Sheffield Gold' bitter – which, after a sequence of images of the steel-production process, mobilises Newton's Third Law of Motion to proclaim that 'to every action [implicitly, hard physical 'graft'] there is an equal and opposite reaction [the need for a 'well-earnt' pint]'.[10]

These iconic representations of Sheffield 'men of steel', shown regularly on commercial television, operate at the level of the local imagination alongside a number of other nostalgic icons of local history, local identity, local forms of masculinity and local workplaces in the industrial and local history museums and also alongside a constantly expanding new trade in the production and sale of local history texts of various kinds available in local bookstores, the Sheffield City Library and other local outlets, which cover much the same ground. This new industry in local history includes, *inter alia*, a number of glossy booklets made from old photographs of the city, a series of quiz books about the history of the city and its people, books on local ghosts, urban myths or 'local trivia', and also some working-class autobiography, written mainly by retired steelworkers. Indeed, it is important to remember that the vast bulk of this literature on Sheffield's industrial past is being produced, quite consciously, for local people – precisely in the moment of the demise of the industrial past it attempts to recall.

It is impossible to see this explosion of local publishing as anything other than a mobilisation of nostalgic 'social memory', of the kind which Alessandro Portelli (1991) so brilliantly discusses in the case of Terni, Italy.[11] Portelli uses oral history to show how memory works in an old industrial city as a kind of myth-making linked to the lost utopian hopes of

Figure 9.4 Still from Stones' Breweries 'Sheffield Gold' television ad, winter 1994.
Photo: courtesy of Bass Breweries Ltd

Figure 9.5 'An equal and opposite reaction': later image from 'Sheffield Gold' television ad. Photo: courtesy of Bass Breweries Ltd

what survives of the local working class and labour movement, often without too strict a regard for empirical detail. But he is also attentive to the ways in which these myths can be reorganised in the current period by spokespeople for new local 'growth coalitions' and other important local figures, including, in some instances, local academics, trading in nostalgia or urban regeneration. Every one of these different memories is suffused with powerful and usually unstated assumptions with respect to gender, age and other social interests, and should be so read. But it is important to understand the significance of the new local industry in *nostalgia* in places like Sheffield as a series of written or oral testimonies about a kind of life that is now understood in these localities *to be extinct*, but to which, by implication, the consumers of this literature are presumed to long to return. The *Shorter Oxford English Dictionary*, after all, defines 'nostalgia' as 'a form of melancholia associated with a prolonged absence from one's country or home' or as 'severe homesickness'.

One of the key issues in respect of these nostalgic texts is whether they should be read merely as a contemporary instance of what Lasch argues is an *interminable* recycling of the past, particularly by the 'conservative' imagination unsettled by any prospect of progress and change (Lasch 1991) or whether the nostalgia of citizens of cities like Sheffield, in the aftermath of the crisis of the local labour market and other connected changes to local provision, accurately grasps the impossibility of 'progress' under present political and economic circumstances in Britain – and, therefore, equally accurately, accentuates its valorisation of a more 'authentic' existence imagined to be available in the past. These are appropriate matters for moral philosophy and psychological enquiry as well as for literature and poetry.[12] Sociologists may also want to investigate the actual prevalence or distribution of this kind of nostalgia, which may be less marked amongst women, new residents or immigrants in an area than amongst men. Our particular purpose, in this chapter, however, is to try and clarify the relationship between this constant re-working of *nostalgic scripts* about the history of 'Sheffield, the City of Steel' (which tries to authorise a continuation of the particular local configuration of hegemonic masculinity) and the particular gender practices and vocabularies exhibited by a group of 'angry young men' in the city in the mid-1990s.

SHEFFIELD STEEL

Before we turn to this analysis of the 1990s, however, we want to look more closely at the television advertisement for 'Sheffield Gold' released by Stones Breweries in 1994. The story told in these advertisements has a specific local (rather than a generalised class or even northern) resonance.[13] The beer is being presented, specifically, as the preferred drink of 'the City of Steel' – a connection that is underwritten by black-and-white footage of different parts of the steel-production process (the stoking of the furnace, the rolling of steel and, finally, the crucible splashing out its molten steel) which then bursts into a gold-tinted image of a pint of 'Sheffield Gold', then focusing on a team of steelworkers, and back to that pint of Gold bitter itself (identified both by name and logo on the side of the glass). The corporate video produced to accompany this new advertising campaign explains how Stones have recently changed their logo into a '1990s-style' image,[14] centred on Vulcan, the Roman god of fire and blacksmiths, and protector of craftsman.[15]

Sharon Zukin observes in her study of Weirton, a steel town in West Virginia:

> No industry has a more powerful image than steel. Its symbolic weight in the national economy reflects a host of material factors: the brute force required to make steel, the volume of capital investment in a mill, the size of the workforce engaged in smelting, pouring, casting and shipping, and the omnipresence of steel in all modern structures, from rail trestles, and bridge girders, to auto bodies, skyscrapers, airplanes and ships. Steel has power because it has been the lifeline of industrial society.
>
> (Zukin 1991: 59–60)

Steel has also always been associated with what Zukin calls 'a male production culture', involving workers using both skill and brawn, in teams, in a collective daily struggle in the workplace with the material world and with employers and managers (the 'Steelmasters'). In the American case:

> Since the days of Andrew Carnegie ... owners and managers have been brusque, forceful and often violent. If a worker was a 'man of steel', he faced no less an adversary than the steel baron, surrounded

by hired security guards and hand-picked elected officials.... The legacy of iron manufacture was a craft-dominated production process in which highly-skilled workers accumulated power on the basis of knowledge and technique. When a monopoly of ownership confronted a monopoly of skill, the resulting power struggles centred on the privileges of craftsmanship.

(ibid.: 61–2)

The development of the steel industry (the so-called 'Heavy Trades') in Sheffield followed on, during the second half of the eighteenth century, from the already-existing 'Light Trade' of cutlery, based in small mills or forges on the banks of the rivers coming down the valleys from the Peak District of Derbyshire and the West Riding. By the beginning of the seventeenth century, cutlery forges or 'wheels' were scattered up and down all five river valleys in 'Hallamshire', and an Act of Parliament of 1624 allowed these craftsmen to establish themselves as a self-governing guild – masters of their own trade – the Cutlers' Company. This company of 'cutlery Mesters' continues in existence to this day, primarily as a dining-

Figure 9.6 Little Mesters: table knife grinding, 1902
Source: Binfield *et al.* (1993)

club for senior figures in Sheffield's commercial middle class. But in the seventeenth century until the early nineteenth century, the idea of a 'proper Little Mester', or craftsman seen as a master of his own trade, was a concept used in Sheffield to refer, specifically and exclusively, to small manufacturers working out of small tenement workshops in the production of specialised high-quality domestic cutlery, knives, swords and related items. As Taylor has shown in a very impressive piece of local industrial research, these small manufacturers, or 'little Mesters', were nearly all of quite limited means, working in confined workshop spaces (Taylor 1993). Frequently, especially when dealing with large orders, these little Mesters would have to subcontract parts of the process out to other, even less well-established 'outworkers', to whom they may have given some kind of basic apprenticeship in certain skills of the cutlery trade. These outworkers, who usually aspired to graduate, in time, to being 'little Mesters' themselves, would rent out 'troughs or sides' (spaces sunk in the ground or corners in a rented tenement building given over to cutlery work) or, if they were very poor, would actually work at home (ibid.: 198).

Some of the 'little Mesters', did not work themselves (and, indeed, did not have craftsmen skills themselves), but existed instead as 'factors' or intermediaries, buying the labour of outworkers to fill particular orders. The little Mesters engaged in 'sweating of labour' were widely resented as 'bullies' and as parasites on the skills both of 'working Mesters' and outworkers. The nostalgic inscription of the working little Mester, sitting across the grinding wheels or working at the bench, and the factor, 'sweating out' the craft work, fudges this contradiction. So also does it suppress the reality of the particular gender order that was institutionalised in local trades. The 'little Mesters' were, by definition, always men – but the 'polishing up' of the finished product in the cutlery trade (and also in the small, but celebrated, pewter industry) would be done by women (the so-called 'buffer girls'). The workshops themselves, however, without exception were the preserve of the little Mester – characteristically older and more experienced than the apprentice outworkers – with a small number of 'buffer girls' working in workshops nearby, and a number of women, increasing in number towards the end of the nineteenth century, in low-paid ancillary tasks. In 1911, some 18 per cent of the total work-force employed in the cutlery industry were women, some in polishing, but others in warehouse work or packaging (ibid.: 207). The majority of these women were young, and would be laid off as soon as they were married. So this was a workplace culture in which 'the lasses' had to know their limited place within the workshop, and from which married women were systematically excluded. It was also a work *place* in which men bonded to other men, working as a group 'sweating up' an order, often against a deadline but with a stubborn craftsman's involvement in the quality of the cutlery produced, or, in the case of steel forgeworkers employed in the nearby Heavy Trades, as 'a team' relying on cooperation and muscle-power in a daily struggle with molten steel and furnaces.

The processes of male-bonding within the workplace, and the connected rituals of group initiation, vulgarity and profanity of humour, camaraderie and resistance to the steel boss and to external authority and convention outside the workplace, should be the subject of extended social historical work. But, as we shall see later, it is difficult to ignore the parallels between these forms of collective group practice amongst steelworkers and cutlers and the confident assertion of the power of young men in groups to defy convention and constraint, even in the absence of the dignity of work.[16]

Sheffield's steel industry developed significantly later than the cutlery trade, initially as a result of Benjamin Huntsman's invention of the casting crucible in 1740. The greatest development occurred over the next 100 years, and the Heavy Trades, of steel and metal manufacturing, reached their heyday (in terms of output and worldwide importance) in the 1840s (Tweedale 1993). In the late nineteenth and early twentieth century, steel production was consolidated amongst a small number of giant firms (the Steelmasters) with a continuing worldwide importance. What is not really detailed in the local histories of Sheffield and its various working-class

Figure 9.7 Stones' Breweries: new corporate logo, 1994.
Courtesy of Bass Breweries Ltd

Figure 9.8 Steel furnace gang, Vanadium Steel Company, Union Lane, Sheffield, early twentieth century. *Source*: Binfield *et al.* (1993)

neighbourhoods are the precise ways in which those employed in the Heavy Trades related to the little Mesters or outworkers in the cutlery trade – whether there was any significant spacial segregation of these occupational groups, of the kind which has been observed in other, larger industrial regions. What was not in doubt in the minds of local historians or other observers (like Edward Carpenter, the utopian socialist who lived just outside Sheffield in the early years of this century) was the strength of local identity and local culture in Sheffield, and its close relationship to the 'dual economy' of cutlery and steel. The social geographer, Nigel Thrift, was particularly impressed by the way that in each of the smaller districts of Sheffield, there had grown up:

> a set of class-specific institutions forming the node around which this way of life could be built: the workshop, obviously, the sick clubs (the proportion of artisans contributing to sick clubs was higher in Sheffield than in any other manufacturing town in England); the Sunday schools (often firmly in artisanal hands); the many small inns and beer houses; the numerous Methodist chapels (Methodism was the major denomination in Sheffield and 'democratic' Methodism was very popular); and the distinctively domestic character of the home (it was a male culture; fewer women worked than in Leeds).
>
> (Thrift 1987: 32)

He concludes:

Workshop-pub-chapel-house: these were the foci of what was almost an enclave mentality and what was certainly a very resistant culture: *a culture that controlled itself.*

(ibid.)

At the centre of this 'resistant culture', of course, was the 'little Mester' – a term which by the end of the nineteenth century was used, locally, to refer generally to all men employed in the Sheffield trades, in the Heavy and Light Trades alike, complicit as these men were in the local gender order. The term 'proper little Mester' is, in fact, double-edged in its local usage. It denotes an actual location in the industrial division of labour (as an employer of other labour) and distils some of the recognition, on the one hand, and resentment, on the other, attached to this local position of power. Specifically local references to 'proper little Mester' connote a man who is very self-important, unyielding, individualistic and intractable on questions of gender order. In its local Sheffield usage, the term is not dissimilar to the idea of a 'proper little madam' – when used as a description of a difficult, demanding, self-centred and spoilt young woman.[17]

Thrift's description of local culture in Sheffield does not address, in any critical way, the other side of this 'very resistant culture'. As early as 1918, for example, the classical economist, Alfred Marshall, had developed a keen interest in Sheffield as an example of what he wanted to call 'an industrial district' – in other words, as a district that had become very heavily dependent, culturally as well as economically, on a narrow industrial base (the metal trades), and which may have altogether become *too* reliant on that base, unable to innovate either horizontally into other industrial or other commercial fields. A continuing criticism of Sheffield steel and cutlery masters throughout the middle years of this century was the 'complacency' they exhibited with respect to the organisation of production, the continually developing international competition, and the effective marketing of steel and cutlery products, especially internationally. The essential conservatism of the dual economy may also be thought to be a faithful reflection of a stubborn and complacent stance of the local 'enclave culture' itself, particularly in respect of gender relations, specifically the kind of misogyny that was evident in the social organisation of the pubs, especially in the vicinity of the steelworks[18] as well as in many aspects of social life in Sheffield.

THE LOCAL CRISIS

The broad context for any analysis of the symbolic worlds and the behaviours of young men in north of England cities is set by the rapid decline of mass manufacturing industry of those cities over the last twenty-five years. If one accepts, following Paul Willis's arguments in the 1970s, that work is a primary institutional setting for the construction of masculinity (Willis 1976, 1977), then the decline of work and the disappearance of work settings and work experience for men will clearly be having a profound impact on male identity. What does not follow, however, is that this 'loss of work' necessarily entails the sudden and total evacuation of men from the *symbolic terrain* of work, or the loss of work references in the discursive construction of hegemonic forms of masculinity. During the ten years from 1979 to 1989, according to one analysis, 94 per cent of all job losses in England and Wales occurred north of a line drawn from the Wash to the Severn (Dickinson 1991: 76), and, although subsequent developments have involved significant unemployment in the south of England, the majority of the cities in the north continue to have official unemployment rates significantly above the national average. The absence of wage-labour, in this sense, is a defining feature of the local experience of many old manufacturing districts throughout the north, and has been so for some considerable time.

However, the crisis of the labour markets of the north of England during this period has taken a different form in different industrial regions or districts – notably, in terms of the first serious *moment of impact* of such a crisis, its *intensity* and *the character of local responses* (for example, in terms of levels of migration and population loss). Sheffield's crisis, in the early 1980s, was quite late to develop, by comparison with the local crises of the north-east (Tyneside, Wearside and the Durham Coalfield, in particular), which had really begun before the war but intensified from the late 1950s onwards (Byrne 1992: 39) and Merseyside, continuously since 1965 (Lane 1987: chapter 5). Unemployment in Sheffield had been steady throughout the 1960s at about 2 per cent of the labour force, increasing steadily in the late 1970s to between 4.3 and 5.1 per cent, with some local anxiety expressed about the small number of vacancies in the long-established cutlery and steel industries. Then, very suddenly:

> The storm broke with full force in the course of 1980. Taking the figures for January, and for the Sheffield travel to work area (TTWA), there was a rapid rise to 27,400 (9.3 per cent) in 1981 and a continuous rise thereafter to a peak of 47,500 in 1987, or 16.3 per cent of the registered labour force. It should be stressed that these were the figures *after* the systematic weeding-out of significant numbers of unemployed people from the official registers by a host of new government regulations. According to some calculations, the real figure was some 15,000 higher. For men the incidence of unemployment was more severe: thus in January 1987 it was 19.4 per cent for men as against only 11.8 per cent for women. It was also noticeable that the Sheffield unemployment rate, hitherto well below the national average, had risen steeply above it. In January 1987, while Sheffield registered 16.3 per cent unemployment, for example, the figure for the United Kingdom was 11.9 per cent.
>
> (Pollard 1993: 277)

What we want to argue here is that the crisis of Sheffield's local economy was also, precisely, a massive crisis for the 'very resistant culture' observed by Thrift, though in no sense a crisis that was interpreted entirely independently of the well-established local belief and understandings.

Nearly two-thirds of the loss of local employment since 1980 can be attributed specifically to the 'radical re-structuring' of the Sheffield steel industry.[19] In the period between 1979 and 1986 in particular, 50,294 of the jobs lost in the local labour market were in 'metal manufacture' – 69 per cent of the total (72,863). A further measure of the decline of metal trades generally in Sheffield was the fact that during the brief 'recovery' of 1987–9 only about 1,000 new jobs were created in 'metal manufacturing' whilst the service and financial sectors added about 8,500 such opportunities (ibid.: 278).

There are two connected, defining features of this local crisis of the labour market in Sheffield. One of these – the enormous loss of full-time jobs within the locality for relatively unskilled manual (male) workers, with some (by no means numerically equivalent) increase in the overall number of poorly-paid, temporary or part-time jobs in the service industries, many of them taken by women – is general to most of the old manufacturing areas, and therefore a large part of the north of England. A rather more specific feature of the crisis in Sheffield, however, is its suddenness and its relatively late development: as late as 1980, in nearly all contemporary accounts, there was still a widespread belief in the locality in the continuing resilience of the long-established 'dual economy' of cutlery and steel, and an equally widespread sense that the local City Council ('the Corporation') and local Labour Party were continuing, competently, to manage local affairs in the universal interest (from transport policy through to local economic futures). The remainder of the decade in Sheffield, however, witnessed a rapid sequence of steel-plant restructuring and closure, with a massive haemorrhaging of jobs and then, within a matter of months, the symbolic razing to the ground of the works that had dominated Attercliffe, Darnall and Tinsley areas throughout the previous 100–150 years. There was a powerful sense in which the 'shock', which has been identified by psychological writers in individuals facing unemployment for the first time, was a 'collective and social shock' for Sheffield as a whole – a sudden and unexpected body blow to a city which had thought it could survive on the self-sufficient regime of its established 'dual-economy'.[20] This sense of shock was certainly informed by a collective sense of the rapidly developing impoverishment of the city – not just in respect of the physical fabric (the condition of the city centre itself being an important symbolic topic throughout this period) but also of its citizens, large numbers of whom fell into a poverty for which they had not been culturally or politically prepared in the 1970s. One measure of the poverty engulfing the city was the survey compiled in 1993 by the Opposition's Spokesman for Industry, Derek Fatchett, identifying the loss of 'gross domestic product' for South Yorkshire between 1979 and 1989 (from 95.7 to 79.1, where 100 was the average of all counties in 1979) as the steepest of any metropolitan county (*Guardian*, 20 December 1993). So, also, was there a powerful local sense that the suddenness and the severity of the crisis in the local labour market was intimately connected to the sudden sharp increase in crime in the city and across the wider county of South Yorkshire (with an absolute increase in the number of recorded crimes of 76 per cent between 1988 and 1993), one of the fastest increases anywhere in England and Wales. The increase in recorded crime in South Yorkshire in 1993 was absolutely the largest of any police force area in the country (14 per cent up on 1992) (*Home Office* crime figures, 19 April 1994) and at the end of 1994, in a year in which some decreases in crime were reported across much of England and Wales, South Yorkshire was one of five police force areas continuing to show an increase (*Guardian*, 28 September 1994). A city and county area which for many years had thought of itself as having a lower rate of crime and related problems than urban areas elsewhere in the north no longer felt it was exempt.

Sheffielders' response to this sudden and fundamental sense of crisis and decline has also exhibited distinctive forms. As in all such crises of the local labour market, some people left – migrating out from the city and region to other parts of the country or abroad in search of work or better prospects. But there are indications that the out-migration from Sheffield during the 1980s, at the height of the crisis, was significantly less marked than in other de-industrialised northern cities: the population loss in the city between the 1981 and 1991 Census was measured at 41,219 (7.2 per cent of the 1981 population of 530,843). South Yorkshire as whole declined in population by only 3.6 per cent.[21] In the same period, Liverpool lost 13.9 per cent of its population and Manchester 12.1 per cent. Beattie has provided a journalistic ethnography describing a wide variety of strategies which have been adopted by local Sheffield people (especially by adult ex-steel workers and other individuals with different kinds of marketable skills) to stay in the city and survive via their activities in the local hidden and night-time economies (Beattie 1986). There is evidence throughout the city in the 1990s of the further development of alternative survival strategies that have been identified, for example, by Mingione in his analysis of various de-industrialised locales across Europe (Mingione 1994), particularly in respect of crime, and also a powerful sense of a popular recognition that no 'quick fix' was available to the problems of de-industrialisation, joblessness and poverty in the 'City of Steel' – relatively unprepared as it was for the new circumstances of global competition.

LITTLE MESTERS OF THE 1990s[22]

We are finally in a position to address the intense focus group discussion held between Karen Evans and Ian Taylor, and eight young men (aged between 16 and 19) on probation orders with the South Yorkshire probation service (Billy, Des, Eddie, Gopher, Mick, Paul, Steff and Zeke) in Sheffield on 27 January 1994.[23] All but one of these young men were born in Sheffield, and all eight were brought up in one of the two most demonised areas of the city ('the Manor', a council estate first developed in the 1930s),[24] and Pitsmoor (part of Burngreave, a well-established Victorian residential area in Sheffield's East End which has recently been constituted as home to second and third generation African-Caribbean Sheffielders).

This discussion was one amongst many conducted in Sheffield on different uses of urban space and the subjective definitions of different groups in the local public about 'recent changes in the city', as part of a larger study on everyday life in north of England cities (Taylor, Evans and Fraser 1996). As in all the other groups, these Sheffield young men were asked primarily for their descriptions of how they spent their days, what they did and where. Given that these young men were all unemployed, we fully expected to hear stories about a variety of time-filling activities, and also about long hours of idleness and domestic parasitism. Beatrix Campbell's study of the Meadow Well Estate in Newcastle on Tyne quotes one of the lawyers for the young men arrested after riots as saying:

> These men live in a twilight world. . . . They're lying around on the sofa in their boxer shorts, watching videos; they have their tea when it's put in front of them, then they go TWOCing and burgling.
> (quoted in Campbell 1993: 178)

Grafting

There was no question that this twilight world existed in Sheffield as much as in Newcastle. Billy informed us he 'probably' would get up about 12 or 1 o'clock, 'mope around the house a bit, go and annoy my social worker'. But what the research really had not anticipated, as a key feature of the way in which local young men were re-fashioning masculinity in the context of poverty, was the committed description of their criminal activity as a demanding daily *regime of work*. Universally, these eight young men referred to this activity – exactly in the manner of their parents' and grandparents' generations' discussion of work in the steel trades – as 'grafting'. They also referred, repeatedly, to their own membership of a 'firm', as if employed by a small, functioning enterprise, or a 'crew', as if they were a member of a working 'team' of manual workers. There was also a suggestion that these crews were structured around a kind of apprenticeship system, helping younger 'lads and lasses' learn the trade. Some local adults, acting as receivers of stolen valuables, seemed to have relevance for these lads, though never to the extent, for example, that the craftsman would have had influence over a young apprentice in the earlier years of the Light and Heavy Trades. The monies obtained through burglary or other theft were seen very definitely as being *well earnt* – the product, indeed, of 'graft', which, it was insisted, involved considerable skill (for example, in tech- niques of quick entry ('doing a snoop') into different kinds of houses). Like thousands of other young men involved in car-theft, joy-riding and 'surf-riding' across the de-industrialised north of England, these young men also placed an enormous value on their knowledge of cars (and notably the speed at which they could immobilise different types of car alarm, and enter and drive different vehicle-types).

It is quite clear that these particular young men, like the 'adult villains' studied by north American criminologists in the early 1970s (Irwin 1970; Letkemann 1973) and the full-time thieves in Sweden interviewed more recently by Akerstrom (1993), saw themselves as being engaged in a kind of 'work', to which, in the absence of what they would consider acceptable alternatives, they expressed a certain fatalistic commitment. There was also a broad recognition, it should be said, that their activities were not thought equivalent to the jobs which their parents may have 'held down'. Paul commented on how,

> I'm 20. I haven't had a job since nineteen eighty something, you know what I mean? They won't give you one. Everybody is going grafting now, aren't they?

Taking unemployment as given, Stuart set out his own style of *carpe diem* calculus. If the only alternative to grafting and doing drugs with his 'crew' is sitting around the house or probation hostel watching telly 'not doing nowt', he counsels another, less enterprising member of the group, to accept the risk of prison:

> Now us, fair enough, we're going to get sent down. You'd be sitting in that house, and we'll be sitting in a cell, but before we get sent down, we'd get smashed out of our heads every day. So we've got something out of it.

However, involvement in this 'alternative lifetime strategy' did not mean that the young men were alienated from *any* idea of work or graft (they saw themselves as skilled and hard-working risk-takers) or even from the idea of a formal labour market, but there was also a clear idea of what might look like a reasonable price for their labour. Paul complained how,

> They put you on YTS, thirty-five pound a week. What the fuck's that, man? It's worse than school, that fucking YTS. I'm not having somebody ordering me about for thirty-five pounds.

There was great reluctance, in particular, to accept the regulation associated with government training programmes. Paul admitted he had been 'on every YTS in Sheffield' and he had been '*sacked* off every one, every single one'. 'Owt you can learn' (There's nothing to be learnt). These young men were not here engaged in an avoidance of work as such, though, *like the little Mesters before them*, they were not prepared to accept 'cut-rate ' wages for their labour. In this sense, the distorted or 'protest' strategic stances which they adopted towards the world resonated the recalcitrant stances of the little Mester and forgeworker in earlier moments of the city's history. In 1908, for example, a local trade union organiser, Robert Holmshaw complained about the culture of the cutlery 'mester' in the following terms:

> Very informal habits [had been] formed, and a set of traditions handed down which it is easy to see arose entirely out of peculiar circumstances under which they worked. To this cause we must attribute the freedom from restraint which is so characteristic a feature of the Sheffield cutlery worker today.
>
> (Robert Holmshaw, quoted in Taylor 1993: 203–4)

We are not arguing that there is a direct and causal connection between historically occurring or 'imagined' masculinities of the past and the protest masculinity of young men in the present. We simply want to underline the ways in which the reference to 'graft' and to local work practices and traditions has a salience in the symbolic re-working of masculinity in which the young unemployed Sheffield men were apparently engaged. We are also wanting to suggest that, whilst the metaphor of 'crime as work' is obviously not unique to de-industrialised Sheffield, the particular discursive inflection placed on vocabularies of crime-as-work do have a specific local-historical character.

Misogyny

Another quite inescapable and defining dimension of these young men's 'protest masculinity' was the exaggerated form of the misogyny they continually articulated. Bob Connell had observed a similar pattern in his group of young men in Sydney, Australia – on the one hand, a resentful dependence on mother for domestic provision, and, on the other, episodic sexual encounters with young women without commitment. The deep misogyny encountered in our Sheffield group, however, involved some specific local language. The younger girls who 'knock about' with 'the crews' were known as 'little scraggies' or 'little nookie tramps', whilst Paul, in particular, insisted with great venom, in respect of the girls of his own age in his own locality (the Manor):

> Manor lasses,[25] you're just talking *mucky*. You don't want to know them. We've all been through them, and now they're gone.

Steff reacted, with equal force, to the group beginning to talk about going to town with 'girlfriends',

> staying with a girlfriend. It's talking to a brick, d'you know what I mean? You can't earn money with a girlfriend. You've got to get about to earn money. If you don't walk nowhere, you can't find it – unless she's the kind of bird what shoplifts. Then you get her to do it all *and* let her get to take rap. Like most people just sit about, you know, with a girlfriend expecting the money or the job to come to them, but it dun't.

> (emphasis in original)

If girls were not 'little scraggies', then they were 'lasses with babbies'. The young men as a whole were clearly dismayed at the thought of girls their own age shouldering responsibility for child-rearing. This may also underscore these young men's awareness that (despite their peripatetic predations across town) they too are compelled to spend large proportions of their daily round within the constraining and shabby space of the estate. These themes (of constraint, disgust and misogyny) are apparent in the many disparaging references made, for example, to council accommodation where there were concentrations of single mothers (like the legendary Kelvin Flats a large block of high-rise deck-access flats, now demolished). In one exchange, Eddie observed how:

> You walk under Kelvin, and you can guarantee tha gonna see a fucking flying saucer, a telly or something.

To which Paul replied, with a show of disgust:

> I walked through, and a big, sweaty, dirty nappy splatted about that far away from me.

It is a moot point, in one sense, whether these expressions constitute simply and only a form of misogyny or whether it is also and primarily a commentary on the demoralised domesticity to which many of them are now condemned. There is certainly a sense, however, in which the misogyny expressed by these lads is a contemporary but highly exaggerated and neurotic expression of the 'traditional' misogyny of Sheffield's cutlers and steelworkers in the earlier post-war period (reading the daily tabloid press and decorating their snap (lunch) cabins with pornography, or the outworkers in the cutlery trade engaged in a ribald daily banter with the 'buffer girls'). In all kinds of ways, there are real continuities between the angry misogyny of this 'protest masculinity' and the more longstanding local forms of misogyny, especially in terms of language, but also in terms of actual practices associated with 'the proper little Mester'. These young men, like their fathers and their grandfathers, had absolutely no interest in the idea of 'going to town, shopping', which they saw by definition as an activity done by women 'with babbies'. They would only 'go to town' on Saturday evenings, to one particular nightclub, *Roxy's*, assuming they had some money. But it is difficult to find evidence that the little Mesters right into the early post-war period behaved very differently, except only that the Saturday evening, if spent 'in town', would have been spent in certain pubs (or on certain pub-crawls or 'runs') rather than nightclubs. What *is* really distinctive about the direction and shape of the misogyny of these little Mesters, we think, is the way in which women and girls in particular, and respectable working-class domesticity in general, are now contemplated: knocking about with younger girls – 'little nookie tramps' – was one thing, but young *women* in general were now identified as a feared and despised Other, alongside members of visible ethnic minorities in the city (feared, in part, because they might be 'doing rather better' in school or in the local labour market).

White trash: 'the bottom rung' in de-industrialised Sheffield

The young men who were interviewed in Sheffield, whose aspirations had been forged around a particular local industrial social structure and a particular gender order, were fighting losing battles on many connected fronts. Surrounded by nostalgic inscriptions of 'proper little Mesters' (on television as well as in many local shopping malls and city centre streets), they seemed to be smarting from the loss of the possibility of re-living these forms of masculinity – in part, because of the crisis of local manufacturing industry, but also, importantly, because of increasing competition within the labour market and changes in the gender order. First, despite the sexual terms in which they express their exaggerated contempt for their female contemporaries, the possibility of their subordinating young women in any kind of traditional domestic arrangement of the respectable working class were increasingly remote. Second, they voiced a specific fear and resentment in respect of race which has two distinct dimensions. On the one hand, there is a palpable fear of 'Rastas' in another area of the city (Pitsmoor/Burngreave) who they perceive to engage in an altogether 'heavier' form of grafting (involving aggressive marketing strategies and guns).

> You can't burgle a house on Pitsmoor. You could do a snoop on Pitsmoor, you could walk in and there would be an eight-foot Rasta looking at you . . . with a shotgun.
>
> (Steff)

According to Eddie, these Rastas would 'beat your head in, if you don't buy their draw' (marijuana). On the other hand, there is a specific and very local resentment of losing out *on their patch* – for example, 'down the social' – to the Somali refugee families who were housed on the Manor and Upperthorpe estates by the City Council in the mid-1980s. Eddie was particularly wounded by (and still smarted from) being called 'white trash' by Somali pupils while still at school. There is a pressing sense creeping through here of what Jack Miles, writing on old industrial areas in the United States, once called 'the struggle for the bottom rung' in a declining market of work, housing and other provision (Miles 1992). There is a barely suppressed sense amongst these young men of being 'white trash', surplus to the requirements of local capital and 'the (white British) nation', a sentiment which might in principle render them ready recruits to some form of fascist movement.

At the same time, it is clear that these Sheffield young men still have a primarily *local* concept of themselves, above all, as 'proper little Mesters' on their own patch – or, in other words, as local sons of their local fathers, looking to do some 'real graft' (for the right price) like some of their fathers or most of their grandfathers. It is in this sense that Stones Breweries' marketing strategy for Sheffield Gold plays on the lads' preferred sense of identity as *local artisans*, even at a time where no serious heavy industry remains. The advertising additionally evokes the rhythm of the working day (punctuated by shift work and ending in the evening in the pub) – a rhythm that is absent from the timelessness of a day spent either 'on blow' in front of the television or on frenetic journeys to crime and grafting. The use of pubs by the young lads is a problem in several other senses. As we indicated earlier, they may or may not have the money for an evening's drinking, depending on the success of their grafting. They are also sometimes nervous about sitting as 'a team' or 'a crew' in a public house which might be visited by the police or by other crews, with whom they might be involved in some territorial or other struggle. Investigative television reporters researching protection rackets in pubs on council estates in Salford, Manchester suggest that one solution to this problem is for crews virtually to colonise a pub for their own use on a more-or-less permanent basis (*The Cook Report*, ITV, December 1994), but we have no evidence on this in Sheffield.

Their own place

The 'grafting' in which these young men and their 'crew' were engaged, however, was conducted along the lines of a sortie, on the one hand, searching out criminal opportunities across a wide variety of areas in the city, and, on the other, looking for spaces which some kind of domination could be achieved (over a stretch of park, street-corner or other location). In a different urban location, in his ethnographic work in inner-city districts in Sydney, Bob Connell noted the attempts being made by young men to achieve some dominance in the interstices of the city (Carrigan, Connell and Lee 1985: 83).

> We don't do it in our own areas. It's like doing it on your own doorstep, int it? We'll just go somewhere else. Go to some area, then go to another area, keep on going round earning money. It all goes on drugs anyway. Skint by next day.
>
> (Steff)

Zeke insisted that the more experienced grafters would move 'well out of their own areas' into neighbourhoods like Bents Green, which he described bluntly as a place 'where there's money' and, rather more lyrically, as somewhere where,

> when you see the sun shining on a tree, you see gold! When you see the sun shining on a tree down here, all you see is muck.[26]

The home territories for these young men, however, were the streets of their own area and their own houses.

> Manor is its own little town. There's not many people who go off to do a graft, and they end up back on the Manor as soon as they've done it.
>
> (Eddie)

On the Manor Estate, there was heavy use in the day of a local church youth club ('on the church'). In the evenings and weekends (which their forebears would have spent in the pubs), they took over the local streets and periodically retreated into their own homes for food, to watch television or videos, or to sleep. The rest of the time, on their return from 'grafting', they might move around the area, within a very small radius, finding a place for a smoke of marijuana ('a draw') or looking 'for a laugh'. The use of chemical drugs did not seem to involve the discovery or colonisation of any one locale, though it might be associated with other activities (including car-driving and even just watching television at home in a family situation). So Steff would,

> sneak 'em in during the day whilst you're sat watching telly. You don't get caught.

In contrast to earlier generations of Sheffield working men, then, these 'little Mesters' had no space of their own (either in the works or the pubs) endowed on them by their role in a local industrial structure. They were actively involved in the creation of an alternative daily life (around the home, 'our street' or 'the church'), interspersed by the 'journey to crime', primarily for 'grafting' but also, in many instances, to purchase drugs. The young men had a clear 'mental map' of the city, associated in their minds with particular patterns and kinds of drug use. Some parts of the Manor Estate, according to Eddie, were dominated by 'smack heads', with one family 'lucky not to have had their house blown up by now'. Burngreave was the place to buy 'good draw' from 'the Rastas'. There was also a developed sense of *the risks* associated with particular areas, not least in respect of apprehension by police or security guards, or other eventualities.[27] There was a clear hierarchical evaluation of different drugs and different patterns of drug use which, in the refined knowledge-claims and commitment brought to these distinctions, was reminiscent of nothing so much as the language and commitment which the Little Mester and the steel forge-worker might, in reality as well as in imaginary representation, bring to the discussion of different beers. So also, the animated and showy discussion of the merits of the different cars they had stolen had its equivalent, linguistically, in the discussion that can be heard in many a commercial office building or read in men's upmarket 'style magazines'. There was less evidence that these young men engaged in talk about football or sport as a way of stressing their local identity or as a way of affirming their relationship to earlier generations of Sheffield men.[28] Indeed, they seemed to be quite disconnected in their grafting activities from older men, apart from the connections they made with older receivers on the estate.

CONCLUSION

The primary purpose of our chapter has been to think about the form of 'protest masculinity' encountered in 1994 in Sheffield amongst a small group of young men in trouble with the law in that city. Our analysis turns on both a discursive and material context. Discursively, the form of protest masculinity being enacted involves an angry and aggressive accentuation of the vocabularies (local slang, folk-sayings, local knowledge and myth) and behaviour and practice (grafting and misogyny) known, locally, to have been characteristic of the 'little Mester' – a *locally* 'hegemonic masculinity', which for all that it was contested, dominated everyday life in that city in the era of steel production. Since the demise of the steel and cutlery industry in the early 1980s, this re-working of masculinity has been profoundly nostalgic. It has coincided with the emergence of a pronounced interest in local heritage and the history of the city and its industry, precisely at the moment of drastic de-industrialisation. It should be noted, of course, that there is little evidence of significant support amongst the enthusiastic consumers of such heritage for the forms of protest masculinity exhibited by the young men of Sheffield, deprived of their entitlements to be Little

Masters in the 1990s. But the re-working of masculinity itself has occurred in circumstances in which the aspiration of 'being a man' through employment in heavy manufacturing industry (graft) or skilled artisanship (craft) are widely understood in the locality to have become remote possibilities indeed. So these young Sheffield men are engaged in a practical struggle for 'the bottom rung' in a desperate local labour market, and many are obviously learning to graft in the hidden economy of crime. It may be that crime is the only practice in which these young lads can gain a little Mastery.

NOTES

1 The first two objectives of this chapter are the product of continuing discussion between ourselves about a city we know well and continue to visit on a regular basis. One author of this chapter (Taylor) was born and bred in Sheffield and was employed at the university between 1971 and 1981, whilst the other (Jamieson) lived and worked in that city between 1974 and 1981. Jamieson's interest in the young offenders in Sheffield arises from her work as a teacher/social worker there during that period.

2 The research in question is the project undertaken from the University of Salford during 1991–4 into 'The public scene of well-being: a taxonomy of publics and space' (ESRC Grant R-000-23-3048). This research is discussed at length in Taylor, Evans and Fraser (1996), but has also resulted in various other reports cf. Evans, Fraser and Taylor (1995), Evans and Fraser (1995) and Evans (1995).

3 There is a striking parallel between Adler's account of the masculine crisis and the account provided of the recruitment of young men into 'subcultures of delinquency' by American sociologists of crime in the 1950s, especially Albert Cohen (1960) and Walter Miller (1958), but this goes unremarked in Connell's discussion.

4 For further details of this statue, and other aspects of the internal and external architecture of the Meadowhall centre, and also the history of its construction, and its impact on the local economy, see the Meadowhall Leisure Shopping Education Pack 1995.

5 The image of a steelworker, with helmet and muffler, was originally submitted to a competition organised by the local evening newspaper, *The Star*. Comprising 30,000 bricks in all, and sponsored by local brick companies, it was completed by the bricklayer Mr Henry Walsh in August 1986 (*The Star*, Sheffield, 2 August 1986). The image presented is reminiscent of some of the socialist-realist imagery produced in the Soviet Union in the 1920s, though we would argue that the gaze of this particular steelworker does not have a Messianic, Soviet quality. Curiously, some other commercial advertising (like the Whitbread Trophy advertisement released in the early 1980s, complete with a direct and confident male gaze and a reference 'to the Republic' (sic) of Yorkshire) does seem to carry this kind of message.

6 The northern associations evoked by the famous Hovis advertisements are very much an historical construction. Even though the original germ bread was first milled, in the late nineteenth century, in Macclesfield, the firm has been based for much of this century in Windsor. The famous 'Bike Ride' commercial, depicting a young boy pushing a load of loaves up hill and then free-wheeling down again, was filmed on Gold Hill in Shaftesbury, Dorset in November 1973, and for several years the 'voice-over' on Hovis advertisements was that of 'Thomas Hardy country' rather than the north.

7 Such a history of beer advertisements would also have to examine the 'decoding' by northern men of Heineken's massive billboard campaign in 1993, foregrounding the Chippendale male strippers, and also the series of mellow beach-scenes in a series of advertisements for Carlsberg Lager, shown in March 1995, both seemingly aimed at women. The 'space' in which beer advertising is encoded and decoded is increasingly 'a contested terrain'.

8 The familiar connection for earlier generations of Sheffield workers between 'graft' and leisure is re-asserted by Wesley, in our focus group, as he asserted that he and his mates

'were grafting [stealing] in the day . . . to get in the pub' (which otherwise they could not afford to patronise). 'It will be that way *all week*,' he continued, 'non-stop.'

9   The use of drink by the 'Little Mesters' proper – the cutlers – is another area of study, though uncontrolled drinking would certainly have imperilled the status they claimed as the local aristocracy of labour. (See also our discussion of the history of drink in the steelworks in note 18.)

10 The use of Newton's law in this advertisement also carries suggestions, of course, of 'the laws' of social life in which Lacanian analysis has shown great interest – notably, the Law of the Father, naturalising particular arrangements of gender inequality.

11 See also the discussion of 'class and group memory in western society' in Fentress and Wickham (1992).

12 We are aware that our discussion of the relationship between 'nostalgic representation' and issues of personal authenticity and identity (including local identification) cuts across important theoretical issues in moral and social philosophy (on the problematic idea of authenticity itself), notably as addressed by Charles Taylor (1991), and also the argument that nostalgia is just one way of suppressing the inescapable 'disappointment' of experience of the life-course, inevitable in any historical period (Craib 1994). We do not want to ignore these issues, but neither do we want to downplay the specific reality or the psychological immediacy of the loss of industrial destiny for Sheffield men in the 1980s and 1990s, and the specific loss of social attachment which this particular economic transformation has produced.

13 One pioneering study of differences in gender relations in manufacturing areas was that of Michael Savage, pointing to local labour markets in different regions in the nineteenth century that were absolutely dominated by men (Tyneside, the Durham and Yorkshire coalfields), labour markets where there was some equality of participation in both formal and informal economies (the north-east Lancashire weaving districts) and market in which relatively large numbers of women were employed, albeit in segregated spaces (Dundee) (Savage 1987).

14 It is intriguing, however, to note the resemblances between Stones' new logo and the logos adopted by the ever-expanding private security industries in different parts of the north of England. The abstract representation in both instances is of a form of 'hard masculinity'.

15 A statue of Vulcan has sat on top of the Sheffield Town Hall for over 150 years as a signifier evoking the pride and self-confidence of the 'City of Steel' itself, and Vulcan was also the name adopted for many years by the straight-talking feature-writer(s) of the local evening newspaper, the *Sheffield Star*.

16 So, for example, Stuart triumphantly proclaimed in the discussion that 'We're idiots when we're on us [our] patch, and we're even worse when we're off.'

17 In Sheffield, the 'proper little madam' description finds local expression in the pejorative reference to any such woman, especially a middle-aged or elderly woman, as 'Lady Muck' or 'Lady Got-nowt'.

18 We know of no history of the public house in Sheffield (though surely there will be one forthcoming as a part of the mushrooming writing of local history in that city). But there is enough scattered information to support the general thesis advanced by Valerie Hey on the pub as 'a patriarchal institution' (Hey 1986). Three qualifications are, however, necessary in the Sheffield case. The taverns and pubs in the vicinity of the steelworks were all set up to accommodate the 'nine o'clock break' during night-shifts – the start and finish of which would be signalled by the works buzzer. This hour of drinking served as some kind of compensation for 'working nights' and was useful for combating dehydration, especially on summer evenings. But it was an hour of disciplined drinking, which experienced forgeworkers knew how to handle. In an industry placing such a premium on disciplined teamwork, the rationales behind the fear of the 'boozer' or the man 'who could not hold his beer' are self-evident. The domination of this kind of pub by steel men was almost total, although there is evidence that workers would sometimes arrange to meet members of their family during this break to complete some unfinished business of the day (cf. Sollit 1983). The second modification to Hey's thesis would be in relation to the public houses situated near to Little Mesters' workshops. These pubs would set aside one part of the pub, often 'the Snug', for the use of the 'buffer girls' and

other women working in 'support jobs' in the Light Trades, so setting up a particularly local segregation of young women and men. Third, however, there is some evidence of the heavy use of public houses on the new post-war council estates by women, perhaps as an alternative to the pre-war wash-house, as their own site of sociability. Joanna Bourne quotes a study of 1954 by Hodges and Smith of a Sheffield estate where over half the women interviewed claimed that they visited a public house on a weekly basis or more regularly (Bourne 1994: 144). Male domination of particular local spaces for all that it is a matter of considerable anxiety, is uneven across different areas and different locations in the city.

19 This reference to 'radical restructuring' of the Sheffield steel industry involves a recognition of the argument that the actual level of steel production in the Sheffield area, on many measures, has actually been maintained, but with a quite massively reduced work-force.

20 For a detailed account of the 1980s' recession in Sheffield, and the initiatives taken by the City Council and also the Sheffield Development Corporation (including the World Student Games of 1991), as well as the responses of different local publics, see Taylor, Evans and Fraser (1996: chapter 3).

21 1991 Census: County Report, South Yorkshire, Part 1, Table B.

22 We are not claiming that the eight young men involved in this research were representative in any straightforward sense either of all men in Sheffield or of the youthful population. But it may help the reader to know that the 1991 Census registered 65,917 people aged 16 to 24 in Sheffield, of which 4.4 per cent (2,900) were on government schemes and another 14.2 per cent (9,360) officially unemployed.

23 The ESRC team would like to acknowledge the help of the South Yorkshire Probation Service, and particularly Christine Shann, in setting up this group discussion.

24 In 1994, a local survey found that unemployment on the Manor Estate as a whole was in the order of about 29 per cent, but also that there were particular streets and small areas where the rate was more than 50 per cent of the population over 18. About one quarter of the people unemployed on the Manor has been unemployed for more than ten years. Martin Halsall 'Sheffield forges new links to help pioneer Job Centres', *Guardian*, 25 January 1994.

25 Manor lasses' is a reference to girls living on the troubled Manor Estate, mentioned earlier.

26 With all respect to its residents, we need to clarify that Bents Green is actually a mixed, predominantly **lower**-middle-class area. However, Bents Green **is** easily accessible by bus and car, and also, from these young men's own point of view, quite prosperous. It has the additional benefit of being a relatively easy area for them to be inconspicuous. (Further discussion of young people's idiosyncratic 'mental image of the city' is advanced in Taylor, Evans and Fraser (1996: chapter 11).) In the more unambiguously affluent areas of the city, like Dore, there was more of a problem, though one of the more experienced young men indicated that the best strategy when challenged in Dore was to claim to be a resident of Limb Lane, a local authority childrens home on the outskirts of this affluent village.

27 Some evidence about the strategic assessments of the dangers associated with particular places in the daily search of young people (of different ethnic backgrounds) for money or drugs in a Californian industrial town is presented, in a series of individual interviews with these young men, by Elliott Currie (1991).

28 The achievement of an intimate and persuasive knowledge of major local football clubs (particularly Sheffield Wednesday in the Premier League) has been made very problematic by the admission prices now charged at the all-seater Hillsborough stadium, and the alternative source of 'football knowledge' – the saturation coverage of football on satellite and terrestrial television – is less reliable as a form of local football 'education' (cf. Taylor 1995).

Part IV

NARRATING CITYSCAPES

10

THIS, HERE, NOW

Imagining the modern city

James Donald

To imagine is to make present to my mind's eye what is absent. As I write, enervated by summer diesel smog and distracted by the noise of drilling from across the road, *imagining* the city may seem, on the face of it, a perverse and redundant activity. The city is hardly *not there*. Why do I need to imagine it?

My argument is that, however insistent this traffic, these buildings, and those inconsiderate bastards may be, my sense of this combination of information and affects as uniquely urban is mediated through a powerful set of political, sociological, and cultural associations. It is these connotations that are condensed in the symbolic space *the city*. You know what I mean about being in the city, not only because your lungs and ears have been assaulted like mine, but because you too operate with the city as a category of thought and experience.

This is the immaterial city which, Ihab Hassan argues, has 'in-formed history from the start, moulding human space and time ever since time and space moulded themselves to the wagging tongue'.[1] It is the city which embodies a will to create social relations that transcend the animal or even the tribal. Implicit in the project of the city, then, are the hubris and the pathos mythologised in the fate of Babel and Babylon. The republican city, the city as public sphere, and the rational, planned city continue to articulate the hopes and the despair of modernity. The ideal of civilisation, the creation of society and the formation of self made possible only through the *civis*, is forever betrayed by the grimy reality of an alien and unhomely environment. But by now, the city also indicates – and perhaps produces – a unique way of seeing and being. Unable to contain the unbounded spread of London, Paris, Berlin, or New York in an all-encompassing image, we recall the city through metonymic images and fleeting events. These include the stereotypes of the Eiffel Tower or the Manhattan skyline. But often we share the pragmatic urban aesthetic shown by the heroine of Virginia Woolf's *Mrs Dalloway*: 'what she loved was this, here, now, in front of her; the fat lady in the cab.'

Does 'the city' also stand for, or demand, a certain style of politics, an art of living together in the *polis*? I think that it may, but that this political craft is not to be found in the utopian dreams and schemes of the great urbanists and planners from Edwin Chadwick to Otto Wagner, Le Corbusier, and Robert Moses. I take seriously a warning from that most practical and commonsensical of urban critics, Jane Jacobs: 'Designing a dream city is easy; rebuilding a living one takes imagination.'[2] Those who fantasise about turning the city into an efficient machine, with all its component parts flawlessly engineered and geared, misrecognise the space of the city. They see it as a territory to be bounded, mapped, occupied and exploited, a population to be managed and perfected. This is the overweening dream of Enlightenment rationality: to render the city transparent, to get the city right, and so to produce the right citizens. It is a dream which, in disavowing them, is doomed to reproduce and repeat the anxieties, repressions, and censorships that provoke the dream. It wishes away the aggression, the conflict, and the paranoia that are also part of urban experience. The city is not a problem that can be solved. It is the eternal, impossible question of how we strangers can live together. Rebuilding a living city – a city which jumbles together multiple and conflicting differences – therefore requires less a utopian plan than a poetics of political imagination.[3]

How would that poetic imagining differ from the hubristic rationalism of the total planners? First, it would show a different understanding of *space*, seeing it as something other and more than a field of mathematical calculation and political instrumentalism. This imagination would be sensitive to the history of modes of mapping and representing space – the cone of vision, perspective, the plane of representation, the conventions of cartography, the simultaneism of cubism, cinematic montage, and so forth – which themselves entail different modes of subjective experience of space. It would therefore also take account of what Victor Burgin, following Freud and Lacan, calls 'the history of psychical, or interior space', space as projection and introjection.[4] The *living* space of the city exists as representation and projection and experience as much as it exists as bricks and mortar or concrete and steel. That is why rebuilding the living city means taking account of this other sense of space.

Where does this other space exist? In Doris Lessing's novel *The Four-Gated City* (1969), the protagonist, Martha Quest, is a Marxist intellectual recently arrived in the London of the 1950s from what was then Rhodesia. Martha Quest is no Le Corbusier, but her disposition is to see London in conventional political and aesthetic terms, as socially deprived and ugly. For Iris, however, a local woman with whom Martha is staying, the neighbourhood is a palimpsest, textured and animated by layers of history and memory.

> Iris, Joe's mother... knew everything about this area, half a dozen streets for about half a mile or a mile of their length; and she knew it all in such detail that when with her, Martha walked in a double vision, as if she were two people: herself and Iris, one eye stating, denying, warding off the total hideousness of the whole area, the other, with Iris, knowing it in love. With Iris, one moved here, in a state of love, if love is the delicate but total acknowledgement of what is.... Iris, Joe's mother, had lived in this street since she was born. Put

her brain, together with the other million brains, women's brains, that
recorded in such tiny loving anxious detail the histories of window-
sills, skins of paint, replaced curtains and salvaged baulks of timber,
there would be a recording instrument, a sort of six-dimensional map
which included the histories and lives and loves of people, London –
a section map in depth. This is where London exists.

This should not be read as a sentimental celebration of secure feminine
identity grounded in working-class community. Nor is the London cityscape
simply there to connect *The Four-Gated City* to a specific geographical
location at a specific historical time, the cultural setting within which the
novel's action can take place.[5] In describing Iris's mundane spatial
projection and introjection of desire and anxiety, Lessing hints at something uncanny in urban space. J. Hillis Miller calls this the atopical.

> This is a place that is everywhere and nowhere, a place you cannot get
> to from here. Sooner or later ... the effort of mapping is interrupted
> by an encounter with the unmappable. The topography and the
> toponymy ... hide an unplaceable place. It was the locus of an event
> that never 'took place' as a phenomenal happening located in some
> identifiable spot and therefore open to knowledge. This strange event
> that took place without taking place cannot be the object of a
> cognition because it was a unique performative event. This strange
> locus is another name for the ground of things, the preoriginal
> ground of the ground, something other to any activity of mapping.[6]

This is a difficult argument, but Miller's phenomenology of space offers
some clues that I shall pursue in my attempt to understand how we imagine
the city. Almost paradoxically, he suggests that we cannot imagine space as
such. What we imagine, he suggests, is always an event or events taking
place. Our imagination is inherently narrative. Space is less the already
existing setting for such stories, than the production of space through that
taking place, through the act of narration. (The argument thus recalls
Heidegger's account of the boundary as the event which produces space,
rather than setting limits to space.) What, then, is the nature of these space-
producing events? Do they simply map spaces or represent events? Not
really, suggests Miller. Rather, they project events onto space; they project
a narrational space.[7]

So narratives about cities imagine events taking place in an urban
topography. They conjure up the space of the city through the projection
of these narrative images: Woolf's fat lady in the cab, for example. It is in
this sense that the real to which they refer is atopical. The events narrated
did not take place, or not like that, although their affect is real enough.
(Think of Toon Town in *Who Framed Roger Rabbit?*) Such narratives are
therefore best thought of as 'potent speech acts'. In telling us what a city is
like, they teach us how to see it. The question is less, how accurate is this
portrait of the city? than, what happens if I do see the city like this?
Imagined cityscapes, suggests Miller, 'have to do with doing rather than
knowing.'[8] This pedagogy of the symbolised city is at work as much in films,

novels, and poetry as it is in architectural plans and political programmes. Equally, though, the atopical – the strange event which never took place and yet which generates representation – is to be found at the heart of the most rationalistic urban utopia.

Hillis Miller links the atopical to the non-transparency of social relations and the obscurity of the self to the self. This opacity is also bound up – this is the second point of difference from planners' dreaming – with a particular imagining of time. Planners and urban sociologists tend to operate with a pretty straightforward view of time. Recollections of past cities either define the problem that is to be solved (if you are Le Corbusier) or offer a nostalgic route to salvation (if you are Prince Charles). Whether you are Le Corbusier or Prince Charles, the present is pretty awful, a failure of the will to change and/or a fall from grace. Plans for the future represent not only a programme for action, or a prediction of what tomorrow's city will look like, but another potent speech act designed to bring that perfect future into being. Put like that, it is clear that we are not dealing with a past of memory, a present of description, and a future of imagination and planning. The past exists as the projection backwards of present concerns. The desire for a good city in the future already exists in the imagination of the past. The future tense of urbanist discourse turns out to be less predictive than optative, although expressed in the present tense of the architectural drawing. Jane Jacobs's description of this staging of urban fantasies as dreaming chimes with Freud's comment that, in the dream-work, and especially in daydreams, 'a thought expressed in the optative has been replaced by a representation in the present tense'.[9]

Expressed in the future perfect, urban reformism often disavows the viscous complexity of the present by representing a desired state as already having been achieved. The event that is yet to occur, and so unknowable, is represented not only as knowable, but as already past.[10] Politically, this naming the unknowable – giving an identity or substance to the people, community, or citizenship – is incompatible with a radical democratic imagination that acknowledges historicity and contingency, and can live in a present which turns out to be a loop within the chain of signifiers, 'the cross-over point between an untrustworthy past and a promised future that has already begun to decay'.[11] The past is a projection as well as a determinant of the present; the future is less a playground for unconstrained speculation, than a summons to 'inventiveness within an inextirpable framework of constraints'.[12] It is this temporal tangle that defines the 'now' that we inhabit.

For Foucault, freedom consists in the critical reflection on this present: quite a different politics from the authoritarian projection of universal principles in dream cities. The imagination necessary to rebuild a living city is equally a product of the Enlightenment tradition, but it works with a different temporality.

> Our history is such that we cannot choose from past possibilities as from a catalogue (we in fact always start somewhere), and such that we cannot project ahead an ideal to resolve in advance all problems

that will confront us (there in fact exists no such ideal).[13]

This is less a politics of the right answer than a suspicious ethical reflection on the structures and styles of urban thought that produce this fantasy of the architect as spiritual policeman. It is not a turn away from politics, but a turning round on politics to question its traditions and codes. It entails fewer moral certainties and no dream cities. It looks instead at the political, institutional, and symbolic grammar of how we see, what we can imagine, how we act. This politics offers not the comforts of familiar rhetorics and conventional ways of solving problems. It is a poetics of imagination in that it makes those codes strange in order to liberate new ways of thinking. If it is the business of imagination to make politics distrust itself, and to remind it that its principles are not literal facts but constructs of imagination, argues Richard Kearney, 'it is also its business to encourage politics to remake itself by remaking its images of the good life'.[14]

So: what sort of *act* is involved in these three modes of imagining metropolitan life: autobiographical remembering, novelistic description, and architecture?

REMEMBERING A CITY

What sort of act is it to remember a city, to make the past city present? I discovered recently that Virginia Woolf grew up in the same London street as me, in Hyde Park Gate – 'that little irregular cul-de-sac which lies next to Queen's Gate and opposite to Kensington Gardens', as Woolf described it. She was there sixty years before me, from the early 1890s through the turn of the century, and hers was a much grander experience than mine. Woolf's family, the Stephens and the Duckworths, were self-conscious social insiders in late Victorian London. But there is a shared sense that living in that place was formative, not because of the topography of the place necessarily but because both Woolf and I remember it as the precursor of later biographical developments and intellectual priorities. 'Though Hyde Park Gate seems now so distant from Bloomsbury, its shadow falls across it', Woolf recalled. '46 Gordon Square could never have meant what it did had not 22 Hyde Park Gate preceded it.'[15] But there is, in Woolf's memoir, also an indication of memory as performative act. She becomes the spectator of her own formation.

> I felt as a tramp or a gypsy must feel who stands at the flap of a tent and sees the circus going on inside. Victorian society was in full swing; George [Duckworth] was the acrobat who jumped through hoops, and Vanessa and I beheld the spectacle. We had good seats at the show, but we were not allowed to take part in it. We applauded, we obeyed – that was all.[16]

Woolf glosses this almost voyeuristic relationship to her past, and her marginalisation to the position of spectator, in terms of 'the laws of patriarchal society'. For me, it provokes other associations, in their own way equally theatrical in their structure. I recall that 8B, our rented flat, was at the top of a building on the corner of Hyde Park Gate, looking over Kensington Gardens in the front and down the cul-de-sac at the back. This gave us a view over a rich cast of characters, although at the time the drama seemed generally quite unremarkable. Down the street lived, at number 20, Winston Churchill, then in the dog days of his final term of office as prime minister and later in resentful retirement. Opposite him, at number 18, lived the sculptor Jacob Epstein, who represented a face of modernism that was acceptable to the English at least to the degree that he had been the butt of endless philistine humour. An interesting conjuncture, now I come to think of it, and one that Woolf herself might have appreciated: the representative of a patriarchal myth of Empire over the road from a cosmopolitan and bohemian artist.

The point of this digression into autobiographical recollection is to show the relevance of Hillis Miller's notion of atopicality to the imaginative recreation of the past. Memory is not just the bringing to mind of past facts. Notoriously, the vivid events recalled from childhood may or may not have taken place, and yet the reworking of the past plays a crucial role in our sense of who we are. These imagined events are a working through of current desires and anxieties, a way of managing them by staging them as a narrative. In my case, the new knowledge that Virginia Woolf lived in Hyde Park Gate too becomes part of my loving narrativisation of the place – a place I have not visited for twenty years or more, but still a place that is central to my imagining of the city and to my experience of myself as formed in and by London. Equally, my rewriting of Hyde Park Gate in terms of a juxtaposition between a politics of national identity and a modernist aesthetics is no doubt a symptom of my present intellectual interests, not how I experienced the place at the time. The future is always already written into the recollected past. There is an uncanny edge to recollections of our past cities which is symptomatic not only of the atopicality of narrative but also of the temporal disjunctures of memory and imagination. 'The individual is debarred from any benign sensation of temporal flow', notes Lacan; 'past, present, and future will always stand outside each other, unsettle each other, and refuse to cohere.'[17]

DESCRIBING A CITY

In order to imagine the unrepresentable space, life, and languages of the city, to make them liveable, we translate them into narratives. We remember or misremember events and imagine them taking place against a symbolic topography. This is true not just of individual memory. It is evident in the intimate connection between the modern metropolis and the development of aesthetic genres and technologies of communication. Most notable of these are the cinema and, before that, the novel.[18] My question here is, what can we learn about an urban imagination from the cities described in novels? What sort of act are these accounts? These are not questions about the aesthetic function of the cityscape. Rather, again, they concern the social function of imagined cities.

The links between the novel and historically specific ways of seeing the city have been documented often enough. It is not just that the popularity of the nineteenth-century novel was made possible by new urban technologies – railways, artificial light, printing, education, and so forth – and the new reading publics that appeared in cities. How the city is narrated in novels – the structure and form of the genre – disseminates certain perspectives, certain ways of seeing, and so certain structures of imagination: the opposition between rural utopia and urban nightmare; the *Bildungsroman* narrative of heroic self-creation in the great city; the Dickensian search for the subterranean networks of community beneath the unreadable and irrational surface of the class-divided city; the social complexity of the city recorded through its demotic idioms and slang by French novelists from Balzac to Zola.

The nineteenth-century novel-city, characterised by frenetic activity and social illegibility, exists as a cast of mind, and is peopled by a type of personality that is recognisably and pedagogically urban. On the one hand, the novel's structural openness to the city's multiple points of view and to the Babel of linguistic diversity gives the genre a semblance of democratic inclusiveness, an urban tolerance of difference. On the other hand, the formal organisation of this plenitude often appears to embody a powerful will to domination, a desire to subjugate urban heterogeneity to the design of an omnipotent, panoptic narrator. This mix of tolerance and paranoia produced a repertoire of responses to the city, from popular melodramas about master criminals and secret conspiracies to the *flâneur*'s contemplative, aestheticising gaze.[19]

The relation between novel and city, then, is not merely one of representation. The text is actively constitutive of the city. Writing does not only record or reflect the fact of the city. It has its role in producing the city for a reading public. The period of the rise of the novel saw the emergence of other genres for recording, for instituting, the truth of the city. Population surveys, police records, sanitary reports, statistics, muck-raking journalism, and photography all rendered the city an object of knowledge, and so an object of government.[20] The boundary between these documentary records and fictional narratives is more permeable than one might suppose. There is a free migration of images and narratives between archive and library. Their circulation provides the symbolic currency through which we recall, describe, and so negotiate the city. It provokes and channels the projection of desire and anxiety onto the city.

At their best, novels imagine the sort of *living* city that Jane Jacobs says is so difficult to rebuild; difficult because the city exists in that complex living, not just in their architecture or design. Novels are speech acts in that they help to construct that living symbolic city. Take two examples, very briefly: *Mrs Dalloway* (1925) by my anachronistic neighbour Virginia Woolf, and *Berlin Alexanderplatz* (1929) by Alfred Döblin.[21] My argument is that their narration of London and Berlin in the 1920s encounters the sort of unmappable – or un-narratable – place that Hillis Miller talks about: the 'place that is everywhere and nowhere, a place you cannot get to from here'.

Neither novel tells of a provincial heroine or hero arriving with high hopes in the capital city only to discover a social and spiritual wasteland (although there is a spectral residue of that plot structure in the character of the shell-shocked ex-soldier Septimus Smith in *Mrs Dalloway*). By the 1920s, after the trauma of total war and with new forms of transport and new media of communication transforming urban life, the discontinuity and complexity of the metropolis had become so intense as to defy narration in that conventional form. These two novels attempt to reproduce the inner speech of the metropolis, the mental life stimulated by its size, speed, and semiotic overload. In their different ways, each of them is modernist both in the way it *sees* the metropolis and in the way it *narrates* the experience of the metropolis. I would argue, for example, that both see the city through a cinematic structure of visibility.

In his review of *Berlin Alexanderplatz* in 1930, Walter Benjamin placed the novel in the *epic* tradition of modernism which he helped to articulate in his collaboration with Brecht. This epic style was one feature of the new realism that emerged as an alternative to expressionism in post-war Germany. The *Neue Sachlichkeit* rejected illusionism in favour of the objectivity of historical facts, it celebrated the possibilities opened up by technological reproduction, and it championed the pedagogic power of gesture rather than characterisation. For Benjamin, Döblin's adaptation of cinematic montage techniques represented an attempt to recreate an epic relationship between artist and public. 'The material of the montage is, after all, by no means random', he commented. 'Genuine montage is based on documents.' Montage thus represents something more than a way of reproducing the multifaceted, disjunctural experience of time and space, the shocks that characterise metropolitan life. Its documentary basis makes a claim to both authenticity and authority by anchoring the work in the life of the people. As a mode of narration, montage promises a more provocative selection and juxtaposition of images, and so a more inter-active, less consumerist and less manipulative experience of reading.[22]

In a review of James Joyce's *Ulysses*, written while working on *Berlin Alexanderplatz*, Döblin acknowledged that 'the movies have invaded the territory of literature', and it is probable that for his experiments in montage Döblin took as his primary model Walter Ruttman's documentary film *Berlin: Symphony of a Great City* (1927).[23] Just as the film opens with shots from a train entering the city, for example, so there is a quasi-cinematic manipulation of time and space in the first chapter of Book 2, 'Franz Biberkopf Enters Berlin'.[24] Ruttman's structure of the passage of a day interspersed with little human dramas is echoed here as the bustle of the day on the Rosenthaler Platz gives way to increasingly intimate encounters and conversations in the late afternoon and then in the evening. The rhythm and use of diagonal motion in Ruttman's editing find literary equivalents in Döblin's focus on the activities in and around Rosenthaler Platz in the East End of Berlin. The stops along the route of the 68 trolley as it runs from north to east are listed, with Rosenthaler Platz in the middle and Herzberge Insane Asylum at the end. The documentation of different aspects of metropolitan activity is linked to the four streets which radiate from the square: the AEG factory, the railway station, commerce, construction, and so forth.

Using montage as a principle of narration enables Döblin to play with shifting and multi-faceted points of view, and to mimic the epic factography of film. Daringly, the chapter opens with a sequence of graphics. The bear of Berlin followed by small stereotypes depicting 'Trade and Commerce', 'Street Cleaning and Transport', 'Health Department' through to 'Finance and Tax Office'. This is followed by a montage of public notices and announcements: 'The scheme for the addition of an ornamental rosette to the street wall of No. 10 An der Spandauer Brücke ... is hereby published'; '– I have granted to Herr Bottich, hunting lessee, with the consent of the Police President, authority, liable to cancellation at any time, for the shooting of wild rabbits and other vermin ...'; '– Albert Pangel, master furrier, who may look back upon an activity of almost thirty years as an honorary local official, has resigned his honorary office ...' (46/7). Then for the first time the presence of the narrator as *metteur-en-scene* is indicated. 'The Rosenthaler Platz is busily active', he announces. The nature of its diverse activities is documented, initially in long shot but then with a cut to a near accident as 'a man with two yellow packages jumps off from the 41' and other vignettes of the messiness of everyday life. These include a double suicide ('In a little hotel over there in that dark street two lovers shot themselves early yesterday morning, a waiter from Dresden and a married woman, both of whom, however, had registered under false names.'), and an account of a 14-year-old boy with a stutter who gets on the no. 4 tram. The latter story incorporates a flash forward to the boy's future life as a tin-smith and his death at the age of 55.

The final section of the chapter closes in on two passages of dramatic dialogue, with explicit narration restricted to stage directions. In the first, a morphine-addicted ex-high school teacher consoles a young man who has been sacked with a mixture of cynical street wisdom and his love of metropolitan life: 'I enjoy the Rosenthaler Platz, I enjoy the cop at the Elsasser corner, I like my game of billiards, I'd like anyone to come and tell me that his life is better than mine' (53). The second dialogue conveys the sexualisation of space in the city. At 8 p.m. a young girl and an elderly man meet for an assignation in Brunnenstrasse.

> Upstairs they smile at each other. She stands in the corner. He has taken off his coat and hat, she lets him take her hat and music-case. Then she runs to the door, switches off the light: 'But not long today. I have so little time, I must get home, I won't undress, you are not going to hurt me?'
>
> (55)

After this fade to black, these characters disappear from the narrative. The epic sweep of *Berlin Alexanderplatz* embraces many such anonymous stories. There are five million stories in the city, as the prologue to *The Naked City* almost used to say, and the story of the ex-prisoner Franz Biberkopf is just one. To some extent, he can be seen as Everyman, or perhaps better as Anyone in the city. Certainly, there is no attempt at detailed psychological analysis.

Virginia Woolf also had aspirations to inclusiveness in *Mrs Dalloway*. 'I want to give life and death, sanity and insanity', she wrote in a diary entry. 'I want to criticise the social system, and to show it at work, at its most intense.' What is striking about the novel, however, especially in comparison with *Berlin Alexanderplatz*, is its introversion, the experience of London as psychic space. The toponymy in the novel, its naming of places, is as detailed and precise as you would find in Dickens, but the references to locations and events are mediated through the subjective thoughts of the main characters. Psychological states are not so much caused by the cityscape, as projected onto it. The boundary between inner and outer is shown early on to be blurred and uncertain:

> For having lived in Westminster – how many years now? over twenty, – one feels even in the midst of the traffic, or waking at night, Clarissa was positive, a particular hush, or solemnity; an indescribable pause; a suspense (but that might be her heart, affected, they said, by influenza) before Big Ben strikes. (4)

Whereas Döblin renders the city in terms of a modernist epic, Woolf offers a modernist impressionism. Like Döblin, Woolf was self-consciously trying to write about the experience of the modern city after Joyce. Notoriously, though, she had a mixed and rivalrous response to reading *Ulysses*. In her diaries, although she was able to recognise its liberating and critical novelty, she admitted feeling 'puzzled, bored, irritated, & disillusioned as by a queasy undergraduate scratching his pimples'.[25] Leaving aside such reservations, the more considered comments in the essay 'Modern fiction' stress Woolf's endorsement of Joyce's rejection of the tyranny of Edwardian narration. He, modern like her, was able to recognise the empirical reality of 'an ordinary mind on an ordinary day' – a mental reality similar also to that diagnosed by Georg Simmel. For Woolf:

> The mind receives a myriad impressions – trivial, fantastic, evanescent, or engraved with the sharpness of steel. From all sides they come, an incessant shower of innumerable atoms.[26]

This bombardment of images and events defines the task of the modern novelist:

> Let us record the atoms as they fall upon the mind in the order in which they fall, let us trace the pattern, however disconnected and incoherent in appearance, which each sight or incident scores upon the consciousness.[27]

What would be the paradigm for a modernist literary aesthetic capable of rendering this pattern in literary form? How might it be possible, Woolf asked elsewhere, to capture in the novel 'the power of music, the stimulus of sight, the effect on us of the shape of trees or the play of colour, the emotions bred in us by crowds, the obscure terrors and hatreds which come so irrationally in certain places or from certain people, the delight of movement'?[28]

However different the outcome, Woolf, like Döblin, turned to the cinema for an analogy, if not inspiration. For her, it was not the explosive epistemological power of montage that was the attraction. Rather, it was the ontological precision of the camera that opened up new ways of recording and dramatising London. Laura Marcus has shown how Woolf used her 1926 essay 'The cinema' 'to explore the roles of space, movement and rhythm in narrative film and fiction'.[29] Despite Woolf's predictable reservations about the stupidity and vulgarity of the medium (and especially of literary adaptations), she saw cinema as potentially the most appropriate form for expressing the complex experience of modernity and the shock effects of the city.

> The most fantastic contrasts could be flashed before us with a speed which the writer can only toil after in vain; the dream architecture of arches and battlements, of cascades falling and fountains rising, which sometimes visits us in sleep or shapes itself in half-darkened rooms, could be realised before our waking eyes. No fantasy could be too far-fetched or insubstantial.... How all this is to be attempted, much less achieved, no one at the moment can tell us. We get intimations only in the chaos of the streets, perhaps, when some momentary assembly of colour, sound, movement, suggests that here is a scene waiting a new art to be transfixed.[30]

The camera, as a recording instrument capable of charting the drama and impressionistic chaos of the city, finds its literary equivalent in the narrative eye of *Mrs Dalloway*.

> In people's eyes, in the swing, tramp, and trudge; in the bellow and the uproar; the carriages, motor cars, omnibuses, vans, sandwich men shuffling and swinging; brass bands; barrel organs; in the triumph and the jingle and the strange high singing of some aeroplane overhead was what she loved; life; London; this moment of June.
>
> (4–5)

But this love of London is not the love of Iris, Joe's mother. It is not the knowing, forgiving love of familiarity, the sense of a self rooted and recorded in place. Rather, the eye of *Mrs Dalloway*, its *recording movement*, mimicks the tracking, panning, and analytical camera of cinema by harking back to the distanciating vision of *flânerie*.

So Peter Walsh, the flawed and disappointed colonial administrator, cuts a swathe (he fancies) through the often kitsch memorials of imperial, post-war London and even has an encounter (he fantasises) with a classic Baudelairean *passante*.[31] The society hostess and MP's wife Clarissa Dalloway moves observing but, as far as she can tell, invisible through the crowds of Bond Street. However frivolous, limited and selfish she may be, Clarissa is the woman of the crowd in the sense that only there, in others, does she exist.

> ... what she loved was this, here, now, in front of her; the fat lady in the cab. Did it matter, then, she asked herself, walking towards Bond Street, did it matter that she must inevitably cease completely; all this

must go on without her; did she resent it; or did it not become consoling to believe that death ended absolutely? but that somehow in the streets of London, on the ebb and flow of things, here, there, she survived, Peter survived, lived in each other, she being part, she was positive, of the trees at home; of the house there, ugly, rambling all to bits and pieces as it was; part of people she had never met; being laid out like a mist between the people she knew best, who lifted her on their branches as she had seen the trees lift the mist, but it spread ever so far, her life, herself.

(10–11)

Her walk through London conjures up a place that she cannot get to, which is herself, her 'precious and reassuring' past (12), but above all her precarious present and future. Clarissa's past – childhood, the country – is not preserved in the 'this, here, now' of the city. On the contrary, her past has become atopical, the irrecoverable locus of identities that might have been, of choices not made, of paths not taken. This past is disquieting as soon as she recalls it here and now: Peter's return puts her decision to reject him for Richard again in question, and also reminds her of Sally Seton and their kiss, with all that promised and threatened. Her walk through London provokes thoughts not of the continuity of identity, but disquiet at the lack of subjective fixity.

She had the oddest sense of being herself invisible; unseen; unknown; there being no more marrying, no more having of children now, but only this astonishing and rather solemn progress with the rest of them, up Bond Street, this being Mrs Dalloway; not even Clarissa any more; this being Mrs Richard Dalloway.

(13)

This narration is not only a record of images, but a projection of multiple selves – past, future, imaginable selves – onto the cityscape being recorded. Clarissa's flash-back to her childhood is both nostalgic and anxious, the recall of a lost self and a sense of multiplying possible selves. In contrast, the bus journey of Elizabeth Dalloway, Clarissa's competent daughter, prompts a flash forward: the busy-ness of Chancery Lane inspires not introspection and retrospection, but fantasies of the great works she will do. Woolf's section map in depth here captures the complex temporality of London in 'this moment in June'; a present which, as in Simmel's Berlin, is regulated by the imposed chronology of the clock. Elizabeth's daydream of the future comes to an end as she remembers: 'She must go home. She must dress for dinner. But what was the time? – where was a clock?' (179).

The simultaneity of past, present, and future in the life of the city tests the limits of novelistic narrative. Döblin's solution is epistemological montage, Woolf's the passage of ontological perception. This tangled temporality also suggests why the experience of the modern city has so often produced hallucination, new types of mental illness, and, in the case of Septimus Smith, suicide. Whereas Peter Walsh fancies himself as a figure in the drama of London, and Clarissa fears that, unless hailed by a member of her social set like Scrope Purvis, she is merely an invisible part of the scenery, in Septimus Smith's paranoid perception of Bond Street he is both out of place and in the way.

> Everything had come to a standstill. The throb of the motor engines sounded like a pulse irregularly drumming through an entire body. The sun became extraordinarily hot because the motor car had stopped outside Mulberry's shop window.... And there the motor car stood, with drawn blinds, and upon them a curious pattern like a tree, Septimus thought, and this gradual drawing together of everything to one centre before his eyes, as if some horror had come almost to the surface and was about to burst into flames, terrified him. The world wavered and quivered and threatened to burst into flames. It is I who am blocking the way, he thought. Was he not being looked at and pointed at; was he not weighted there, rooted to the pavement, for a purpose? But for what purpose?
>
> (18–19)

At the beginning of *Berlin Alexanderplatz*, Franz Biberkopf too hallucinates as he readjusts to what seems the chaos of Berlin in comparison with the ordered confinement and routine of prison. The crowd in the streets seem lifeless, like the wax mannequins in a shop window: 'Outside everything was moving, but – back of it – there was nothing! It – did not – live!' (12). Inanimate objects like trams seem terrifyingly alive, and Biberkopf has the first attack of his recurring vertiginous fear that the roofs will slide off the houses. Like the hysterical Septimus Smith and Clarissa Dalloway with her 'panic fear' in the metropolis, Biberkopf cannot draw a line between inner and outer states.

Septimus Smith is very much the type described by Simmel in 'The metropolis and mental life'. Far from Baudelaire's detached and aristocratic *flâneur*, he is the newcomer to the city, subjected to 'the intensification of emotional life due to the swift and continuous shift of external and internal stimuli'. With every crossing of the street, says Simmel, the city 'creates in the sensory foundations of mental life ... a deep contrast with the slower, more habitual, more smoothly flowing rhythm of the sensory-mental phase of small town existence'.[32] Although traumatised by the war – *Mrs Dalloway* is set only five years after its end – Septimus Smith's mental instability is exacerbated by the unbearable normality of the city.

> London has swallowed up millions of young men called Smith; thought nothing of fantastic Christian names like Septimus with which their parents have thought to distinguish them. Lodging off the Euston Road, there were experiences, again experiences, such as change a face in two years from a pink innocent oval to a face lean, contracted, hostile.
>
> (110)

Both *Mrs Dalloway* and *Berlin Alexanderplatz* follow Simmel in linking the *experience* of the metropolis to what might be called the psychic and spatial diseases of modernity: Smith's hysteria, Biberkopf's agoraphobia, Clarissa's neurasthenia. Many such diseases appeared towards the end of the nineteenth century, as an emerging psychological discourse displaced a primarily medical paradigm for describing the dangers of great cities.[33] All of them, even though most of the people treated for them were probably men, were linked not only to degeneracy but also to the perceived feminisation of metropolitan life and modern culture.[34] In the city dweller's psychic space of projection and introjection, the danger was that the boundaries between self and environment, like those between past and present, or male and female, become uncertain and unreliable. Such disorientation produces a retreat into an interiority, either mental or physical, or both, and a disabling inability to admit feelings. Life in the city becomes un-narratable, and so, in a more acute sense, un-imaginable. These transient diseases – 'neurasthenia' was dropped as clinically meaningless in the 1930s – were themselves attempts to name, and so manage, the mental life of the metropolis.

The aesthetic architecture of *Mrs Dalloway* and *Berlin Alexanderplatz* enacts these modern spatial phobias. Once such phobias were recognised and acknowledged as a feature of modern experience and its modernist representation, argues Anthony Vidler, 'neurasthenia found its role as a veritable stimulus for aesthetic experiment'. The forms it took were those of 'stream of consciousness, of entrapment, of intolerable closure, of space without exit, of, finally, breakdown and often suicide'.[35]

This neurotic motivation behind modernism seems to indicate an aesthetic of despair. Franz Biberkopf is incarcerated in Herzberge Insane Asylum; Septimus Smith's suicide is announced at Clarissa's party by the crass and incompetent nerve doctor, Sir William Bradshaw. But another, perhaps surprising, feature common to the two novels is the note of hope, however constrained and uncertain, on which they both end. In the asylum Biberkopf confronts death and is, however implausibly, redeemed and reborn, both subjectively and politically. He is thus, as Benjamin ironically observed, granted 'access into the heaven of literary characters' and – against all the odds and all the evidence – the narratability of the city is reasserted.[36] Clarissa Dalloway's partial redemption is bought at the price of Smith's suicide. He becomes her surrogate:

> A young man had killed himself. And they talked of it at her party – the Bradshaws, talked of death. He had killed himself – but how? Always her body went through it first, when she was told suddenly, of an accident; her dress flamed, her body burnt.... They went on living (she would have to go back; the rooms were still crowded; people kept on coming).... Death was defiance. Death was an attempt to communicate, people feeling the impossibility of reaching the centre which, mystically, evaded them.
>
> (241–2)

Having confronted the atopicality of being – 'the centre which, mystically, evaded them' – the novel ends with a reaffirmation of Clarissa's being, even if that being is contingent on the specular gaze of another. That is about as grounded as subjective existence gets in modernity.

'I will come,' said Peter, but he sat on for a moment. What is this terror? what is this ecstasy? he thought to himself. What is it that fills me with extraordinary excitement?
It is Clarissa, he said.
For these she was.

(255)

IMAGINING A DIFFERENT CITY

What sort of speech acts are *Mrs Dalloway* and *Berlin Alexanderplatz*? They enact a way of seeing which can be linked to the perceptual technology of cinema, and a subjective experience of the city that is manifested elsewhere as phobic spatial diseases. How, then, do the novels help us to respond to Jane Jacobs's dictum: 'Designing a dream city is easy; rebuilding a living one takes imagination'?

First, they remind us, if a reminder were needed, of the dangers of the total planning associated above all with Le Corbusier. Perhaps we treat Le Corbusier as too easy a villain these days, paying too little heed to the ironic and polemical edge to his writing. It is therefore interesting to read him as a contemporary of Döblin and Woolf. Le Corbusier too had a sense of space being mediated and transformed through the mass media. His huge horizontal windows, for example, in effect turned the outside world into a cinematic spectacle, and so structured into his architecture modernist uncertainties about outside and inside, about public and private. [37] But what stands out most clearly from his more ambitious plans is the atopical terror that motivates his therapeutic modernism, the desire for a space cleansed of all uncanny mental disturbances, or even, it seems, of events.[38] The radiance, air and transparency that make up his image of the good city in the perfect future are symptoms of a phobic reaction against the narrative reality of the street, the disgust at the possibility of being touched by strangers diagnosed by Simmel.

> The street is full of people: one must take care where one goes ... every aspect of human life pullulates throughout their length ... a sea of lusts and faces. ... Heaven preserve us from the Balzacian mentality of [those] who would be content to leave our streets as they are because these murky canyons offer them the fascinating spectacle of human physiognomy![39]

It is this phobic disgust – is it claustrophobia, a paradoxical agoraphobia, or simply ochlophobia? – which drove his desire to reduce the messiness of people in cities to the abstraction of geometric order. Without this order, changes in modern life were swamping the city: 'The resultant chaos has brought it about that the Great City, which should be a phenomenon of power and energy, is today a menacing disaster, since it is no longer governed by the principles of geometry.' His response, madder by far than anything in *Mrs Dalloway* or *Berlin Alexanderplatz*, was to dream up his City of Tomorrow in which mathematical order displaces narrative: 'Little by little, and basing each point on cause and effect, I built up an ordered system of the grouping of such cells as would replace with advantage the present chaos to which we are subject.'[40]

The second lesson I would take from a reading of Döblin and Woolf is about the nature of the *living* city Jane Jacobs talks about. The city exists in lives as complex, as opaque, and as painful as those the novels depict. But is that not a lesson already well learned? In today's anti-modernist backlash, no one is proposing – are they? – Le Corbuiser's apocalyptic aesthetic of urban planning. Discussion starts from the existing cultures and communities of cities, and asks how they might be regenerated. Postmodern traditionalists share Prince Charles's dream of urban design which would be able 'to nurture human life and to give dignity, imbuing people with a sense of belonging and a sense of community'. More radical architects like Richard Rogers and urban theorists like Franco Bianchini and Ken Worpole argue for a revitalised and re-enchanted city, one that people can imagine or narrate to themselves, one that is designed to encourage civilised encounters with strangers: 'a potential place for commonality, where some form of common identity could be constructed and where different ages, classes, ethnic groups and lifestyles could meet in unplanned, informal ways'.[41] These enthusiasts paint a seductive picture of an urbane and cosmopolitan life – a vision of Habermas's public sphere in which the strenuous republican disciplines of public life often seem less important than a good meal and a decent bottle of wine in a pavement café.

Sadly, I agree with Kevin Robins that, in both the traditionalists and the cosmopolitans, 'there is an imaginative deficit in the claimed "re-imagination" of urban culture'.[42] What is missing, Robins suggests, is any real sense of the city not only as the space of community or pleasurable encounters or self-creation, but also as the site of aggression, violence, and paranoia. That is why I have insisted that imagining the city in ways that can encompass such forces should be prior to any attempts to rebuild actually existing cities. To reject traditional modes of planning is not to give up hope, even though the hope that I detected in *Berlin Alexanderplatz* and *Mrs Dalloway* may now look like reckless optimism in comparison with the representational urban space to be found not only in more recent novels, but also in academic urban studies. Think of the incisive migrant's view of Ellowen Deeowen in Salman Rushdie's *Satanic Verses*; the London saturated by poisonous histories in Iain Sinclair's *Downriver*; the demented and impenetrable semiotic networks of urban California described by Thomas Pynchon in *The Crying of Lot 49*; Mike Davis's *film noir* political economy of Los Angeles; or the sci-fi cyber-city of capital flows, information flows, and power flows conjured up by writers like Manuel Castells, William Gibson, and Saskia Sassen.[43]

Faced with this often paranoid, sometimes scatological and yet in some ways sublime poetics of the city, how is it still possible to imagine intentional urban change? For a start, cautions Doreen Massey, don't get over-excited: 'most people actually still live in places like Harlesden or West Brom. Much of life for many people, even in the heart of the First World, still consists of waiting in a bus-shelter with your shopping for a bus that never comes.'[44] It is certainly true that there is an uneven development of ways of seeing and experiencing the city, and probably most of us operate with 'residual' modes most of the time. Perhaps that is why Kevin Robins argues less for change in the city than for change in the way we live in the city. He imagines a post-feminist heroism which forgoes the illusion of wholeness, coherence, or narratability in favour of a tolerant, melancholic acknowledgement of, and engagement with, complexity – a postmodern version of Iris, Joe's mother, perhaps, and her loving intimacy with the city. He quotes Elizabeth Wilson:

> The heroism – for both sexes – is in surviving the disorientating space, both labyrinthine and agoraphobic, of the metropolis. It lies in the ability to discern among the massed ranks of anonymity the outline of forms of beauty and individuality appropriate to urban life.[45]

But isn't this heroic attitude still trapped within the narcissistic aestheticism of *flânerie*? Detecting the poetic in the everyday, or the eternal in the transitory is, in the end, a way of domesticating the city, turning its public spaces into your interior world. It avoids the stubborn reality of difference and the opacity of others. The problem is not just how to live in the city, but how to live together.

Is it then possible to imagine change that acknowledges difference without falling into phobic utopianism, communitarian nostalgia, or the disavowal of urban paranoia? To start at the other end, how would one imagine the spatial manifestation of a radical democracy? For a start, one would have to acknowledge, as I have tried to do here, the historicity and contingency of the spatial representations and projections which allow and constrain such imagining. Second, therefore, the imagining would take the form not of a dream city, but a re-thinking of the processes and technologies of change. It is the impossibility of representing the social relations of the city in a single normative image or an all-encompassing narrative that lends this style of imagination its sublime edge and, Ernesto Laclau might agree, places it within a radical democratic imaginary. His account of society as 'mere event' perhaps goes too far in the opposite direction from Le Corbusier's dream of the city as pure space. But read Laclau with Hillis Miller's account of space as constituted by event (and so inherently temporal) in mind, and then he does offer a political imagination couched in terms of narrative rather than *topos*, of pragmatics rather than representation, of living cities rather than dream cities.

> Society, then, is ultimately unrepresentable: any representation – and thus any space – is an attempt to constitute society, not to state what it is. But the antagonistic moment of collision between the various representations cannot be reduced to space, and is itself unrepresentable. It is therefore mere event, mere temporality.... [T]his final incompletion of the social is the main source of our political hope in the contemporary world: only it can assure the conditions for a radical democracy.[46]

This approach to social space as event would have to acknowledge, and in a quiet way might even celebrate, the fictional element in all architecture, its necessary attempt to imagine social relations taking place. Architecture to that degree is also a critical commentary, a making strange of what is. The important point is to avow this proper degree of fantasy in the architectural imagination, and not to make the mistake of assuming any particular piece of design or planning will have social consequences that are wholly predictable. Such an architecture would therefore have two aspects: a critical power of remembering in grasping urban space as historically and temporally layered; and an imagination that combines aesthetics and ethics in formulating possible changes to the fabric of the city. The question, then, is how a poetics of political imagination might be effectively allied to a pragmatics of architecture and design.

Something of this style can be found in the work of Bernard Tschumi, in the 1960s an architectural activist influenced by the Situationists who more recently has collaborated with Jacques Derrida. His starting-point is that, in contemporary urban society, 'any cause-and-effect relationship between form, use, function, and socio-economic structure has become both impossible and obsolete'. If that is true, how can you improve people's experience of the social by changing the urban environment? No longer can you assume that people's experience of space will be determined by your plan for that space; that buildings and the uses of buildings are the same thing; or that there is a transparent relationship between space and the movement of bodies within space. Instead, Tschumi calls for an architectural imagination which starts from 'the pleasurable and sometimes violent confrontation of spaces and activities'. It is the *disjunction* between use, form, and social values which gives architecture its subversive and creative power. The space in and on which architects work is neither coherent nor homogeneous nor marked by clear boundaries:

> ... we inhabit a fractured space, made of accidents, where figures are disintegrated, *dis*-integrated. From a sensibility developed during centuries around the 'appearance of a stable image' ('balance', 'equilibrium', 'harmony'), today we favor a sensibility of the disappearance of unstable images: first movies (twenty-four images per second), then television, then computer-generated images, and recently (among a few architects) disjunctions, dislocations, deconstructions.[47]

When offered the chance to transform the Parc de la Villette in Paris, this was the spatial imagination Tschumi brought to bear. He did not want either to create a conventional architectural masterpiece, or to fill in the gaps in what existed, scribbling in the margins of the architectural text. This left him two options. Either:

> Deconstruct what exists by critically analysing the historical layers that preceded it, even adding other layers derived from elsewhere – from other cities, other parks (a palimpsest).

Or:

Search for an intermediary – an abstract system to mediate between the site (as well as all given constraints) and some other concept, beyond city or program (a mediation).[48]

Tschumi had explored the possibilities of the palimpsest model in earlier projects, but here he felt that 'its inevitably figurative or representational components' were incompatible with the programmatic, technical, and political constraints on the project. He went for the strategy of *mediation* which would, he hoped, allow 'a strong conceptual framework while simultaneously suggesting multiple combinations and substitutions'.

Where did Tschumi turn for his mediating system and concept at La Villette? His answer is both familiar and surprising. His first mediation involved a grid of *Folies*: a reference not just to eighteenth-century architectural follies, but to a spatial understanding of madness and the psychoanalytic relation of transference. This was the deconstructive or critical aspect of the project. The other mediating principle was one of construction or assemblage, a means of exploring 'the set of combinations and permutations that is possible among different categories of analysis (space, movement, event, technique, symbol, etc.), as opposed to the more traditional play between function or use and form or style'. His first analogy for this style of imaginative construction is the type of *montage* to be found 'in Dziga Vertov's or Sergei Eisenstein's work in the cinema'.[49] As far as I can see, Tschumi was making no great polemical point about madness as urban experience nor cinema as urban perception. Nevertheless, he did take the theme of madness and the techniques of cinema which I detected in *Berlin Alexanderplatz* and *Mrs Dalloway* and translate them into an apparently arbitrary principle of construction.

What appeals to me about Tschumi is his acute awareness that architectural imagination is contingent on technologies of vision and perception as well as the codes and traditions of architecture as a discipline – and, of course, the political and economic realities that will determine, often in the first instance, how urban space gets changed. Tschumi's is an architecture that works through dis-juncture, dis-location, and dis-integration. What he was aiming for in his schemes for La Villette was a plan, certainly, but not a *telos*; a strategy for rebuilding a living city park, rather than a dream park or a theme park. Aware of the city as temporal palimpsest, he remembered the past and acknowledged that we in the present cannot legislate the future. His plan therefore had flexibility, tolerance, difference, restlessness, and change built into it.

One part could replace another, or a building's program be revised, changing (to use an actual example) from restaurant to gardening center to arts workshop. In this manner, the park's identity could be maintained, while the circumstantial logics of state or institutional politics could pursue their own independent scenarios. Moreover, our objective was also to act upon a strategy of differences: if other designers were to intervene, their projects' difference from the *Folies* or divergence from the continuity of the cinematic promenade would become the condition of their contributions.[50]

'An organizing structure that could exist independent of use, a structure without center or hierarchy': that seems pretty close to a future-oriented architecture that displays inventiveness within a framework of constraints.[51]

This style of imagining, aesthetically daring and yet scrupulously ethical, does not stop you from rebuilding a living city. It should make you think differently about what you are doing, and why you are doing it. You are not going to produce total social transformation. You are not going to make the city into a home, at least not in the sense of expunging all traces of the uncanny from it, nor filling out its atopicality, nor domesticating all traces of alterity and difference. The point of examining the imaginary cities constructed in novels and films is that it is often artists rather than urbanists who have found the language and images to teach us not only the joyous potential of cities, but also that, as Anthony Vidler puts it, 'no amount of space or structure can make a home where no home can exist'.[52]

What can we hope for from cities? What, in particular, can we hope for from imagining the city differently? All of us long for a place that is bounded and secure, where the noise stops, and where we are sustained by the love of those we love, or – more desperately – by infantile fantasies of plenitude and security. This urgent desire for home is real enough, and should not be dismissed as hopeless nostalgia. Equally, though, we have to admit that, in the end, no such place exists this side of the grave. That is why Le Corbusier's Radiant City has the chill of the Necropolis about it, and why the urbane life of café and square can transmogrify so easily into an Expressionist Dance of Death. City life as a normative ideal acknowledges not only the necessary desire for the security of home, but also the inevitability of migration, change, and conflict, and so too the ethical need for an openness to unassimilated otherness.[53] The city becomes the symbolic space in which we act out our more or less imaginative answers to the question which defines our *ethos*: 'how to be "at home" in a world where our identity is not given, our being-together in question, our destiny contingent or uncertain: the world of the violence of our own self-constitution.'[54]

The drillers have packed up and gone home now, and the rush hour traffic has reduced to an occasional bus or car. There is a scent of rosemary from my tiny town garden. From the pub over the road drifts the sound of the juke box and the whoop of an over-excited drinker. Here, now, in front of me, a moment of peace this summer evening in the city. Tomorrow, I imagine, the aggravation starts again.

NOTES

Thanks to Rachel Bowlby and Laura Marcus for their comments on an earlier draft of this article.

1 Ihab Hassan (1981: 94).
2 Cited ibid., p. 97.
3 On this characterisation of the city, see Iris Marion Young (1990). On imagination, see Richard Kearney (1991).
4 Victor Burgin (1991). See also Anthony Vidler (1993: 32–3).

5 See J Hillis Miller (1995: 6).
6. ibid., p. 7.
7 Henri Lefebvre makes a similar point through his distinction between the representation of space and representational space. See Lefebvre (1991).
8 Miller, p. 8
9 Cited in Malcolm Bowie (1993: 18).
10 Bowie, pp. 34, 26.
11 ibid., p. 35.
12 ibid., p. 45.
13 John Rajchman (1991: 145–6).
14 Kearney (1991: 226).
15 Virginia Woolf (1976: 159–60).
16 ibid., p. 132; cited in Susan M. Squier (1988: 20).
17 Bowie (1993: 26).
18 See Donald (1995).
19 Christopher Prendergast (1992: 221). See also Raymond Williams (1973); D. A. Miller (1988); and Klaus R. Scherpe (1989).
20 See Donald (1992).
21 Virginia Woolf (1992); Alfred Döblin (1978). Page references given in the text.
22 Dietrich Scheunemann (1978: 176); cited in David B. Dollenmayer (1988: 69).
23 Scheunemann (1978: 167–74, 182–3). The case for the influence of Ruttman's film is strengthened by viewing Phil Jutzi's 1931 film of *Berlin Alexanderplatz*, for which Döblin wrote the script.
24 In this reading I follow Dollenmayer (1988).
25 Quoted in Maria Dibattista (1983: 96).
26 Woolf (1993: 8).
27 ibid., p. 9.
28 Quoted in John Mepham (1983: 137).
29 Laura Marcus (1995: 28).
30 Virginia Woolf (1994: 595); see Marcus (1995: 31–2).
31 See Rachel Bowlby (1992) and Jeremy Tambling (1989: 141).
32 Georg Simmel (1995: 31).
33 See Donald (1992).
34 See Vidler (1993: 35).
35 ibid., pp. 43, 45.
36 Quoted Scherpe (1989: 173). On the narratibility of the city, see pp. 167–68.
37 See Beatriz Colomina (1994).
38 Vidler (1993: 36ff.).
39 Quoted ibid., pp. 41–2. I am following Vidler's argument closely here.
40 Le Corbusier cited in Kevin Robins (1995: 50, 51).
41 Bianchini and Schwengel, cited Robins (1995: 47).
42 Robins (1995: 47).
43 Mike Davis (1990); Manuel Castells (1989); Saskia Sassen (1991).
44 Doreen Massey (1994a: 163).
45 Robins (1995: 53).
46 Ernesto Laclau (1990: 82).
47 Tschumi (1994: 217).
48 ibid., pp. 191 ff.
49 ibid., pp. 181, 185.
50 ibid., pp. 193.
51 See note 11.
52 Vidler (1993: 48).
53 This is Iris Marion Young's phrase in *Justice and the Politics of Difference*.
54 Rajchman (1991: 144).

11

(RE)PLACING THE CITY

Cultural relocation and the city as centre

Tim Hall

INTRODUCTION

This chapter offers a deconstruction of certain myths that have become associated with the process of urban regeneration in the 1980s and 1990s in British cities. It seeks to illustrate the multi-faceted representation of the process of urban regeneration and the ways in which this representation has established a definitional discourse of urban change. Both the anatomy of this discourse and its implications are examined.

The chapter is particularly concerned with the related notions of power and geography in the representation and re-imagination of place. It advances an approach to understanding place representation that makes reference to the allied concepts of internal regionalisation and cultural relocation. It is argued that the representation of locales involves the production or transformation of a cultural system of space internal to the locale, in which an imagined geographical order of centre and periphery are achieved through the processes of enclosure and disclosure. However, the transformation of the locale's internal geography in turn affects its position within the overlapping cultural systems of space associated with locales of greater span, reorienting it with regard to their systems of centre and periphery. The chapter is specifically concerned with the reorientation of various cultural systems of space around Birmingham, in the United Kingdom, as part of the media discourses associated with a major project of urban regeneration, the International Convention Centre Birmingham (ICC). It is concerned with the ways in which these media challenge the prevailing structures of expectation that have evolved within the cultural systems of space which are deeply embedded within national culture. The chapter argues that in remapping and redefining its own internal geographies, the city is implicated in a concomitant relocation within external systems of cultural space. It concludes that challenging these prescriptions, and the consequent relocation within wider cultural spaces, most notably the 'European' and the 'international', has been vital to the re-imagination of the city.

REPRESENTATION AND CULTURAL RELOCATION

Recent sociological and geographical perspectives have recognised that space is socially constructed (see Lefebvre 1974). Representation is a process whereby cultural systems of space are envisioned into being. There is nothing natural or universal about these systems of space. Prevailing social constructions of space tend to be relativist. Therefore, any movement within them (physical or cultural) can only be understood as change (relocation). The sedimentation of power relations and the evolution of regionalised cultural space establishes a discursive basis within which action is situated. In representing space as relative, the notion of transformation is inherent. The reproduction of power relations requires that agents situate themselves within this geography and that they accept the discourse of spatial relativism. Consequently, a common tactic in the reproduction of power is the physical or symbolic claiming of the centre and a consequent imagination of associated peripheral zones. The discursive nature of the prevailing spatial language is evident in the scripting of a number of phenomena; these include the narration of the geographical dimensions of national space and the subsequent re-imagination of places within this context. Deeply embedded cultural systems of space such as these establish the dimensions from within which individual places must extricate themselves if they are to assert their own identities above those they are ascribed by virtue of their position within these systems.

SCRIPTING SPACE

Academic interpretations of social, economic and cultural processes have tended to reify the relativist construction of space. The danger is that this can lead to the valorisation of space, whereby the fortunes of one place are understood entirely in their relation to other places. The script provided by academic geographers has two political consequences. Most immediately, in reproducing the idea that geographies can be understood as patterns of centre and periphery it further projects marginal identities across space. Second, and more fundamentally, it perpetuates a perspective in which places are understood only in so far as they conform to or deviate from measurements established or present in a designated centre. Said (1994) has read this sort of relationship as imperialist, one in which the histories and cultures of one place are rendered invisible and irrelevant through the hegemony of comparisons with other spaces.

Such discursive scriptings have opened up around the emergence of a number of spatial formations. These have included the north–south envisioning of economic, social, political and cultural patterns within the UK and the emergence of the European Community. The academic reading of the emergence and formation of a European political and economic community, for example, has predominantly been under the hegemony of spatial relativism. This story has been understood primarily as the opening up of a new series of centres and peripheries across European space. It is disappointing, but perhaps inevitable given the legacy of imperialism in western thought, that geographers have been unable to understand the emergence of modern Europe in anything other than a paradigm characterised by these unfortunate political effects. While there has been some dismantling of terms such as the 'third world' because of the political projections and identities that they engender, there has been little or no dismantling of the discourse of 'peripheral' Europe. Clearly, these places – Southern Europe and parts of Northern and Eastern Europe – are peripheral from certain perspectives but there exist many other perspectives, mainly indigenous, where this peripherality and the notion of their emplacement as peripheral and consequently their construction as 'other' to a dominating, defining centre, is not recognised.

However, while noting that the 'imperialist' tendencies in much contemporary academic scripting of space is only a secondary aspect of this chapter, it does emphasise the importance of cultural systems of space and the dimensions with which 'peripheral' places must engage if they are to assert their own identities in the current fight to win investment. The emergence, since the early 1980s, of narratives of identity from places such as the formerly industrialised regions of the UK can be read as an attempt to extricate them from the legacy of these wider and external discourses of space and to rescript and reorientate the contours of these geographies around themselves. This chapter offers an example of the way in which one such marginal space has sought to do this through a major flagship project of urban regeneration.

RE-IMAGINING AND (RE)PLACING MARGINAL PLACES

The symbolic representation of cities in narratives of place promotion involves two geographical relations: within cities, or internal regionalisation, and between cities and systems of space at other levels, such as the region, nation or international region. The literature on the economic and material geographies of these relationships is extensive and includes contributions from sources as diverse as Anthony Giddens' (1984) *The Constitution of Society* and the 'spatial division of labour' school of economic geography (see Massey and Meegan 1982; Massey 1984). However, there is relatively little on the *symbolic* regionalisation of places. The closest we get are those works that have examined the symbolic representation of de-industrialised regions (see Burgess and Wood 1988; Watson 1991; Kearns and Philo 1993; Short *et al.* 1993; Gold and Ward 1994). While useful, this literature is limited by its failure to examine the role of these representations in the reproduction or transformations of wider systems of cultural space. This section considers two examples that illustrate how these geographical relationships affect, and in turn are affected by, the cultural systems of space envisioned in the narratives of place representation. These emphasise the importance of narrative in the scripting of new geographies of cultural space and the overlapping geographies of different cultural systems of space.

Short *et al.* (1993) considered the attempts by the city of Syracuse to reconstruct its image. They investigated the relative 'visibility' of certain elements of the environment of the city, built and otherwise. Prominent in their analysis was the Onondaga Lake and the industrial townscape of the city. The reproduction of two civic logos from contrasting periods illustrate the relative degrees of enclosure and disclosure afforded to different elements of the city's environment at different times. The first example, from 1848, showed a city of industrial capital in which the only visible elements on the logo were the factory units, with an accompanying industrial iconography. Importantly, the lake was not represented on the logo. The current city logo, by contrast, was produced at a time of radically different attitudes towards industrial capital and the environment, and consequently the elements that are disclosed and enclosed differ radically from those in the earlier logo. In the current city logo no industrial elements are present, and the lake, reflecting an emerging discourse on environmentalism, fills up the foreground of the logo, a stark disclosure or centring of this element of the city environment. The lake comes to dominate both the foreground of the logo and the cultural centre of the locale of Syracuse.

Syracuse's redefinition of its identity was achieved by the deployment of both material and symbolic resources in the selective enclosure and disclosure of elements of the city's environment. Material resources were deployed in an effort to rid the city of the effects of pollution, and symbolic resources were deployed in the representation of the city through the press and promotional literature. The effect of this was an internal region-alisation of the city.

This example demonstrates the ways in which media discourses can affect the internal regionalisation of locales. The archaeology of this type of process of enclosure and disclosure is a major aspect of the analysis presented here. The elements that get enclosed and those which are disclosed in dominant civic discourse and city images reflect the power and ability of agents and institutions to get their favoured images promoted above those of others. This process involves the differential access to these discourses, definitions of their rules and prescriptions and of their content. The implications of this for various groups within the power-economy of the city are obviously important.

The internal regionalisation of locales cannot be understood entirely by looking within the locale. It has a crucial bearing upon, and it is in turn influenced by, its relationship with locales of greater span and, therefore, by its relationships with its constituent locales of lesser span. The deploy-ment of symbolic and material resources within, say, a city not only affects its own internal geography. It also constitutes part of the internal geography of locales further up the spatial hierarchy, such as the region, the nation and, increasingly, spaces beyond.

The city, for example, will either be central or peripheral to the cultural system of space that makes up the internal geography of the region or nation. Again, the deployment of both material and symbolic resources will affect the position of the city within this larger space. Cities may be held in positions of economic peripherality by the establishment of relationships between headquarters and branch manufacturing or assembly plants. This position can be altered, however, by the deployment of material and symbolic resources within the city and by institutions associated with it, although in many cases external institutions associated with wider regions, such as the national government or an international organisation, are important. If, for example, material resources are deployed within the city through the planning or property system, the result may be an economic boom. This will not only affect the internal regionalisation of the city, but will also affect the internal geography of the larger region. This economic boom may involve the relocation of economic facilities from the previous centre to the city in question. As well as affecting the internal region-alisation of the city, the result of this might be to establish a new set of centre–periphery relations in the wider economy and hence affect a transformation of the geography of that wider region. Should important 'central' economic functions relocate to the city, then, within the cultural system of national space, that city will be brought closer to the centre of national life. The corollary of this will be that areas previously close to the centre may be expelled to the peripheries of national life.

The work of geographers is replete with examples that hint at the nested, hierarchical nature of regions and the importance of social, economic, political and cultural context (Eyles 1987; Ley 1987; Domosh 1989; Jacobs 1992). While certainly being of value and suggesting that the geographical literature is potentially receptive to the approaches and concepts discussed here, it must also be concluded that this work is limited. At the risk of over-generalisation, the works cited above aim, with reference to wider contexts, to 'explain' the internal geographies of sites of relatively restricted span (the building, the housing estate, neighbourhood or city). They are relatively unconcerned with the connections running the other way, from the smaller space outwards. They fail (understandably, as this is not their stated aim) to consider how the internal geographies of places affect their position within larger cultural spaces and hence transform the geographies of the larger spaces, the region or the nation, for example.

Perhaps the closest study to the perspective adopted in the current project is Eyles and Peace's (1990) iconological study of the Canadian 'steeltown', Hamilton. The authors examined the deployment of symbolic resources by agents and institutions in the city, namely, the discourse of the local press and politicians regarding the poorly perceived external image of Hamilton. These discourses effected a selective enclosure and disclosure of elements of the city. Much of this was a direct refutation of prevailing external impressions of the city.

> This is a tale of two cities. Both are called Hamilton. One is the city you see and hear and smell when you pass without stopping on the Queen Elizabeth Way. The other is the whole city, the city of culture and parks, commerce and academics and scenery second to none.
> (*The Hamilton Spectator* 6 September 1980, quoted in Eyles and Peace 1990: 81)

Despite allusions towards 'the whole city', this short extract clearly illustrates the processes of enclosure and disclosure with regard to elements of the environment of Hamilton. Elements of culture, parkland, employment structure and scenery enjoy disclosure, while those elements of functionality and industry are rigorously avoided, rendered invisible, and are thereby enclosed. It is likely that programmes of urban planning and investment were designed to achieve a similar enclosure and disclosure of the city's various environmental elements.

Eyles and Peace attributed Hamilton's poor image to a number of factors. Perhaps the most important was the city's economic life, which was associated with unappealing, unattractive functionality and its peripheral economic and cultural position within the larger regional locale, the 'Golden Horseshoe' (the Niagara–Oshawa corridor), particularly its subordinate position with regard to Toronto. Through an imbalance in material and symbolic resources, Toronto had achieved a position of centrality, both locally within the 'Golden Horseshoe' and within wider Canadian culture. The striking centre–periphery opposition that has characterised the relationship between Toronto and Hamilton is illustrated by the metaphorical descriptors that have been attached to them: 'Toronto is the rich kid and Hamilton the poor country cousin' (Eyles and Peace 1990: 84).

This relationship was traced back to the internal regionalisation of each city. Toronto's centrality derived in large part from its economic life: '[Toronto] experienced growth in terms of financial and corporate power' (ibid.: 83). This, along with its political climate, ethnic diversity, absence of civic disorder and successful planning '[c]ontributed to Toronto's metaphor – the liveable city. Toronto's status has also been enhanced by its international profile' (ibid. 1990: 84). Hamilton, by contrast '[i]s known for traditional features, particularly steel making. Steel is also industry, an unfashionable way for a city to make its money in the 1980s and 1990s' (ibid: 85).

Hamilton's vigorous attempts at internal regionalisation, attempts to 'talk the city up', can be interpreted as a response to its subordinate, peripheral position within the regional locale of the 'Golden Horseshoe'. Should this effort prove successful the internal regionalisation of the 'Golden Horseshoe' area would be transformed by what was a purely internal redeployment of symbolic (and material) resources within the locale of Hamilton. Clearly, the activities of agents and institutions in Hamilton were involved in a contest for centrality within the region and the nation. The 'Golden Horseshoe' region exhibits a demonstrable politics not only of place but also of position.

Writing from the perspective of geography, the previous discussion has inevitably promoted the role of space at the expense of time. While this chapter is more concerned with the spatial realm, the temporal realm cannot be ignored in locale formation and the sedimentation of cultural systems of space. Giddens addressed the relationship between endurance in time and embeddedness in space. He argues that, despite the potential for transformation, centre–periphery patterns do tend to endure; the struggle for endurance is part of the political struggle for position:

Centre/periphery distinctions tend frequently to be associated with endurance in time. Those who occupy centres establish themselves as having control over resources which allow them to maintain differentiations between themselves and those in peripheral regions. The established may employ a variety of forms of social closure to sustain distance from others who are effectively treated as inferiors or outsiders.

(Giddens 1984: 131)

Centre–periphery oppositions frequently display a lengthy temporal endurance. There are many examples of this, such as the relationship between the 'first' and the 'third' worlds and the north and south of England. The activities of individuals and institutions in reproducing these geographic dimensions often represent the unconscious reproduction of deep historical patterns. To have such cultural patterns accepted as 'natural' is an integral part of the deployment of power in the establishment of position.

NORTH AND SOUTH: RELATIVE GEOGRAPHY AND ENGLISH NATIONAL CULTURE

Individual places are situated within a series of cultural geographies associated with ethnic, political, economic, informational, cultural and religious formations. There has evolved a powerful but not uncontested hegemony associated with those systems of space linked to the nation. Frequently, these derive from a particular historical period and endure, despite subsequent changes. Raymond Williams has argued that the 1840s formed the 'decisive period' in the emergence of modern English national identity (1970: 11), during which an enduring narration of national space began to unfold (see Pocock 1978; Wiener 1981; Colls and Dodd 1986; Smith 1989; Chambers 1990; Shields 1991). The effect of this was the sedimentation of a cultural system of space into ideas of English, national identity. These mythologies had their roots in the processes of rapid industrialisation and urbanisation that significantly re-ordered the economic and social geographies of the nation.

During this period, England became increasingly envisioned through a discourse of 'the two nations.' This construction first appeared in a series of novels published in rapid succession between 1848 and 1866 that have become labelled the 'industrial novels'. These included works such as Mrs Gaskell's *North and South,* Dickens' *Hard Times* and Disraeli's *Sybil or The Two Nations* (Williams 1958). A central theme of these and many other narratives of the time was the apparent uneven economic development between the north and the south and the different styles and conditions of life that this economic geography engendered. There emerged a process of association between different economic, social and cultural characteristics and each region, and an enduring space myth of the British nation.

The north–south envisioning of the nation has since come to dominate a number of discourses, including the academic, and has proved an enduring way of understanding spatial variation across the nation (Smith

1989). Broadly, the north–south comparisons highlight a divide between two ways of life. The north represented here is an undifferentiated unity in which the bleak, the functional and the working class are disclosed, while alternatives, 'southern' characteristics – the genteel, picturesque, the 'cultured' and the rural – are enclosed. Shields offers a summary of the representation of the two regions in this prevailing discourse of national space.

'North'	'South'
Peripheral region	Centre, hub
Working class	Economic, political elites
Bleak countryside	Tamed landscapes
Industry, factories	Stockbroking, management
Rugged leisure pursuits (football, dale walking)	High culture (opera, ballet)
Wet and cold climate	Warmer climate
Gemeinschaft	*Gesellschaft*
Sociality, emotional community	Social structure, institutions

Source Shields 1991: 231

Shields argues that various British myths – the pastoral and that of nineteenth-century industrial blight – were organised, deployed and reproduced by a variety of class-based and geographical interests in such a way that 'London and the South [are] the cultural, spiritual and political heartland of the nation' (1991: 245).

While the origins of this construction were political – to hide the realities of conditions among the poor in the south (ibid.: 211) – more importantly, so are its consequences. The system of space fundamental to this construction of the nation offered a differential valorisation of spaces and places. Most basically, it represented the equation of the south as centre and the north as periphery. The geography that underpinned this construction was based on the cultural distance between the imagined lives of each region and the imagined ideal 'Englishness' that was concomitantly emergent at the time and was constructed in opposition to the actual economic geography of industrialisation.

The effects of this marginalisation or 'otherisation' of the north were evident in its subsequent construction as alien, strange or even foreign to what is regarded as 'English.' Orwell expressed this well when he referred to the north as 'a strange country' (1959: 106). This discourse of the north as other is further evident in, for example, the construction of the 'northerner' in tones that reflect the construction of the 'foreigner' as other in early anthropological literature, concentrating on the strange accent, the alien landscape and unfathomable cultural practices.

DISPLACING BIRMINGHAM: THE PECULIAR
MARGINALITY OF THE ENGLISH MIDLANDS

Any cultural system of space is replete with silences, omissions and contradictions. The system of space associated with English national identity is no exception. Contradictions include spaces in the geographical north which are more 'southern' in their cultural identity, and visa versa. However, major silences include the enclosure of spaces and practices within each region, but also of regions that fail to fit into the north–south division of national space. Perhaps the most major silence in this regard is the exclusion of the English Midlands.

The north was invented as a way of consigning and enclosing the unpleasant characteristics of the industrial revolution and their resultant localities (Wiener 1981; Shields 1991). The spaces of the nation were then consigned to one of these two cultural spaces. The system of space that emerged as a result of the collision between the social and economic changes of the industrial revolution and southern interests was imposed 'from above'. It acted as a way of obliterating the complex reality that existed within these two spaces. When viewed from this perspective, the English Midlands was not a problematic space to accommodate. The English Midlands contains elements as 'English' as the deep England of the Herefordshire, Worcestershire and Warwickshire countryside and elements as 'unEnglish' as Black Country factories and Birmingham workshops. Accommodating the English Midlands within the north–south geography of English culture involved little more than consigning the former elements to the cultural south and the latter to the cultural north. This division of the English Midlands has consequently been legitimised in other representations of the 'divided nation' discourse, including the academic, through an enduring silence.

However, that the legitimacy of this division derives from the hegemony of certain cultural perspectives is rarely acknowledged; to do so would involve an expansion or a destabilisation of the parameters of this system of space. This hegemony has tended to remain unchallenged within debates surrounding the question of the geographical dimensions of English national space. The ascription of northern and southern identities to the Midlands simply does not tally with the experience of Midlanders. The north and the south are not: ' "our" places where "we" feel we belong' (Paasi 1986: 129). That this system of space was and continues to be at variance with the experience of the majority of Midlanders is not the point; it was neither designed for them nor constructed and legitimised from 'their' perspective.

The city of Birmingham is doubly marginalised within the cultural geographies of England. First, it is geographically located a space largely denied legitimacy within the prevailing cultural geographies of national space. Following this is a second realm of marginality whereby it has been consigned to the cultural north. Being so consigned affects, to a large degree, the representation of the city. Prevailing representations of Birmingham have demonstrated a considerable correspondence with the identity of the cultural space within which it has been placed (see Murphy 1987: 156; Jennings 1995). This *dis*placement of Birmingham has provided the prevailing structures of expectation against which the city has had to compete to assert an identity of its own making.

REPRESENTING THE PROCESS OF URBAN REGENERATION

[Myth] has turned reality inside out, it has emptied it of history and has filled it with nature, it has removed from things their human meaning so as to make them signify a human insignificance. The function of myth is to empty reality.

(Barthes 1972: 142–3)

The identity of urban regeneration emergent through its representation is not a natural, universal relationship but rather a social construction. This identity makes appeal to the dual notions of the internal regionalisation of cultural space and relocation or centring within external systems of cultural space. The intentions of the representation of the process of urban regeneration are to achieve an internal regionalisation of civic space and to implant or relocate the city in external cultural systems of space. Some of these systems of space are well-established, such as those associated with the nation. Others are more recently emergent such as those associated with ideas of Europe. The aims of this representation are to make the equation of the process of urban regeneration and transformation appear 'natural' by developing a discourse of urban regeneration based upon the processes associated with cultural relocation. This section examines this process with reference to the three media most closely associated with urban regeneration: the local press, promotional materials and public art. It seeks to examine ways in which these media, despite their obvious differences, are attuned to the question of cultural position and aim to achieve their goal of cultural relocation. It examines the construction of both myths of position and myths that seek to engage with the contents of identities ascribed within systems of cultural space.

THE INTERNATIONAL CONVENTION CENTRE BIRMINGHAM

The idea of a convention centre for Birmingham (ICC) was first raised in 1981 at the height of the economic recession in the UK. It was regarded as something of a panacea for the effects of de-industrialisation afflicting the West Midlands region at the time. Work began on the ICC in 1986, following the securing of a European Regional Development Fund grant of £49.75 million. The ICC was eventually completed, at a cost of £180 million, in 1991. It was officially opened by the Queen in June of that year. The ICC (Figure 11.1) consists of eleven halls of varying size. One of which, Symphony Hall, was designed specifically as an international concert venue.

Figure 11.1 The International Convention Centre

The ICC is situated within the Broad Street Redevelopment Area, an extensive area ten minutes walk west of the Birmingham city centre.

Three discourses of cultural relocation

I The city as phoenix: the social construction of urban regeneration as transformation (the local press)

Between 1981 and 1991 the Birmingham local press[1] produced almost 500 articles on the ICC. Within these accounts a number of themes were dominant and recurrent. There is little doubt that the imagery that underpinned the representation, and consequently the identity, of urban regeneration in the 1980s and 1990s was that associated with transformation (Thomas 1994). However, merely to recognise this is to fail to understand the implications of the representation and the imagination of the process of urban change. First, the equation of urban regeneration with transformation is discursive. The implications of this are that in relation to a contestable process, such as urban regeneration, this construction legitimised certain perspectives while marginalising others. The representation of urban regeneration provided a map of power and established the limits to contest. This chapter argues that if contest or resistance are to be effective they need to recognise this discursivity and seek to destabilise it. While this chapter does not seek to offer any alternative it highlights the basis by which representations of urban change perpetuate hegemonies.

The notion of cultural relocation offers the best way of understanding the social construction of urban regeneration as transformation. This identity was achieved in two ways. First was the construction of transformation as a myth of cultural centrality which is achievable through the process of urban regeneration. This necessitated a particular imagination of change which was derived from the cultural geographies of national space. The construction of Birmingham's present and recent past during the 1980s, and hence the definition of its needs, resonated with the myths of northern and industrial space derived from the deeply rooted narrative geographies of national space. The association also acted to define the characteristics that the city aimed to refute or alter through the process of urban regeneration. In the first instance, in recognising itself only as peripheral the question of the necessity for transformation was automatically legitimised, rendered natural and unquestionable. For example:

> Bitten by recession in the 70s and 80s, the city was wandering in a void of uncertainty.
>
> *(Birmingham Evening Mail,* 2 April 1991)

> The International Convention Centre opens next Tuesday and is the missile which will launch Birmingham over the moon and into the 21st century. Like it or lump it, it is the future for Birmingham and the whole of the West Midlands. It's a firm footing to a fine future. A future in which the people and the city of Birmingham can be confident and proud.
>
> *(Birmingham Evening Mail,* 28 March 1991)

Further, this had the effect of regionalising cultural space within the city according to its relationship with the peripheral spaces of British national identity or the imagined spaces of international, 'high' culture, the two cultural spaces that the city was imagined as moving between. Those cultural practices and the associated spaces that reflected identities ascribed to the periphery in British national identity were excluded from the imagined spaces of the civic future. These were replaced by those landscapes and cultural practices concomitant with the cultural spaces of which the local press increasingly imagined the city to be part. This was a tactic that effectively circumvented the complexities of need and difference. The re-imagination of the city was achieved by the imagination of the internal space of the city through a geography of visibility and invisibility. This is explored further in the following section.

II Sites of utmost modernity: marketing the ICC and Symphony Hall (promotional materials)

As the previous section indicated, the process of cultural relocation is based upon the material or symbolic regionalisation of locales. In this instance the promotional narratives of the ICC were, and continue to be, vital in the envisioning of a geography of visibility and invisibility within the city. This was evident in the re-imagination of certain sites within the city as spectacular and theatrical, and the consequent marginalisation, or enclosure, of other cultural spaces, practices and geographies.

The most apparent examples of this are the opening up of a series of highly spectacular spaces within the city. The ICC itself was an obvious example, as was the construction of an identity for, and selling of, its cultural 'flagship' the Symphony Hall concert hall. This promotion involved the construction of a geography of culture within the city. This was one that conferred notions of legitimacy upon certain cultural practices within the city and exclusion and marginalisation upon others.

The image of the ICC was based around the usual attributes of the post-industrial economy: technical excellence, flexibility/versatility, modernity, choice, prestige, purpose, design, professionalism and uniqueness. However, beyond this inventory, what was of interest was the visualisation of the space and its creation as a centred, definitional site. The promotional materials that advertised the ICC unknowingly provided an apt descriptive metaphor of the construction of the site's identity, 'industrial theatre' (*International Convention Centre Birmingham* n.d.: 4). As with the realm of culture in the case of Symphony Hall, the realm of industry was rendered a theatrical production. The emphasis within the materials was firmly on *display*. The representation of industrial presentations within the materials visually resembled theatrical productions and were presented in such a way as to suggest the staging of theatre. These were played on a stage in front of large audiences. They existed in model form or were shots of actual or simulated 'life-size' productions. These were typically spectacular, either in their staging and lighting sets (*International Convention Centre Birmingham* n.d.: 4) or through the scale of either the production itself or elements of it, for example, the inclusion of full-size lorries on stage (leaflet *International Convention Centre Birmingham*, n.d.). While these clearly suggested that spectacular productions can be staged, they also acted as a referent for the ICC as a very spectacular production itself. This was reinforced by the imagery of display within the Centre which strongly echoed the construction of stage scenery and the conspicuous display of the technical 'backroom' support of the Centre.

The identity of Symphony Hall was established as a site of spectacular modernity. This was anchored around the combination of refined cultural practice and displays of technical prestige. In incorporating specific classical musicians of world standing into its promotional strategies, Symphony Hall acted as a receptor of their prestige. The musicians acted as emblems of international or world class accreditation. Further, the utmost modernity of the Hall was rendered visible through the conspicuous display of its essentially invisible components, acoustic and technical facilities.

Simon Rattle (conductor, City of Birmingham Symphony Orchestra) described Symphony Hall as a musical instrument that is itself 'played' by orchestras performing in it. This is appropriate in more than just the musical sense. The metaphor captures the integral nature of the relationship between the Hall and the spectacle of performance. The Hall itself was transformed into an object of display rather than merely being a backdrop. It is as integral to the experience of witnessing a performance there as the performers and their activities themselves. Rather than being rooted in the cultural activities of the site, the promotion of Symphony Hall represented a spectacular, architectural articulation of place identity. This is consistent with the theatrical metaphor that underpinned the promotion of the ICC as a whole. Symphony Hall, when it is not in use, is a popular tourist attraction in its own right. It is open to the public who are shown around and who have the dimensions, technical capabilities, specifications, details and costs pointed out to them by guides.

Two implications of this highly visualised representation of the sites follow. The first is the establishment of the city within external cultural space. The second is the implication of this deliberate centring upon the internal cultural geography of the city. In establishing a series of defini-tional centres the city imagined itself within certain cultural spaces, those of high culture, international culture and spectacle. These were oriented explicitly around dominant ideas of European, rather than British, national space. This alignment with international space can be read as an attempt to challenge the ascriptions of the cultural geography of British national space. This was explicitly spelled out in the promotional materials issued by the ICC:

> In April 1991, the world of music will witness the opening of the UK's finest concert hall – Symphony Hall Birmingham. Modelled on the great concert halls, such as the Musikvereinssaal, Vienna and the Concertgebouw, Amsterdam, Symphony Hall's classic elegance bene-fits from the latest technology to make it a truly versatile venue for all forms of music Seating 2,220 people in style, Symphony Hall will provide a platform for the finest orchestras and artists in the world.
> (Symphony Hall Birmingham, n.d.: 1)

This cultural positioning affected a concomitant re-ordering of the cultural spaces of the city into a series of centres and peripheries according to their compatibility with the cultural practices of the wider space. It imagined a geography of visibility and invisibility. The implications of these imagined geographies, which are inherent in this type of cultural centring, were articulated by one group which felt marginalised by the actions of the city:

> The city's policy shifted around then [1989] from providing growth locally to top-shelf stuff they can advertise in the international arena. There are only about four fringe theatre companies left in Birming-ham. Five years ago there were twenty-five. There hasn't been confidence in the work produced locally so they bring it in, as with Sadler's Wells and the D'Oyly Carte. There were good ballet com-panies in Birmingham but they didn't put the seed money in. There are more touring companies coming in now than local companies performing. I'm not against high-quality international work, but investing in local people has got to be a priority.
> (Chris Rozanski co-ordinator of the Theatre of the Unemployed, Birmingham, quoted in Lister 1991: 57)

III A tradition of transformation: imagining civic history
(public art)

The representation of urban regeneration affected a progressive equation of civic identity with the process of transformation. Civic history has been recast from within identities currently emergent as a tradition of transformation. This is most clearly evident in contemporary representations of civic history in the programme of public art associated with the ICC.

The word 'industry' and the identities and images that it evokes are highly problematic for the promotion of cities within the context of the post-industrial economy. This is so for a number of reasons. First, it evokes a whole series of negative, 'unfashionable' images. It is emblematic of peripherality within the narrative geographies of English national identity (see Wiener 1981; Shields 1991). It is also emblematic of dereliction within the narratives of recession from which the wave of 1980s urban regeneration projects were born (Eyles and Peace 1990; Watson 1991). However, despite this it remains an enduring thread of regional self-identity in the English Midlands. Furthermore, industry has been used as the basis for resistant identities constructed in opposition to the official cultures of urban regeneration (Boyle and Hughes 1991). This political identity is one that needs to be countered and an alternative inserted in its place if this identity is not to taint the narration of a new cultural geography of the city through the media of urban regeneration. The way in which these associations were avoided was through the process of *re-semanticisation*. The previous section examined the ways in this was achieved through the representation of industry in promotional materials. This section concentrates on its re-semanticisation through the medium of public art.

Central to many landscapes of urban regeneration are projects of public art and sculpture (Hall 1992, 1994; Goodey 1994). This is particularly so in Birmingham which has implemented, through the Public Art Commissions Agency, a percent for art scheme. One product of this has been the extensive commissioning of works of public art in association with the ICC. The most prominent element of this programme is Raymond Mason's sculpture in yellow fibreglass, *Forward* (Figure 11.2). *Forward* narrates the emergence of civic pride through the figurative representation of numerous 'Brummies' and is replete with references to a number of historical periods.

Within the topography of the sculpture, industry occupies a central, nexical space between a grim, anonymous past and an optimistic, 'bright' future. The significance of this space is that it is, Mason argues, where a recognisable civic identity emerged and took on tangible form. Human figures increase in both size and detail and become distinguishable as recognisable individuals rather than simple members of a crowd. References to specific individuals, activities and institutions also begin to appear at this stage. Central to this narrative of an emergent identity is an iconography of industry.

Mason's representation of industry through *Forward* is not one that either seeks to exclude the functional elements of industry or simply makes reference to industry through exceptional 'pioneers' or 'heroes'. Rather, Mason's industrial heritage is one of 'ordinary' working *men* (which

Figure 11.2 An iconography of industry, *Forward*, by Raymond Mason

excludes the role of women in Birmingham's industrial heritage) engaged in a process of production. However, Mason reconciles the fact of industry's unappealing functionality through a very 'humanised' reading. This he achieves through the development of a myth of industry as a human rather than a mechanical saga. This is a trope he readily recognises within his work:

> 'FOR ONE precise moment in history Birmingham was unique,' says Raymond Mason the sculptor who was born and raised there but now lives in France. 'It founded a tradition of fine craftsmanship and fine machinery. That shouldn't be forgotten.' Nor will it be if Mason achieves his aim. . . .

> 'They tore the heart out of Birmingham,' he says. 'When I was asked to do a monument I said yes – if I could evoke the city they has taken down. It would be a great pity to forget what was a great moment in the human saga of fine work.'
>
> (Weideger 1991: no page given)

Mason constructed this human saga in a number of ways. The representation of the human and industrial elements within the sculpture is not to scale but is biased towards the human. The human elements typically enjoy heavy idealisation both in their appearance, for example in the case of the prominent muscled figure, and in their construction as archetypes of particular human attributes, most usually strength and skill.

The industrial 'hardware' represented in *Forward* is not that of mass production, but rather it is of those elements that require animation through human attention. This is essentially a derivation from a specific historical period, prior to the mechanisation of the production process with the consequent skill-shifting of industrial production. Mason draws upon various masculine myths of the industrial workplace where pride is forged through 'hard graft' and the 'sweat of the brow' that allow him to gloss over Birmingham's recent troubled industrial history. Mason essays his saga from within that enduring body of mythology that sees Birmingham's 'wealth and reputation' being founded upon the industrial revolution (see Slim 1986). Mason's representation of industry is a celebration of the power of the body, rather than the machine. Mason's workers echo less the alienated proletariat of the Marxist vision, more the 'noble' worker of Stalinist propaganda.

CONCLUSION

By 1991 when the ICC opened, the notions of transformation, spectacle and centrality had become roundly appropriated by those agents involved in, and representing, the process of urban regeneration. First, the equation of transformation with the realm of urban regeneration had the effect of distancing it from any potentially radical or subversive meanings. Its dominant signification spirals were established around the realm of urban regeneration. Second, the notion of transformation was actively used by agents to implant Birmingham centrally within certain positively valorised cultural spaces. This cultural relocation acted to challenge the prevailing structures of expectation associated with systems of space linked to the nation. The effect of this was that it reflected back within the city and opened up a series of centres and peripheries according to their compatibility with the identities of these wider spaces. Through the processes of cultural relocation and internal regionalisation, a politics of centring and exclusion was affected by the narration of a 'new' city. This discourse was crucial to the framing of change in the built environment.

NOTE

1   The local press in Birmingham is dominated by three newspapers from the same group, the daily, morning *Birmingham Post*, the daily, evening, *Evening Mail*, and the weekly *Sunday Mercury*. Also available in Birmingham is the Wolverhampton-based *Express and Star*.

12

ANGLICISING THE AMERICAN DREAM

Tragedy, farce and the 'postmodern' city

Julie Charlesworth and Allan Cochrane

It is by now widely recognised that development in and of particular places can only be understood by setting them in a wider (global) context (see Cooke 1990; Massey 1995). Such a starting-point may appear to be little more than common sense, but it is important, not least because it undermines approaches which imply that the world is constituted merely as the aggregate of a series of static and bounded 'localities' or even 'communities'. Much locality-based research has found it difficult to move beyond the geographical boundaries which it uses to define its objects of study. So, for example, despite Cooke's attempt to escape from such a framework in his introductory chapter, this seemed to be the message of the case studies arising from the ESRC's Changing Urban and Regional System research programme, which were reported in Cooke (1989) and Harloe, Pickvance and Urry (1989). Although the case studies are of interest in themselves, the links between them are limited, and each seems almost hermetically sealed from the outside world (despite the inclusion of broad statements which acknowledge the importance of world-wide economic restructuring).

The significance of global processes is, perhaps, clearest in discussions which focus on the economic aspects of urban development. The growth or decline of cities is closely related to, and influenced by, the investment decisions made by major corporations and by the changing structures of global markets (see Hamnett 1995). One consequence of recognising the significance of economic globalisation has been the emergence of a rhetoric in which people and places are automatically rendered powerless. All that matters, it appears, is the impersonal power of the global markets (see Allen 1995 for a critical review of this position). But it is important to recognise that urban development is not just the inevitable outcome of the workings of these markets. There are more subtle processes at work, too, which both enable and constrain cities (their residents and elites) allowing (and sometimes requiring) them to position themselves in particular ways within the global system. The global system not only generates uneven development and inequality, but is itself the product of competition and contestation which draws on that unevenness.

Place-marketing is an increasingly important element within these processes (see Kearns and Philo 1995; Gold and Ward 1994) and Harvey's notion of urban entrepreneurialism helps to explain its dynamic (Harvey 1989). The lived experience of urban residents is shaped by their position in the context of global competition, but their own understandings and interpretations also help to construct the spaces of social and political interaction locally and globally (see Massey 1995). It is no longer possible, if it ever was, to identify some self-contained and bounded urban space within which social relations can safely be left to work themselves out, since those relations themselves stretch across the globe in complex and overlapping patterns, not only in the field of economics but also, for example, in those of culture and politics (see Allen 1995; Anderson, Brook and Cochrane 1995; Gilroy 1993a). Nor is it possible to identify some simple process through which global pressures feed through to find clear-cut expressions in particular places. Instead, an active process of interpretation, borrowing and representation helps to shape the parameters of urban existence.

In this chapter, we explore just one of the ways in which global representations of urbanisation come together with place-marketing to produce particular expressions in and of one place. We will be considering the remarkable power of the American dream as it is translated to a European and, indeed, specifically English context. In developing this argument we shall be drawing mainly on the example of Milton Keynes and representations of it, but doing so within the broader context of urban change in the south-east of England. We aim to show the power of global image-making in shaping and influencing particular developments, but also to identify some of the ways in which those images may be negotiated to generate different meanings in specific places. Our arguments focus on some of the complex social and political negotiations that influence the outcomes of place-marketing.

THE POWER OF US IMAGERY

It is hard to escape the dominance of the US model in discussions of urban form. The construction of the US as universal 'future' is well-established across a wide range of social phenomena (a point noted by Hall *et al.* as long ago as 1978 in their discussion of the importation of 'mugging' to England's inner cities). That 'future' or, perhaps more accurately, those 'futures' are a powerful amalgam of utopian and dystopian visions, often coexisting within the same understanding. This can be summed up with the help of just one recent example – that of Los Angeles – although many others could also be used.

Los Angeles has become a paradigmatic symbol of the postmodern city. In Mike Davis's version we are offered the promise of excavating the future – and not just that of the West Coast of the USA (Davis 1990), while in Ed Soja's famous phrase 'it all comes together' in Los Angeles which also seems to provide the evidence that space has finally become more important than time (Soja 1989). Los Angeles, says Soja, is 'exemplary or symptomatic of the new urbanisation' (Soja 1995: 128). Zukin points out that Los Angeles has become most interesting as a 'spatial metaphor'. We are fascinated by it, she argues, 'because we think it shows us the future' (Zukin 1991: 220). As long ago as 1971 Banham was claiming that 'Los Angeles cradles and embodies the most potent current version of the great bourgeois vision of the good life in a tamed countryside' (Banham 1971: 238). More recently we have been told that, as the 'great grand-daddy of Edge Cities', Los Angeles offers the dominant model of urbanisation for the late twentieth century (Garreau 1991: 129). In the European popular imagination Los Angeles has become the latest in a long line of US based 'futures' which offer us both the frisson of fear and the promise of paradise (also expressed in Rieff 1993).

The main empirical focus of this chapter is on the experience of Milton Keynes,[1] and at first sight the counterposition of Los Angeles and Milton Keynes (even in this form) may simply appear absurd. Los Angeles is exciting, a lotusland familiar from television, films, music and the news, yet somehow threatening and different, a place which undermines the traditional certainties of European culture. Milton Keynes, by contrast, remains hopelessly familiar, even – perhaps particularly – for those who have never been there: its resolute suburbanism and 'successful' Thatcherite growth leave it as somewhere easy to dismiss, as what has been described as a 'non-place place' (Zukin 1991: 20) or might more charitably be labelled an 'ordinary place' (Pinch 1992). Every discussion of Milton Keynes in press or magazine seems to be accompanied by a reference to Gertrude Stein's famous comment about Oakland: there's no *there* there (see, among many others, Dalby 1992; Marks 1992; Marling 1993: 55).

Yet it is precisely the sharpness of the contrast which highlights the global power of 'Los Angeles' as an image, or representation, of postmodernity, influencing interpretations of urbanism in Europe as much as America, while itself being reinterpreted and reshaped to fit in a different context. Looking at Milton Keynes through the prism of 'Los Angeles' is helpful, not only in understanding what is happening there (and in the south-east of England more generally), but also in highlighting some of the key processes of change in contemporary urban society. The arguments which follow make no pretence to being a comparison between Los Angeles and Milton Keynes. Even at their most ambitious, they only draw on journalistic and popular accounts of Los Angeles – images which dominate European understandings not only of Los Angeles, but also of 'Los Angeles' as archetype of the postmodern city and, increasingly, of 'America' as symbol of our shared future – in order to explore the ways in which they have been reflected and reinterpreted in changing urban forms within the UK.

THE MAKING OF MILTON KEYNES

Milton Keynes is a (third wave) new town – or new city, according to its planners – located on the edge of the south-east of England. The new town was designated by the Labour government in 1967 as one of the last gasps of Wilsonian modernisation; a master plan was drawn up by the consultants Llewellyn-Davies, Weeks, Forestier-Walker and Bor and a development corporation was appointed with the task of bringing the plan to fruition.[2] The history of the town's development was not entirely trouble-free – in the 1970s its growth relied extensively on public sector investment in housing and infrastructure and in the early 1980s unemployment soared to unprecedented levels as the traditional industries of railway manufacture and light manufacturing (which predated the new town) were hit by recession. In the end, however, the Thatcher years were kinder. At the start of the 1990s Milton Keynes was the settlement with the fastest-growing population in the UK over the previous decade with a total population of around 200,000. However, it remains resolutely suburban, not only as a significant commuting source for London, but also for other settlements in the south-east. According to the 1991 Census some 21 per cent of its resident work-force travel to work outside the area, although there is a similar number of inward commuters.

From the air, the result spread out at the start of the 1990s: Milton Keynes looks like a middle-sized town in the US mid-West, with its drive-in fast food outlets, its shopping malls and related chunks of low-rise office development. Journalists have had little hesitation in drawing parallels with the US. So, for example, Marler simply says that it is 'England's most American city' (Marler 1993: 63), while Williams (1992) confirms that Milton Keynes is 'described by many as "American"'. John Daniel (now Vice Chancellor of the Open University) returning to the UK after many years in Canada suggests that 'if you have lived in North America, Milton Keynes is just the place to return to' (quoted in Adonis 1992). Marks (1992) reports that one of the *Superman* series of films 'used aerial views of it to depict an archetypical American city'. Hill (1993) says 'close your ears to the accents and you could be in Minneapolis'. Mars (1992) enthusiastically endorses a vision of Milton Keynes as 'Little Los Angeles in Bucks'. He even claims that the Pacific beaches of Los Angeles find their middle English expression in Milton Keynes' extensive network of parks – 'what the beaches are to LA, the parks are to Milton Keynes' (ibid.: 25).

These references also find an echo in the planning history of Milton Keynes. Particularly in the early years of its planning the Development Corporation was directly influenced by European readings of Los Angeles, as interpreted by Reyner Banham, whose arguments had a wide degree of currency in the early 1970s (Banham 1971). His stress on the low-density development of Los Angeles linked by an extensive freeway system found a clear echo in early decisions which rejected proposals to plan the new city around a public transport network (an early proposal for a new town in North Buckinghamshire included plans for a monorail system) (Mortimer 1976: chapters 6 and 7). This would necessarily have implied a denser population. Instead, as Mortimer (ibid.: 178) notes, 'unrepentantly impressed by Los Angeles', the plan is based the assumption of high car ownership levels. The road system is organised around one kilometre square grids, and a low population density (8 per acre) is projected for the year 2000. Even Banham's scepticism about town planning found some reflection in the Development Corporation's plans, with explicit reference to Banham's support for 'non-plan' and Webber's notion of 'permissive planning' appearing in its Interim Report (Bendixson and Platt 1992: 67).

More direct borrowing from the US came through Webber (Professor of Urban and Regional Development at Berkeley) himself, who set out a very clear message for Milton Keynes in early seminars for the Development Corporation in 1967: Milton Keynes, he argued, would not be the product of the 'middle industrial era', but rather of a 'post-industrial era', 'in which the nature of the city is radically changing'. Moving away from the manufacturing to the information economy was seen to be the key: 'Milton Keynes will be, in a sense, spearhead of this changing phase in urban civilisation'. The task facing Milton Keynes' planners was the 'planned invention of the future' (ibid.: 47). Webber's work on southern California, which led him to develop the notion of 'non-place urban realm' – of 'community without propinquity' – fed into the early plans. The future was to be a modest version of 'Los Angeles', with high levels of car ownership and little public transport.

Indeed, even the muted denials of the Development Corporation's official historians (Bendixson and Platt 1992) simply confirm the power of US-based imagery, if only because it was the common sense of the time. The message borrowed brought a commitment to low-rise housing, spread out in a grid system of roads, with an attempt to avoid having a single centre to reproduce the 'unfocused ubiquity' which Banham (1971: 211) saw as typical of Los Angeles. Milton Keynes was to be decentralised and diverse, with different land uses and employment sources being distributed around the city. And, of course, it was above all to be car-based with the main roads operating much like freeways. In general, Milton Keynes was to be characterised by single family housing and vernacular rather than heroic architecture – there was not even to be any high-rise commercial or housing development (with a six-storey limit on commercial developments in central Milton Keynes, and a three-storey limit elsewhere).

UNDERSTANDING MILTON KEYNES

Although it only stretches over twenty-five years, Milton Keynes' planning and architectural history is a highly contested one. One version (espoused by Bishop 1986; Mars 1992; Ward 1993, among others) suggests that an attempt was made in the early 1970s to pervert the flexible aims of the master planners by imposing a modernist vision of urbanism. According to this version, the architects tried to take over, imposing almost brutalist styles of geometrically arranged public housing in the grid squares for which they were given responsibility. Bishop (1986: 18) reports stories of an archi-tectural department largely made up of young men 'known as the "undertakers" because of their penchant for black suits', whose designs were generally disliked by residents. If the initial plan appeared to draw on images from southern California, the architect-planners in power tended to utilise images from European urban culture, with Milton Keynes emerging as a contemporary expression of that culture, with even the grid roads being explained as 'our Venice canals' (see Walker 1981, 1994).

By the end of the decade, however, it was suggested that the logic of the master plan, coupled with the preferences of residents, had finally succeeded in undermining these grand metropolitan ambitions. It is in this context that Bishop argues that 'MK is a success ... despite the planners' (Bishop 1986: 3) while Bendixson and Platt (1992: 105) similarly celebrate 'The replacement of "Bauhaus regimentation" by "fishing village romantic"' in the late 1970s. Residents interviewed by Bishop and his research team at the end of the 1970s implicitly questioned visions of Milton Keynes which defined it as a city, instead interpreting it as a series of connected 'villages' or 'neighbourhoods', while actively taking advantage of urban facilities located outside their own areas (Bishop 1986: 100).

In the 1980s, any possibility of imposing a coherent 'modernist' vision on the development of Milton Keynes was lost in the shift from public to private sector housing development (particularly towards the building of executive housing). The new estates ranged from the explicitly American 'California Collection' to the more modest red-brick vernacular of the cul de sac and borrowings from English tradition. Some are 'versions of Southfork for people with normal-sized shoulders/incomes/families' (Marling 1993: 63), while elsewhere, 'favourite names for estates and house types are redolent of old England' (Hanson 1992: 37). 'Judging by its show homes,' says Hanson, 'Milton Keynes is a futuristic city which goes in for collective nostalgia.'

Alongside the consciously US-oriented borrowing of malls, boulevards and drive-thru restaurants, the 'pioneers' of Milton Keynes seem equally dedicated to constructing a bucolically English retreat into a simulacrum of village life. Most romantically, one Development Corporation report described Milton Keynes as 'a quilt of secluded but connected villages' (quoted in Bendixson and Platt 1992: 172). The 'history' which survives is largely constructed as pastiche, with one estate in land-locked Milton Keynes being described as having the features of a small fishing village (Bendixson and Platt 1992: 102), another juxtaposing a brand new thatched cottage next to a brand new Queen Anne mansion (both – of course – with double garages), while a conscious attempt is made to evoke a rural landscape which never existed along the main roads, with the claim that the grid road plan is 'quintessentially English' (p. 54) and the ghosts of Capability Brown and Repton are called on for inspiration and support.

Even the explicitly urban styles also borrow images from the past. A new Tesco superstore includes in its windows a picture of the interior of the Victorian railway works which it replaced – and the workers depicted are of course safely Victorian and distant. The road lay-out in central Milton Keynes is described as 'Wren-like' by Bendixson and Platt (ibid.: 135) and the new Church of Christ the Cornerstone is a consciously miniaturised version of St Paul's Cathedral, with its very own prefabricated dome. One architectural commentator claims that Milton Keynes' plan reminds him 'most of all of the West End of London in the seventeenth and eighteenth centuries, with its kilometre grid of through-roads' (Rasmussen 1994: 13).

The grid roads have come to define the city (as 'green corridors' or 'soft city'), as much as the rather uninspiring buildings in any of the grid squares formed by their interaction (Owens 1992: 30), their 'Englishness' expressed not only in borrowings from great landscape gardeners of the past, but also in the resolute use of roundabouts, rather than cloverleaf junctions (or even traffic lights) at all major intersections.

SUBURBANISING THE DREAM

At the core of the construction of Milton Keynes as a place has been the dual process of explicitly and deliberately creating comforting images about a stable English society while making claims to (post)modernity through the enthusiastic embrace of symbols borrowed from the US. Even the, presumably conscious, *hommage* to Sunset Boulevard expressed in the naming of Midsummer Boulevard is balanced by the almost mystical reference to the England of ley lines and druids in the naming of Silbury Boulevard, the parallel road which encloses central Milton Keynes. In Milton Keynes, the need for change is formally acknowledged, but the legacy of planning ensures that threats to reproduction of stable 'Englishness' through growth are effectively resisted. Migration has been managed to ensure that the closest Milton Keynes gets to what Davis (1992) calls the 'Bladerunner scenario' is in the naming of its ice rink.

As a result, Milton Keynes looks more like a prime example of an 'edge city' or what Soja more accurately calls 'exopolis', than part of the core or a core in its own right. In his analysis of Los Angeles Davis focuses on the effect of edge city growth on the city: here we are looking at the creation of an edge city itself – one of those areas which Davis has blamed for the decline of the urban cores. In the US, he argues, instead of the 'spatial "trickle-down" from national economic growth' going to the 'chastened entrepreneurial city it has actually been centrifuged off to Edgeland' (Davis 1993: 14). In the context of the south-east, Milton Keynes has one of the greatest claims to fitting the edge city paradigm outlined by Garreau (1991). It has all (or at least most) of the functions of cities, it is a city of immigrants (if not pioneers) far from the old downtown, and it has grown dramatically on the site of farmland over the last thirty years (doubling in population over the course of the 1980s). Ward argues that the ultimate factors in Milton Keynes' success are 'not those which would have been uppermost to an economist, but the ones which would have occurred to an estate agent' (Ward 1993: 71), which fits in well with Garreau's identification of property developers as the drivers of urban change. If Garreau (1991: 109) is right to suggest that the 'London area [by which presumably is meant the urbanised south-east] today functions a great deal more like Los Angeles than sentimentalists care to acknowledge', largely because of the edge cities it has spawned more than thirty miles from its centre, then Milton Keynes is an integral part of this new 'south east'.

Unlike Garreau's 'edge city' paradigm, however, Milton Keynes is a planned settlement. The state has provided the framework and infrastructure, limiting entrepreneurial risks, so that developers have been able to invest with security. Its 'Englishness' also places it within a longer tradition of garden suburbs and garden cities, drawing on the visions of Ebenezer Howard, as well as the wider new town movement (see Schaffer 1970). Milton Keynes is clearly more than a suburb, at least as suburbs have traditionally been understood. Bendixson and Platt summarise the position positively to conclude that: 'Milton Keynes is a place for suburban living where the whole is greater than the parts. It is a city' (Bendixson and Platt 1992: 179). But the extent of the urban vision is fundamentally limited since, according to the same authors, 'It is suburban. It is a city of trees. Its uniqueness is that it is also a grand design. No comparable claim can be made for Solihull or Bromley' (ibid.: 167). One critic puts the same point less positively. For him, Milton Keynes 'is the garden suburb adapted for the car, and oh, so carefully, planned' (Amery 1992).

Milton Keynes is not a city in any traditional sense, because of its decentralised and dispersed settlement pattern. It is part of a wider system of edge cities which stretch in a quadrant across the south-east of England beyond the M25, from Cambridge right down to Southampton. As a result, it is difficult to find the sort of local structural coherence which Goodwin *et al.* (1993) identify in the cases of Sheffield, Bracknell and Camden as the basis on which locally specific forms of social regulation are able to develop. It is the interaction and interdependence of places within the wider sub-regional system that helps to give Milton Keynes (and places like it) its rather fluid identity. Milton Keynes itself is internally divided, with much of its population and many of its employers effectively focused outwards to other sources of employment or demand. Those who spend money in its shopping malls are drawn from a very wide swathe of the urbanised south-east, with special buses even coming from London.

Milton Keynes can be understood as a much bigger – state-sponsored – version of the way in which urban expansion has spread across the edges of the south-east as development has been tacked on to villages and small towns, with shopping centres and superstores on the edges. The new developments increasingly overwhelm the core from which the name is taken, and are effectively indistinguishable one from the other across the home counties. Although it appears to take its name from some unholy marriage between the economic gurus of Thatcherism and social democracy, Milton Keynes, too, borrowed its name from a pre-existing village. And the planners have now had the confidence to rewrite history again by renaming that village Middleton (which is, according to the Borough Council's newspaper, perhaps unsurprisingly, a name taken from some still earlier 'history').

The traditional images of Englishness mobilised in the development of Milton Keynes are, of course, not innocent. They carry with them an emphasis on single family housing and equally traditional domestic divisions of labour, in a quasi-rural setting. In Milton Keynes the proportion of women in paid employment remains significantly lower than in the region (and country) as a whole, largely because its population is also concentrated in the younger age range, but also because of the nature of the new employment and the lack of part-time job opportunities. Even before the recession the figures for women's employment in the city suggested that they were excluded even from many of the low-paid part-time jobs available in other places. At the end of the 1980s, only 42 per cent of the Milton Keynes work-force was female, compared with 47 per cent in Great Britain. This places women in a particularly unfortunate position within the labour market: not only are there fewer part-time job opportunities, but a higher proportion of them are taken up by men than in the rest of the country, so women are doubly excluded (Chesterton Consulting 1989: 10–13). Since men generally have first claim on the use of household cars for travel to work, the planners' emphasis on car-based transport, coupled with the still limited extent of car ownership, means women are frequently left reliant on what is universally agreed to be inadequate public transport, or are effectively confined to their decentralised and dispersed housing estates (Bishop 1986: 64). The 'quilt of secluded but connected villages' may also be an effective means of fostering exclusion and isolation for many women.

Images such as these, emphasising linkages to a 'rural' English past, also play an important role in the construction of a regional ethnicity which is predominantly 'white', inviting residents 'to draw comfort from a mythic sense of the past as it is reconstructed as historical memory in the present' (Gilroy 1993b: 29), and doing so all the more effectively precisely because it is not directly linked to the new racism whose genesis Gilroy is exploring. While there are some towns in the south-east with large minority ethnic group populations (such as Bedford, Luton and Slough), these represent the high water mark of a previous round of growth, based on (Fordist) mass production manufacturing industry, particularly the car industry. The new growth areas reflect clear divisions along lines of ethnicity. Where there is growth, there are relatively few members of minority ethnic groups. Instead the ethnicity of the new south-east is overwhelmingly white – and the symbolic representations with which it is associated are those of a romanticised Englishness, of cottages, villages and small towns (even if, in practice, the representations are frequently incongruously expressed in modern estates with rural addresses) (see Charlesworth and Cochrane 1994).

In this context, it is perhaps hardly surprising that planned Milton Keynes, too, has a predominantly white population, despite an initial commitment to encouraging a social mix which initially left it with a higher (if rapidly declining) share of public sector housing than elsewhere in the south-east. Despite being (or perhaps because it is) a place most of whose residents have been relatively recent migrants, Milton Keynes has a minority ethnic group population slightly below the national (English) average. According to the 1991 Census, just over 94.2 per cent of the resident population categorised themselves as white, 1.6 per cent as black, and 2.5 per cent as being of Indian, Pakistani or Bangladeshi origin. In the south-east as a whole, only 90.1 per cent of the population characterise themselves as white, although for the outer south-east this proportion rises dramatically to 97.8 per cent. The figures for Milton Keynes, it may be unnecessary to stress, are in marked contrast to the population of those parts of London from which the new town was originally intended to draw its population. In Greater London as a whole the proportion of the population which characterises itself as white is only 79.8 per cent, while in Inner London the proportion is 74.4 per cent. Most strikingly, perhaps, in Inner London, some 13.5 per cent of the population describe themselves as black, in sharp contrast to the Milton Keynes figure.

Milton Keynes has always had its own image makers, attempting to construct an Anglicised (and sanitised) version of lotusland. Television and other forms of advertising have emphasised the features which might be expected – with easy access to work, leisure facilities and the countryside being highlighted alongside the space available to young families and children. Famous television advertisements have focused on children releasing large numbers of red balloons, or on the early morning cycle ride through manicured fields to easily accessible fishing. Meanwhile, other advertisements blared about the numbers of Japanese and German firms which have located there. Milton Keynes had set out to construct an image of itself as the ultimately successful suburb well before the discovery of edge cities. Where other cities locate their malls on the outskirts, Milton Keynes city centre – central Milton Keynes – is itself almost reducible to its enclosed, protected and policed shopping mall, and even the big retail warehouses are clustered around the central railway station. The central mall bestrides the city centre, leaving an unfillable hole after dark, around which local residents have to drive or walk, but may not enter (growing local concerns about this are reflected, for example, in Milton Keynes Forum 1993). Instead of operating as an enclosed and protected 'high street', as some hoped it might, the mall has become privatised space, protected from local residents after dark by their exclusion from it (see Ward 1993: 99ff).

Milton Keynes is characterised by subtle, and not so subtle, processes of social segregation almost as impressive as those of any US city, although in Milton Keynes the grid roads, with their external banks of earth, walls of trees and limited access from main roads, operate effectively enough without the need for other defensive ramparts. It is almost immediately clear (and is certainly part of the local urban common sense) which grid squares have the highest levels of unemployment, poverty and other social problems and which contain the 'executive housing' whose shortage was at one stage supposed to be limiting further growth. The harsh realities of life for those in some of the large public sector housing estates, where poverty and unemployment are endemic, also help to define the extent to which those residents are marginal to the overall project. Lord Campbell (first chair of the Development Corporation's Board) commented retrospectively in 1993 that 'Our original goal was not to have a west end for the rich and east end for the poor. That has gone completely out of the window!'

Conway (1992: 2) identifies sixteen (out of seventy-one) estates within the new town area in which there is a significantly higher concentration of referrals to the Social Services Department and notes that 'where need is greatest resources are least'. Almost all (fifteen) of these estates were built before 1981, and all are dominated by public sector housing. Lone parent households are overrepresented in five estates (over 9 per cent of households in all and 16 per cent in one) with lone pensioner households generally being concentrated in a different set of estates (around 26 per cent of households in one) although with some overlap at lower levels (Conway 1992: Tables 2 and 3). On one estate (the subject of investigation by an interagency working group) nearly 40 per cent of households did not own a car – a matter of some importance in a city in which transportation and accessibility are based on car ownership – while over 22 per cent of the economically active population were unemployed or on government schemes (MKBC 1993). The different estates have quite distinctive local reputations, which reflect their positions in the urban social hierarchy, and this is being reproduced in the new private housing estates, whose 'housing layouts speak eloquently of status divisions' (Hanson 1992: 37).

Not surprisingly, given the obstacles to effective public transport, household car ownership levels in Milton Keynes are higher than the British and regional averages. But the imagery of universal car ownership borrowed from the US remains some distance away – 25 per cent of households in the Borough (27 per cent of those in the new town's designated area) have no car and 47 per cent have only one (Chesterton Consulting 1995). Surveys conducted on behalf of the Borough Council in 1995 highlighted the inadequate public transport system as one of the main areas in which residents want improvements, and similar concerns were raised by residents in the late 1970s (Bishop 1986: 76). There are regular campaigns and complaints in the local press about bus services and through citizens' organisations such as Milton Keynes Forum. The Development Corporation was always reluctant to admit the full logic of its transport planning assumptions and claimed that a policy of heavily subsidising fleets of minibuses would provide an effective system of public transport (see Potter 1976: 152). Not surprisingly, as Potter predicted, such subsidies have not been forthcoming in the longer term, and it takes a remarkably Panglossian analysis to claim that the deregulation (and privatisation) of the buses has solved the problems, just because it has brought expensive (and half empty) minibuses to the estates (Bendixson and Platt 1992: chapter 15).

INTERPRETING NEW URBAN SPACES

The politics of growth in Milton Keynes is driven by what Davis calls the mythology of entrepreneurialism. It is difficult not to agree with the conclusions of the authors of *MK 2k* – a strategic planning document prepared by the Borough Council – that the economic growth of the Borough over the last twenty years 'has been directly attributable to the success of attracting new jobs to the area' by the Milton Keynes Development Corporation (BMK 1988: 16). Yet, in this case the ambiguity of urban entrepreneurialism is particularly noticeable. Milton Keynes would not and could not exist without substantial state intervention (for a brief summary of its planning history, see Chesterton Consulting 1992). It is the product not only of the growth pressures which faced the south-east in the 1970s and 1980s, and of private sector investment which accompanied this, but also of the greenbelt, new town policy and even road-building programmes. Its growth was explicitly predicated on a planning policy which restricted growth in the southern part of Buckinghamshire (see Buckinghamshire County Council 1988). In the later 1980s, it was alone among settlements within the planning region to be identified by SERPLAN (the regional planning authority) as a growth pole.

Without the extensive investment in infrastructure during the 1970s and the movement of population associated with it, the expansion of the 1980s would not have been possible. Development Corporation officials acknowledged the role of public sector investment in the 1970s, but suggested that by the 1980s the emphasis changed towards private sector initiatives (conveniently coinciding with the replacement of the Labour government by a Conservative one) (Interview with authors, January 1992). In that respect, Milton Keynes can be seen to be a precursor of the more extensive public–private partnership programmes which were initiated later in the decade, with public sector initiatives continuing to underpin and guarantee investment carried out by the private sector. In an extreme form, at least by UK standards, Milton Keynes' planners operated in an entrepreneurial fashion: first investing and then seeking extensive returns through promotion and marketing.

They did so with little democratic involvement or participation either by the pre-existing population or by those who have come to live in the area. The emerging forms of local governance make it unlikely that matters will change significantly in future since patterns of development will effectively be determined for some time to come by the outline plans of the past as they are reinterpreted by development companies. Until 1992 the politics of Milton Keynes was effectively dominated by an unelected agency. Although formally responsible to central government, the Development Corporation proudly operated as an independent development agency, and one which worked closely with the private developers on which it relied. It played a major part in setting up the local Chamber of Commerce and various joint organisations associated with training and marketing. The privatisation of many of its divisions (including planning and development, and landscaping) in the 1980s, alongside guarantees of contracts to them, reinforced this delegation of governmental responsibility to private sector agencies. Lock (1992), who worked for the Development Corporation until the early 1980s, and who continues to operate as a planning consultant and developer in Milton Keynes, commented that:

> The privatisation process survived the scrutiny of the Audit Commission [and, incidentally, the National Audit Office] but has not wholly achieved its objectives; some former employees became overnight very rich indeed, yet the staff they were paid to shelter have drifted away; some to collect the redundancy the Corporation said it would continue to honour, some because there is too little work in the present recession, and others because they wanted to do something completely different.
>
> (Lock 1992: 6)

On its departure in 1992,[3] although it failed in attempts to transfer its housing stock to housing associations rather than the local authority, the Corporation was more successful in other areas, in parcelling out much of its land to private consortia in the form of Large Development Opportunities with planning permission; in setting up a trust to manage some 'community' assets and act as a source of funding for community groups and arts activities; and – despite a challenge in the courts from the Borough Council – in passing its extensive parkland to a trust with non-elected directors. The central Milton Keynes shopping mall, with all its apparently *public* space, was passed to a private consortium, which apart from policing it in the customary way to exclude undesirables, now also closes it at night, leaving a massive hole in the middle of what might otherwise begin to provide a civic focus. Of course, much of this is consistent with moves currently taking place throughout the British welfare state at the local level (see Cochrane 1993: chapters 6 and 7). But the experience of Milton Keynes highlights the extent to which complex political networks which are emerging which make it more and more difficult to distinguish between public and private sector interests in the operation of urban politics (and associated state forms).

These are the new forms of urban development which are spreading inexorably across the south-east. They represent more than suburbs, and the direction of change cannot simply be summarised as decentralisation to small towns and villages. The emerging urban forms are generating messier networks of urban spaces, which help to construct new mechanisms of social exclusion. Even in the US there is a recurrent concern that the new cities don't have 'soul', 'history' or 'community' (sometimes paradoxically reflected in an obsessive reference to community in promotional literature). Despite his general sympathy for the freebooting developer, even Garreau expresses concerns about the relationship between land and development. 'Each piece of the new world we build caters to our dreams of freedom. But right now the totality does not make us feel like individuals. It makes us feel like strangers. Strangers in our own land' (Garreau 1991: 413). The search for individuality may create sameness: so, for example, wanting to be able to move frequently means people have to live in housing which is standardised and easy to sell.

At first glance Milton Keynes – following Soja – looks like the ultimate confirmation that we have reached the end of history and achieved the victory of space. It was placed in a more or less undeveloped area of low grade agricultural land between London and Birmingham (Giles and Ansell 1985: 7), and its neighbourhoods have been put together in a remarkably short time with the help of a grid system drawn on an initially virtually empty map, linking existing settlements at its corners. The notion of city as 'theme park' (see Sorkin 1992) might almost have been tailor-made for Milton Keynes, with the Development Corporation (and later the Commission for New Towns) playing the part of public sector Disney, in collaboration with the development industry. Trying to get hold of the precise 'theme' which underpins the urban 'park', of course, is by no means so easy, not least because planners are keen to emphasise their flexibility.

But some aspects are reasonably clear, as attempts are made to draw on imagery both from the US and from English 'tradition' to point towards a new white world of car-borne consumption and secluded villages coupled with policed public space and renewed forms of social segregation.

NOTES

1   This chapter arises out of work done as part of a project on the politics of local economic policy-making in a 'growth' region and funded by the ESRC (Ref No. R000 23 30007), in the context of a wider programme of research on the south-east of England being undertaken at the Open University.

2   In the context of recent discussions about non-elected local governments (see Cochrane 1993), it is perhaps worth noting that new town development corporations were single-purpose development agencies with boards appointed from above and subject to no local electoral (or democratic forms of) accountability. When Michael Heseltine, as Secretary of State for the Environment, created the first urban development corporations at the start of the 1980s, he explicitly drew on the new town experience to justify the model.

3   In 1990 The Borough Council and the County Council combined (MKBC/BCC 1990) to argue for an extension of the life of the Development Corporation, but the government was unsympathetic to their request, and the Corporation was wound up on schedule, although an office of the Commission for the New Towns was based in Milton Keynes to deal with some aspects of continuing land disposal and promotion.

Part V

VIRTUAL CITIES

13

CYBERPUNK AS SOCIAL THEORY[1]

William Gibson and the sociological imagination

Roger Burrows

The intrinsically hyper-dynamic nature of contemporary technological developments provides one of the most concrete examples of Giddens's 'runaway world' where 'not only is the pace of social change much faster than in any prior system' so is its 'scope and ... profoundness' (Giddens 1991: 16). As Rucker *et al.* (1993: 16) in *Mondo 2000* more colourfully put it:

> Technology escalates on your very block: Knives turn to pistols, pistols become Uzis. Cocaine turns to crack, crack to nuke. Charles Atlas turns to Arnold Schwarzenegger, 48DD turns to 64GG, Mick Jagger sings 'Sympathy for the Devil' on the easy-listening station, and after an evening of techno hard-core sounds, the first Sex Pistols album sounds mellow and quaint.

And it does!

It is not just technology which appears to be accelerating towards meltdown, so are our cultural and sociological understandings of the world. The speed at which new theoretical discourses emerge, are disseminated and then become passé is now absurd. It is almost as if the second that one begins to engage with some new conceptual development it becomes unfashionable. The recent literature on things 'cyber' is a case in point. Reading it makes the latest pile of books on the postmodern, globalisation, reflexive modernisation (last year's model?) and the like appear mellow and quaint. Never mind who now reads Marx? or even Foucault? Who now reads Baudrillard?

This process of sociological *passéification* is, of course, not unconnected with '*fin-de-millennium*' pessimism and our general loss of visions of utopian transcendence and hope in a better future. Our inability to adequately account for our changing world in sociological terms has led, not just to an ontological insecurity but to ever more frantic attempts to provide some sort of sociological frame for a constantly moving target. In the recent conceptual scramble some analysts have begun to turn to sources of inspiration beyond traditional social scientific and political discourses in order to try and make some sort of sense of our contemporary condition. In particular the fictional world of cyberpunk has been seized on by some as a resource of analytic insights into the new dimensions of human, or even post-human existence, which are supposedly now upon us.

For Jameson (1991: 419n) cyberpunk, the work of William Gibson in particular, represents 'the supreme *literary* expression if not of postmodernism, then of late capitalism itself'. Indeed, the work of Gibson has been held up as the prime exemplar of postmodern poetics (McHale 1992a, 1992b). This might well be so, but for others cyberpunk represents much more. Perhaps the most extreme claim made for cyberpunk comes from Timothy Leary who declares that Gibson:

> has produced nothing less than the underlying myth, the core legend, of the next stage of human evolution. He is performing the philosophic function that Dante did for feudalism and that writers like Mann, Tolstoy [and] Melville ... did for the industrial age.
>
> (cited in Kellner 1995: 298)

Slightly less extreme is the claim by Stone (1991) that the work of Gibson represents the dividing line between different social epochs based upon different modes of communication. For Stone (ibid.: 85–99) the advent of cyberspace is most appropriately considered as paradigmatic of an emerging mode of communication which, by its character, constructs a new 'virtual community'. She views it as representing the most recent of four epochs each of which is evidenced by a marked change in the character of the technology of human communication. Although roughly the same quantity of data is exchanged within each epoch, each differs dramatically due to the increasing velocity of information circulation. (cf. Lash and Urry 1994).

Stone (1991) suggests a periodisation beginning in the mid-1600s with the advent of printed texts which concluded in the early 1900s (the second epoch) with the beginnings of electronic communication and entertainment media – the radio, the motion picture and, of course, television. The third epoch, began in the 1960s with computer-based information technologies reaching its apogee with the development of BBSs from the mid-1970s onwards. The fourth epoch, that of cyberspace, began in 1984 with the development of early virtual reality systems at the level of technology and with the publication of *Neuromancer* at the level of culture. For Stone, the publication of *Neuromancer*:

> crystallised a new community.... [It] reached the hackers ... and ... the technologically literate and socially disaffected who were searching for social forms that could transform the fragmented anomie that characterised life in ... electronic industrial ghettos.... Gibson's powerful vision provided for them the imaginal public sphere and refigured discursive community that established the grounding for the possibility of a new kind of social interaction ... [It] ... is a massive textual presence not only in other literary productions ... but in technical publications, conference topics, hardware design, and

scientific and technological discourses in the large.

(ibid.: 95)

Other writers, clearly not just influenced by the fictional world of cyberpunk, but by technological change itself, have begun to construct a sociological agenda exploring the realities of what some have termed *cybersociety* (Jones 1994). As Stone notes in the above quote, the cyberpunk literature remains 'a massive textual presence' in even the most atheoretical and empiricist explorations of the Internet and virtual reality. However, whilst cyberpunk has a radical and dystopic edge to it much of the work on cyberculture more generally has, hitherto, been overly utopian (Robins 1995). Indeed, there are some striking parallels between the utopianism of much of the current phase of technological development – the construction of the so called 'information superhighway' – and the construction of the interstate highway system in the US. First, it was the father of Vice-President Al Gore – one of the greatest political advocates of the new technologies – who was instrumental in the development of the federal highway system. Second, in both cases it was the US military who provided the initial rationale for the construction of both systems (Jones 1994: 10). And, as in the previous period, the utopian hyperbole surrounding the new technologies may come to be viewed as representing little more than the politically interested discourse of the 'organic intellectuals' of a new class – a 'virtual class':

> compulsively fixated on ... technology as a source of salvation from the reality of a lonely culture and radical disconnection from everyday life ... [a virtual class of] would-be astronauts who never got the chance to go to the moon [driven by the] will to virtuality.
>
> (Kroker and Weinstein 1994: 4–5)

Nevertheless, despite the hyperbole and the mythology surrounding it, it is still possible to decipher within its literary concomitant, cyberpunk, a *sociologically* coherent vision of a very near future, which is, some argue, about to collapse on the present (Csicsery-Ronay 1991: 186; Kellner 1995: Rucker *et al.* 1993). A future which is characterised as a,

> transition to the post-human world of cyberspace.... Many of the new attitudes toward the body and the new modes of social behavior do not seem particularly significant in isolation, but viewed together they demonstrate a decided trend toward a radically new model of the self and of social behavior ... that is likely to make society ... ready ... for the truly radical technologies that are soon to come.
>
> (Deitch 1992: 39)

Cyberspace began life as a word without any concrete referent. It was, Gibson claims, constructed like a William Burroughs 'cut-up' before finally being given some solidity of meaning as a central concept in a novel. As he explains it:

> Assembled word cyberspace from small and readily available components of language. Neologic spasm: the primal act of pop poetics.

Preceded any concept whatever. Slick and hollow-awaiting received meanings. All I did: folded words as taught. Now other words accrete in the inerstices.

(Gibson 1991: 28)

Whether William Gibson intends it or not, his fiction *can* be systematically read as social and cultural theory in that it not only paints 'an instantly recognizable portrait of the modern predicament', but also shows 'the hidden bulk of an iceberg of social change' that 'now glides with sinister majesty across the surface of the late twentieth century' (Sterling 1986: 2–3). Indeed, for Kellner (1995) cyberpunk fiction is a far more insightful and dynamic analytic resource for understanding the postmodern than the recent work of cultural critics such as Baudrillard. Whilst for Mike Davis (1992: 3), the work of Gibson provides:

> stunning examples of how realist 'extrapolative' science fiction can operate as prefigurative social theory, as well as an anticipatory opposition politics to the cyber-fascism lurking over the next horizon.

Thus the Gibsonian concept of *cyberspace* has begun to transmute into a tangible *reality* – his technological vision has fed back into both computer and information systems design and theory (Benedikt 1991a; Biocca 1992a; McFadden 1991) financially underwritten by the Pentagon, Sega, Nintendo and various other global corporations. Equally, many of Gibson's fictional perspectives on cultural, economic and social phenomena have begun to find their way into social and cultural analyses as viable characterisations of our contemporary world.

Reading cyberpunk as social theory tends not to be a unidirectional activity. The relationship between cyberpunk literature and social theory is, if anything, recursive (Clark 1995). Cyberpunk and sociological analyses which draw upon it have a 'habit' of 'folding into' each other in a recursive relation between the fictional and the analytic. For example, issues of public space and urban surveillance are themes taken up by Gibson throughout his work, but most fully in *Virtual Light* (Gibson 1993). It is a book profoundly and explicitly influenced by Davis's (1990) analysis of Los Angeles, *City of Quartz*, itself adorned by a quote from Gibson (Bukatman 1993a: 144). This recursivity continues in Davis's (1992) *Beyond Blade Runner: Urban Control, the Ecology of Fear* where an explicitly 'Gibsonian' map of the contemporary urban condition is presented. A map instantly recognisable in *Virtual Light* and, in a much more extreme form in Stephenson's *Snow Crash* (1992).

Kellner (1995) also recognises a recursivity between cyberpunk and postmodern social theory. In a paper which is stimulating, polemical but very discourteous he argues that:

> cyberpunk science fiction can be read as a sort of social theory, while Baudrillard's futuristic postmodern social theory can be read in turn as science fiction. This optic also suggests a deconstruction of sharp oppositions between literature and social theory, showing that much social theory contains a narrative and vision of the present and future,

and that certain types of literature provide cogent mappings of the contemporary environment and, in the case of cyberpunk, of future trends.

(Kellner 1995: 299)

And continues:

at the very moment when Baudrillard dropped the theoretical ball, losing his initiative, Gibson and cyberpunk picked it up, beginning their explorations of the new future world which Baudrillard had been exploring.

(ibid.: 327)

Gareth Branwyn writing in *Mondo 2000* provides a useful description of cyberpunk as both a literary perspective and worldview:

The future has imploded onto the present. There was no nuclear Armageddon. There's too much real estate to lose. The new battle-field is people's minds. . . . The megacorps *are* the new govern-ments. . . . The U.S. is a big bully with lackluster economic power. . . . The world is splintering into a trillion subcultures and designer cults with their own language, codes and lifestyles. . . . Computer-generated info-domains are the next frontiers. . . . There *is* better living through chemistry. . . . Small groups or individual 'console cowboys' can wield tremendous power over governments, corporations etc. . . . The coa-lescence of a computer 'culture' is expressed in self-aware computer music, art, virtual communities, and a hacker/street tech subculture ... the computer nerd image is passé, and people are not ashamed anymore about the role the computer has in this subculture. The computer is a cool tool, a friend, important human augmentation. . . . We're becoming cyborgs. Our tech is getting smaller, closer to us, and it will soon merge with us.

(Rucker, Sivius and Queen 1993: 64–6)

Perhaps the overriding theme of Gibson's work (for summaries see: Kellner 1995; McHale 1992a, 1992b; Csisery-Ronay 1991; and various of the contributions to McCaffrey 1991) is the knowledge that, as Bukatman (1993a: 5) puts it '[t]echnology and the human are no longer so dichotomous'. The boundaries between subjects, their bodies and the 'outside world' are, like everything else, being radically reconfigured (Haraway 1991; Plant 1993). The division between technology and nature is dissolving as the analytic categories we draw upon to give structure to our world – the biological, the technological, the natural, the artificial, *and* the human – begin to blur (Stone 1991: 101–2; McCarron 1995; Rawdon Wilson 1995; Tomas 1995). Cosmetic surgery and the rise of biotechnology, genetic engineering and nanotechnology have led some to contemplate that the next generation could very well be the last of 'pure' humans (Deitch 1992). A programmatic users' guide on new technological develop-ments (Rucker, Sivius and Queen 1993: 100) suggests:

We are *already* cyborgs. My mother, for instance, leads a relatively normal life thanks to a pacemaker. Beyond that, genetic engineering and nanotechnology ... offer us the possibility of literally being able to change our bodies into new and different forms ... a form of postbiological humanity can be achieved within the next fifty years.

If the increasing acceptance by some consumers of cosmetic surgery and other associated technological interventions on the body (Glassner 1995) are at all indicative of future trends then the next fifty years could see ever more radical plastic surgery, computer-chip brain implants[2] and gene splicing become routine. More importantly for the cyberpunk vision than such bodily transformations, however, are technologies which do not alter the human body *per se* but allows it to be *transcended* – technologies that promise, literally, a new world in which we can *represent* our bodies with a degree of flexibility that parallels the reflexive transformation of our self-identities invoked by the late modern condition. Technologies which have collectively become known as *cyberspace.*

The literature on cyberspace is now a central part of our popular culture[3] and cyberspace is best considered as a generic term which refers to a cluster of different technologies, some familiar, some only recently available, and some still fictional, all of which have in common the ability to simulate environments within which humans can interact (Sterling 1990). Other writers prefer the term computer-mediated communication (CMC) to refer to much the same set of phenomena: *Barlovian cyberspace*; *virtual reality* (VR); and *Gibsonian cyberspace* (Jones 1994).

Barlovian cyberspace – named after John Barlow,[4] a founder of the political action group called Electronic Frontier Foundation (Sterling 1990: 54) – refers to the existing international networks of computers. The Internet is now a 'ragged ... world-spanning electronic tangle' (ibid.: 54) consisting of some 40 million people. In a sense such a simple form of cyberspace is little more than an extension of existing telephone systems, substituting text and some icons for voice. Indeed, for Barlow cyberspace 'is where you are when you're talking on the telephone' (Rucker *et al.* 1993: 78). Clearly both telephones and computer network systems rely upon only a limited range of human senses and (although interactions via these mediums can be extremely rich (Stone 1991; Rheingold 1994; Wiley 1995). They are perhaps no substitute for 'face-to-face' (ftf) interactions, because contemporary social life still tends to operate with an implicit physiognomic notion that the face and the body are the only 'true' sources of the character of a person (Featherstone 1995a, 1995b). Thus, other advanced forms of cyberspace attempt to more vividly simulate such interactions by the use of co-ordinated multi-media systems, such as virtual reality, which stimulate our other senses.

The term 'virtual reality' (VR) was first coined by Jaron Lanier[5] (former head of VPL Research Inc. California), and has recently been defined as a 'real or simulated environment in which the perceiver experiences telepresence' (Steur 1992: 76–7; Heim 1995). It is a system which provides a sense of being in an environment. This sense of presence, which is achieved by means of a communications medium, is what is meant by 'telepresence'.

Unlike Gibsonian cyberspace, VR, although at the moment in its infancy, is already with us. VR is a computer-generated visual, audible and tactile multi-media experience. Using stereo headphones, head-mounted stereo television goggles ('eyephones') able to simulate three dimensions, wired gauntlets ('datagloves') and computerised clothing ('datasuits'), VR aims to surround the human body with an artificial sensorium of sight, sound and touch. VR systems are also truly interactive in the sense that the computer which produces the simulated environment in which a person is immersed constantly reconfigures that environment in response to body movements. Currently, the technology is relatively crude. There is sometimes a lag between movements of the body and the reconfiguration of the environment, graphics resolution is relatively low and many environments rely upon line-drawings and/or cartoon-like iconic represenations. Nevertheless, all the indications are that the level of realism attainable will continue to improve (Lanier and Biocca 1992).

Gibsonian cyberspace, as defined in *Neuromancer* (the inspiration for the generic term) is:

> A consensual hallucination experienced daily by billions of legitimate operators, in every nation, by children being taught mathematical concepts.... A graphic representation of data abstracted from the bank of every computer in the human system. Unthinkable complexity. Lines of light ranged in the nonspace of the mind, clusters and constellations of data. Like city lights receding.
>
> (Gibson 1984: 51)

In this fictional world cyberspace is a global computer network of information which Gibson calls 'the matrix' which operators can access ('jack-in') through headsets ('trodes') via a computer terminal ('cyberspace deck'). Once in the matrix operators can 'fly' to any part of the vast three-dimensional system of data coded into various colourful iconic architectural forms laid out beneath him/her like a vast metropolis: a city of data (Bukatman 1993a: 103–82). Once a particular location has been selected it is possible to move inside the three-dimensional representation of the data in order to scan particular areas. Gibsonian cyberspace also allows for highly 'realistic' interactions between iconic representations of operators (what Stephenson (1992) in *Snow Crash* terms 'avaters' or what we might term 'cyberbodies') so that co-presence can be simulated within a myriad of highly vivid environments. However, other 'intelligent' entities can also 'exist' in cyberspace. Some are previously downloaded personality constructs of humans, whilst others are autonomous posthuman artificial intelligences (AIs) which live in cyberspace 'like fish in water' (Sterling 1990: 54). In effect, Gibsonian cyberspace represents an imagined merger between the Internet and VR systems.

This imagined merger is given its most detailed rendition in Stephenson's (1992) Gibsonian-inspired *Snow Crash* through the description of the 'Metaverse'. The following extract from *Count Zero* by Gibson (1986) provides a graphic example of the idea. It describes a fictional state-of-the-art 'simstim' (simulation stimulation) interaction between two characters,

Marley Krushkhova, a 'disgraced former operator of a tiny Paris gallery', and Joseph Virek, the 'head' of a massive global corporation. On presenting herself for an interview at Virek's office in Brussels, Marley is ushered into a room and told to grasp a brass knob which provides a sensory link for the simstim:

> As her fingers closed around the cool brass knob, it seemed to squirm, sliding along a touch-spectrum of texture and temperature in the first second of contact.
>
> Then it became metal again, green-painted iron, sweeping out and down, along a line of perspective, an old railing she grasped now in wonder.
>
> A few drops of rain blew in her face.
>
> Smell of rain and wet earth.
>
> A confusion of small details, her own memory of a drunken art school picnic warring with the perfection of Vireks's illusion.
>
> Below her lay the unmistakable panorma of Barcelona, smoke hazing the strange spires of the Church of the Sagrada Familia. She caught the railing with her other hand as well, fighting vertigo. She knew the place. She was in Guell Park, Antonio Gaudi's tatty fairyland. . . .
>
> 'You are disorientated. Please forgive me.'
>
> Joseph Virek was perched below her on one of the park's serpintine benches, his shoulders hunched in a soft topcoat.
>
> His features had been vaguely familiar to her all her life. . . . He smiled at her. His head was large and beautifully shaped beneath a brush of stiff, dark grey hair. . . .
>
> 'Please.' He patted the bench's random mosiac of shattered pottery with a narrow hand. 'You must forgive my reliance on technology. I have been confined for over a decade to a vat. In some hideous industrial suburb of Stockholm. Or perhaps of hell. I am not a well man, Marley. Sit beside me.'
>
> (ibid.: 24–5)

The world of cyberspace is itself an urban environment – 'a simulation of the city's information order' in which the 'city redoubles itself through the complex architecture of its information and media networks' (Davis 1992: 16). The city is a digitised parallel world which from 'above' might appear as rationally planned (Le Corbusiers metropolis), but from 'below' reveals itself as a Benjaminesque labyrinth, in which no one can get the bird's eye view of the plan, but everyone effectively has to operate at street level in a world which is rapidly being re-structured and re-configured (Featherstone 1995b). This digitised urban hyper-reality connects in various ways with the technological reality of the street, not least in the way in which the socio-geography of the digitised city mirrors that of the built city. Davis (1992: 16) notes for example how the imploding communities of Los Angeles are 'a data and media "black" hole; an 'electronic *ghetto* within the emerging *information city*', reinforcing extant racisms.

The intersection of the digital domain with the technology of the street produces a complex continuum of human/machine fusions (Tomas 1989, 1991; Balsamo 1995). At one end we have 'pure' human beings and at the other fully simulated disembodied '*post*-humans' which can only exist in cyberspace ('AIs' in Gibson and 'Daemons' in Stephenson). If we move out from the human body, the first area of interest is concerned with the aesthetic manipulation of the body's surface through cosmetic surgery, muscle grafts and animal or human transplants which blur visual cues. Second, there are alterations and enhancements to the functioning of the inner body. Here we have a range of alternatives including biochip implants, upgraded senses and prosthetic additions. Both these areas of intervention enable the body to be disassembled and reassembled with a high degree of functional specialisation. Moving along the continuum, the next area is what Tomas (1991: 41) refers to as 'classical hardware interfaced cyborgs', which exist in cyberspace. These are the operators who move around in cyberspace whose 'bodies' are wired up to computers for input and output flows of information.

The idea of the cyborg has its clearest expression not in Gibson but in the form of the 'avaters' (the iconic representation of the bodies of people logged into the Metaverse) in *Snow Crash* by Stephenson. They represent examples of 'decoupling the body and the subject' (Stone 1991: 99; Lupton 1995; McCarron, 1995). Although late modern reflexive self-identity increasingly relies upon an ability to transform the body, with the development of a parallel 'social' world of cyberspace, the manner in which one can represent one's embodied subjectivity becomes much more flexible than the fleshy constraints of the 'physical' body (even with radical medical enhancements). Despite the dominance of embodied physiognomic notions of the 'true self' in contemporary social life, there is some evidence to suggest that the new technology is opening up the possibility of radically new disembodied subjectiv*ities* (Balsamo 1995; Land 1995). In Gibson (1984: 12) there exists 'a certain relaxed contempt for the flesh' which is regarded as 'the meat' by those addicted to 'life' in the 'matrix'. Some, like Robins (1995) regard such claims as unfounded and the new identities being created as banal. The cyberpunk vision, others suggest, is an epoch within which self-identity derived from 'real', 'authentic', 'embodied' experiences is unable to compete with ones derived from the 'erotic ontology' (Heim 1991) of 'hyperreal', 'simulated', 'disembodied' cyberspace (but see Sobchack (1995) for a powerful corrective to this view).

As already indicated, the cyberpunk view of the world is also one which recognises a shrinking public space and the increasing privatisation of many aspects of social life. It suggests that close face-to-face social relationships, outside those with kin and some others within highly bounded *locales*, are becoming increasingly difficult to form. Social and geographical mobility increase the fluidity of social life and undermine the formation of strong social bonds. The spectacle of consumer culture, manifest in the commodified 'simulation' of the shopping mall as authentic public space, although providing a forum for the display of self-identity and the outcomes of associated body projects, in the end only results in the construction of a 'lonely crowd'. This promotes a retreat into an increasingly fortified technologised privatised world away from the increasingly remote and ungovernable spaces occupied by the *repressed* (Bauman 1988), which serves to further contract the more proximate 'social' sources of self-identity. For many all that is left is technology. As Elwes (1993: 65) views it:

> computer technology was developed to promote and speed up global communication and yet somehow the effect is one of disconnection and distance. Individuals are increasingly locked into the isolation of their homes (it isn't safe to go out) and they only make contact with the outside world through telecommunications and networked computer-information systems. Not so much distance learning as living at a distance.

And Lanier agrees:

> California is the worst example.... Individuals don't even meet on sidewalks anymore ... we live in this constant sort of fetal position where we are seated in a soft chair looking at the world through a glass square, be it the windshield of the car or the screen of a television or computer. It's sort of constant, and we're in a little bubble.
> (Lanier and Biocca 1992: 157)

The privatised retreat into television and video has been followed by engagements with increasingly interactive technologies: camcorders, multimedia interactive CDs, computer games and so on. Technology is beginning to mediate our social relationships, our self-identities and our wider sense of social life to an extent we are only just beginning to grasp. The portable telephone, the portable fax, the notepad computer have become essential for social life in the 'densely networked centres of the global cities' (Lash and Urry 1994: 319) and, increasingly, beyond. The seemingly ubiquitous camcorder endlessly records not just the 'spectacle' but also the 'mundane' to such an extent that 'lived experience' in and of itself becomes secondary to gaining a taped 'representation' of it for later 'consumption'.[6]

The proliferation of new technologies has initiated the spread of electronically mediated communication from primarily workplace settings to the private sphere. Cyberpunk as social theory suggests that the social preconditions for the creation of a new cyberculture are being firmly established as we increasingly communicate via the telephone, the fax, the modem, the video, BBSs, and, in the foreseeable future, VR systems, and less and less through face-to-face interactions. In Japan, Deitch reports, there has been a discussion on a new type of personality emerging in response to these technological changes, known as *Otaku*.

> Otaku people are defined more by their possessions than by their inherent character. They can be described as a concept of person-as-information. Travellers to Tokyo are often amazed by the proliferation of vending machines for all sorts of goods and services ... research has shown that much of the popularity of these vending machines is

due to the preference of young Japanese for interacting with machines instead of with real people.

(Deitch 1992: 40)

One might view the popularity of Japanese films such as *Akira* and *Tetsuo*, and indeed of cyberpunk images and text (Tatsumi 1991) – all of which emphasise the merging of technology and humanity – as an indicator of such a tendency. It is in Japan that Gibson locates his Chiba City with its much quoted 'sky above the port ... the color of television tuned to a dead channel' (Gibson 1984: 9) where this merging is at its most developed with a myriad of clinics at 'the cutting edge' of body modification through technological augmentation, neurosurgery, nanotechnology and the like. For Tatsumi (1991: 372), although, 'Gibson's Chiba City may have sprung from his misperception of Japan'; however 'it was this misconception that encouraged Japanese readers to correctly perceive the nature of post-modern Japan'.

In engaging in these and other activities we are, it is claimed, beginning to create new 'on-line' or 'virtual communities', new sets of social relationships, new disembodied modes of interacting and, for some, as we have seen, embryonic Gibsonian cyberspace itself. Of course these new sets of relationships mirror in many ways existing patterns of access, interaction and power; considering gender relations, for example, suggests that at the moment cyberspace is a sexist male-dominated (non) place! Despite this some (cyber) feminists such as Sadie Plant (1995) claim that the new technologies are a sign of hope for women. Haraway (1991), in particular, argues that the new technologies allow an escape from the conceptual dualisms of culture/nature and mind/body and open up the potential for a host of post-gendered possibilities. Following Haraway, Plant (1993: 13) suggests that the relationship between women and machinery is beginning to evolve into 'a dangerous alliance' in which '[s]ilicon and women's liberation track each other's developments'.

I want to argue that the manner in which sociology has been parasitic upon the cyberpunk tradition has not only been in terms of the substantive themes of writers such as Gibson. More importantly it is the impact of writers such as De Landa (1991, 1992, 1993) who explore the methodo-logical implications and their consequences for the human sciences of the cyberpunk vision.

De Landa not only draws upon many of the themes inherent to cyberpunk, robots, cyborgs, Artificial Intelligence, non-human agency and so on in his work, but he also utilises many elements of the aesthetics of cyberpunk in his everyday practice. He is a computer graphics designer working outside the academic mainstream drawing upon an eclectic range of the human and physical sciences in order to construct a radical and compelling vision of what he terms 'the emergence of synthetic reason' (De Landa 1993). He cogently argues that the human sciences are fettered by many of their domain assumptions to such an extent that they are simply unable to provide any useful analysis of the contemporary condition. By drawing upon a materialist non-metaphorical reading of Deleuze and

Guattari (1982) he has outlined a theory of 'stratification' in which the complementary operations of 'sorting out' and 'consolidation' are shown to be behind many (physical and social) structural forms.

De Landa concludes that the future of social theory will be in the construction of new 'epistemological reservoirs' based upon complex computer simulations of cultural, social and economic processes in cyberspace. Those of us familiar with the analytical insights popular simulations such as *Sim City 2000* can afford will have had a small glimpse of the sort of thing De Landa has in mind, even if the sociological operationalisation of such an approach is currently less than convincing (Gilbert and Doran 1994; Gilbert and Conte 1995).

The methodological 'purging' involved in the project is profound. First, De Landa suggests that we must once and for all abandon ideal typical analytic thinking and begin to take seriously 'population' thinking. Rather than conceptualising phenomena as more or less imperfect versions of some ideal essence we must recognise that it is only *variation* which is real – a complete inversion of the classical paradigm. There is then for De Landa no such thing as a pre-existent collection of traits which define some phenomena (biological, physical, social or cultural); rather each trait develops along different lineages which accumulate in a population under different selection pressures; selection pressures which are themselves dependent upon *specific* and *contingent* histories. Traits accumulate through the operation of a 'searching device' (which results from the coupling of any kind of spontaneous variation to any kind of selection pressures) and are the product of a more or less stable solution in relation to the various contingencies within a given environment. Drawing upon developments in artificial life (AL) research, especially work on genetic algorthims, De Landa suggests that such points of stability are likely to be multiple rather than singular. But if there is no Darwinian survival of the fittest what is the source of stability (however brief) in systems? The answer to this question leads De Landa to call for a second 'purge' – this time against notions of equilibrium thinking in the human sciences.

The importation into the human sciences of notions of stability from equilibrium thermodynamics premised upon the idea of 'heat death' – that stability was some function or other of all useful energy being transformed into heat – has had a profound effect upon modern social thought. It has underpinned our conceptualisation of closed systems from which some static socio-economic solution can be derived. Most obviously our conceptualisation of markets within which the operation of the laws of supply and demand generate a unique and stable solution in terms of prices and outputs has reverberated throughout the social sciences via game theory, exchange theory, functionalism and systems thinking more generally.

De Landa suggests that this closed and static notion of (physical and socio-economic) stability has been superseded by the new science of 'dissipative' systems based upon an understanding of the continual flow of energy and matter. The importation of ideas derived from the science of such systems – nonlinear dynamics – into the human sciences fundamentally alters how we conceptualise the world. Most important is the idea of 'deterministic chaos' in which the processural flux of dynamic systems is conceptualised as an 'attractor' and the transitions which transform one attractor into another are conceptualised as 'bifurcations'. It is quite possible, indeed very common, to find systems 'stabilised' in such a way that the properties of the population system as a whole are not manifest in the isolated, individual members of the population. Examples of such *synergistic interactions* include long waves of capitalist economic development (Kondratieff cycles), neural networks, the emergence of organisational cultures and so on.

De Landa suggests that by combining the insights of both nonlinear dynamics and anti-ideal typical population thinking,

> we get the following picture: the evolutionary 'searching device' constituted by variation coupled with selection ... [which explores] ... a space 'preorganzied' by attractors and bifurcations.
>
> (De Landa 1993: 798–9)

Such insights can only be explored by constructing cyberspatial virtual environments within which such processes can be examined. Clearly, if we are to take the study of emergent processes seriously an analytic approach that categorises a population into its components will lose sight of those properties generated by the configuration of the individual elements within the system. Computer simulations thus provide us with a tool within which we can synthesise rather than analyse systems.

This vision of the future of social theory will not be to the taste of everyone. The prospect of understanding social processes by staring at sociological simulcra on a computer screen is not such a comfortable scenario. Nevertheless, such an approach to social analysis can also be conceptualised more positively in terms of the generation of a new form of *post-symbolic communication*. In effect cyberpunk sociology may not be in the form of the written word but instead the product of our sociological endeavours might be a simulation or a virtual world, which our audience will be able to enter, explore and understand, a creative merger of aesthetic and technical considerations – a virtual environment within which the cities we imagine can be synthesised.

NOTES

1 Some of what follows derives from the introduction to Featherstone and Burrows (1995).
2 For an interesting discussion of representations of the social and cultural possibilities of both plastic surgery and biochip implants in the cyberpunk literature see Tomas (1989, 1991) and Featherstone (1995b).
3 The concept now even has its very own 'for beginners' volume (Buick and Jevtic 1995) published in the same month as *Postmodernism for Beginners* (Appignanesi and Garratt 1995), a profound indication indeed of its contemporary ubiquity.
4 Barlow is an interesting figure in the history of contemporary technological developments. He is a Republican rock lyricist for the 1960s rock group The Grateful Dead.
5 Sterling (1990: 54) claims that 'Lanier is aware of the term "cyberspace" but considers it too "limiting" and "computery"'. Levy (1992: 3) notes that the term 'virtual reality' has perhaps superseded 'cyberspace' as a term, whilst Featherstone (1995b) and Rucker et al. (1993) treat them as related but distinct phenomena. As will be apparent the present

author, following Sterling (1990), Benedikt (1991b) and Rheingold (1994), prefers to treat 'cyberspace' as a generic term and 'virtual reality' as one important example of it.

6   It is little wonder that the analysis offered by the Situationist International in the late 1960s on the emergence of 'the society of the spectacle' has recently been recognised as *the* crucial antecedent to Baudrillard's meanderings on hyperreality, simulcra and the like (Plant 1992; Rojek and Turner 1993).

14

CITIES, SUBJECTIVITY AND CYBERSPACE

Graham B. McBeath and Stephen A. Webb

Communities are to be distinguished, not by their falsity/genuineness, but by the style in which they are imagined.

(Benedict Anderson)

INTRODUCTION

There are many confusions haunting cyberspace. Primarily the confusions can be located at the level of metaphors which are invoked to characterise the nature of cyberspace. There are two images in particular which strike us as inimical, yet are frequently uttered in tandem in many of the fashionable journals and articles about the Internet and so forth; namely – cyberspace as community and cyberspace as city. By way of brief examples we could note the title of Howard Rheingold's new book *The Virtual Community* (1994b), and that of Peter Hinssen's article in the first issue of *Wired*: 'Life in the digital city' (*Wired* 1.01, April 1995, p. 53). Indeed in the Rheingold volume, the author at various junctures refers to cybernets as the basis for a community, that is, people coming together creating a web of personal relationships, and as the basis for civic democracy which, in effect, is describing a digital city-state.

Internet magazines stress both the possibility of bringing people together into greater or lesser degrees of community, and the possibility of sailing the boundless, resource-rich seas of the net without home port for security. We are puzzled about the co-presence of these two metaphors in descriptions of cyberspatial relations because community is about closed systems and reified relations, and city about openness and change. This difference is predicated upon different life-worlds and modes of appropriating space resulting from each system respectively. However, much widely available literature portrays cyberspace to be simultaneously possessed of the properties of community and the city.

Our focus is upon the role of the territorial imaginary in the construction of space, and how the metaphor of 'net' allows for the conflations of city/community, and virtual city/virtual community. And furthermore, to consider how these bastard spaces are given an 'objective' correlate in the form of network models of urban space that visualise space as enclosed. It is the relation of the pre-figure (the city) to the current figures of understanding space (cyberspace) that forms the basis of this chapter. More simply, we want to use readings of the nature and meaning of city space to interrogate and critique cyberspace and its surrounding hype. In so far as we argue that there are parallels between how we imagine the city and how we imagine cyberspace, we will be arguing by analogy. But in doing so we will try to expose some of the false analogies which attempt to ontologise the cyberworld as a parallel universe to our own – as a space apart with its own terms and conditions into which we are inserted as nodes of communication and as identities constituted as a function of the meanings internal to the virtual realm. Part of the problem is that we are not only led to envisage cyberspace as a self-constituting realm, but at the same time to entertain ideas of virtual communities, or virtual cities, which are taken from conceptions of ideal cities or communities fashioned for the purposes of living in the non-virtual world. The language we use to try to grasp the structure of cyberspace thus trades equally, on notions of radical difference and sameness.

Towards the end of the chapter we will argue that the idea of cyberspace as an alternative structure in which new forms of social and intra-personal relations are mediated is illusory; that cyberspace and how we relate to it is little different from how *fin-de-siècle* social theorists, such as Simmel and Kracauer, described the phenomenology of experiencing the city and how Bachelard described the movement of the poetic image. Despite the force of the metaphors of city and community, we want to argue that the dominant mode of understanding cyberspace is as community, but that it is better conceived as a city space, uncoded by the petrifying effects of spatial net analysis, the latter removing the *flâneur*-like role of the subjective consciousness roving from one virtual space to another. We ought to see cyberspace as movement and individualised flows of subjective consciousness, and the nature of the relation between user and cyberspace as dithyrambic. The transcendental and metaphysical mode of talk about cyberspace is but a poetics of space, and with this in mind we will draw on the work of Gaston Bachelard to understand the moments of what we will identify as absorbed consciousness – the spirit taken by its own poetic images, and the mind taken by the form of its activity as if there were no alternative. From the standpoint of theory, the basic problems we address are: How is the virtual imaginary constructed? What are its shapes? What description can we give to the flow of the construction of that spatial imaginary? As we intimated at the beginning, we will look at ways in which theorists have construed urban space, and then at how those readings have their counterparts in first, a misconceived grasp of cyberspace, and second, in what we believe to be a more plausible, less magical account of cyberspace.

MODELLING THE CITY AS PHENOMENOLOGY OF COMMUNITY

One of the major foci of urban geography has been how one can best represent the city – as a capitalist city with flows of money and labour; as an aestheticised space *à la* Simmel; and among others, as a formal systems-theoretic net of lines and points marking out such things as communication and transport patterns and points of population or housing densities, and so forth. The latter approach provides a schematic diagram bounded by defined city limits, and internally enriched (or not) by the range of social, economic, political factors represented. This kind of modelling is common to control systems analysis, and found in the traffic control operations rooms of police, city planners' offices, and electricity companies' offices wherein the National Grid is represented. Such a grid mapped onto the city encloses the city, but equally will spread according to its own rules of construction as the city spreads. Such a way of envisaging the city offers us a construction of the structurally regulated features of the city carrying intimations of an integrated community. Network analysis sponsors the notion of city as community. It does this by its enclosing of space, of regulating and rationalising that space, of seeing the city not as an anomic, amorphous sprawl, but as a structurally integrated whole constituted by the interdependency of the parts. Allan Pred refers to the net approach in his essay 'The social becomes the spatial' where he notes:

> Places and regions, however arbitrarily delimited, are the essence of traditional human geographic inquiry . . . [and] whether presented as elements within a spatial distribution, unique assemblages of physical facts and human artefacts, as units interacting with one another in a system, or as localised spatial forms, places and regions have been portrayed as little more than frozen scenes for human activity.
>
> (Pred 1985: 337)

In *Mille Plateaux* (1988), Deleuze and Guattari analyse this kind of coding by net structures in relation to a variety of human resources such as the state, language, the town, war, and so forth. They describe how the *abstract machine* of the net reterritorialises spaces made of discrete places of intensity. For instance, the city is a plane or plateau on which there are intensities of population, road intersections, cars, danger zones, high crime. In the order of the material world these particular spaces are separated, but under the net they are reterritorialised by being connected into a whole by the grid lines that re-place the city structure. If we were to imagine the city as made up of a series of towns (intensity-places) we might see what Deleuze and Guattari mean when they say that:

> It (the town) is a phenomenon of transconsistency, a network, because it is fundamentally in contact with other towns. It represents a threshold of deterritorialization, because whatever the material involved, it must be deterritorialized enough to enter the network . . . to follow the circuit of urban and road recoding. . . . Towns are circuit points of every kind, which enter into counterpoint along horizontal lines; they effect a complete . . . town-by-town, integration.
>
> (Deleuze and Guattari 1988: 432)

Here then the authors are showing that a net structure recodes the spatially discrete through the deterritorialisation/reterritorialisation couplet connecting towns together in a large yet integrated circuit. By analogy, we would argue that the effect of net analysis of the city works in the same way. The abstract machine of the net is:

> an abstract machine of overcoding: it defines a rigid segmentarity, a macrosegmentarity, because it produces or rather reproduces segments ... laying out a divisible homogeneous space striated in all directions.

> (ibid. p. 223)

For our purposes, the effect of the net is to put the discrete domains of intensity within the whole space of the city 'fundamentally in contact'. This 'drawing together' is how we are invited to see the machinic reterritorialisation of city space; that is an imagery which resonates with the character of community.

Community, that most contemporary and ancient word connoting stability, order, regularity and, at least in today's terms, security, perhaps even ontological security, is about the diminution of the feeling of distance between persons. The warmth suggested by the term 'community' is at root importantly signifying the desire to have a sense of shared space, orderly and respectful of personal space. Communities tend to be self-regulating, because of the shame and guilt one will feel, and often be made to feel, if one acts irresponsibly towards another member of the community. This is a function of proximity to others, and that one cannot get away quickly enough to avoid the real or imagined disapprobation of others. Thus the handling of risky actions and trust in the community setting is mediated through mechanisms of reflexivity not dissimilar to the 'invisible hand explanation' found in Adam Smith's *The Theory of Moral Sentiments* (1754). The tentatively held belief that such mechanisms will work underlies hope for a more orderly, graspable world.

Network analysis images large spaces as, in fact, contiguous cells, showing persons and resources in proximity with each other. Such grids of intelligibility are by implication grids of nearness to each other. Fishman (1995) comments on this image looking like 'the network of superhighways as seen from the air, crowded in all directions, uniting a whole region into a vast super-city'. We would suggest that we are given the impression that cities are essentially built inside boundaries of the net, such that we imagine cities as developing internally rather than spreading outward. Cities can be represented as determinate spaces which fill up with people and things drawing us ever closer allowing the invisible hand mechanism to work, disciplining our behaviours, obliging us to act responsibly towards others.

Phenomenologically, networking or 'gridding' the city does not invite us to extend the grid outwards, but to work inside the boundaries of the net structure. In this we oppose the view of Frank Lloyd Wright who argued that such grids implied boundlessness, extension in all directions. Grids are synchronic models of a particular space, and the image of movement is determined by the rods and lines which make up the model. Our idea of the city is encrypted by the structure and limits of the model, and not the other way round. Furthermore, the net structure simplifies our sense of distance and the complexity of spaces that would otherwise signify alienation. This is analogous to the feeling that a place is not so very far away if we can identify a route to it made up of a clear series of connecting roads punctuated by identifiable settlements confirming that we are on the right route. It is the very ease of seeing the route and being able to access it by using road numbers that makes even a long journey appear simple, and our destination close at hand. In short, it seems that 'we are never too far away'. To paraphrase de Certeau (1984): The net model of the city (the Concept-city), like a proper name (e.g. M1, A52, B3429), provides a way of conceiving, simplifying, and construing space on the basis of a finite number of stable, isolatable, and interconnected properties (see de ibid.: 94). The point here is that the rhetoric of these formal models can s(t)imulate a way of seeing cities as possible communities by mapping the city as an enclosure, a matrix of proximities rather than of distances. Such analyses feed into the hope for unity – for co-munity.

THE IMAGINARY AND THE CYBERNETIC COMMUNITY

We have argued that one way of imagining the city is as a community, and that this image is a projection of formal network graphs and grids. In as much as this way of visualising the city-as-community is taken to reveal a proper way (a desired way) of making sense of the city, phenomenologically the model stands as the truth of the real (itself a simulacrum), and of course the real is the model. This inversion is familiar to us through the writings of Baudrillard, but equally the inversion of the real and the imaginary at the level of persuading us to see the world in a particular way is to be found at the heart of Althusser's theory of ideology. Trading on Heidegger's celebrated essay 'The question concerning technology' (1955), we might say that our mode of being is made through the enframing (*gestell*) – through an ordering structure which sets-upon. We 'get the picture' of the world which permits us movement through space. Thus we plan our route, but this route has already been planned for us by the technical enframing of the cartographer. But in not reflectively grasping this hermeneutic, this 'pre-disposing', we continue to believe that rationality and freedom are not inimical. In other words, we defend the voluntarism of the will and imagination. Our desire always to affirm our choice of action is an attempt to give expression to the truth of self – to 'unconceal' self to ourself. And we live that expressive aesthetic truth through technological ordering. Our only crime is that we deny the ordering patterns our movements, to preserve our sense of self-possession.

However, what we can cope with is a squaring of self-affirmation, as a claim of origin, with the originary ordering of nature, so long as that nature is benign or affirming of self. It is the clash between nature and self that is the mother of technological invention – a point Marx knew only too well. The harmony between nature and self when it can coexist is the original community. Things stand well to each other when nature is inert and we produce simply to reproduce ourselves – that is, when there is an order of the same. Such arrangements are predicated upon a pastoral vision of a fertile earth yielding up her riches prompted by a non-rapacious husbandry. This essential community is preserved even if extended to encompass similar activities by others. Heidegger might recognise this as a structure of social relations in the condition of standing-reserve, that is, a letting things be, uncorrupted by the enframing of technology. Technology becomes dangerous when it is manipulated by the ambitions of man. In our modern world ambition is executed in the mode of hyperactivity continuously pressed by the demands of capital. Heidegger writes of the technological enframing as destiny, but this is to historicise man and it is the fate of the hyperactive world of technology and capital to obscure time so as to appear to live only in the present. Further, this present is singular moments of now-time; we never know what the next moment will bring. Above all, the city is the place of the hyperactive, the focus of technology and capital variably circuiting in the interests of opportunities for profit. From Hayek and his teacher Mises we learn this. Mises drives home the message that we live *ex ante* in anticipation of outcomes which are derailed by the contingent actions of others. The modern city is the space of endless activity and insecurities, not a structure of standing-reserve. If we can but neutralise this restlessness, then the city may become a more understandable, orderly space. This is what we do by our mediated imagination – we place the city under the net.

Net analysis freezes the city. It is at once an enframing which is also in standing-reserve. The rhizomatic movement is arrested by the set flows of horizontal and vertical lines. It is this which structures the heuristic imaginary. In simplifying space, *more geometrico*, we can re-take possession of ourselves. In a more determinate world we can let things be. We can trust and feel secure. The metaphor of the net connotes an integrated interdependency of all the parts, co-ordinated by a benign structure of rules and regulations. We have here the ground of the imagined community, a space absent from the fear of contingency and without neurotic attachment to rule-systems. Our dream of community is of an enclosed soft system in which the absence of threat encourages us to be open – to express our thoughts, feelings, and concerns. This aesthetic ideal presumes a regularised circuit of flows which is not a totalitarian product of human artifice but is voluntarily reciprocal with the other. Thus, such an image of the genesis of community is squared with nature – our original nature as free willing self-possessing beings.

In cyberspace the same relation of the aesthetic to the technological obtains. We see technology as if it were benign, and dream of virtual community where we exist in the virtually shared. The lived imaginary of virtual community activates the forgetting of the technological, and the latter goes into standing-reserve. The ideals of virtual community are basically the same as those of the ideals of non-virtual community, superimposed upon uncongenial spaces and modes of living. At the level of human subjectivity the possibility of life in cyberspace can, at least in part, be construed as motivated by a resistance to the uncongenial, and ultimately as the manufacture of an illusion of self-possession. We will develop the latter points below. The way the meaning of cyberspace is conceived is, then, analogous to the way that network analysis persuades us to conceive of the city; that is, as a community. Of course not all cybersurfers see cyberspace as a community, but many do. We want to explore for a moment how those who do talk about the net or parts of the net as a community. The proselytiser and editor of the very first issue of *On-line World* (March 1995), Clive Grace, comments: 'The net has been in the public eye for months now. . . . Over the years it's developed in a community of people all eager to share, enjoy and communicate.' Even more preposterous, but altogether more seriously meant is the comment of Thomas Moore in *Net Guide*. Moore, a lecturer in archetypal psychology living in . . . no, not California, but New York, says that:

> The age of therapy is ending, the age of the therapist and patient in one room, one to one. I truly believe this. The new therapy that replaces it will occur outside of a room, in a kind of nurturing community, which the Internet might provide. It will be a community of support and understanding where people with like minded problems talk about the soul, about the heart.
> (*Net Guide*, February 1995: 39–40)

His interviewer asks: 'Group therapy in Cyberspace?' Moore answers: 'Why not?' For Moore, we can even undergo analysis of the self on the net. The Harvard academic, Dorothy Zinberg, in a recent edition of the *Times Higher Education Supplement* noted in more cynical vein:

> Everywhere I turn, whether it is trendy new magazines like *Wired* or *Internet*, or to the mesmerised users of the equipment at the latest hot spot in town, the cybersmith, where access to state-of-the-art cyberspace technologies can be rented, or even while lurching along the *Infobahn* myself, I am bombarded with 'data' that proclaims, the arrival of a new community in cyberspace.
> (Zinberg 1995: 14)

Broadly, we sympathise with the scepticism of Zinberg. At best the virtual community is but a projection of community, it is an imagined community which lacks both ontological and emotional security.

The title of Benedict Anderson's 1983 book is now very familiar, *Imagined Communities*, and many writers have latched on to the phrase as giving expression to the phenomena of humans wishing to *image* as communities the web of relations to persons with whom they are in regular contact. But even if this is what many understand by Anderson's phrase, they ignore a dimension of community which is central to the concept, namely, its affective aspect, the dimension of fellow-feeling bound to 'being together'. This is the emotional/feeling strand of solidarity that Williams (1976) refers to this as the persuasive 'community . . . of feelings'. Community is not merely proximity to the other obliging us to be responsible toward the other and toward the community. Bruce Murray's submission to the *Aspen Workshop* on 'Society, cyberspace and the future' goes further when he states that: 'for communities to be harmonious externally as well as internally they must provide not only a sense of belonging and wholeness for their members, but incorporate and tolerate diversity' (Murray 1993).

It is this stress upon belonging and wholeness which we would suggest is not properly a feature of cyberspace interaction. Instead it is held out as a *possibility*, a mythic projection of the desire for a community in the face of a fatalistic belief that we will never discover a true community or a satisfying life in the everyday world. Virtual communities are not imagined because they are virtual, to grasp the virtual we have to make a leap of imagination, but imagined because people wish to refuse the sense of alienation that they may feel in relation to the apparently unstable world around them. Disalienating effects may be promoted by imputing to cyberspace the properties of a benign objective world, or at least to the parts cybernauts use. They construct what de Certeau might have called a 'Concept–community' which is a law unto itself, an 'in-itself, comprehensible and complete world for its initiates. The basis for community on the nets is the security afforded by the illusion of being in another world having left behind a troubling environment. We will suggest below that this kind of alienation is registered as dissatisfaction, disappointment, and frustration as opposed to the grand forms of alienation discussed by Marx. As Simmel notes: 'The lack of something definite at the centre of the soul impels us to search for momentary satisfaction in ever new stimulations, sensations and external activities,' (cf. *Philosophy of Money*, 1907/1978: 114). Cyberspace offers a fantastical world through which we can live in an apparent proximity to others, talk to them, share views and express feelings. Rheingold, in his recent *The Virtual Community*, cites the comment of sociologist Marc Smith: 'Virtual communities require an act of imagination to use, and what must be imagined is the idea of the community itself' (Rheingold 1994: 64). What Smith does not point out is that somehow to successfully project the net as a community we must in engage in what Nietzsche called an 'active forgetting', that is, that we imagined it as a community in the first place. The structure of a projection of virtual community is a double movement of alienation from the 'real' everyday world of objectified culture into the atomised private life-world and then to the 'virtual' community world, an illusion as humanly rich as the ideals of community in the everyday world.

Contemporary alienation is not the materially grounded function of dispossession by the capitalist, the removal of surplus value, and the waste of labour power, but the expression, at the level of feeling, of the lack of a meaningful life even if one has no meta-narrativised project to bridge the gulf between how one feels and how one might feel. Baudrillard in *Cool Memories* picks up on aspects of this when he notes:

> If in days gone by, it was sound strategy to accumulate the effects of alienation, today it is safer to stockpile the effects of indifference....
> Or yet again to become nothing but a ghostly hologram, a laser outline – so that it may then be all the easier to disappear without being noticed, leaving others prey to reality.

> (Baudrillard 1990: 14)

For Marx and others the condition of alienation fed utopian projects that needed alienation as a cumulative force ready to motivate revolutionary action. But Baudrillard's account is of an aestheticised, contemporary version of alienation, more about feeling disaffected and enervated than motivated. Alienation in positive terms is drift and indifference; that is, having no motivation to make positive choices, other than when we are 'grabbed' by the moments of the appearance of the spectacle. For some the spectacle becomes interesting, offering a mode of 'creating' output, of achieving an end. When this happens a small fissure in the apparent totality of indifference opens and the possibility of a local emergence of the teleological self of modernity. This is a self which, perhaps at a subliminal level, posits the limited horizon of 'I could get into this'. But still the frame of indifference prevails allowing people to drift from one activity or person to another. Any change towards 'being-interested' is often gradual and discrete. For many the backdrop to 'doing something' is the generalised feeling that 'I ought to do something to fill my time'. Perhaps we can describe these moments as the attitude of 'indifferent purpose'. Shotter (1980) comments on such processes of social action as unfolding in time, writing of people as 'form-creators' and as rule makers, i.e., actively creating a personal form of life:

> To take such a creative view of human action is to treat it as a formative process in its own right, as a sequence of transformation rather than as merely a sequence of discrete events, as a developing process rather than as merely a (changing) medium through which other (more constant) factors exert their determining influence.... Viewing human actions not as a sequence of well-defined events but as something which develops in time, which involves a passage from something less to more definite, emphasises the fact that while we can, on occasions, act deliberately, according to rule, plan or script, we do not always necessarily do so. Often we act simply on the basis of our 'thoughts and feelings' we say in terms of the situation 'as we saw it'.
>
> (Shotter 1980: 31–2)

The move to travelling into cyberspace is accidental to the extent that one could have done otherwise, it is not the product of a logic of necessity, but a falling through an access point pushed by the relatively gentle forces of curiosity, boredom, opportunity and social pressure. Why, exactly, do we pick on *this* rather than *that* activity? At root the personal motive to do something else may be as Kracauer suggests:

> travel is one of the greatest possibilities for society (self) to hold itself from a confrontation from itself ... it leads to the splendours of the world in order that its ugliness goes unobserved.
>
> (Kracauer 1975: 299)

Some may see this process as 'taking flight', but in our view such an image would be mistaken. Often people drift away from uncongenial situations to engage in an activity which will placate the people putting them under pressure. It is more a response of 'OK, I'll have a go at this.' 'Doing computers' is one way of filling one's time and, more importantly, satisfying the demands for a show of purposefulness. Computers are perfect for this as they promote a bounded, focused activity which carries intimations of science, knowledge and production. In 'doing computers' one is doing something with purpose. It is not accidental that recent TV ads for computers place a stress on multi-tasking and educational values. We may of course just play with the machines for a few hours, demonstrating that we are capable of a purposeful life, but some will keep going, acquiring a word-processor, a graphics card, a CD-ROM, a modem, access to the Internet and who knows maybe even full-blown immersion in virtual worlds.

The medium of computing and virtual worlds offers us the power to convert the negative unfocused alienation – the disappointment in and indifference towards the world – into a positive good alienation. That is *becoming* in a world away from the irritations and boredom of everyday life. In becoming a cybernaut, *ex ante* alienation is simply an avowal of tiredness, but *ex post* seems with hindsight to have been a disaffection with one's life as a whole. If the latter occurs – the 'I wish I'd got into this sort of thing earlier' – the person concerned may become the committed enthusiast, and then a cyber-evangelist.

We now come to the final section of this chapter where we offer a phenomenological reading of the poetics of self-possession in the realm of the virtual. To execute this we have drawn on the extraordinary writing of Bachelard whose *The Poetics of Space* (1969) explores how the poetic image takes the spirit into the image. Here we are concerned with the absorption of the self into the spectacular surface of cyberspace. We try to show that the relation of self to cyberspace is an illusion of radical otherness, the projecting of an objective world *totally* different from the non-virtual world in which we live disappointingly. We will conclude with some remarks about how we believe the relation between self and cyberspace actually stands, suggesting that it is more like the city – hyperactive, lacking in basic structures of security and trust, and ultimately what we could call, without fidelity to Heidegger's words, inauthentic.

A PHENOMENOLOGY OF CYBERSPACE?

As we noted above, Baudrillard writes of how one can disappear, 'leaving others prey to reality' (1990) Of course, one does not literally disappear, but becomes immersed and absorbed by the technical operation of the medium and the virtual world which one enters, and to which one is subject. Absorption is the collapse of indifference and the emergence of a gradually lost difference between self and cyberspace. To be absorbed is to *become oneself inside a frame where boundaries do not matter. The more one becomes on the inside the less one is aware of an outside.* In our view, becoming absorbed is the move into virtual space. It is a fascination with the spectacle or the play of the game that lets us forget that we are fascinated. As with Merleau-Ponty, we become an embodied self inside a frame, but the boundaries are of no account. Thus, this space has no meaning as *this* space, but rather has meaning for the cybernaut from its interior, an interior of which the cybernaut is part:

> The image offered us . . . now becomes really our own. It takes root in us. It has been given us by another, but we begin to have the impression that we could have created it, and that we should have created it. It becomes a new being in our language, expressing us by making us what it expresses; it is at once a becoming of expression, and a becoming of our being.
>
> (Bachelard 1969: xix)

The arborescence of the flow of images offered entices us yet further into the depths of hierarchical virtuality, yet we do not see the hierarchy. If we think of the way we use the World Wide Web we should realise that we do not perceive hierarchy. Phenomenologically, each page seems to be lying at the same level as any other page. What we see is the florescent text as we scan it for a keyword to click. The seeming endlessness of available information intimates no boundaries but provokes exploration. Yes, we can use the Web in utilitarian fashion, but how few of us do this? There is always something else to look up, just as the gambler will play another hand. Once absorbed, we live in the domain of cyberspace. As Bachelard notes: 'But poetry is there with its countless surging images, images through which the imagination comes to live in its own domain' (ibid.: xxv). In other words, the property of being truly seduced by the virtual realm is to forget that we have been seduced, that we have an imaginary life inside the virtual. Baudelaire in his *Journaux Intimes* puts it well: 'In certain almost supernatural states, the depth of life is entirely revealed in the spectacle however ordinary, that we have before our eyes, and which becomes the symbol of it' (cited in ibid.: 29). Of course the depth of life is always on the surface, on screen. Our absorption into a virtual world is the space of our own growing confidence, as such it is a felicitous space of which Bachelard says:

> Attached to its protective value . . . are also imagined values which soon become dominant. Space that has been seized upon by the imagination cannot remain indifferent space subject to the measures and estimates of the surveyor. It has been lived in, not in its positivity, but with all the partiality of the imagination. For it concentrates being within limits that protect.
>
> (ibid.: xxxii)

From the perspective of the user she is in the electronic communal womb, the intimate immensity of cyberspace offering her space for support and growth. But, on reflection, is she not living a solipsistic life in an anomic universe? In this space we do not reflect upon the machine codes and rule structures that control what happens on screen. Rather, we live our modes of engagement with others with the horizonal knowledge that we can virtually go elsewhere. We can drop in and drop out, come across things by accident and click on. Cyberspace is a lawless world that has its counterpart in the dangerous city. We do not know who is going to pop up on the discussion groups or whether we are going to suffer viral infection. We may live through cyberspace as if a participant in a communal setting, but this is a transmutation of practices by the imagination. The seeming immensity of cyberspace made manifest by the possibility of 'always somewhere else to go', the anomic quality of cyberspace, and the absence of perception of hierarchy (for hierarchy always posits origins and ends) produces wonderment. And as Bachelard notes: 'The surest sign of wonder is exaggeration' (ibid.: 112). Only by phenomenological reflection do we grasp this movement. For Bachelard, the wonder is constrained by intimacy with technology, the relation between the screen image and the user. As we have pointed out this distance is erased by the processes of fascination and absorption.

When we are involved in a group conversation in cyberspace we are not in intimate relations with other persons, only an intimacy with ourselves, with the excitement of what is going to come on screen next, or what one is going to say in response, ultimately with the magic of the immediate presence of the image into which we are incorporated. Screen images appear as if by magic, we do not perceive the causes of their appearance. They just happen. 'When considered in transmission from one soul to another, it becomes evident that a poetic image eludes causality' (ibid.: xx).

There are no hidden depths in cyberspace, all is on screen, and because of this we imagine that we reveal all at a touch of the mouse. This is an illusion of the totally public, of an open access democracy, whereas, in fact, we are always hidden. Hidden from sight. We can hide our identities and change our identities, become woman, become man. We can deceive or choose to tell the truth, but nobody can trust the statements we make. All the norms of validation which are part of the communicative structures of the life-world, the public world, are undone. The lessons which Grice and Habermas taught us are inverted so that we live in a regime of invalidity claims. The manufacture of trust and obligation upon which the construct of community rests becomes unstable, and we are thrown back into the imaginary world of the indeterminate city, the city that contains the fleeting, the spectacle, the symptoms of anxiety.

When we finally do step back from absorbed time, we may see that our relation with cyberspace is one overcoded with hope. This is the hope that our suspicion of a technological jungle will turn out to be a land of plenty and security. That the deterritorialised alien space of city/cyberspace will permit reterritorialisation by the figures of community which we try to pretend are not a projection of the imagination. Sadly, these are but daydreams of the intimacy of the immense. Or as Bachelard says: 'The mind sees and continues to see objects, while the spirit finds the nest of immensity in an object' (ibid.: 190). Thus we are finally caught between reflexive reason and the poetics of hope that finds re-presentation in the oppositions of city/community and exteriority/interiority.

Tell your readers that the Internet is a dangerous place.
(Dr. F. Cohen, *Personal Computer World*, May 1995: 545)

BIBLIOGRAPHY

Adams, T. (1995) 'Elegy to the Bullring', *The Observer* 'Life' magazine, 5 March.

Adonis, A. (1992) 'Evidence of special attachment', *Financial Times*, 3 April.

ADUML (1991) *Plan de Développement Urbain de la Communication*, Agence de Développement D'Urbanisme de la Métropole Lilloise.

Akerstrom, M. (1993) *Crooks and Squares*, New York: Transaction Books.

Allen, J. (1995) 'Global worlds', in Allen, J. and Massey, D. (eds) *Geographical Worlds*, Oxford: Oxford University Press.

Althusser, L. (1971) *Lenin, Philosophy and Other Essays*, trans. B. Brewster, London: New Left Books.

Amery, C. (1992) 'Milton Keynes: the view from the grid', *Financial Times*, 27 January.

Amin, A. (ed) (1994) *Post-Fordism*, Oxford: Blackwell.

Amin, A. and Thrift, N. (1994) 'Globalisation, institutional "thickness" and the local economy', in Healey, P., Cameron, S., Davoudi, S., Graham, S. and Madani Pour, A. (eds) *Managing Cities: The New Urban Context*, London: Wiley.

Amis, K. (1954) *Lucky Jim*, Harmondsworth: Penguin.

Anderson, B. (1983) *Imagined Communities: Reflections on the Origins and Spread of Nationalism*, London: Verso.

Anderson, J., Brook, C. and Cochrane, A. (eds) (1995) *A Global World? Reordering Political Space*, Oxford: Oxford University Press.

Anspacher, H. and Anspacher, R. (eds) (1958) *The Individual Psychology of Alfred Adler: A Systematic Presentation in Selections from his Writings*, London: George Allen & Unwin.

Anthias, F. and Yuval-Davis, N. (1993) *Racialized Boundaries*, London: Routledge.

Appadurai, A. (1987) 'Disjuncture and difference in the global cultural economy', *Culture and Society* 7.

Appadurai, A. (1992) 'Putting hierarchy in its place' in Marcus, G. E. (ed.) *Re-reading Cultural Anthropology*, Durham, N.C.: Duke University Press.

Appignanesi, R. and Garratt, C. (1995) *Postmodernism for Beginners*, Cambridge: Icon Books.

Archbishop of Canterbury's Urban Priority Commission (1984) *Faith in the City*, London: Church House Publishing.

Auster, P. (1988) *In the Country of Last Things*, London: Faber & Faber.

Bachelard, G. (1969) *The Poetics of Space*, Boston: Beacon Press.

Back, L. (1995) *New Ethnicities and Urban Cultures* London: ULL.

Baker, P. L. (1993) 'Chaos, order and sociological theory', *Sociological Inquiry* 63.

Balibar, E. (1991) 'Racism and nationalism' in Balibar, E and Wallerstein, I. *Race, Nation, Class*, London: Verso.

Balsamo, A. (1995) 'Forms of technological embodiment: reading the body in contemporary culture' in Featherstone, M. and Burrows, R. (eds) *Cyberspace/Cyberbodies/Cyberpunk: Cultures of Technological Embodiment*, London: Sage.

Balzac, H. (1979) *Lost Illusions*, trans. H. J. Hunt, Harmondsworth: Penguin.

Bane, M. (1992) *White Boy Singin' the Blues: The Black Roots of White Music*, London: Da Capo Press.

Banham, R. (1971) *Los Angeles: The Architecture of Four Ecologies*, London: Allen Lane/Penguin.

Bannister, N. (1994) 'Go-slow on the European multimedia superhighway', *Guardian*, 26 October.

Barrell, J. (1991) *The Infections of De Quincey*, Boston: Yale University Press.

Barthes, R. (1972) *Mythologies*, London: Jonathan Cape.

Batifol, I. (1930) *The Great Literary Salons*, Paris: Musée Carnavalet.
Batty, M. (1990) 'Invisible cities', *Environment and Planning B*, 17: 127–130.
Baudrillard, J. (1990) *Cool Memories*, London: Verso Press.
Bauman, Z. (1988) *Freedom*, Milton Keynes: Open University Press.
Bauman, Z. (1989) *Modernity and the Holocaust*, Cambridge: Polity.
Bauman, Z. (1991) *Modernity and Ambivalence*, Oxford: Polity Press.
Bauman, Z. (1992) 'Soil, blood and identity', *The Sociological Review*, 40(4).
Baumgartner, M. P. (1988) *The Moral Order of a Suburb*, New York: Oxford University Press.
Beattie, G. (1986) *Survivors of Steel City*, London: Chatto & Windus.
Bendixson, T. and Platt, J. (1992) *Milton Keynes: Image and Reality*, Cambridge: Granta Editions.
Benedikt, M. (ed.) (1991a) *Cyberspace: First Steps*, London: MIT Press.
Benedikt, M. (1991b) 'Cyberspace: some proposals' in Benedikt, M. (ed.) *Cyberspace: First Steps*, London: MIT Press.
Benewick, R. (1972) *The Fascist Movement in Britain*, London: Allen Lane.
Benjamin, W. (1979) 'Berlin chronicle' in Benjamin, W., *One Way Street*, London: Verso.
Benvenuto, B. and Kennedy, R. (1986) *The Works of Jacques Lacan*, London: Free Association Books.
Bhabha, H. (1986) 'Remembering Fanon', Foreword to, Franz Fanon's *Black Skin, White Masks*, London: Pluto Press.
Bhabha, H. (1990) 'DisseminNation' in Bhabha, H. (ed.) *Nation and Narration*, London: Routledge.
Bhabha, H. (1994) *The Location of Culture*, London: Routledge.
Biocca, F. (1992a) 'Communication within virtual reality: creating a space for research', *Journal of Communication*, 42(4).
Biocca, F. (1992b) 'Virtual reality technology: a tutorial', *Journal of Communication*, 42(4).
Bird, J., Curtis, B., Putnam, T., Robertson, G., Tickner, L. (eds) (1993) *Mapping the Futures: Local cultures, global change*, London: Routledge.
Birmingham Evening Mail (1991) '16 page special', 2 April.
Birmingham Evening Mail (1991) 'Jewel in our crown', 28 March.
Bishop, J. (1986) *Milton Keynes – the Best of Both Worlds? Public and Professional Views of a New City*, Bristol: School for Advanced Urban Studies.
Bishop, J. and P. Hoggett (1986) *Organizing around Enthusiasms: Mutual Aid in leisure*, London: Comedia.
Blackman, T., Keenan, P. and Coombes, M. (1994) 'Developing GIS for urban policy and research in local government in the UK', *Newcastle City Council* mimeo.
Blackside, Inc. (1994) 'Malcolm X: make it plain', *TV Documentary* – The Voice of Sharon X (Amina Rahman) USA.
BMK (1988) *MK 2k. The Next Step. Strategic Plan. Interim Statement*, Milton Keynes: Borough of Milton Keynes.
Borrie Commission (1994) *Report on Social Justice* London: Vintage.
Bourne, J. (1994) *Working Class Cultures in Britain: Gender, Class and Ethnicity*, London: Routledge.
Bowie, M. (1993) *Psychoanalysis and the Future of Theory*, Oxford: Blackwell.
Bowlby, R. (1992) 'Walking, women and writing: Virginia Woolf as Flâneuse', *Still Crazy After All These Years*, London: Routledge.
Boyer, C. (1986) *Dreaming the Rational City*, London: MIT Press.
Boyer, C. (1993) 'The city of illusion: New York's public places', in Knox, P. (ed.) *The Restless Urban Landscape*, Englewood Cliffs, N.J.: Prentice Hall.
Boyle, M. and Hughes, G. (1991) 'The politics of the representation of "the real": discourses from the Left on Glasgow's role as European City of Culture, 1990', *Area* 23(3): 217–228.
Bradbury, M. (1959) *Eating People is Wrong*, Harmondsworth: Penguin.
Braine, J. (1957) *Room at the Top*, Harmondsworth: Penguin.
Brunn, S. and Leinbach, T. (1991) *Collapsing Time and Space*, London: HarperCollins.
Buckinghamshire County Council (1988) *County Structure Plan. Monitoring Statement 1988*, Aylesbury: Buckinghamshire County Council.
Buick, J. and Jevtic, Z. (1995) *Cyberspace for Beginners*, Cambridge: Icon Books.
Bukatman, S. (1993a) *Terminal Identity*, Durham, N.C.: Duke University Press.

Bukatman, S. (1993b) 'Gibson's typewriter' in Dery, M. (ed.) *Flame Wars: The Discourse of Cyberculture*, Durham, N.C.: Duke University Press.

Bunder, T. (1953) *The Real East End*, London: Allen & Unwin.

Burchell, G., Gordon, G. and Miller, P, (eds) (1991) *The Foucault Effect*, London: Harvester Wheatsheaf.

Burgess, I. and Wood, A. (1992) *Decoding Docklands*, London: Media Matters.

Burgess, J. and Wood, P. (1988) 'Decoding Docklands: place advertising and decision making strategies of the small firm', in Eyles, J. and Smith, D. (eds) *Qualitative Methods in Human Geography*, Cambridge: Polity Press.

Burgin, V. (1991) 'Geometry and abjection', in Donald, J. (ed.) *Thresholds: Psychoanalysis and Cultural Theory*, London: Macmillan.

Burke, P. (1978) *Popular Culture in Early Modern Europe*, London: Temple Smith.

Byrne, D.S. (1992) 'What sort of future?' in Collis, R. and Lancaster, B. (eds) *Geordies: Roots of Regionalism*, Edinburgh: Edinburgh University Press.

Byrne, D. S. (1989) *Beyond the Inner City*, Milton Keynes: Open University Press.

Byrne, D. S. (1994) 'Deindustrialization, Planning and Class Structures', unpublished Ph.D. thesis, University of Durham.

Byrne, D. S. (1995a) 'Deindustrialization and dispossession', *Sociology* 29: 95–116.

Byrne, D. S. (1995b) 'Radical geography as "mere political economy" – the local politics of space', *Capital and Class* 56: 117–38.

Calhoun, C. (1986) 'Computer technology, large-scale social integration and the local community', *Urban Affairs Quarterly*, 22(2): 329–49.

Campbell, B. (1993) *Goliath: Britain's Dangerous Places*, London: Methuen.

Campbell, C. (1987) *The Romantic Ethic and the Spirit of Modern Consumerism*, Oxford: Basil Blackwell.

Carrigan, T., Connell, R. W. and Lee, J. (1985) 'Towards a new sociology of masculinity', *Theory and Society* 14(5): 551–604.

Carter, R., Harris, C. and Joshi, S. (1987) 'The 1951–55 Conservative government and the racialisation of black immigration', *Policy Papers in Ethnic Relations*, no. 11 , University of Warwick, England.

Cartwright, T. J. (1991) 'Planning and chaos theory', *Journal of the American Planning Association* 57: 44–56.

Castells, M. (1977) *The Urban Question: A Marxist Approach*, London: Edward Arnold.

Castells, M. (1985) 'High technology, economic restructuring and the urban–regional process in the United States' in Castells, M. (ed.) *High Technology, Space and Society*, London: Sage.

Castells, M. (1989) *The Informational City: Information Technology, Economic Restructuring and the Urban-Regional Process*, Oxford: Blackwell.

Casti, J. L. (1994) *Complexification*, London: Abacus.

Certeau, M. de (1984) *The Practices of Everyday Life*, Berkeley: University of California Press.

Chambers, I. (1990) *Border Dialogues: Journeys in Postmodernity*, London: Routledge.

Chaney, D. (1993) *Fictions of Collective Life: Public Drama in Late-modern Culture*, London: Routledge.

Chaney, D. (1994) *The Cultural Turn: Scene-setting Essays on Contemporary Cultural History*, London: Routledge.

Channel 4 (1994) *Once Upon a Time in Cyberville*, London: Programme transcript.

Charlesworth, J. and Cochrane, A. (1994) 'Tales of the suburbs. The local politics of growth in the south-east of England', *Urban Studies*, 31(10): 1723–38.

Chaudhary, V. (1994) 'The pub from hell', *Guardian* 1 November.

Chesterton Consulting (1989) *Milton Keynes Employers' Survey Report 1989*, Milton Keynes: Chesterton Consulting, on behalf of Milton Keynes Development Corporation.

Chesterton Consulting (1991) *1991 Milton Keynes Employment Survey*, Milton Keynes: Chesterton Consulting on behalf of Milton Keynes Development Corporation and Milton Keynes and North Bucks TEC.

Chesterton Consulting (1992) *The Planning of Milton Keynes*, Milton Keynes: Chesterton Consulting on behalf of Milton Keynes Development Corporation.

Choay, Françoise (1980) *La règle et le modèle: sur la théorie de l'architecture et de l'urbanisme*, Paris: Seuil.

Christopherson, S. (1994) 'The fortress city: privatized spaces, consumer citizenship' in Amin,

A. (ed.) *Post Fordism: A Reader*, Oxford: Blackwell.

Clark, N. (1995) 'Rear view mirrorshades: the recursive generation of the Cyberbody' in Featherstone, M. and Burrows, R. (eds) *Cyberspace/Cyberbodies/Cyberpunk: Cultures of Technological Embodiment*, London: Sage.

Cochrane, A. (1993) *Whatever Happened to Local Government?*, Buckingham: Open University Press.

Cohen, A. K. (1960) *Delinquent Boys: The Culture of the Gang*, New York: The Free Press.

Cohen, P. (1988) 'The perversions of inheritance' in Cohen, P. (ed.) *Multi-racist Britain*, London: Macmillan.

Cohen, P. (1996) 'Labouring under whiteness', in Frankenberg, R. (ed.) *Localising Whiteness*, Berkeley: University of California Press.

Cohen, S. (1985) *Visions of Social Control*, London: Polity.

Cole, T. (1987) 'Life and Labour on the Isle of Dogs', unpublished Ph.D. thesis.

Colls, R. and Dodd, P. (eds) (1986) *Englishness: Politics and Culture 1880–1920*, London: Croom Helm.

Colomina, B. (1994) *Privacy and Publicity: Modern Architecture as Mass Media*, Cambridge, Mass.: MIT Press.

Connell, R. W. (1987) *Gender and Power: Society, the Person and Sexual Politics*, Cambridge: Polity Press.

Connell, R. W. (1995) *Masculinities*, Cambridge: Polity Press.

Connolly, W. (1991) *Identity/Difference*, London: Cornell University Press.

Conway, D. (1992) *Locality Planning, Research Summary*, Report of a research project looking at social need within the Milton Keynes Grid Square System, unpublished: prepared for Buckinghamshire County Council Social Services Department.

Cooke, H. and Blankley, D. (1977) 'The Ripper's shadow hangs over Scott Hall Ave', *Daily Express*, 27 June.

Cooke, P. (ed.) (1989) *Localities: The Changing Face of Urban Britain*, London: Unwin Hyman.

Cooke, P. (1990) *Back to the Future?*, London: Unwin Hyman.

Cooper, W. (1950) *Scenes from Provincial Life*, Harmondsworth: Penguin.

Corner, J. (1995) *Television Form and Public Address*, London: Edward Arnold.

Coward (1995) Superintendent Coward, West Yorkshire Police, Minutes of Chapeltown South Police Community Forum.

Craib, I. (1994) *The Importance of Disappointment*, London: Routledge.

Csicsery-Ronay, I. (1991) 'Cyberpunk and Neuromanticism' in McCaffery, L. (ed.) *Storming the Reality Studio*, Durham, N.C.: Duke University Press.

Currie, E. (1991) *Dope and Trouble: Portraits of Delinquent Youth*, New York: Pantheon.

Cuthbert, C. (1995) 'Under the volcano: postmodern space in Hong Kong' in Watson, S. and Gibson, K. (eds) *Postmodern Cities and Spaces*, Oxford: Blackwell.

Dalby, S. (1992) 'Success on many fronts', *Financial Times*, 3 April.

Daniels, S. (1977) *The Paint House*, Harmondsworth: Penguin.

Davidoff, L. and Hall, C. (1987) *Family Fortunes: Men and Women of the English Middle Class 1780–1850*, London: Hutchinson.

Davies, J. K. and Kelly, M. P. (eds) (1993) *Healthy Cities*, London: Routledge.

Davis, M. (1990) *City of Quartz: Excavating the Future of Los Angeles*, London: Verso.

Davis, M. (1992) *Beyond Blade Runner: Urban Control, the Ecology of Fear*, Westfield, N.J.: Open Magazine Pamphlets.

Davis, M. (1993) 'Who killed LA? A political autopsy', *New Left Review* 197: 3–28.

De Gournay, C. (1988) 'Telephone networks in France and Great Britain' in Tarr, J. and Dupuy, G. (eds) *Technology And The Rise Of The Networked City In Europe And North America*, Philadelphia: Temple.

De Greene, K. B. (1994) 'The rocky path to complex system indicators', *Technological Forecasting and Social Change* 47: 171–88.

Deitch, J. (1992) *Post Human*, Amsterdam: Idea Books.

De Landa, M. (1991) *War in the Age of Intelligent Machines*, New York: Zone Books.

De Landa, M. (1992) 'Non-organic life' in Crary, J. and Kwinter, S. (eds) *Zone 6: Incorporations*, New York: Zone Books.

De Landa, M. (1993) 'Virtual environments and the rise of synthetic reason' in Dery, M. (ed.) *Flame Wars*, Durham, N.C.: Duke University Press.

Deleuze, G. and Guattari, F. (1982) *A Thousand Plateaus*, London: Athlone Press.
Deleuze, G. and Guattari, F. (1988) *Mille Plateaux A Thousand Plateaus: Capitalism and Schizophrenia*, trans. and foreword by B. Massumi, Minneapolis: University of Minnesota Press.
Deleuze, G. and Guattari, F. (1994) *What is Philosophy*, London: Verso.
Dennis, N and Erdos, G. (1992) *Families without Fatherhood*, London: Institute for Economic Affairs.
Derrida, J. (1973) *Speech and Phenomena*, Evanstone: Northwestern University Press.
Derrida, J. (1976) *Of Grammatology*, London: Johns Hopkins University Press.
Derrida, J. (1981) *Positions*, London: Athlone Press.
Derrida, J. (1982) *Margins of Philosophy*, London: Harvester Wheatsheaf.
Derrida, J. (1987) *Dissemination*, Chicago: Chicago University Press.
Deutsch, K. (1966) 'On social communications and the metropolis' in Smith, A. (ed.) *Communication and Culture*, London: Holt, Rinehart & Winston.
Dibattista, M. (1983) 'Joyce, Woolf and the modern mind', in Clements, P. and Grundy, I. (eds) *Virginia Woolf: New Critical Essays*, London: Vision and Barnes & Noble.
Dickens, P., Goodwin, M., Gray, F. and Duncan, S. (1985) *Housing, States and Localities*, London: Methuen.
Dickinson, M. (1991) *Goodbye Piccadilly: the History of the Abolition of the Greater Manchester Council*, Manchester: Intercommunication Publishing.
Döblin, A. (1978) [1929] *Berlin Alexaderplatz*, trans. Eugene Jolas, Harmondsworth: Penguin.
Docklands Forum (1993) *Race and Housing*, London: LDDC.
Docklands Forum (1994) *Once Upon a Time in Docklands*, London: LDDC.
Dollenmayer, D. B. (1988) *The Berlin Novels of Alfred Döblin*, Berkeley: University of California Press.
Domosh, M. (1989) 'A method for interpreting landscape: a case study of the New York World Building', *Area* 21 (4): 347–55.
Donald, J. (1992) 'Metropolis: the city as text', in Bocock, R. and Thompson, K. (eds) *Social and Cultural Forms of Modernity*, Cambridge: Polity.
Donald, J. (1995) 'The city, the cinema: modern spaces', in Jenks, C. (ed.) *Visual Culture*, London: Routledge.
Drake, St. C. Cayton, R. (1945) *Black Metropolis: A Study of Negro Life in a Northern City*, New York: Harcourt, Brace & Co.
Dutton, W., Blumler, J. and Kraemer, K. (eds) (1987) *Wired Cities: Shaping the Future of Communications*, Washington D.C.: Communications Library.
Dyos, H. J. (ed.) (1985) *Victorian Cities*, London: Routledge.
Eade, J. (1994) *Local/Global Relations in a London Borough*, Roehampton: Mimeograph.
Eade, J. (1995) *Profiting from Places*, BSA conference paper.
Easthope, A. (1990) *What a Man's Gotta Do: The Masculine Myth in Popular Culture*, London: Routledge.
Elees, C. (1993) 'Gender and technology', *Variant* 15.
Ellin, N. (1995) *Postmodern Urbanism*, Oxford: Blackwell.
Elliott, D. (1995) 'The battle for art', *Art and Power: Europe under the Dictators 1939–1945*, London: Hayward Gallery.
Ellison, R. (1952) *Invisible Man*, London: Penguin.
Elwes, C. (1993) 'Gender and technology', *Variant* 15.
Emberley, P. (1989) 'Places and stories: the challenge of technology', *Social Research* 56: 741–785.
Epstein, N. D. (1985) 'The social explorer as anthropologist', in Dyos, H. J. (ed.) *Victorian Cities*, London: Routledge.
Esser, J. and Hirsch, J. (1994) 'The crisis of fordism and the dimensions of "post-fordist" regional and urban structure' in Amin, A. (ed.) *Post-Fordism*, Oxford: Blackwell.
Eubanks, G. E. (1994) 'President and Ceo Symantec', *Business And Technology Magazine*: 42.
Evans, K. (1995) *Black British, Segregation, Surveillance and the Reconstructed Late Modern City*, BSA Conference Paper.
Evans, K., Fraser, P. and Taylor, I. (1995) 'Going to town: routine accommodations and routine anxieties in respect of public space and public facilities in two cities in the north of England', in Edgell, S., Walklate, S. and Williams, G. (eds) *Debating the Future of the Public Sphere*, Aldershot: Avebury.

Evans, K. and Fraser, P. (1995) 'Difference in the city: locating marginal use of public space' in Sampson, C. and South, N. (eds) *Conflict and Consensus in Social Policy*, London: Macmillan.

Everitt, B. (1974) *Cluster Analysis*, London: Heinemann.

Eversley, D. (1990) 'Inequality at the spatial level – tasks for planners', *The Planner* 76.

Eyles, J. (1987) 'Housing advertisements as signs: locality creation and meaning systems', *Geografiska Annaler* 69B(2): 93–105.

Eyles, J. and Peace, W. (1990) 'Signs and symbols in Hamilton: an iconography of Steeltown', *Geografiska Annaler,* 72B(2–3): 73–88.

Fainstein, S., Gordon, I. and Harloe, M. (1992) *Divided Cities*, London: Blackwell.

Fanon, F. (1967a) *Black Skins, White Masks*, New York: Grove Press.

Fanon, F. (1967b) *Wretched of the Earth*, Middlesex: Penguin.

Farrar, M. (1981) (aka Paul Holt) 'Riot and revolution: the politics of an inner city' *Revolutionary Socialism – the Journal of Big Flame* Winter, 2.

Farrar, M. (1986) 'A slice of the empire in Leeds' *Focus* 1.

Farrar, M. (1988) 'The politics of black youth workers in Leeds', *Critical Social Policy* 23, Autumn.

Farrar, M. (1989) *Living history: some biographies for Harehills and Chapeltown, Leeds*, Leeds: Leeds City Council.

Farrar, M. (1992) 'Racism, education and black self-organisation', *Critical Social Policy* 36, Winter.

Farrar, M. (1994a) 'The word is out on the street', *New Statesman and Society*, 21 January.

Farrar, M. (1994b) 'Slaying Goliath: riot, "race", men and the inner city', *Regenerating Cities* 6, February.

Farrar, M. (1994c) 'Meeting my mugger', *New Statesman and Society*, 25 November.

Farrar, M. (1995) 'Re-presenting the inner city', *Regenerating Cities* 7, January.

Farrar, M. (1996) 'Black communities and processes of exclusion' in Haughton, G. and Williams, C. C. (eds) *Corporate City? Partnership, Participation and Partition in Urban Development in Leeds*, Aldershot: Avebury.

Fazey, I. H. (1993) *The Financial Times*, 28 January.

Featherstone, M. (1991) 'The aestheticization of everyday life', *Consumer Culture and Postmodernism*, London: Sage.

Featherstone, M. (1995a) 'Personality, unity and the ordered life' in Featherstone, M. *Undoing Culture: Postmodernism, Globalization and Identity*, London: Sage.

Featherstone, M. (1995b) 'Post-bodies, ageing and virtual reality' in Featherstone, M. and Wernick, A. (eds) *Images of Ageing*, London: Routledge.

Featherstone, M. and Burrows, R. (1995) *Cyberspace/Cyberbodies/Cyberpunk: Cultures of Techno-logical Embodiment*, London: Sage. Also published as a special double issue of the journal *Body & Society* 1(3/4).

Feldman, D. and Jones, S. (eds) (1991) *Metropolis*, Routledge.

Fentress, J. and Wickham, C. (1992) *Social Memory*, Oxford: Basil Blackwell.

Finnegan, R. (1989) *The Hidden Musicians: Music-making in an English Town*, Cambridge: Cambridge University Press.

Fishman, R. (1987) *Bourgeois Utopias: The Rise and Fall of Suburbia*, New York: Basic Books.

Fishman, R. (1995) 'Megalopolis unbound' in Kasinitz, P. (ed.) *Metropolis: Centre and Symbol of Our Times*, London: Macmillan.

Forrest, R., Murie, A. and Williams, P. (1990) *Home Ownership: Differentiation and Fragmentation*, London: Unwin Hyman.

Forum meeting of 27 July 1995, West Yorkshire Police Authority, Wakefield.

Foster, J. (1992) 'Living with Docklands redevelopment', *London Journal* 17(2).

Foucault, M. (1972) *The Archaeology of Knowledge*, London: Tavistock.

Foucault, M. (1979) *Discipline and Punish*, New York: Vintage Books.

Franks, A. (1986) 'Where trouble waits on the corner', *The Times*, 1 April.

Frieman, T. (1994) 'Making sense of software: computer games and interactive textuality' in Jones, S. (ed.) *Cybersociety*, London: Sage.

Frisby, D. (1985) *Fragments of Modernity: Theories of Modernity in the Work of Simmel, Kracauer and Benjamin*, Cambridge: Polity Press.

Frith, S. (1988) 'Playing with Real Feeling – Jazz and Suburbia', in *Music for Pleasure: Essays in the Sociology of Pop*, Cambridge: Polity Press.

Garreau, J. (1991) *Edge City: Life On The New Frontier*, New York: Doubleday Anchor.

Gartner, L. P. (1960) *The Jewish Immigrant in England, 1970–1914*, London: George, Allen & Unwin.

Gashè, R. (1986) *The Tain of The Mirror*, London: Harvard University Press.

Gibson, W. (1984) *Neuromancer*, London: HarperCollins.

Gibson, W. (1986) *Count Zero*, London: HarperCollins.

Gibson, W. (1991) 'Academy leader' in Benedikt, C. M. (ed.) *Cyberspace: First Steps*, London: MIT Press.

Gibson, W. (1993) *Virtual Light*, London: Viking.

Giddens, A. (1979) *Central Problems in Social Theory*, London, Macmillan.

Giddens, A. (1984) *The Constitution of Society*, Cambridge: Polity Press.

Giddens, A. (1991) *Modernity and Self-Identity: Self and Society in the Late Modern Age*, Cambridge: Polity Press.

Gilbert, N. and Conte, R. (eds) (1995) *Artificial Societies: The Computer Simulation of Social Life*, London: UCL Press.

Gilbert, N. and Doran, J. (eds) (1994) *Simulating Societies: The Computer Simulation of Social Phenomena*, London: UCL Press.

Giles, A. K. and Ansell, D. J. (1985) *Milton Keynes 1967–84: The Farming Story*, Miscellaneous Study No. 73, Department of Agricultural Economics and Management, Reading: University of Reading.

Gillespie, A. (1992), 'Communications technologies and the future of the city' in Breheny, M. (ed.) *Sustainable Development And Urban Form*, London: Pion.

Gillet, L. (1930) 'Introduction', in Batifol, I. *The Great Literary Salons*, Paris: Musée Carnavalet.

Gilman, S. (1985) *Degeneration*, New York: Columbia.

Gilroy, P. (1987) *There Ain't No Black in The Union Jack*, London: Allen & Unwin.

Gilroy, P. (1993a) *Promised Lands: Modernity, Utopia and Emancipation in the Black Atlantic*, London: Verso.

Gilroy, P. (1993b) *The Black Atlantic: Modernity and Double Consciousness*, London: Verso.

Gilroy, P. (1993c) *Small Acts: Thoughts on the Politics of Black Cultures*, London: Serpent's Tail.

Glassner, B. (1995) 'In the name of health' in Bunton, R., Nettleton, S. and Burrows, R. (eds) *The Sociology of Health Promotion*, London: Routledge.

Godbolt, J. (1984) *A History of Jazz in Britain 1919–1950*, London: Quartet Books.

Godbolt, J. (1989) *A History of Jazz in Britain 1950–70*, London: Quartet Books.

Godfrey, D. and Parhill, D. (1979) *Gutenberg Two*, Toronto: Porcepic.

Goffman, E. (1971) *The Presentation of Self in Everyday Life*, London: Penguin.

Gökalp, I. (1992) 'On the analysis of large technical systems', *Science, Technology and Human Values* 17(1): 578–87.

Gold, J. (1985) 'The city of the future and the future of the city' in King, R. (ed.) *Geographical Futures*, Sheffield: Geographical Association.

Gold, J. (1990) 'A wired society? Utopian literature, electronic communications and the geography of the future city', *National Geographic Journal Of India* 36(1–2): 20–9.

Gold, J. and Ward, S. (eds) (1994) *Place Promotion: The Use of Publicity and Marketing to Sell Towns and Regions*, Chichester: John Wiley.

Goldberg, D. T. (1993) *Racist Culture*, Oxford: Blackwell.

Goldin, H. (1937) *East End My Cradle*, London: Heinemann.

Goldmark, P. (1972) 'Tomorrow we will communicate to our jobs', *The Futurist*, April: 55–9.

Goodey, B. (1994) 'Art-ful places: public art to sell public spaces?' in Gold, J. R. and Ward, S. V. (eds) *Place Promotion: The Use of Publicity and Marketing to Sell Towns and Regions*, Chichester: Wiley.

Goodwin, M., Duncan, S. and Halford, S. (1993) 'Regulation theory, the local state and the transition of urban politics', *Environment and Planning D: Society and Space*, 11: 67–88.

Gordon, C. (ed.) (1980) *Michel Foucault: Power and Knowledge*, Hemel Hempstead: Harvester Wheatsheaf.

Gordon, P. (1990) *Racial Violence and Harassment*, London: Runneymede Trust.

Gould, S. J. (1989) *Wonderful Life: The Burgess Shale and the Nature of History*, London: Penguin.

Graham, G. (1992) 'Postfordism as politics: the political consequences of narrative on the left', *Society and Space* 10: 393–410.

Graham, S. (1995) 'Cities, nations and communications in the global era: urban telematics policies in France and Britain', *European Planning Studies* 3(3): 357–80.

Graham, S. (1996) 'Cities in the real-time age: telecommunications as a paradigm challenge to the conception and planning of urban space', *Environment and Planning A* (forthcoming).

Graham, S. and Marvin, S. (1996) *Telecommunications and the City: Electronic Spaces, Urban Places*, London: Routledge.

Grossberg, L. (1992) *We Gotta Get Out of This Place: Popular Conservatism and Postmodern Culture*, New York: Routledge.

Grosz, E. (1994) *Volatile Bodies*, Indiana: Indiana University Press.

Hall, P. (1989) *London 2001*, London: Unwin Hyman.

Hall, S. (1978) 'Racism and reaction' in CRE, *Five Views of Multi-Racial Britain*, London: Commission for Racial Equality.

Hall, S. (1991) 'The local and the global', in King, A. D. (ed.) *Culture, Globalisation and the World System*, London: Macmillan.

Hall, S. and Jefferson, T. (eds) (1976) *Resistance through Rituals: Youth Subcultures in Postwar Britain*, London: Hutchinson.

Hall, S., Critcher, C., Jefferson, T., Clarke, J. and Roberts, B. (1978) *Policing the Crisis*, London: Macmillan.

Hall. T. R. (1992) *Art and Image: Public Art as Symbol in Urban Regeneration*, Working Paper No. 61, School of Geography, University of Birmingham.

Hall, T. R. (1994) 'Urban regeneration and cultural geography: The International Convention Centre Birmingham', unpublished Ph.D. thesis, School of Geography, University of Birmingham.

Hamnett, C. (1995) 'Controlling space: global cities' in Allan, J. and Hamnett, C. (eds) *A Shrinking World? Global Unevenness and Inequality*, Oxford: Oxford University Press.

Hanson, J. (1992) 'Setting the dream', *Architectural Journal* 195(15): 36–7.

Haraway, D. (1991) *Symians, Cyborgs and Women: The Reinvention of Nature*, London: Free Association Books.

Harker, D. (1985) *Fakesong: The Manufacture of British 'folksong' 1700 to the Present Day*, Milton Keynes: Open University Press.

Harloe, M., Pickvance, C. and Urry, J. (eds) (1989) *Place, Policy and Politics: Do Localities Matter?*, London: Unwin Hyman.

Harrison, M. (1995) *Visions of Heaven and Hell*, London: Channel 4 Television.

Harvey, D. (1973) *Social Justice and the City*, London: Edward Arnold/Baltimore, M.D.: Johns Hopkins University Press.

Harvey, D. (1989) *The Condition of Postmodernity*, Oxford: Blackwell.

Hassan, I. (1981) 'Cities of mind, urban words', in Jaye, M. C. and Chalmers Watts, A. (eds) *Literature and the Urban Experience*, New Brunswick, N.J.: Rutgers University Press.

Haughton, G. and Whitney, D. (eds) (1994) *Reinventing a Region: Restructuring in West Yorkshire*, Aldershot: Avebury.

HCRO (Hertfordshire County Records Office) Documents as numbered in their files.

Healey, P., Cameron, S., Davoudi, S., Graham, S. and Madani-Pour, A. (eds) (1995) *Managing Cities: The New Urban Context*, Chichester: John Wiley.

Hebdige, D. (1992) 'Digging for Britain: an excavation in Seven Parts' in Strinati, D. and Wagg, S. (eds) *Come on Down? Popular Media Culture in Post-war Britain*, London: Routledge.

Hegedus, J. and Tosic, I. (1994) 'The poor, the rich and the transformation of urban space', *Urban Studies* 31: 989–93.

Heidegger, M. (1955) 'The question concerning technology' in Krell, D. (ed.) *Basic Writings*, New York: Harper & Row.

Heim, M. (1991) 'The erotic ontology of cyberspace' in Benedikt, M. (ed.) *Cyberspace: First Steps*, London: MIT Press.

Heim, M. (1995) 'The design of VR' in Featherstone, M. and Burrows, R. (eds) *Cyberspace/Cyberbodies/Cyberpunk: Cultures of Technological Embodiment*, London: Sage.

Hellawell, K., Chief Constable of West Yorkshire Police (1994), personal communication, 28 February 1994.

Hennessy, P. (1993) *Never Again*, London: Arrow.

Heptinstall, B. (1995) Leeds Taxi Drivers' Association, Minutes of Chapeltown South Police

Community Forum meeting of 27 July 1995, West Yorkshire Police Authority, Wakefield.

Hesse, B. (1993a) 'Racism and spacism in Britain' in Francis, P. and Matthews, R. (eds) *Tackling Racial Attacks*, Leicester: Centre for the Study of Public Order, Leicester University.

Hesse, B. (1993b) 'Black to front and Black again: racialization through contested times and spaces' in Keith, M. and Pile, S. (eds) *Place and The Politics of Identity*, London: Routledge.

Hesse, B. Rai, D. K., Bennett, C. and McGilchrist, P. (1992) *Beneath the Surface: Racial Harassment*, London: Avebury.

Hewison, R. (1987) *The Heritage Industry: Britain in a Climate of Decline*, London: Methuen.

Hey, V. (1986) *Patriarchy and Pub Culture*, London: Tavistock.

Hill, D. (1993) 'The last Tories', *Sunday Times*, 16 May.

Hill, R. L. and Feagin, J. R. (1987) 'Detroit and Houston: two cities in global perspective' in Smith, M. P. and Feagin, J. R. (eds) *The Capitalist City: Global Restructuring and Community Politics*, Oxford: Blackwell.

Hill, S. (1988) *The Tragedy of Technology*, London: Pluto.

Hinshaw, M. (1973) 'Wiring megalopolis: two scenarios' in Gerbner, G., Gross, L. and Melody, W. (eds) *Communications Technology and Social Policy: Understanding The New 'Cultural Revolution'*, London: Wiley.

Hirsh, A. (1981) *The French New Left*, Boston: South End Press.

Hobbs, D. (1989) *Doing the Business*, Oxford: Oxford University Press.

Hobsbawm, E. and Ranger, T. (eds) (1983) *The Invention of Tradition*, Cambridge: Cambridge University Press.

Hoggart, R. (1988) *A Local Habitation*, London: Chatto & Windus.

Holmes (1876) *Leeds Street Directory*.

hooks, b. (1992) *Black Looks*, London: Turnaround.

Hostettler, E. (1991) *An Outline History of the Isle of Dogs*, London: Island History Trust.

Humphries, A. (1989) *Travels in a Poor Man's Country*, Cambridge: Cambridge University Press.

Hunt, A. and Wickham, G. (1994) *Foucault and Law*, London: Pluto Press.

Husbands, C. (1982) 'East end racism 1900–1980', *London Journal* 8.

International Convention Centre Birmingham (n.d.) Brochure.

International Convention Centre Birmingham (n.d.) Leaflet.

Irwin, J. (1970) *The Felon*, Englewood Cliffs, N.J.: Prentice Hall.

Jackson, D. (1990) *Unmasking Masculinity: A Critical Autobiography*, London: Routledge.

Jackson, K. T. (1985) *Crabgrass Frontier: The Suburbanization of the United States*, New York: Oxford University Press.

Jacobs, J. (1961) *The Death and Life of Great American Cities*, Harmondsworth: Penguin.

Jacobs, J. M. (1992) 'Cultures of the past and urban transformation: the Spitalfields market development in East London' in Anderson, K. and Gale, F. (eds) *Inventing Places: Studies in Cultural Geography*, Australia/North and South America: Longman Cheshire/Wiley Halstead Press.

Jameson, F. (1984) 'Postmodernism, or the cultural logic of late capitalism', *New Left Review* 146: 53–92.

Jameson, F. (1991) *Postmodernism or the Cultural Logic of Late Capitalism*, London: Verso.

Jay, M. (1988) 'Scopic regimes of modernity' in Foster, H. (ed.) *Vision and Visuality*, Dia Art Foundation, Discussions in Contemporary Culture no. 2, Seattle: Bay Press.

Jennings, C. (1995) *Up North: Travels Beyond the Watford Gap*, London: Little Brown.

Jones, S. (ed.) (1995) *Cybersociety*, London: Sage.

Kadrey, R. and McCaffery, L. (1991) 'Cyberpunk 101: a schematic guide to *Storming the Reality Studio*' in McCaffery, L. (ed.) *Storming the Reality Studio*, Durham, N.C.: Duke University Press.

Karim, B. (1995) quoted in Malcolm X *Make It Plain*, an oral history edited by Greene, C. Y. with Strickland, W. and the Malcolm X Documentary Production Team. London: Penguin.

Kauffman, S. (1993) *The Origins of Order*, London: Oxford University Press.

Kearny, R (1991) *Poetics of Imaging: From Husserl to Lyotard*, London: HarperCollins.

Kearns, G. and Philo, C. (eds) (1993) *Selling Places: The City as Cultural Capital Past and Present*, Oxford: Pergamon.

Keating, P. J. (1985) 'Fact and fiction in the East End' in Dyos, H. J. (ed.) *Victorian Cities*, London: Routledge.

Keith, M. (1993a) *Race, Riots and Policing: Lore and Disorder in a Multi-racist Society*, London: UCL Press.

Keith, M. (1993b) 'From punishment to discipline?: racism, racialisation and the policing of social control' in Cross, M. and Keith, M. (eds) *Racism, The City and the State*, London: Routledge.

Keith, M. and Pile, S. (eds) (1993) (eds) *Place and the Politics of Identity*, London: Routledge.

Kellner, D. (1995) 'Mapping the present from the future: from Baudrillard to cyberpunk', in *Media Culture*, London: Routledge.

Kelly, M. P., Davies, J. K. and Charlton, B. (1993) 'Healthy cities: a modern problem or a postmodern solution' in Davies, J. K. and Kelly, M. P. (eds) *Healthy Cities*, London: Routledge.

Kern, S. (1983) *The Culture of Time and Space, 1880–1918*, London: Weidenfeld & Nicolson.

Knight, R. and Gappert, G. (eds) (1989) *Cities in a Global Society*, London: Sage.

Kohn, M. (1994) *Dope Girls*, London: Quartet.

Kracauer, S. (1975) 'The mass ornament', *New German Critique* 2.

Kroker, A. (1992) *The Possessed Individual: Technology and Postmodernity*, London: Macmillan.

Kroker, A. and Weinstein, M. (1994) *Data Trash: The Theory of the Virtual Class*, Montreal: New World Perspectives.

Laclau, E. (1990) *New Reflections on The Revolution of Our Time*, London: Verso.

Laclau, E. (1994a) 'Hegemony, deconstruction, pragmatism', unpublished paper, Department of Government, Essex University.

Laclau, E. (ed.) (1994b) *The Making of Political Identities*, London: Verso.

Laclau, E. and Mouffe, C. (1985) *Hegemony and Socialist Strategy*, London: Verso.

Land, N. (1995) 'Meat (or how to kill Oedipus in cyberspace)' in Featherstone, M. and Burrows, R. (eds) *Cyberspace/Cyberbodies/Cyberpunk: Cultures of Technological Embodiment*, London: Sage.

Landry, C. and Bianchini, F. (1995a) 'The lifting of city limits', *Guardian*, 21 December: 20.

Landry, C. and Bianchini, F. (1995b) *The Creative City*, London: Demos.

Lane, T. (1987) *Liverpool: Gateway of Empire*, London: Lawrence & Wishart.

Lanier, J. and Biocca, F. (1992) 'An insider's view of the future of virtual reality', *Journal of Communication* 42(4).

Lasch, C. (1991) *The True and Only Heaven: Progress and Its Critics*, New York: W. Norton.

Lash, S. and Urry, J. (1994) *Economies of Signs and Space*, London: Sage.

Latour, B. (1987) *Science in Action: How to Follow Scientist and Engineers Through Society*, Milton Keynes: Open University Press.

Law, J. and Bijker, W. (1992), 'Postscript: technology, stability and social theory' in Bijker, W. and Law, J. (eds) *Shaping Technology, Building Society: Studies in Sociotechnical Change*, London: MIT Press.

Lazenby, P. (1980) 'Chapeltown – a special enquiry' *Evening Post* 28 May.

Leary, T. (1994) *Chaos and Cyberculture*, Berkeley, Calif.: Ronin.

Lefebvre, H. (1974) 'La production de l'espace', *Homme et la societé*, 31–32: 15–32.

Lefebvre, H. (1976) 'Reflections on the politics of space', *Antipode* 8(2), May (translated by M. J. Enders from the French journal *Espaces et Societies* 1, 1970).

Lefebvre, H. (1979) 'Space: social product and use value' in Freiberg, J. W. (ed.) *Critical Sociology: European Perspectives*, New York: Irvington.

Lefebvre, H. (1991) *The Production of Space*, Oxford: Blackwell.

Lefebvre, H. (1996) *Writings on Cities*, trans. E. Kofman and E. Lebas, Oxford: Blackwell.

Lessing, D. (1974) *The Memoires of a Survivor*, London: Octagon Press.

Letkemann, P. (1973) *Crime as Work*, New York: Prentice Hall.

Levy, D. (1992) 'Introduction', *Journal of Communication* (special issue on virtual reality) 42(4).

Lewin, R. (1993) *Complexity*, London: Phoenix.

Ley, D. (1987) 'Styles of the times: liberal and neo-conservative landscapes of inner Vancouver 1968–1986', *Journal of Historical Geography* 13(1): 40–56.

Lister, D. (1991) 'The transformation of a city: Birmingham' in Owen, U. and Fisher, M. (eds) *Whose Cities?*, Harmondsworth: Penguin.

Littell, R. (1993) *The Visiting Professor*, London: Faber & Faber.

Little, K. (1948/1972) *Negroes in Britain*, London: Routledge & Kegan Paul.

Lock, D. (1992) 'Milton Keynes at twenty-five', *The Planner*, 24 January: 6–7.

Lowenthal, D. (1985) *The Past is a Foreign Country*, Cambridge: Cambridge University Press.

Lupton, D. (1995) 'The embodied computer/user' in Featherstone, M. and Burrows, R. (eds) *Cyberspace/Cyberbodies/Cyberpunk: Cultures of Technological Embodiment*, London: Sage.

Lyttelton, H. (1954) *I Play as I Please: The Memoirs of an Old Etonian Trumpeter*, London: MacGibbon & Kee.

McCaffery, L. (ed.) (1991) *Storming the Reality Studio*, Durham, N.C.: Duke University Press.

McCarron, K. (1995) 'Corpses, animals, machines and mannequins: the body and cyberpunk' in Featherstone, M. and Burrows, R. (eds) *Cyberspace/Cyberbodies/Cyberpunk: Cultures of Technological Embodiment*, London: Sage.

McClelland, K. (1991) 'Masculinity and the "representative artisan"' in Roper, M. and Tosh, J. (eds) *Manful Assertions: Masculinities in Britain since 1800*, London: Routledge.

McFadden, T. (1991) 'Notes on the structure of cyberspace and the ballistic actors model' in Benedikt, M. (ed.) *Cyberspace: First Steps*, London: MIT Press.

McHale, B. (1992a) 'POSTcyberMODERNpunkISM', *Constructing Postmodernism*, London: Routledge.

McHale, B. (1992b) 'Towards a poetics of cyberpunk', in *Constructing Postmodernism*, London: Routledge.

MacKinnon, N. (1993) *The British Folk Music Scene: Musical Performance and Social Identity*, Buckingham: Open University Press.

McLuhan, M. (1964) *Understanding Media*, London: Sphere.

Maffesoli, Michel (1995) *The Time of the Tribes*, London: Sage.

Maisonrouge, J. (1984) 'Putting information to work for people', *Intermedia* 12(2): 31–3.

Mandelbaum, S. (1986) 'Cities and communication: the limits of community', *Telecommunications Policy* June: 132–40.

Marcus, L. (1995) 'Women, modernism, cinema', in Donald, J. and Donald, S. (eds) *The City, the Cinema: Modern Spaces*, CulCom Research Papers in Media and Cultural Studies, 3, Falmer, University of Sussex.

Marcuse, P. (1989) 'Dual city – a muddled metaphor for a quartered city', *International Journal of Urban and Regional Research* 13: 697–708.

Marks, L. (1992) 'City of sky and myth', *Sunday Times*, 19 January.

Marler, S. (1993) *American Affair: The Americanisation of Britain*, London: Boxtree.

Marriott, J. (1995) 'Sensation of the abyss – the urban poor and modernity', unpublished paper.

Mars, T. (1992) 'Little Los Angeles in Bucks', *Architectural Journal* 195(15): 22–6.

Marsh, C. and Dale, C. (1993) *The 1991 Census Users' Handbook*, London: HMSO.

Mason, R. and Jennings, L. (1982) 'The computer home: will tommorow's housing come Alive', *The Futurist*, 16(1): 35.

Maspero, F. (1993) *Roissy Express: A Journey Through the Paris Suburbs*, London: Verso.

Massey, D. (1984) *Spatial Divisions of Labour: Social Structures and the Geography of Production*, London: Macmillan.

Massey, D. (1992) 'Politics and space/time', *New Left Review*, 196: 65–84.

Massey, D. (1994a) *Docklands a Microcosm of Trends*, London: Docklands Forum.

Massey, D. (1994b) *Space, Place and Gender*, Cambridge: Polity Press.

Massey, D. (1995) 'Rethinking radical democracy spatially', *Environment and Planning D, Society and Space* 13: 283–8.

Massey, D. and Meegan, R. (1982) *The Anatomy of Job Loss: The How and Why and Where of Employment Decline*, London: Methuen.

Mayo, S. (1994) 'Stories from the Island Docklands', *Dyelines*, University of East London.

Mazzoleni, D. (1993) 'The city and the imaginary' in Carter, E., Donald, J. and Squires, J. (eds) *Space and Place*, London: Lawrence & Wishart.

Melly, G. (1977) *Rum, Bum and Concertina*, London: Weidenfeld & Nicolson.

Mepham, J. (1983) 'Mourning and modernism', in Clements, P. and Grundy, I. (eds) *Virginia Woolf: New Critical Essays*, London: Vision and Barnes & Noble.

Miles, J. (1992) 'Blacks vs. browns: the struggle for the bottom rung', *Atlantic Monthly*, October: 41–68.

Miles, R. (1989) *Racism*, London: Routledge.

Miles, R. (1993) *Racism After Race-relations*, London: Routledge.

Miles, R. and Phizacklea, A. (1983) *Labour and Racism*, London: Routledge.

Miller, D. A. (1988) *The Novel and the Police*, Berkeley: University of California Press.

Miller, J. Hillis (1995) *Topographics*, Stanford: Stanford University Press.

Miller, W.B. (1958) 'Lower class culture as a generating milieu of gang delinquency', *Journal of Social Issues* 15: 5–19.

Mingione, E. (1994) 'Life strategies and social economies in the postfordist age', *International Journal of Social and Economic Research* 18(1): 24–45.

Mitchell, D. (1995) 'The end of public space? People's park, definitions of the public and democracy', *Annals of the Association of American Geographers* 85(1): 108–33.

Mitchell, W. (1995) *City of Bits: Space, Place and the Infobahn*, Cambridge, Mass.: MIT Press.

MKBC (1993) *A Summary of the Work of the Neighbourhood Interagency Planning Services Group (NIPS) 1991–93*, Milton Keynes: Milton Keynes Borough Council, Community Development Division.

MKBC/BCC (1990) *Milton Keynes: Safeguarding the Future*, Milton Keynes and Aylesbury: Milton Keynes Borough Council and Buckinghamshire County Council.

Moores, S. (1993) *Interpreting Audiences: The Ethnography of Media Consumption*, London: Sage.

Morgan, G. (1993) 'Local culture and politics in docklands', *Environment and Planning D: Society and Space* 11.

Morley, D. (1992) *Television, Audiences and Cultural Studies*, London: Routledge.

Morley, D. and Robins, R. (1995) *Spaces of Identity*, London: Routledge.

Mortimer, P. (1976) 'Urban Development in North Buckinghamshire 1930–1970', M.Phil thesis, Milton Keynes: Open University.

Mosco, V. (1988) 'Introduction: information in the pay-per society' in Mosco, V. and Wasko, J. (eds) *The Political Economy of Information*, Madison: University of Wisconsin Press.

Moss, M. (1987) 'Telecommunications, world cities and urban policy, *Urban Studies* 24: 534–46.

Motion, A. (1993) *Philip Larkin: A Writer's Life*, London: Faber & Faber.

Mouffe, C. (ed.) (1992) *Dimensions of Radical Democracy*, London: Verso.

Mouffe, C. (1993) *The Return of the Political*, London: Verso.

Mouffe, C. (1995) 'Post-Marxism: democracy and identity' *Environment and Planning D: Society and Space* 13: 259–65.

Moyal, A. (1992) 'The gendered use of the telephone: an Australian case study', *Media, Culture and Society* 14(1): 51–72.

Mudimbe, V. Y. (1988) *The Invention of Africa*, London: James Currey.

Mudimbe, V. Y. (1994) *The Idea of Africa*, London: James Currey.

Mulgan, G. (1989) 'The changing shape of the city' in Hall, S. and Jacques, M. (eds) *New Times*, London: Lawrence & Wishart.

Mulgan, G. (1991) *Communication And Control: Networks and The New Economies Of Communication*, Cambridge: Polity Press.

Murdock, G. (1993) 'Communications and the constitution of modernity', *Media, Culture and Society* 15: 521–39.

Murphy, D. (1987) *Tales From Two Cities: Travels of Another Sort*, Harmondsworth: Penguin.

Murray, B. (1993) 'Society, cyberspace and the future', *Aspen Workshop Papers* (taken from a web page).

Murray, C. (1990) *The Emerging British Underclass*, London: Institute for Economic Affairs.

Murray, C. (1994) 'Underclass – the crisis deepens', *Sunday Times*, 22 May and 'The New Victorians', *Sunday Times*, 29 May.

Naisbitt, J. and Aburdene, P. (1991) *Megatrends 2000 – Ten Directions for the 1990s*, New York: Avon Books.

Naylor, D. (1973) *Yorkshire Evening Post*, 27 June.

Naylor, D. (1975) 'Boarded windows greeted the thug threat', *Yorkshire Evening Post*, 1 November.

Negrier, E. (1990), 'The politics of territorial network policies: the example of video-communications networks in France', *Flux*, Spring: 13–20.

Negroponte, N. (1995) *Being Digital*, London: Hodder & Stoughton.

Neveu, C. (1991) 'Espace et Territoire', *Spitalfield Habitations* 23.

Newton, F. (1961) *The Jazz Scene*, Harmondsworth: Penguin.

Nicolis, G. and Prigione, I. (1989) *Exploring Complexity*, New York: W.H. Freeman & Co.

O'Connor, J. (1982) 'The meaning of crisis', *International Journal of Urban and Regional Research* 5: 301–28.

O'Sullivan, T., Hartley, J., Saunders, D., Montgomery, M. and Fiske, J. (1994) *Key Concepts in Communication and Cultural Studies*, London: Routledge.

Olalquiaga, C. (1992) *Megalopolis: Contemporary Cultural Sensibilities*, Minneapolis: University of Minnesota Press.

Oliver, P., Davis, I. and Bentley, I. (1981) *Dunroamin': The Suburban Semi and Its Enemies*, London: Barrie & Jenkins.

OPCS (1991) *Office of Population Census Statistics*, enumeration district analysis of small area statistics, London: OPCS.

Orwell, G. (1959) *The Road to Wigan Pier*, London: Secker & Warberg.

Owens, R. (1992) 'The great experiment', *Architectural Journal* 195(15): 30–5.

Paasi, A. (1986) 'The institutionalisation of regions: a theoretical framework for understanding the emergence of regions and the constitution of regional identity', *Fennia* 164(1): 105–46.

Palmer, T. (1977) *All You Need Is Love: The Story of Popular Music*, London: Futura.

Parkinson, M. (1994) 'European cities towards 2000: the new age of entrepreneurialism?', mimeo.

Pascal, A. (1987) 'The vanishing city', *Urban Studies* 24: 597–603.

Pinch, P. (1992) 'Ordinary places? The social relations of the local state in two "M4-corridor towns"', *Political Geography* 11(5): 485–500.

Plant, S. (1992) *The Most Radical Gesture: The Situationist International in a Postmodern Age*, London: Routledge.

Plant, S. (1993) 'Beyond the screens: film, cyberpunk and cyberfeminism', *Variant* 14.

Plant, S. (1995) 'The future looms: weaving women and cybernetics' in Featherstone, M. and Burrows, R. (eds) *Cyberspace/Cyberbodies/Cyberpunk: Cultures of Technological Embodiment*, London: Sage.

Pocock, D. C. D. (1978) *The Novelist and The North*, University of Durham, Department of Geography, Occasional Publications, new series, no. 12.

Pollard, S. (1993) 'Labour' in Binfield, C. *et al.* (eds) *The History of the City of Sheffield 1843–1993*, Sheffield: Academic Press.

Pool, I. (ed.) (1977) *The Social Impact of the Telephone*, Boston: MIT Press.

Portelli, A. (1991) *The Death of Luigi Trastulli and Other Stories*, Albany: State University of New York.

Potter, S. (1976) *Transport and New Towns, Volume 2. The Transport Assumptions underlying the Design of Britain's New Towns 1946–1976*, Milton Keynes: New Towns Study Unit, The Open University.

Pred, A. (1985) 'The social becomes the spatial' in Gregory, D. and Urry, J. (eds) *Social Relations and Spatial Structures*, London: Macmillan.

Prendergast, C. (1992) *Paris and the Nineteenth Century*, Cambridge: Cambridge University Press.

Priestley, J. B. (1977) [1984] *English Journey*, Harmondsworth: Penguin.

Privat D'Anglemont, A. (1861) *Paris Inconnu*, Paris: Adolphe Delahays.

Rabinow, P. (ed.) (1986) *The Foucault Reader*, Harmondsworth: Penguin.

Rajchman, J. (1991) *Truth and Eros: Foucault, Lacan and the Question of Ethics*, London: Routledge.

Rasmussen, S. E. (1994) 'Reflections on Milton Keynes' in Walker, D. (ed.) 'New Towns', *Architectural Design*, Profile 111.

Rattansi, A. (1995) Review Essay, 'Forget postmodernism? Notes from de bunker', *Sociology* 29(2): 339–49.

Ravetz, A. (1973) *Model Estate*, London: Croom Helm.

Rawdon Wilson, R. (1995) 'Cyber(body)parts: prosthetic consciousness' in Featherstone, M. and Burrows, R. (eds) *Cyberspace/Cyberbodies/Cyberpunk: Cultures of Technological Embodiment*, London: Sage.

Redhead, S. (1990) *The End-of-the-Century Party: Youth and Pop Towards 2000*, Manchester: Manchester University Press.

Redhead, S. (1993) *Rave Off: Politics and Deviance in Contemporary Youth Culture*, Aldershot: Avebury Press.

Reed, M. and Harvey, D. L. (1992) 'The new science and the old: complexity and realism in the social sciences', *Journal for the Theory of Social Research* 22: 353–80.

Rex, J. (1978) 'Race in the inner city' in CRE *Five Views of Multi-racial Britain*, London: Commission for Racial Equality.

Rheingold, H. (1991) *Virtual Reality*, London: Mandarin.

Rheingold, H. (1994a) *The Virtual Community: Finding Connection in a Computerized World*, London: Secker & Warburg.

Rheingold, H. (1994b) *The Virtual Community: Surfing the Internet*, London: Mandarin Paperbacks.

Richards, G. (1989) 'Masters and Servants: The Growth of the Labour Movement in St Christopher-Nevis, 1896 to 1956', Dissertation submitted for the Ph.D. degree at the University of Cambridge.

Ricoeur, P. (1988) *Time and Narrative*, vol. 3, Chicago: Chicago University Press.

Rieff, D. (1993) *Los Angeles: Capital of the Third World*, London: Orion Books.

Ritzer, G. (1992) *The McDonaldization of Society: An Investigation into the Changing Character of Contemporary Social Life*, London: Sage.

Robins, K. (1995a) 'Cyberspace and the world we live in' in Featherstone, M. and Burrows, R. (eds) *Cyberspace/Cyberbodies/Cyberpunk: Cultures of Technological Embodiment*, London: Sage.

Robins, K. (1995b) 'Collective emotion and urban culture' in Healey, P., Cameron, S., Davoudi, S., Graham, S. and Modani-Pour, A. (eds) *Managing Cities: The New Urban Context*, Chichester: John Wiley.

Robins, K. and Hepworth, M. (1988) 'Electronic spaces: new technologics and the future of cities', *Futures*, April: 155–76.

Robson, B. (1969) *Urban Analysis*, Cambridge: Cambridge University Press.

Rogers, R. (1996) *The Reith Lectures*, BBC Publications: London.

Rogers, R. (1996) 'Britain's urban gardener', *The Higher* 26 January.

Rojek, C. and Turner, B.S. (eds) (1993) *Forget Baudrillard?*, London: Routledge.

Rose, N. and Miller, P. (1992) 'Political power beyond the state: problematics of government', *British Journal of Sociology* 43(2): 173–205.

Rucker, R., Sirius, R.U. and Queen Mu (1993) *Mondo 2000: A User's Guide to the New Edge*, London: Thames & Hudson.

Runnymede Trust (1994) *Neither Unique nor Typical*, London: Runnymede Trust.

Runnymede Trust (1995) *Island Stories – Imagined Communities of Race and Class in the Remaking of East Enders*, London: Runnymede Trust.

Rustin, M. (ed.) (1996) *Rising in the East*, London: Lawrence & Wishart.

Rydin, Y. (1993) *The British Planning System*, London: Macmillan.

Sack, R. D. (1986) *Human Territoriality: its Theory and History*, Cambridge: Cambridge University Press.

Said, E. (1978) *Orientalism*, London: Penguin.

Said, E. (1993) *Culture and Imperialism*, London: Vintage.

Said, E. (1994) *Culture and Imperialism*, London: Chatto & Windus.

Samuel, R. (1981) *East End Underworld*, London: Routledge.

Santucci, G. (1994), 'Information highways worldwide: challenges and strategies', *I & T Magazine*, Spring: 614–23.

Sassen, S. (1991) *The Global City: New York, London, Tokyo*, Princeton: Princeton University Press.

Sassen, S. (1994) 'The urban complex in a world economy', *International Social Science Journal* 139: 43–62.

Saunders, P. (1980) *Urban Politics*, London: Penguin.

Savage, M. (1987) *The Dynamics of Working-Class Politics*, Cambridge: Cambridge University Press.

Savage, M. and Warde, A. (1993) *Urban Sociology, Capitalism and Modernity*, Macmillan: Basingstoke.

Sayer, A. (1985) 'The Difference that Space Makes' in Gregory, D. and Urry, J. (eds) *Social Relations and Spatial Structures*, Basingstoke: Macmillan.

Scannell, P. (1989) 'Public service broadcasting and modern public life', *Media, Culture and Society* 11(2).

Schaffer, F. (1970) *The New Town Story*, London: McGibbon & Kee.

Scherpe, K. R. (1989) 'The city as narrator: the modern text in Alfred Döblin's *Berlin Alexanderplatz*', in Huyssen, A. and Bathrick, D. (eds) *Modernity and the Text: Revisions of German Modernism*, New York: Columbia University Press.

Scheuneman, D. (1978) *Romankrise: Die Entstehungsgesctriche der modernen Romanpoetik in Deutschland*, Heidelberg: Quelle Du Meyer.

Schiller, D. and Fregaso, R. (1991) 'A private view of the digital world', *Telecommunications Policy*, June: 195–207.

Schroeder, R. (1994) 'Cyberculture, cyborg post-modernism and the sociology of virtual reality technologies', *Futures* 26(5): 519–28.

Seigel, J. (1986) *Bohemian Paris: Culture, Politics and the Boundaries of Bourgeois Life, 1830–1890*, New York: Viking.

Sennett, R. (1970) *The Uses of Disorder*, Harmondworth: Penguin.

Sennett, R. (1971) *The Uses of Disorder*, London: Faber.

Sennett, R (1990) *The Conscience of the Eye: The Design and Social Life of Cities*, London: Faber & Faber.

Sennett, R. (1994) *Flesh and Stone*, London: Faber & Faber.

Sennett, R. and Cobb, R. (1973) *The Hidden Injuries of Class*, New York: Vintage.

Sherman, B. and Judkins, P. (1993) *Glimpses of Heaven, Visions of Hell*, London: Hodder & Stoughton.

Sheth, J. and Sisodia, R. (1993) 'The information mall', *Telecommunications Policy*, July: 376–89.

Shields, R. (1991) *Places on the Margin: Alternative Geographies of Modernity*, London: Routledge.

Short, J. R., Benton, L. M., Luce, W. N. and Walton, J. (1993) 'Reconstructing the image of an industrial city', *Annals of the Association of American Geographers*, 83(2): 207–24.

Shotter, I. and Geiger, K. (1989) *Texts of Identity*, London: Sage.

Shotter, J. (1980) 'Action, joint-action and intentionality' in Brenner, M. (ed.) *The Structure of Action*, New York: St Martins Press.

Sibley, D. (1995) *Geographies of Exclusion*, London: Routledge.

Silverstone, R. (1994) *Television and Everyday Life*, London: Routledge.

Simmel, G. (1950) 'The metropolis and mental life' in Wolff, K. H. (ed.) (1950) *The Sociology of Georg Simmel*, New York: The Free Press.

Simmel, G. (1978) *The Philosophy of Money*, London: Routledge.

Simmel, G. (1995) 'The metropolis and mental life', in Kascnitz, P. (ed.) *Metropolis: Centre and Symbol of Our Times*, London: Macmillan.

Simpson and Darling (1994) 'The Missing Millions' *Journal of Social Policy* 23(4).

Sizemore, C. (1984) 'Reading the city as palimpsest: the experiential perception of the city in Doris Lessing's The Four Gated City' in Squier, S. (ed.) *Women Writers and the City: Essays in Feminist Literary Criticism*, Knoxville: University of Tennessee Press.

Slim, J. (1986) 'Visions of our future', *Birmingham Evening Mail*, 29 January.

Small, S. (1994) *Racialised Barriers*, London: Routledge.

Smith, A. (1754) *The Theory of Moral Sentiments*

Smith, B. (1974) 'Spotlight on Leeds mecca of vice', *Evening Post*, 31 January.

Smith, D. (1989) *North and South: Britain's Economic, Social and Political Divide*, Harmondsworth: Penguin.

Smith, S. (1989) *'Race' and the Politics of Residence*, Cambridge: Polity.

Smith, S. J. (1989) *The Politics of Race and Residence*, London: Polity Press.

Sobchack, V. (1995) 'Beating the meat/surviving the text, or how to get out of this century alive' in Featherstone, M. and Burrows, R. (eds) *Cyberspace/Cyberbodies/Cyberpunk: Cultures of Technological Embodiment*, London: Sage.

Soja, E. (1989) *Postmodern Geographies: The Reassertion of Space in Critical Theory*, London: Verso.

Soja, E. (1991) 'Poles apart: New York and Los Angeles', in Mollenkopf, J. and Castells, M. (eds) *Dual City: The Restructuring of New York*, New York: Russell Sage Foundation.

Soja, E. (1992) 'Inside expolis: scenes from Orange County', in Sorkin, M. (ed.) *Variations on a Theme Park: The New American City and the End of Public Space*, New York: Hill & Wang/Noonday Press.

Soja, E. (1995) 'Postmodern urbanization: the six restructurings of Los Angeles' in Watson, S. and Gibson, K. (eds) *Postmodern Cities and Spaces*, Oxford: Blackwell.

Soja, E. (1996) *Third Space: Journeys to Los Angeles and Other Real-and-Imagined Places*, Oxford: Blackwell.

Soja, E. (forthcoming) *Postmetropolis*, Oxford: Blackwell.

Sollitt, K. (1983) *Man of Steel*, Sheffield: Sheaf Publishing.

Sollors, W. (ed.) (1989) *The Invention of Ethnicity*, Oxford: Oxford University Press.

Solomos, J. (1989) *Race and Racism in Contemporary Britain*, London: Macmillan.

Sorkin, M. (ed.) (1992) *Variations on a Theme Park*, New York: Hill & Wang.

Squier, S.M. (1988) *Virginia Woolf and London: The Sexual Politics of the City*, Chapel Hill: University of North Carolina Press.

Squires, J. (1994) 'Ordering the city: public spaces and political participation' in Weeks, J. (ed.) *The Lesser Evil and the Greater Good: The Theory and Politics of Social Diversity*, London: Rivers Oram Press.

Stallabrass, J. (1995) 'Empowering technology: the exploration of cyberspace', *New Left Review* 211: 3–32.

Stalleybrass, P. and White, A. (1986) *Politics and Poetics of Transgression*, London: Methuen.

Stedman Jones, G. (1983) *Outcast London*, Harmondsworth: Penguin.

Stephenson, N. (1992) *Snow Crash*, New York: Bantam Books.

Sterling, B. (1986) *Mirrorshades: The Cyberpunk Anthology*, New York: Arbor House.

Sterling, B. (1990) 'Cyberspace (TM)', *Interzone* 41.

Steur, J. (1992) 'Defining virtual reality: dimensions determining telepresence', *Journal of Communications*, 42(4).

Stevens, L., Karn, V., Davidson, E. and Stanley, A. (1981) *Ethnic Minorities and Building Society Lending in Leeds*, Leeds: Leeds Community Relations Council.

Stilgoe, W. J. (1988) *Borderland: Origins of the American Suburb 1820–1939*, New Haven: Yale University Press.

Stone, A. R. (1991) 'Will the real body please stand up? Boundary stories about virtual cultures' in Benedikt, M. (ed.) *Cyberspace: First Steps*, London: MIT Press.

Stott, R. (1956) 'There's really no such place as Chapeltown', *Yorkshire Evening News*, January.

Stowell, G. (1929) *The Story of Button Hill*, London: Victor Gollancz.

Sudjic, D. (1993) *The Hundred Mile City*, London: Flamingo.

Symphony Hall Birmingham (n.d.) Brochure.

Tambling, J. (1989) 'Repression in *Mrs. Dalloway*', *Essays in Criticism* 39.

Tatsumi, T. (1991) 'The Japanese reflection of mirrorshades' in McCaffery, L. (ed.) *Storming the Reality Studio*, Durham, N.C.: Duke University Press.

Taylor, C. (1991) *The Ethics of Authenticity*, Cambridge, Mass.: Harvard University Press.

Taylor, I. (1995) 'It's a whole new ball game', *Salford Papers in Sociology*, no. 17.

Taylor, I. and Jamieson, R. (1995) 'Little Mesters', paper given at the British Sociology Association Conference. (Reproduced in this volume)

Taylor, I., Evans, K. and Fraser, P. (1996) *A Tale of Two Cities: Global Change Local Feeling and Everyday Life in the North of England*, London: Routledge.

Taylor, S. (1993) 'The industrial structure of the Sheffield cutlery trades 1870–1914' in Binfield, C. *et al.* (eds) *The History of the City of Sheffield 1843–1993*, Sheffield: Academic Press.

Thomas, H. (1994) 'The local press and urban renewal: a South Wales case study', *International Journal of Urban and Regional Research* 18(2): 315–33.

Thomas, N. (1994) *Colonialism's Culture*, Cambridge: Polity Press.

Thompson, E. P. (1978) *The Poverty of Theory*, London: Merlin.

Thompson, P. (ed.) (1990) *Myths We Live By*, London: Routledge.

Thoresby, R. (1816) *Ducatis Leodensis*, Leeds: Whittaker.

Thorns, D. (1972) *Suburbia*, London: Paladin.

Thrift, N. (1987) 'The geography of nineteenth-century class formation' in Thrift, N. and Williams, P. (eds) *Class and Space: The Making of Urban Society*, London: Routledge.

Thrift, N. (1993), 'Inhuman geographies: landscapes of speed, light and power' in Cloke, P., Doel, M., Matless, D., Phillips, M. and Thrift, N. (eds) *Writing the Rural: Five Cultural Geographies*, London: Paul Chapman.

Toffler, A. (1980) *The Third Wave*, New York: Morrow.

Tomas, D. (1989) 'The technophiliac body', *New Formations* 8.

Tomas, D. (1991) 'Old rituals for new space' in Benedikt, M. (ed.) *Cyberspace: First Steps*, London: MIT Press.
Tomas, D. (1995) 'Feedback and cybernetics; reimaging the body in the age of the cyborg' in Featherstone, M. and Burrows, R. (eds) *Cyberspace/Cyberbodies/Cyberpunk: Cultures of Technological Embodiment*, London: Sage.
Treen, C. (1982) 'The process of suburban development in North Leeds, 1870–1914' in Thompson, F. M. L. (ed.) *The Rise of Suburbia*, Leicester: Leicester University Press.
Tschumi, B. (1994) *Architecture and Disjunction*, Cambridge, Mass.: MIT Press.
Tweedale, G. (1993) 'The business and technology of Sheffield steelmaking' in Binfield, C. *et al.* (eds) *The History of the City of Sheffield 1843–1993*, Sheffield: Academic Press.
Urry, J. (1985) 'Social Relations, Space and Time' in Gregory, D. and Urry, J. (eds) *Social Relations and Spatial Structures*, Basingstoke: Macmillan.
Valentine, G. (1990) 'London's streets of fear' in Thornley, A. (ed.) *The Crisis of London*, London: Routledge.
Van Kempen, E. T. (1994) 'The dual city and the poor: social polarisation, social segregation and life chances', *Urban Studies* 31: 995–1015.
Vidler, A. (1993) 'Bodies in space/subjects in the city: psychopathologies of modern urbanism', *Differences*, 5(3): 32–3.
Virilio, P. (1987) 'The overexposed city', *Zone* 1(2).
Virilio, P. (1993) 'The third interval: a critical transition' in Andermatt-Conley, V. (ed.) *Rethinking Technologies*, London: University Of Minnesota Press.
Wacquant, L. (1989) 'The ghetto, the state and the new capitalist economy', *Dissent*, Fall: 508–20.
Waldrop, M. M. (1992) *Complexity*, London: Viking.
Walker, D. (1981) *The Architecture and Planning of Milton Keynes*, London: Architectural Press.
Walker, D. (ed.) (1994) 'New towns', *Architectural Design*, Profile 111.
Walkovitz, J. (1992) *City of Dreadful Delight*, London: Virago.
Waller, D. (1991) *Town, City and Nation*, Manchester: Manchester University Press.
Wallerstein, I. (1974) *The Modern World System: Capitalist Agriculture and the Origins of the European World-Economy in the Sixteenth Century*, New York: Academic Press.
Wallerstein, I. (1979) *The Capitalist World-Economy*, Cambridge: Cambridge University Press.
Wallerstein, I. (1984) *The Politics of the World-Economy*, Cambridge: Cambridge University Press.
Ward, C. (1993) *New Town, Home Town*, London: Calouste Gulbenkian Foundation.
Ward, D. (1960) 'The Urban Plan of Leeds', MA Thesis, Department of Geography, University of Leeds.
Ward, D. (1962) 'The pre-urban Cadaster and the urban pattern of Leeds', *Annals of the Association of American Geographers* 52(2): 150–66.
Wark, M. (1988) 'On technological time: Virilio's overexposed city', *Arena* 83: 82–100.
Watson, S. (1991) 'Gilding the smokestacks: the new symbolic representations of deindustrialised regions', *Environment and Planning D: Society and Space* 9(1): 59–70.
Watson, S. and Gibson, K. (eds) (1995) *Postmodern Cities and Spaces*, Oxford: Brackwell.
Webber, M. (1964) 'The urban place and the non place urban realm' in Webber, M., Dyckman, J., Foley, D., Guttenberg, A., Wheaton, W. and Whurster, C. (eds) *Explorations into Urban Structure*, Philadelphia: University of Pennsylvania Press.
Webber, M. (1968) 'The post-city age', *Daedalus*, Fall.
Weideger, P. (1991) 'Larger than life tribute to Brum's golden age!', *The Independent*, 8 June.
Westwood, S. (1990) 'Racism, black masculinity and the politcs of space' in Hearn, J. and Morgan, D. (eds) *Men, Masculinities and Social Theory*, London: Unwin Hyman.
Wiener, M. (1981) *English Culture and the Decline of the Industrial Spirit 1850–1980*, Harmondsworth: Penguin.
Wieviorka, M. (1995) *The Arena of Racism*, London: Sage.
Wiley, J. (1995) 'No body is "doing it": cybersexuality as a postmodern narrative', *Body & Society* 1(1).
Williams, R. (1958) *Culture and Society 1780–1950*, London: Chatto & Windus.
Williams, R. (1970) 'Introduction' in Dickens, C. *Dombey and Son*, Harmondsworth: Penguin.
Williams, R. (1973) *The Country and the City*, London: Chatto & Windus.
Williams, R. (1976) *Keywords*, London: Fontana Press.
Williams, R. (1980) *Problems in Materialism and Culture*, London: Verso.

Williams, R. (1992) 'Milton Keynes comes of age', *Management Today*, March.
Willis, P. (1976) *Profane Culture*, London: Routledge & Kegan Paul.
Willis, P. (1977) *Learning to Labour: How Working Class Kids Get Working Class Jobs*, Farnborough: Saxon House.
Wilson, E. (1988) *Hallucinations*, London: Radius.
Wilson, E. (1991) *The Sphinx in the City*, London: Virago.
Wilson, E. (1992) *The Sphinx in the City: Urban Life the Control of Disorder and Women*, Berkeley: University of California Press.
Wilson, E. (1995a) 'The invisble flâneur' in Watson, S. and Gibson, K. (eds) *Postmodern Cities and* Spaces, Oxford: Blackwell.
Wilson, E. (1995b) 'The rhetoric of urban space', *New Left Review* 209: 146–60.
Winant, H. (1994) *Racial Conditions: Politics, Theory, Comparisons*, Minneapolis: University of Minnesota Press.
Woolf, V. (1976) *Moments of Being: Unpublished Autobiographical Writing*, Jeanne Schulkinol (ed.), New York: Harcourt Brace Jovanovich.
Woolf, V. (1992) [1925] *Mrs Dalloway*, Oxford: Oxford University Press.
Woolf, V. (1993) 'Modern Fiction', *The Crowded Dance of Modern Life*, Rachel Bowlby (ed.), Harmondsworth: Penguin.
Woolf, V. (1994) 'The Cinema', *The Essays of Virginia Woolf*, Andrew McNeillie (ed.), Volume 4, 1925–1928, London: Hogarth Press.
Wright, P. (1985) *On Living in an Old Country*, London: Verso.
Wright, R. (1990) [1940] *Native Son*, London: Pan Books.
WYAS (West Yorkshire Archive Service) Documents as numbered in their files.
Yallop, D. A. (1981) *Deliver Us From Evil*, London: Macdonald Futura.
Young, A. (1996) *Imagining Crime*, London: Sage.
Young, E. D. K. (1986) 'Where the daffodils blow: elements of communal imagery in a northern suburb' in Cohen, A. P. (ed.) *Symbolising Boundaries: Identity and Diversity in British Cultures*, Manchester: Manchester University Press.
Young, I. M. (1990) *Justice and the Politics of Difference*, Princeton: Princeton University Press.
Young, K. (1992) *Tale Worlds and Story Realities*, The Hague: Nijhof.
Young, T. R. and Kiel, L. D. (1994) 'Chaos and management science: control, prediction and nonlinear dynamics', by Internet 1994.
Zeman, J. (1977) 'Pierce's theory of signs' in Sebeok, T. (ed.) *A Profusion of Signs*, Bloomington: Indiana University Press.
Zinberg, D. (1995) *Times Higher Educational Supplement*, 7 April.
Zukin, S. (1982) *Loft Living Culture and Capital in Urban Change*, Baltimore: Johns Hopkins University Press.
Zukin, S. (1991) *Landscapes of Power: From Detroit to Disney World*, Berkeley: University of California Press.

INDEX